THE GANNET

THE GANNET

by BRYAN NELSON

Illustrations by JOHN BUSBY

BUTEO BOOKS
Vermillion, South Dakota

First published in 1978 by T. & A. D. Poyser Limited
281 High Street, Berkhamsted, Hertfordshire, England

Published in 1978 in USA by Buteo Books
PO Box 481, Vermillion, South Dakota 57069, USA

ISBN 0-931130-01-8

Library of Congress Catalog Card Number 78-57690

Text set in VIP Melior and printed and bound
in Great Britain at The Pitman Press, Bath

Contents

Pen and wash drawing from Taylor's Laws of the Isle of Man (c. 1652).
The original is in sepia except for the gannets' bills and feet which are
coloured grey-blue. The original caption reads: 'A Landskip with
Gaunts being birds that mount Like faulcons i'th Aire and when they
see their Prey Strike into the water.'

List of figures

List of tables

List of plates

Preface

It is surprising that Gurney's *The Gannet* has stood for over 60 years as the standard account of the gannet* *Sula bassana*, which, and not only in my biased eyes, is our most spectacular seabird. This deficiency, however, is partly a historical accident, for the late and lamented James Fisher wanted to write a monograph on the gannet and indeed, I believe, harboured plans for joint authorship with me more than ten years ago.

Writing the book has given me a deal of pleasure for the simple reason that much fascinating material begged to be integrated. There was, for example, the uniquely complete information on the world population of gannets; the many years' records of breeding biology and behaviour on Bass Rock; exciting comparative data from Bempton Cliffs, Ailsa Craig and Bonaventure Island; recent research on the closely related African and Australasian gannets and a detailed treatment of the whole family, to say nothing of several seminal studies of other seabirds. The time, therefore, was right. This was in part, also, because I had recently completed a much larger work on the entire family, *The Sulidae*, from which, may I assure the reader, the present volume is not an extract; neither book is any substitute for the other. This one, *The Gannet*, has been written afresh and with a different approach. The larger volume is unsuitable for the general ornithologist and bird-watcher in Britain because most of its content (boobies) is peripheral to his interests, and because it is too expensive to find its way onto his shelves, and too large to be carried around. I have tried to make this monograph on the gannet as complete as anybody but the specialist could want, yet without cluttering it with too much detail, and I hope many copies will even see a gannetry in the flesh.

Throughout, the emphasis is equally on fact, integration and interpretation, because I am sure that a book like this should leave the reader feeling that (s)he understands the subject; knows why, for instance, the gannet's breeding strategy is what it is and why it displays as it does. It is as important to ask why gannets do not feed their free-flying young as it is to describe the plumage of a two-year-old, even though the one cannot be answered as fully and factually as the other can be described. I hope that those who read this book will find their understanding and enjoyment of the lovely 'white bird of the herring' greatly enhanced.

* This perhaps unfairly excludes Reinsch's excellent little account in German.

Acknowledgements

This book is based on field work in which, especially in the early years, I have been greatly aided by my wife; my deepest appreciation is offered. I am extremely grateful to Sarah Wanless and Joan Fairhurst for allowing me to use some of their unpublished information on the gannets of Ailsa Craig and Bempton. The following people kindly answered queries or provided help or information: R. Appleby, W. R. P. Bourne, R. Broad, R. G. G. Brown, H. O. Bunce, D. Cabot, J. Cudworth, R. Dennis, Th. Einarsson, D. C. Emerson, P. Evans, A. C. B. Henderson, P. Hopkins, M. F. Jarvis. Ph. Milon, B. Montevechii, D. Nettleship, M. Richardson, C. J. Robertson, R. F. Ruttledge, B. Sage, B. Sinclair (for J. McGeoch), J. C. Young, K. Wodzicki.

It is a pleasure to acknowledge my debt to Sir Hew Hamilton Dalrymple for allowing me to study the Bass gannets and for consistent interest in them. Similarly, Fred Marr has always been outstandingly helpful, as well as skilful, in ferrying me to and fro the Bass these last eighteen years. I have now enjoyed the help and friendship of three generations of Marrs. To the many stalwart keepers of Her Majesty's Commissioners of Northern Lighthouses, I offer my warmest thanks. The old coal-fires of 1960 have long since perished; television and hot, running water has arrived, formica has replaced wood, but the same friendly spirit prevails.

This is the fourth book which John Busby has illustrated for me, and without detracting in the least from the others, I believe the drawings in this volume are surpassingly evocative.

Finally, but by no means least, I am pleased to thank Bob Duthie for his sensitive work in preparing Figs 1, 3, 4, 5, 19 and 29; and Andy Lucas for printing many of the photographs. Miss Edna Watson kindly and cheerfully typed most of the manuscript. For these and other facilities Professor G. M. Dunnet of the Zoology Department, and the University of Aberdeen, deserve warm acknowledgements.

The bird introduced

The reader may find it helpful to start with a thumb nail sketch of the
essential gannet to arm him for the chapters to come.

It is the heavyweight among the plunge-divers of the world, if one
excludes the amateurish and ungainly pelican. Many a fine mackerel
and herring ends up in the gannet's capacious craw. Its nesting habits
are equally dramatic. Gannets breed in colonies, often huge and always
dense, preferably on precipitous islands. They are confined, as breeding birds, to the North Atlantic, chiefly on the eastern side from
Norway to Brittany, with the heartland to the west and north of
Scotland. Rock, wind, waves, seaweed, guano and fish, together with
constant interaction with its fellows, are the stuff of a gannet's life.

The squab (a suitably ugly word) hatches after 43 days from the
single, stained and roughened egg, securely couched in the cup of the
pedestal nest and incubated underfoot (the gannet has no brood patch).
It grows rapidly, tended unremittingly by at least one parent. From an
appealing, fluffy chick it changes to a black-feathered juvenile, laden
with fat. The juvenile, not the parent, decides when to sever the link. At
the age of about 13 weeks, and whilst still being amply fed, it jumps off
its ledge and glide-flies down to the sea. Unable to rise from the water,
it swims away on the first leg of the journey south, which eventually
may take it to equatorial waters off western Africa.

It returns to home waters as an immature bird in pied plumage,
usually in its third year, and often to a colony other than the one of its
birth. For two summers or more it plays around, joining the 'club' of
immature and adult-plumaged non-breeders, displaying incipiently,
wandering the sea lanes in extended foraging trips, and departing
again long before the established site-owners leave their precious sites
for a brief period of winter nomadism.

In its fourth or fifth year (that is, after its third or fourth birthday) the
male establishes a site in or at the edge of the colony and 'advertises' for
a mate. The females, prospecting as ever and often a little younger than
the males, respond, and a pair is formed. The next season, they breed
for the first time and continue to attempt yearly breeding for the rest of
their lives, which on average last 16 years more. During this time, the
gannet will typically remain faithful to site and mate in successive
years, although for one reason or another very few keep one site or one
mate all their lives. Year after year it flies back and forth from its

wide-flung fishing grounds to its sea-girt rock. Season after season it sits there through sleet-laden wind, hot sun, enveloping mist; it fights, displays, nest-builds, incubates and rears its young. One day, its harsh but curiously fascinating life comes to an end. Usually, it will be as the result of a fishing accident involving man's nets and lines, or his irritation with the importunate birds; or of an accident at the colony; perhaps it breaks a wing or becomes entangled in waste cordage. A few become oiled. A very, very few will be driven inland, or starve in bad weather. But it takes a lot to starve a gannet.

This figure, in Pontoppidan's work of 1753, is given a shag-like crest, described in his text as red. Gurney speculates that Pontoppidan confused the gannet with the drake king eider, but that species has a frontal shield rather than a crest of feathers

Names

The North Atlantic Gannet, *Sula [bassana] bassana* (L).

Cunningham[26] and, later, Gurney[48] treated the etymology of gannet names exhaustively and certainly this bird has collected more than its share of synonyms. The gannet is essentially a Scottish bird and 'soland goose' was for long the proper, and predominantly Scottish name, with an ancient pedigree and a clutch of variants: solem(ne), sol(l)en, solan(e), soland(e), solend(ae), solent, sollem, solayne, sule, sulan, sullen. Gurney favours Martin's (1698) derivation, from 'sou'l-er', related to the Gaelic 'suil' or eye, as in 'suileach', sharp-sighted, referring to the gannet's proverbially keen sight. However, 'solan' apparently stems from 'sula-n', from 'sula-hin' ('the' gannet in Icelandic). Morris[80] suggests 'sula' derives from 'sulao', to rob or spoil.

According to Cunningham, the name gannet, as also the word gander, is a modification of the ancient British 'gan' or 'gans' (modern German 'Gans'; corresponding to old High German 'Kans', and to the Greek $X\grave{\eta}\nu$, Latin *anser*, and the Sanskrit 'hansa'. All of them mean 'a goose'. The association of these words with the act of gaping or yawning (to 'gant', or 'gaunt'), if genuine, presumably comes from the goose's habit of gaping as it hisses.

The bird has some names in common English besides solan goose – thus, great booby, spotted booby (juvenile plumage); and for the young one with a wig, Parliament goose. 'Saithor', which is Cornish for arrow, is a lovely name with an interesting and little-known history (I quote from M. Nance[81]). 'In the old vocabulary "saithor" is given for a diver or plunger, and it has been supposed that the bird of this name was a cormorant or gull. The gannet was evidently unknown to those who have so rendered "saithor". Derived from "seth", an arrow, "sethor" means archer and paints in a word the bent Scythian bow made by the bird's outstretched wings as it takes aim aloft, and the arrow-like dart and splash as it rushes with closed wings on its prey. This wonderful name seems to be of Cornish invention and is not known elsewhere.' In a later footnote Nance says 'Lhuyd in his manuscript Cornish vocabulary, now in the National Library of Wales, gives "Zethar" (i.e. Saethwr) a gannet, *Larus cinereus major*. He had probably heard this as a living word and it is curious that the true meaning should have been passed over in all other dictionaries.' Gaelic names include Ian Ban an Sgadan (the white bird of the herring), Amhasan, Amhasag, Asan and the well known guga (young gannet). Other vernacular names are (Welsh) Gwydd Lygadlon (clear-eyed goose), Gwylan Wydd (gull goose) and Gans; (Icelandic) Hafssúla; (Greenland) Konksuk; (Danish) Havsula, Tossefugl; (Swedish) Sillebas, Hafssula, Bergshammar; (Finnish) Suula; (German) Bass-Tölpel, Schottengans, Solendgans, Seerabe; (Dutch) Jan van Gent, Basaangans; (French) Fou de Bassan, Fou Tacheté; (Normandy French) Boubie, Harenguier, Marga; (Spanish) Alcatraz; (Portuguese) Ganso-patôla, Mascato, Facão; (Italian) Sula bianca. Booby is derived from el bobo (clown or dunce) and the Russian name, Olusha-glupish, Северная олуша, similarly means simpleton or dolt.

The scientific nomenclature is dominated by the issue of the status of the gannets within the family Sulidae (see Chapter 6), the choice resting between a separate genus (*Morus*, from *Moris*) for gannets, and *Sula* for boobies. Both generic names have been and are extensively used. My own preference is for one genus, *Sula*, because there are no grounds, anatomical, morphological, ecological, behavioural or biochemical (protein analysis) on which it can reasonably be split. On the other hand, the three gannets clearly are distinct from the boobies; it is simply that the boobies themselves can as sensibly be split as can the gannets from the boobies. Whether one calls the three gannets (Atlantic, African and Australasian) *Sula* or *Morus*, their own relationship has to be decided. Again, there have been and are two schools of thought, some people giving each gannet specific status and others sub-specific. Whilst they are clearly more than sub-species, they are nevertheless extremely closely related and it seems best to express this relationship by embracing all three within a superspecies, thus: *Sula [bassana] bassana*, *S. [b.] capensis* and *S. [b.] serrator*. In this way it is clear that they are more than sub-species but perhaps less than full species.

Old scientific names for the gannet were: *Anser bassanus* or *scoticus*, used by Gesner, Aldrovandus, Jonston, Willughby and most other early authors; *Sula hoieri*, used by Clusius, Willughby and Ray; *Pelecanus bassanus* of Linnaeus, Gmelin, Latham and others; *Sula bassana* of Mathurin Brisson (the first naturalist to give the gannet a generic name, in 1760, Linnaeus in 1758 having included it in 'Pelecanus') and modern authors; *Sula alba* of Mayer, Temminck and Fleming, and *Dysporus bassanus* of Illiger. Yet other synonyms used for the specific name have been: *americana*, *lefevri*, *melanura*, *vulgaris* and *major*. *Morus* was (and still is) the alternative generic name, attributed to Vieillot as *Morus bassanus* (Viellot) this author having, in 1817, changed the Moris conferred by Leach in 1816. *Sulu bassana* (Linnaeus), Yarrell, iv, p. 155; Saunders, p. 365; *Pract. Handb.*, ii, p. 404, from *Pelecanus bassanus* Linnaeus, *Syst. Nat.*, ed. x, i, p. 133 (1758 – Scotland, America), the former now shortened to *Sula bassana* (L.) is now the most widely used scientific name. If the superspecies concept be applied to the gannet it becomes *Sula [bassana] bassana* (L.).

1: Plumage, shape, structure and voice

The Hav Sule is a large Sea-bird which somewhat resembles a goose: the head and neck are rather like those of a Stork, excepting that the bill is shorter and thicker, and is yellowish: . . . towards the head it is green mixed with black, and on the top there is a red comb.

Pontoppidan: *Natural History of Norway* (1752)

The gannet, like the puffin, is familiar, at least from pictures, to everybody with the slightest interest in birds. Its distinctive outline adorns the publications and car badges of the British Trust for Ornithology, as that of the avocet decorates those of the RSPB. The severe, binocular gaze of the gannet's icy blue eyes meets us from countless photographs. It is one of those birds with a special aura. The peregrine has it; so, too, have the owls, the nightjar and the swallow. There has to be something especially wild, austere, mysterious or irresistibly charming to qualify.

Plumage and morphology are highly adaptive in hunting and this aspect is discussed under 'fishing'. The gannet is about 90 cm (36 in) long, with a total wing-span, including body width, of about 170–180 cm (66–70 in). See Table 1 for measurements. It looks streamlined due to the sharply tapered beak, head characteristically held so that it merges with the cigar-shaped body (the thickened appearance in flight may be partly due to inflated air sacs in the neck region), and long, pointed tail. Its wings are basically long and narrow. The normal flight is steady and powerful with shallow wing beats (about three per second) interrupted by glides, angled turns and banks. The wings are typically slightly flexed rather than fulmar-stiff, and the body carried at an angle to the horizontal.

The adult is pure white except for the yellow head and the black primaries (which show as broad black wing tips and are actually black-brown, paler on the inner webs, with blackish shafts when new, bleaching when old), black primary coverts and alulae, and black-and-white lesser primary coverts. The exact pattern is best seen in a photograph. There are ten large primaries and one vestigial. Primary 10 (outermost and longest) is emarginated on the inner web for the distal 70 mm (3 in). The outer vane of primary 9 narrows markedly in the distal 100 mm (4 in) and the inner in the distal 70 mm (3 in). The steps in length by which each primary exceeds the previous, starting with primary 10, are: 6 mm; 23; 39; 42; 39; 35; 31 and 23 mm ($\frac{1}{4}$, 1, $1\frac{1}{2}$, $1\frac{5}{8}$, $1\frac{1}{2}$, $1\frac{3}{8}$, $1\frac{1}{4}$ in).

The secondaries, which number 26 or 27, are short and rather broad with rounded tips. The tail (usually twelve feathers) is long, the central pair of feathers especially so, and stiff. Often, the central feathers become so abraded that only the rachis, by now yellow, remains, with a few tattered barbs.

The bill is pale blue, tending to grey-blue, with black indented lines (nasal grooves) running along the mandible on each side and merging into the black skin on the lores, which in turn encircles the eye and runs, as a line, backwards and slightly downwards from the angle of the gape. The mandibles are serrated and the upper one abuts onto a movable plate which continues backwards to the angle of the gape and, together with the naso-frontal hinge (which allows the upper mandible to move upwards) imparts added flexibility to the gannet's beak movements. Some of these features are shown in Fig. 1. The upper mandible is downcurved at the tip and ends sharply; it slightly overhangs the lower, and this helps the bird to lacerate and grip fish more firmly. A narrow line of black skin divides the forehead feathers from the base of the upper mandible and delineates the insertion of the lower mandible, becoming, in the mid-line between the rami, a wider strip extending down onto the throat. The inside of the mouth is blackish. These black lines and black skin, on pale blue and white, give the gannet's face its clear, sharply-cut appearance. The orbital ring is cobalt blue and the iris clear, pale blue-grey with a fine, dark outer ring. There is an old (1919) record of a Bass gannet with black eyes. The pupil appears small. Oddly, the colour of the eye appears to have given much trouble to birdwatchers and artists. Often, it is described and figured as hazel or yellowish. Even one of the early colour photographs has it yellow. I am at a loss to know why.

The black gape is 'presented' to rivals during ritualised menacing, but it is a dull colour compared with the bright gapes of birds (such as kittiwakes and auks) that use them a lot in display. I do not consider that the gannet's gape is well developed as a visual marker, though the whole face and head is certainly highly conspicuous and may well be important in this respect. The legs and feet are black with conspicuous yellowish, greenish or bluish lines along the tops of the toes, converging to run up and across the front of the 'leg' (tarsus); the feet are used conspicuously in the important skypointing display. These lines on feet and legs vary from lime green with a strong hint of yellow, to a deep turquoise-green, the former tending to occur in males and the latter in females. There is, however, a middle range in which it is very difficult to assign sex. Young adults sometimes have pale grey webs and legs and are birds which have recently come to the colony, probably after a prolonged period at sea. The legs and webs darken later in the season. The gannet's web has an area of about 63 cm^2 (10 in^2); the toes, excluding claws, measure about 95, 90, 70 and 30 mm ($3\frac{3}{4}$, $3\frac{1}{2}$, 3 and $1\frac{1}{4}$ in), outer to inner respectively.

The only difference between summer and winter (breeding and non-breeding) plumage is that the head colour becomes progressively paler in winter; and, in the female, conspicuously spotted with white as summer advances.

The yellow head is interesting and puzzling. Coloured facial skin, bills and feet are of course a characteristic feature of the sulids (booby, bobo, clown) and depend upon a number of pigments, presumably taken in with the birds' food. In January, over 90% of males at the colony are pale headed, at best a pale yellowish, whereas in April a fully buff head is an eggshell smooth, deep yellow with orange-brown overtones – a superb colour. At this time, 85% of females are just as dark and lovely. The colour is at its best in April, though only 72% of females are as dark as males, dropping to 33% in June–July. After April the female begins to pale and becomes spotted with white. By August, sometimes earlier, females are noticeably pale and very patchy; some are almost white-headed and only one per cent are as dark as males. Some males at that time are still very dark, others paler and a few 'spotty'. Some females begin to darken again by October. Thus head colour shows most difference between the sexes late in the breeding season, and is then usually marked.

Clearly, the colour is associated with the birds' reproductive physiology and is not simply due to pigment, say from crustaceans taken in with food, otherwise one would not have the clear cut sex differences. Nor is the female's spottiness due to the male's nape-biting, for unmated females go pale and spotty, as do a few males. So, too, do females with contrasting reproductive histories – successful breeders and those who lost eggs or chicks at various stages. Nor is the colour gained from pigment in the plumage-proofing oil from the preen gland, on which gannets rub the back of their head prior to 'rolling' the oil onto their back and wings. Again, this would not explain the sexual and seasonal pattern. The spottiness is probably due to the moulting of head feathers and their replacement by white 'winter' plumage, although if this is so, a sex difference in moulting pattern is implied.

On a comparative note, the red-foot (white morph) *Sula sula* shows in some areas much the same yellowish tinge, but all over the body too, and the brown or part-brown morphs are obviously more gingerish on the head, where the yellow shows through. By contrast, the masked or white booby *S. dactylatra*, in the same area, is dazzling white without ever showing the faintest trace of yellow.

The whiteness of the gannet's plumage helps it when fishing. The white underparts are hunting camouflage, making it less conspicuous to the fish when seen against the sky, and the white upperparts have a signalling function, drawing other gannets to the scene and by so doing helping all of them to fish more successfully. The black wing tips may simply be anti-abrasive, since melanin is thought to strengthen feathers.

The adult plumage is simple, but that of the many immature stages is not. The newly hatched chick is virtually black, because the few tracts of sparse down fail to hide its dark skin; then it becomes pure white and fluffy; then black, in its juvenile plumage, and finally white again

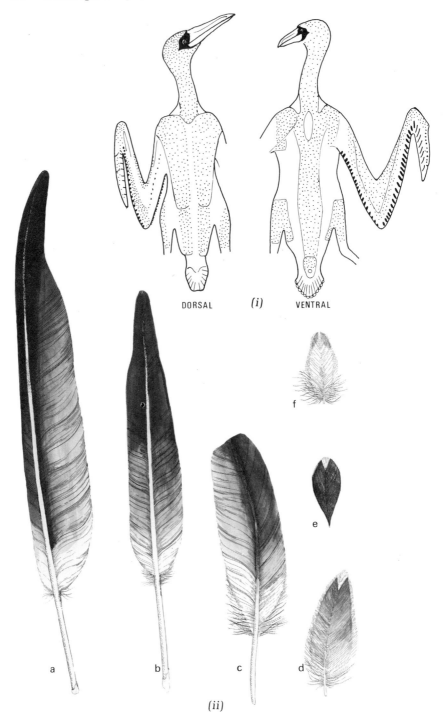

DORSAL   *(i)*   VENTRAL

a   b   c   d

e

f

(ii)

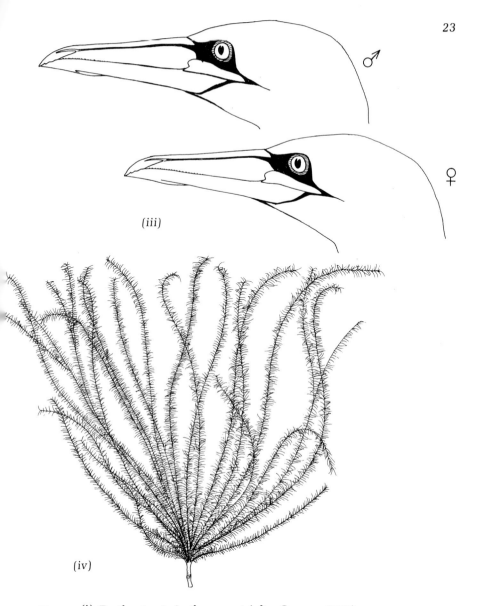

(iii)

(iv)

Fig. 1. (i) *Feather tracts in the gannet (after Gurney, 1913)*
    (ii) *(a) Outermost primary feather, left wing: note emargina-*
        tion (air slot)
      (b) One of the central tail feathers
      (c) Outermost secondary feather, left wing: note broad tip
      (d) Juvenile back feather, scapular area
      (e) Juvenile rump feather
      (f) Juvenile breast feather
    (iii) *Gannet head and bill: note serrated cutting edge to mand-*
      ibles and lack of external nostrils
    (iv) *Down from gannet chick (flanks)*

after a complex series of intermediate 'pied' plumages that last about four years. The chick-stages are described along with its growth; I will begin, here, with the juvenile and work through the various stages of immature plumage. The main source of confusion is the great variation at each chronological age; at, say, 24 or 36 months after hatching, the bird may be like another a year younger or older.

JUVENILE

The young gannet loses its last traces of down when it is 11 to 12 weeks old and practically fully grown – a grey-black replica of its parents. The slaty upper plumage is speckled white, the 'spots' (white tips to the feathers), bigger and fewer on the back, scapulars and wing coverts, are fine and dense around the leading edges of the wings and on head, neck and throat. Later, these finely speckled areas are the first to whiten. There is a conspicuous V-shaped white patch on the lower rump, with its apex pointing backwards and including the base of the tail. Beneath, and particularly on the abdomen, the juvenile is generally paler than on top, and may be whitish. The primaries and secondaries are blackish-brown and glossy, with straw coloured bases to the shafts, and the inner secondaries are tipped white. The tail feathers are black-brown with small white tips. The tail coverts have white tips and mostly white outer webs. The axillaries are paler than the underwing coverts, though both often appear uniformly lighter than the upper wing.

There is great variability in the overall darkness of the juvenile. Some are almost coal-black, with few and small white spots, whilst others are light, silvery grey above and extremely pale beneath. Most are in-between, dark grey above, conspicuously marked with rows of small white spots, and paler beneath. Taking the rather light birds together with the more extreme form, the proportion of dark:intermediate:light is roughly 1:5:2. I have seen one albino, on Ailsa Craig (1973). It had creamy (or slightly darker) white plumage, and dirty pink eyes, bill and feet.

The dark brown or black bill becomes slightly greyer in older juveniles; feet and legs are black, sometimes dark grey with lines faintly discernible on the webs. The iris is usually dark so that the eye appears dull blueish or black from a distance, but it may be greyish, though not nearly as clear as the adult's.

Function of the black plumage

It is a curious fact that whilst one juvenile booby (Abbott's) is virtually indistinguishable from the adult male, others (Peruvian and brown) have dingier and browner versions of the adult's plumage and yet others (the masked, and the red-footed) are considerably different. None has taken the plumage difference as far as the gannet; the black juvenile is as different from the adult as it could be. Why? It is unlikely that the black plumage helps in what one might suppose would be a crucial time in the youngster's life, namely its first period at sea. It is widely held that the extreme commonness of white underparts, or white forehead in plunge-diving birds is because these features make birds harder to see from the fishes' view, so that the fish react less rapidly and are more easily caught. This general phenomenon has been experimentally demonstrated.[107] Yet the young gannet is dark, even on the undersurface, just at the time when its very survival depends on its acquisition of fishing skills, from scratch, without parental support. And, of course, a great many young gannets fail at precisely this time. Furthermore, the gannet's black plumage has been convincingly shown[111] to be a poorer insulator than white, so the youngster uses more energy to keep warm, which means that it makes greater inroads into its fat store and thus reduces the time available to acquire self-sufficiency. It can last without food only as long as its fat store allows. So what *is* the value of its black plumage?

One function, above all, fits well in the gannet's scheme of things, and that is the role of the black plumage in reducing the male parent's tendency to attack its offspring, possibly dislodging it from the nest, thereby with fatal results. The chapter on behaviour describes the male's aggressiveness towards his mate; he bites her each time they re-unite at the nest, and during copulation, and often he re-directs his aggression to her when circumstances inhibit him from attacking the object which elicited it. Sometimes his attacks knock her, a strong adult, from the nest. It is reasonable to suppose that if the chick had the plumage of an adult, it would be at least as likely to trigger the male's attack. Its black plumage, therefore, may be seen as primarily an inhibitor of its father's aggression. After all, it sits on the nest for several weeks during which, on cliffs, even *one* attack could be fatal. Once fledged, it gains white underparts quickly, followed by a white head, just as one would predict.

It is fascinating to find that in Abbott's booby, in which the chick closely resembles the male, even in bill colour, the adults notably lack contact aggression. They have, in fact, an extremely effective *internal* inhibition against any avoidable contact behaviour,[89] whether against rivals or between mates. They do not fight, or jab, and their meeting ceremony and aggressive display is conducted at a distance. All this is, I believe, to reduce the risk of falling beneath the jungle canopy in which they nest. Since, therefore, the checks have been built, as it were, into the birds, so that a conspecific in full adult plumage does *not* release dangerous contact behaviour, it is quite unnecessary for the chick to have *external* checks in the form of different plumage. So it does not in fact have any at all, and is the only sulid to dispense with them.

Post juvenile (fledging to first birthday)
Some birds almost a year old greatly resemble a newly-fledged juvenile, although they have become browner above and have lost the white spots on the back, appearing more uniform and in some cases

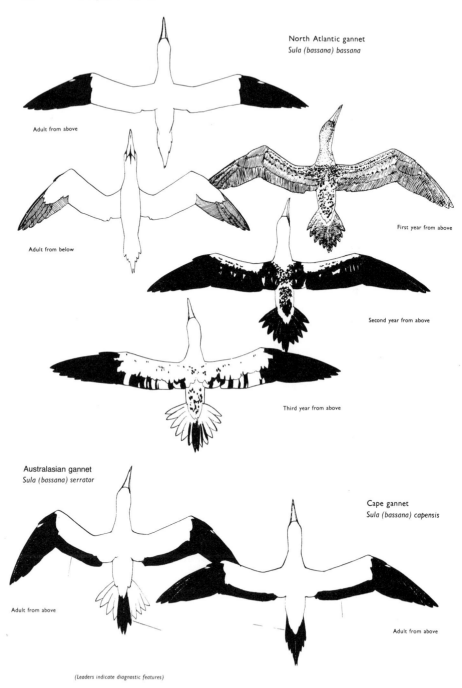

North Atlantic gannet
Sula (bassana) bassana

Adult from above

Adult from below

First year from above

Second year from above

Third year from above

Australasian gannet
Sula (bassana) serrator

Cape gannet
Sula (bassana) capensis

Adult from above

Adult from above

(Leaders indicate diagnostic features)

Fig. 2. (i) Plumages of North Atlantic, Australasian and African
(Cape) gannets

Fig. 2. (contd) (ii) Variations in plumage of immature North Atlantic gannet: (top) first year, (centre) second year, (bottom) third year

very dark. However, they could easily be mistaken for juveniles and may be responsible for some records of apparently exceptionally early fledging. Usually, the juvenile pattern of fine spots on head and neck has begun to disintegrate. Often, a light patch develops just below the lores and ear coverts, giving a capped appearance; at other times the entire head, nape and neck become mottled brownish on white. Frequently, there is more whitening on the throat and the sides of the neck than in the area around the upper breast and on the back of the lower neck. Since the underparts also whiten, this dark area remains as a throat band and (often) as a dark stripe on the hind neck. The throat band may continue to the base of the neck but, even if it does, it is usually separated from the brown back by a paler patch where the neck runs into the back. In a few birds the head and neck clear completely and begin to show the yellowish suffusion. A few brown speckles, perhaps clumped, may remain anywhere on the head; or a whole tract of brownish feathers, from the forehead, say, through the lores and ear coverts and right down the side of the neck, may persist in combination with the yellow suffusion. A very common feature is the retention of brown thigh and flank patches. Combinations of these features occur, so that, for example, one may have a one-year-old bird that is completely brown above, including neck and head, and brown on throat and extreme upper breast, but with a sharp demarcation between this and the white underparts. A new juvenile, by contrast, even if it were a pale specimen, would not show such a demarcation line. Similarly, the pale area may be only a shade lighter than the head, but it indicates the beginnings of the breakdown of the uniformity which characterises the new juvenile and is enough to show that the bird is a year old rather than newly fledged. The most advanced one-year-olds have white or yellowish heads and white or whitish 'epaulettes' – the leading edge between the carpal joint and elbow – and the brown back is beginning to break up, particularly in the mid-back and upper rump areas.

A captive bird kept by Gurney from the age of about 15 weeks to about 26 months, grew darker at the age of six to nine months. It began moulting in about April of its first year at some nine months of age and just before it was fully 12 months old had acquired some white at the base of the neck and become wholly white beneath. Its head, neck and throat were brown and white, the forehead retaining many dark speckles. Two birds which I kept from before fledging, started moulting from April of their first year.

The bill may show signs of blue, though it first passes through a lead colour to a nondescript, suffused one. The eye may be becoming pale, though it is not yet clear.

Year two

From my colour-ringed birds of known age it emerges that, even when fully two years old, the more retarded individuals are still all brown above except for white epaulettes, head and neck and the rump V-patch. Their underparts are white. At the other extreme I have a

record of a bird hatched in June 1961 which in June 1963 had a few
dark feathers among the wing coverts, a mixture of dark and white
secondaries, and one or more black tail feathers, being otherwise like
an adult. In this case it is probable that the bird had been moulting
since March/April and in June had just assumed the plumage which
was due to last almost another year. In plumage it was thus a very new
third-year bird, though scarcely past its second birthday. Between
these extremes, the 'typical' plumage of a bird during most of its
second year is boldly patterned blackish (or deep brown) and white on
the rump, back, scapulars and wing coverts, with a mixture of black
and white secondaries and some black tail feathers. Underneath it is
white; brown patches may persist on thighs and, variably, on the back
of the head and nape, which is suffused yellow. The leading edge of the
wing is broadly white. The bill, face and eyes are already blueish.

Gurney's bird became very black on the back when about one year and five months, but then began to fade or abrade. Its head and neck lost almost all their remaining brown feathers around November/ December (i.e. between the ages of 17 and 18 months). The conspicuous white epaulettes appeared at about 22 months (in one of my birds they had become conspicuous at 13 months), and as the bird approached a full two years large white blotches appeared on its dark back and wing coverts, and continued to increase in size at the beginning of its third year.

Year three

The more immature-looking birds late in their third year have 'piano key' secondaries, with variably sized black blocks, conspicuously black and white scapulars, and some black or part black feathers in the wing and upper tail coverts, and several black tail feathers. Thus, in flight, they retain a boldly patterned appearance, though with white predominating, whereas in the typical boldly patterned bird late in its second year, it is difficult to say whether white or black predominates. At the other extreme, though rarely, the late third-year plumage may be almost adult. Between these extremes the typical bird has several black secondaries during most of its third year, one or two black tail feathers, and may well show a trace of black on scapulars or wing coverts. There are no records of immature gannets with *all* secondaries and tail-feathers black but no black elsewhere, except of course for the primaries. There is a description of such a bird in Macgillivray[71] but, in fact, it was an African gannet, said to have been collected on the Bass in 1831. Thus he says that the bird, sent to him by a Mr William Stables, of Nairnshire, had a black gular strip extending down the neck to more than half its length, and dark secondaries and tail feathers. It was smaller than a typical Atlantic gannet (he gives a wingspan of 64 in (162·5 cm) against 70·3 in (178·6 cm) for some Bass gannets measured at the same time) with a shorter bill. These features show conclusively that it was an African gannet and in fact this would be the first British record for this species. But perhaps there must remain some slight doubt about the authenticity of the record, since there is no unimpeachable first-hand testimony that it was collected on Bass Rock. Indeed, it appears that Mr Stables had shipping interests! Nonetheless, he *had* sent immature gannets, collected on the Bass, to Macgillivray on previous occasions, so he clearly was on the look-out for gannets in unusual plumage. Also, he made no claim about its identity; he merely sent it. Even if the record is rejected, it is still worth noting that this undoubtedly African gannet did reach Macgillivray and that this fact has hitherto attracted rather little notice.

Because most birds are back at the breeding colony in the latter half of their third year or earlier, I have a greater number of accurately aged records among three-year-olds. Of 70 sightings, eleven had black on the scapulars; nine of these were seen before June of their third year (i.e. before they were fully three) and a moult fairly soon after the sighting could, in all cases, have disposed of the black scapulars. In addition, they all had several to many black secondaries and two or more black tail feathers. Twenty-five had several to many black secondaries and some black tail feathers (it is usually impossible to see the exact number), but no black elsewhere. Eight had several black secondaries but no black tail feathers; 14 had one, two or three black secondaries and one central black tail feather; two had a single black secondary only; two had one black or part-black tail feather only, and three seemed fully adult. The remainder had various combinations of the above features, including seven with some black on upper tail coverts and two with a few small black lesser wing coverts, in addition to some black secondaries and tail feathers. All the adults were, in fact, seen in the first few days of July and thus were, technically, very early four-year-olds, though it is highly improbable that all would have been more immature a few days earlier. Nevertheless, it is likely that they had shed some immature feathers in April, May or early June.

Two three-year-old males found in May (towards the end of their third year) showed individual differences and, also, their right and left wings differed and presumably had not moulted synchronously.

Year four

Just under half of the fourth-year birds seen in the breeding colony before June of their fourth year (i.e. probably before the moult that would take them into their fifth-year plumage) already looked adult. The remainder had a single central black tail feather (commonest), one or two black secondaries at the outer (distal) end of the row or, in a few cases, both of these features, except for four cases in which the birds had several black secondaries and more than one black tail feather. I specify 'in the breeding colony' because it is possible, though perhaps unlikely, that these represented a more advanced sample than the four-year-olds to be found in the pre-breeders 'club', of which I have insufficient known-age records to make a direct comparison.

Year five onwards

It is unusual to find a fully five-year-old bird with any immature plumage, but earlier, during their fifth year, traces of immaturity are not uncommon. A very few aberrant individuals retain a single black feather indefinitely. We know one breeding female, at least ten years old, with a single black feather in the wing coverts; and a breeding male, at least 15 years old, with a black secondary and a voice which has never 'broken' from the high pitched squeak of the juvenile. However, one breeding female, just after her sixth birthday, still had a black central tail feather which she would later definitely lose, so caution in ageing such breeding birds is indicated.

To sum, a gannet may attain fully adult plumage, at the earliest, a few months before its fourth birthday, that is, when still a three-year-old. Usually, it does so during its fifth year, probably near the end, that is when four years old. Late birds do not lose the black central tail feathers and/or the remaining black secondaries until they are into their sixth year (five years old); whilst rarely a bird may be actually six years old and still retain traces of black which will probably be lost a few weeks later. Gurney's estimate of two-and-a-half years to reach adult plumage was well out!

It is useful to separate the various age classes seen at sea and in the clubs of non-breeding birds at gannetries. The problem areas lie at the two ends of the scale. We know that birds in their second and third years are common in our coastal waters, and at colonies in the breeding season, from May to August, and their movements back from the areas to which they migrated as post-juveniles are fairly straightforward. Similarly, they are reasonably easy to identify in the clubs and breeding colonies, where even third year birds will not be breeding. But the very retarded first year birds that, by August, are beginning their second year, pose a real problem in their resemblance to some post-juveniles a few weeks old; and since there are some little-understood features of the latter's movements it is necessary to make careful identifications. In poor light and at a distance this may be impossible, but on many occasions the brownness and the demarcation lines shown by late one-year-olds on the upper breast, or on the head, are useful. Also, anything seen *on the wing* before August cannot be a bird of the year; and anything before mid-August is unlikely to be. It is just at this time, and in September, that confusion is likely to arise and to be most damaging, because there are many problems concerned with when and where, after their days or weeks of swimming, most of the young from our own colonies manage to get on the wing; how they learn to fish; their relations with adults at sea; their rate of progress south, and so on.

In fifth and even fourth year birds, the degree of immaturity can be so slight as to be easily overlooked; and the analysis of clubs, the interpretation of immature, site-establishing and breeding birds, and the investigation of sex differences in the plumage of birds of the same age, depend on careful definition of the plumage and time of year. Particular attention should be paid to apparent adults seen far from land in the breeding season. Records could, helpfully, specify the degree of immaturity by reference to the presence of black secondaries, tail feathers and scapulars in their varying degrees.

MOULT

In the gannets and boobies wing-moult follows an unusual pattern. Instead of the flight feathers all being renewed annually, moult is semi-continuous. It begins with the shedding of the juvenile's inner-most primary feather (generation one) about six or seven months after fledging and continues towards the outermost primary at the rate of about one feather per month (a flight feather probably takes about three or four weeks to grow). When the bird is a year old it has already

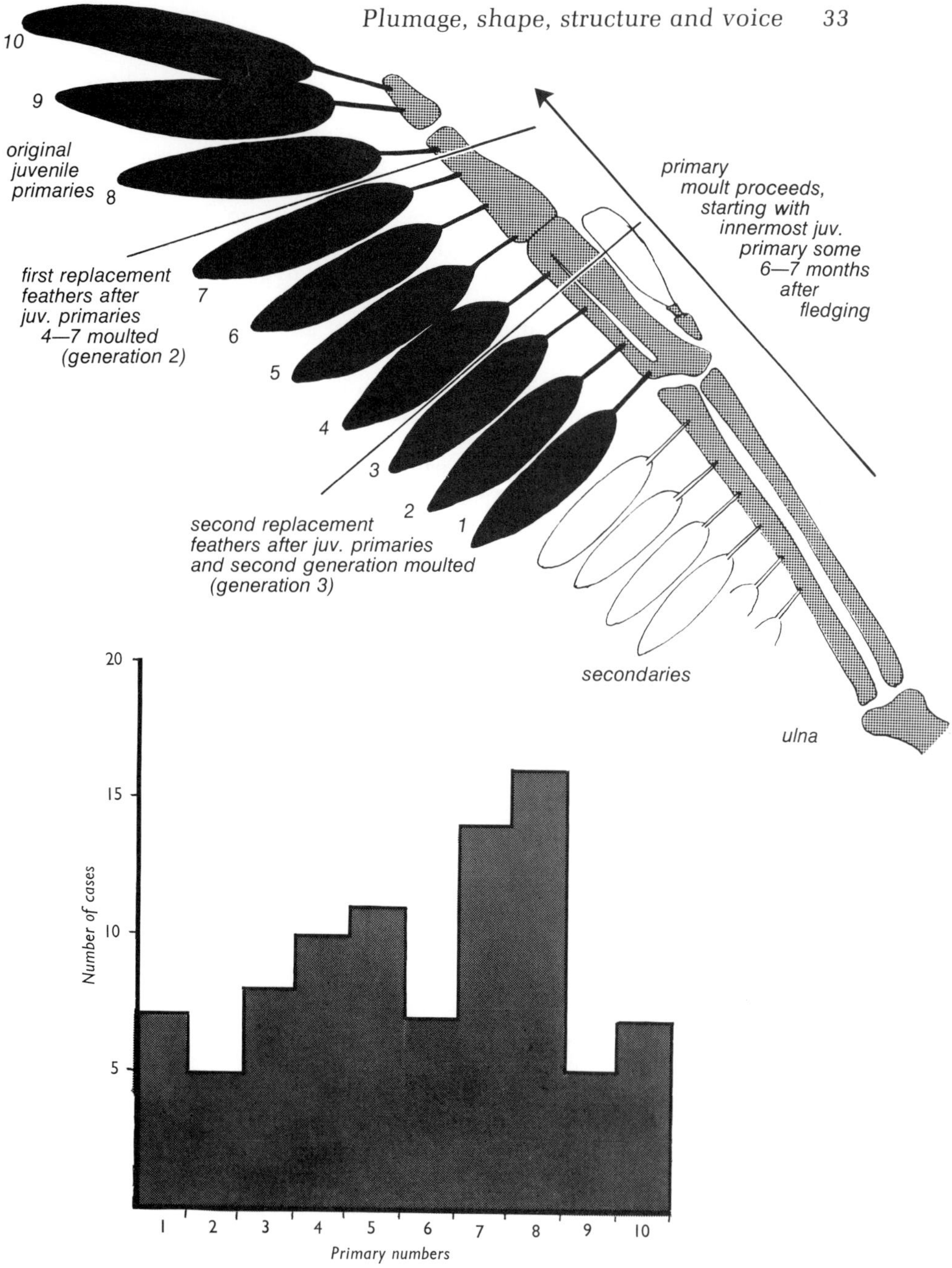

10

9

original
juvenile
primaries 8

first replacement
feathers after
juv. primaries
4—7 moulted
(generation 2)   6

7

5

4

3

2   1

second replacement
feathers after juv. primaries
and second generation moulted
(generation 3)

primary
moult proceeds,
starting with
innermost juv.
primary some
6—7 months
after
fledging

secondaries

ulna

20

15

10

5

Number of cases

1   2   3   4   5   6   7   8   9   10

Primary numbers

Fig. 3. (i) Gannet wing at the age of about one year, showing two
waves of moult and three co-existing generations of
primaries
(ii) Primaries absent or growing in breeding gannets, June/July

replaced primaries one to (about) six. Primary seven, of this new (second) generation, is just growing whilst primaries eight, nine and ten are still the original juvenile feathers. However, by now, primary one is ready to be replaced again (by generation three). Thus three generations of primary feathers co-exist in the wing; the distal feathers still belong to the first generation, the middle ones to the second and the innermost to the third, and moult is said to be continuous-staged-descendant.[127] The secondaries moult in similar manner, but the tail feathers apparently more irregularly and asymmetrically. Birds may grow up to six primaries at a time, three in each wing, though it is unusual to find three absent primaries in each wing; usually one or two primaries are missing or partly grown at any one time.

In 65% of cases, wing-moult was symmetrical; in the remainder the wings had unequal numbers of missing or growing primaries. Because of the staggered cycles, adjacent primaries are never absent together and there are always at least two fully grown primaries between the nearest missing feathers.

It costs energy to replace feathers, therefore moult is best undertaken when the bird is least stressed. For this reason, it is interesting to find that, contrary to what several people had supposed, gannets moult whilst feeding their voracious young – a telling comment on the ease with which they can gather food. They suspend moult around January February and resume it just before the egg hatches. This fits perfectly with my suggestion that, for gannets, the most taxing time of year is that between the return to the colony and the laying of the egg, for this is the period when, despite the short, cold winter days, birds spend long periods on their sites and display vigorously. Compared to the demands which this schedule makes on them (particularly, perhaps, on the male), feeding the chick, despite its huge appetite, is easy. Thus, of 46 adults examined whilst incubating, 41 were full-winged and the five in moult were late in incubation. None of 41 adults examined before, or early, in incubation was moulting. By contrast, 15 out of 18 birds with chicks were moulting primaries. The replacement of secondaries and tail feathers may start a little earlier in the season, from about laying time onwards.

The moult of body feathers becomes most noticeable in late May, when eggs are hatching and the feathers lie in deep piles between the nests. At this time the birds clearly feel 'itchy', and the incidence of rotary-head-shaking (the movement which dislodges loose feathers) is much increased. Once resumed, moult continues until at least November or December. Again, the period at sea, though it occurs in winter, would seem to be 'easy' for the gannet, which not only moults, but returns fat to the colony, as the St Kildans well knew.

Since moult is probably similar in all sulids, it is worth adding a few comments concerning one of the boobies, which bring out additional points. In the masked (white) booby,[29] once the second generation of replacements began, the rate appeared to slow down to about one feather in two months (three feathers in five months was an actual case). The rate at which it occurred left enough time for a pause of perhaps two months a year (which is less than in the gannet). An unmated bird, captured five times between 12 August 1958 and 15 July 1959, paused in August 1958 and July 1959, whilst in between it grew some primaries belonging to three different generations. Since at any one time, three generations were in the process of replacement, the primary in each position would be replaced annually. The pause in moult does not depend on reaching any particular point in the cycle of replacement; the process can halt anywhere, and in this species, as in the gannet, does so prior to egg-laying. This should mean that an individual would be at the same stage in moult at roughly the same time each year, and the records obtained appeared to substantiate this. In fact, though, if suspension of moult is linked with the pre-laying period, and birds lay at different times in successive years (as some do in aseasonal, tropical environments), they could not be expected to maintain this yearly correspondence for a long span. The pattern just described is not absolutely invariable and the same primary, if injured, may be grown twice within a few months. Also, there is likely to be some (perhaps considerable) individual variation in the rate of moult.

MORPHOLOGY

The gannet stands out clearly from the rest of the sulids. Its main features are greater weight, due in good part to fat, a particularly powerful bill and a longer 'arm' (humerus) in relation to 'hand' (radio-ulna and carpals.)* These may be seen as specialisations which have evolved to enable the gannet to cope with the opportunities and challenges of the northern seas. As I try to show in the chapters on ecology and fishing, the opportunities stem from the presence of large shoals of nutritious fish all year round but especially in summer. This all but guarantees breeding success for the gannet; starvation is almost unknown, in great contrast to the boobies of the tropical seas. The challenges have to do with the rigours of the northern climate and the difficulties of coping with deep-swimming and powerful prey. The ways in which the gannet's specialisations help it to cope with these are fairly obvious. Its fat, as weight, helps it to penetrate when plunging, keeps it warm and enables it to subsist on its reserves without stress during long periods of stormy weather or fruitless foraging. Its strength helps it to hold the muscular mackerel struggling for life. Its body, pointed at both ends, tapering gracefully from a thickset anterior third, with long, narrow wings, is ideally suited for penetration of air and water and for economic flying in turbulent airs. Its long upper arm may reduce the stress imposed on the wing in diving, which would be greater if the distal portion was longer.

The gannet is unusual among the sulids in that the sexes are alike in size as well as plumage. In fact, the male is very slightly larger, reversing the trend in the family as a whole. This can be understood in

* *Abbotti* is aberrant among boobies in resembling the gannet in this respect.

relation to the male gannet's extraordinarily developed site competitiveness. An especially large and powerful bill is presumably an
advantage in fighting and would be favoured in evolution. The large
and powerful bill, as such, is of course mainly a feeding tool and is
equally useful to the female; it may be simply that the dual use has
produced a slightly greater size in the male, though there is little in it.
Because both sexes are thus capable of exploiting large fish they can
take equal advantage of their abundant food and ensure the rapid
growth of their chick, with the important result that it fledges as early
as possible and has a better chance of surviving.

It is worth noting that several boobies have been forced to evolve a
considerable difference in size between the sexes, possibly to allow
each to exploit a particular band of the food spectrum more efficiently.
This also happens in some other fish-eating birds where two or more
species live in the same area. In some sympatric kingfishers, for
example, the males and females are *exactly* alike in plumage, but one is
half the size of the other. Since the sympatric species are themselves
different in size, a gradation of sizes, and thus of prey-catching
abilities, results. Moreover, the bill may be reduced in different ratio to
body size, further sub-dividing prey catching abilities. That the gannet
has been under no such selection pressure may be because, as mentioned, it is the *sole* occupant (by virtue of its far-foraging and
deep-diving) of an extremely rich food source. The close resemblance
in plumage between male and female gannets is not in the least
unusual in seabirds. Fulmars, auks, terns, kittiwakes and shearwaters
show little, or extremely little, difference between the sexes. This is
perhaps to be understood in terms of similar selection pressures acting
on both sexes, since they feed alike and share to the full the various
activities involved in breeding. Where, as in eiders and red grouse, the
sexes have differing roles, their plumage is correspondingly different.

It is interesting, in passing, to recall that raptors often show a marked
difference in the size of the sexes. Whilst this may reflect prey
preferences, it could also be a device to protect the female (who is
usually larger). The male, if larger, would be a potential threat to the
female, but not vice-versa. Certainly a huge male gannet and a
diminutive female would be a most unhappy match.

The gannet's shape, obviously, determines how it flies. Its long
narrow wings, with the highest aspect ratio of any British bird, and its
high wing-loading, together with relatively small pectoralis major
muscles and shallow sternum keel, all mean that it is designed to use
wind to assist fast flight. Its wing muscles comprise only 13% of its
weight. It cannot easily remain buoyant, like a gull, in calm airs, nor
power-rise from flat surfaces, like a pheasant or a teal. Good streamlining is essential to the gannet, and this, as we have seen, it certainly
possesses. The pointed tail streamlines the rear, but provides little
surface area for increasing drag to allow the bird to fly slowly and to
manoeuvre. It is helped by its feet, which it uses extensively to increase
tail-area and, by placing the webs on the top or sides, to press down the

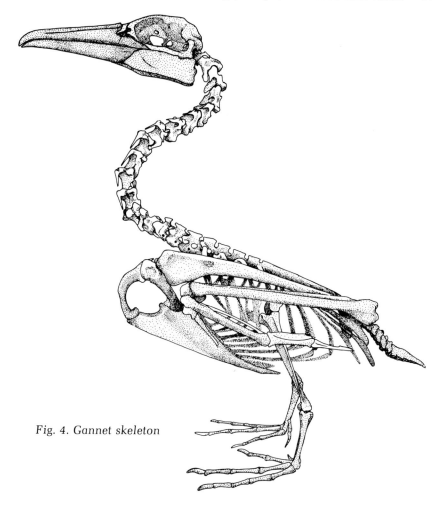

Fig. 4. Gannet skeleton

tail. Even so, it has relatively poor manoeuvrability, a fact of which great skuas take advantage in piracy. It is difficult for a heavy bird with narrow wings, a high wing-loading, and small flight muscles to land delicately among a mass of hostile neighbours or on a tiny ledge, and for this reason, among others, windy islands and cliffs are sought. Landing involves the use of the emarginated outer primaries, which are spread and provide wing-slots, and of the alulae, which are automatically raised so that a slot is opened just before the wing stalls.

The pectoralis minor, which raises the wing to prepare for the power stroke downwards, is particularly small, so that wing recovery for the next stroke is relatively slow. Long wings exacerbate this difficulty and in calm conditions take-off may need up to 20 strokes. In a combination of calm conditions and heavy swell, gorged gannets may be quite

unable to rise, which is what happened at Sennen Cove, Cornwall, when a large flock drifted ashore.

Gannets land on water either by gliding close over the surface and touching down with feet forward and tail spread and lowered or, most commonly, by a shallow dive. Casual flight in calm conditions has been timed at between 55–65 km/h (34–40 mph), but much higher estimates, more than 80 km/h (50 mph) have been reliably made from fast moving ships. When flying over waves in wind, gannets flap and glide, using up-currents deflected by the waves. In really strong wind, gannets use dynamic soaring, gliding down or across wind, turning into it and, with a few flaps to accelerate further, shooting steeply upwards into a faster air layer. When enough height has been gained the process is repeated. In this, weight and streamlining are a great help. Soaring in standing waves is common on the leeward side of the

Bass Rock. Soaring columns are not as common off Ailsa Craig, though they do occur, and they have been noted elsewhere, too. The base of the column is about 15 m (50 ft) above the sea and the top often 200 m (650 ft). Between fifty and several hundreds of birds may ascend, all circling in the same direction. Presumably they use the height to set off on foraging trips or to return to the nest site, but often they seem to do it for pleasure. Thus, gannets use slope soaring, dynamic soaring and soaring in standing waves.

VOICE

Gannets are noisy birds and the clamour of a great colony in uproar is exciting, even to us; to them it must be like the contagious fever of a football crowd. No wonder it gives the old hormones a stir. I have sometimes crouched in the heart of a nesting mass, in the sunset of a fine July evening, when the flood of incomers stimulated the group to a frenzy of calling.

The basic call is a harsh sound, a rasping 'arrah-arrah' or 'urrah-urrah' as powerful and uncompromising as the bird, all vigour and sharp edges. It is given at about two calls per second when flying in to the site (it appears to become louder and faster just before touch-down) and when displaying (territorial display or bowing, and the pair meeting ceremony), or fighting, or threatening. At its loudest, say from a frightened but defiant bird at close quarters, it is quite deafeningly loud and strident. This call thus forms the background noise at a gannetry. The excited calling which occurs when gannets are fishing or gathering nest material (both of them communal activities) is rather shorter ('rah 'rah) and often gruffer, and one can easily tell whether one is listening to noise from a colony or from a fishing group, though the individual calls are not markedly different. Their noisy calling at sea presumably gave them the old German name Seerabe (sea-raven) and, indeed, one sometimes hears, from gannets in flight (in my experience, steady, level flight) over the colony, a soft and extremely raven-like 'crok-crok'.

A quite different note is uttered as the bird begins to take off, or after a hop or a short run. It is a soft, drawn-out 'oo-ah', the second syllable often descending in a hollow moan (it has been described as a 'sepulchral groan'). This noise is typically accompanied by the special posture (skypointing) which precedes movement. Because the note is often given from a strained position, neck stretched and tail acutely depressed for lift during take-off, it has been suggested that it is the involuntary result of contortion, but it is in fact quite voluntary, a true vocalisation. Incidentally, it is the 'same' note as the boobies use when *they* skypoint, though in their case, skypointing has become a sexual display and the bird just skypoints and 'whistles'.

The Atlantic gannet lies at the end of a gradation of sex-differences in sulid calls. In some of the boobies (blue-foot, S. *nebouxii*, white, and brown, S. *leucogaster*, in particular) there is a marked difference between male and female voices (males whistle, females grunt or shout) due to structural differences in the syrinx. In the Australasian and African gannets there is a detectable difference (male higher pitched), but in the Atlantic gannet virtually none at all to the human ear. In fact, even sound spectrograph analysis[140] shows that there are no consistent individual or sex differences in the qualities of the calls, although differences in the pattern of calling, and possibly in its loudness, allow individual 'profiles' to be built up, and play-back demonstrates that gannets respond to the call of their mate. It can be observed that chicks, too, recognise the calls of their incoming parent, and that neighbours can recognise each other's voice.

The gannet, then, has a smaller repertoire than, say, the kittiwake, but, in conjunction with its conspicuous displays, quite enough to convey the information necessary for effective communication within the group. Like kittiwakes, the volume and persistence of noise is impressive, and undoubtedly contributes to development of the gonads and thus to the timing of breeding.

Thomas Bewick's (1805) picture shows the gannet's binocular vision and the totipalmate foot with the light-coloured line up the tarsus

SUMMARY

1. The gannet's shape is adapted for penetration of air and water. Its white plumage is an adaptation to make fishing gannets conspicuous to others.

2. There are 10 large primaries, 26–27 secondaries and usually 12 tail-feathers.

3. The web-lines tend towards yellow in males and turquoise (green/blue) in females. The web has an area of about 63 cm^2.

4.   The yellow head shows seasonal changes and sex differences. Early in the year sexes are alike; later, females are much paler and spottier.

5.   Juveniles are black, and differ more from adults than in almost any other seabird. The black plumage is argued to be mainly an adaptation to reduce the likelihood of the male parent attacking its chick.

6.   Immature plumages are described in detail.

7.   Moult begins with the shedding of the juvenile's innermost primary and 'descends' in 'stages', with pauses between, so that there are up to three generations of feathers in the wing at any one time.

8.   The gannet's morphology and anatomy is adapted for diving with deep penetration (wing-proportions, shape, weight), handling of large prey (bill strength), tolerance of periods of cold and stormy weather when prey inaccessible (fat layer for fuel and insulation, also as weight for penetration).

9.   The gannet has basically three calls, one of which (the 'urrah' call) accounts for almost all vocalisations. It is extensively used during social interactions and the auditory stimulation thus produced is a significant factor in promoting gametogenesis. Mates recognise each other's voice, and chicks that of their parents.

2: Numbers and distribution

The Solan geese are always the surest sign of herrings, for wherever the one is seen, the other is never far off.

Martin Martin, 1698

For a long time we knew more about the numbers of gannets in the world (Tables 3 and 4) than about any other aspect of their biology. Gurney's pioneering work was followed by the enthusiastic investigations of Fisher and Vevers[38] which laid the foundations of our present knowledge. No other common seabird is so thoroughly documented and for none can we calculate, as we now can for the gannet, the rate of increase of almost every colony in the world during this century. Much of this we owe to the fortunate fact that gannets are reasonably easy to count and their colonies are not completely overwhelming. Also, they grip the senses to an extraordinary extent, so that people are keen to count them. Puffins are more popular, but no bird is more thrilling. Furthermore, the Australasian and African gannets, also, have been well studied and a comparison between these three close relatives is now possible. In this chapter I propose to deal with each gannetry and then to discuss the main features of gannet populations. The term 'gannetry', incidentally, we owe to Gurney.

GENERAL ASPECTS OF BREEDING DISTRIBUTION

Food

First, however, there are some general aspects of the gannet's distribution to consider. The Atlantic gannet inhabits cold, rich waters overlying continental shelves; it is not a bird of the deep ocean. It nests only within foraging distance of its principal prey, chiefly herring and mackerel in the breeding season. All gannetries are near herring fisheries. There is summer herring fishing north of the Faeroes, off Iceland and in the boundary zone between polar waters and the Arctic, and major grounds near to all our west coast colonies, whilst the east coast birds have the North Sea herring fisheries. The Canadian gannetries in the Gulf of St Lawrence exploit an area almost half as big as the North Sea, rich in minerals and fed by currents laden with primary material on which the fish feed. In spring, the herring move north to George's Bank off the southern tip of Nova Scotia and are abundant there, and off Newfoundland, from May to October. North of George's Bank, massive shoals of spawners ascend to surface waters, even on

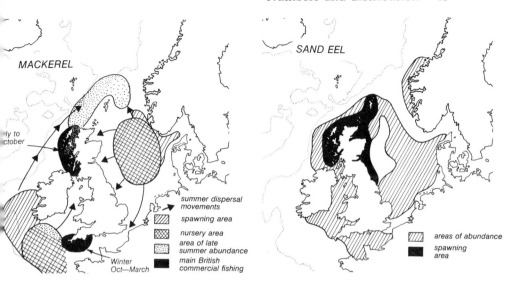

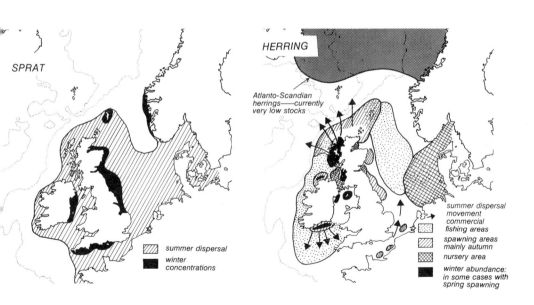

Fig. 5. Distribution maps of mackerel, sand-eel, sprat and herring around British Isles

sunny days, in September and October. Throughout its breeding range the gannet can rely, too, on plentiful inshore mackerel from June to September. These powerful fish are particularly nutritious. Only the gannet has the weight to plunge deeply enough to catch them and the strength to handle them, and so it is virtually the exclusive occupant of this rich feeding niche. Cormorants, though as heavy as gannets, do not forage far enough to compete. As we shall see, the gannet's breeding regime is firmly based on its ability to rely on rich and seasonally predictable fishing. Nor are herring and mackerel all, for many colonies are near to rich capelin fisheries and all gannets within foraging distance of the mid-North Sea, and the Shetland colonies, can rely on abundant sprats and sand-eels.

The northern limits of the gannet's breeding range are probably fixed, principally, by the shortness of the available breeding season. Herring go beyond the gannet's limits, to the Barents Sea and north of the Norwegian colonies, but Norwegian gannets are already within the Arctic circle, well north of the Canadian colonies, and compressed though their reproductive cycle is, it is too long for the high Arctic. The southerly limit may, on the other hand, be fixed by food, for the south-westerly limits of the herring are about at the entrance to Biscay, and the eastern Atlantic gannet's southernmost colony is at Rouzic, Brittany. It is not simply a matter of catching enough fish to keep alive, but of catching large quantities quickly and dependably, for that is what its breeding strategy requires.

Nesting sites

Besides good fishing, gannets need islands, and usually cliffs, partly for protection against large mammalian predators (a menace in the past more than now) but also for wind. Gannets are heavy birds and have the wrong build for easy landing and take-off; up-draughts are a great help. The right combination of islands and fishing occur notably to the north and west of Britain and here, in the eastern North Atlantic, most of the world's gannetries are located. The St Kilda complex is now the largest colony, though its population of some 50,000 pairs is less than half that of Bird Rocks, in the St Lawrence, early last century. In addition to St Kilda, the offshore waters north and west of Scotland hold Myggenaes, Hermaness, Noss, Sule Stack, and Sula Sgeir, altogether some 80,000 pairs or nearly 40% of the world's population. Moreover, there are now tiny new colonies at Fair Isle and Foula. North of this concentration lie the Icelandic colonies, altogether some 21,000 pairs. Grimsey used to be the gannet's most northerly station but that distinction now belongs to the Norwegian colony of Syltefjord, at 70° 35′ N well within the Arctic circle. The colonies in Faeroes and Shetland link Iceland with the cluster of gannetries off north-west Scotland, south of which the predominance of the west coast continues with large colonies at Ailsa Craig, Grassholm and Little Skellig, and small ones at Scar Rocks and Bull Rock. With the establishment of colonies in the Channel Islands and Brittany the gannet has extended its range south to about 48° N on the eastern side of the Atlantic, although on the western side Cape St Mary at 46° N is still the species' southernmost colony. It thus spans over 22° of latitude, compared with 8° 07′ and 14° 14′ for the Cape and Australasian gannets, respectively.

The east coast of Britain has many fewer suitable islands, though a fine exception, the Bass Rock, has dominated this seaboard for centuries. The western seaboard of Europe is little favoured, despite its fishing, and, until the recent establishment of colonies at Rouzic and the Channel Islands in the south, and the Norwegian colonies in the north, entirely lacked gannetries. This may be due to the absence of high and cliff-girt islands. Norwegian colonies are, on the whole, on low islands and, even today, suffer severely from interference. Indeed man, as early as the Stone Age, may well have been an important predator, deterring gannets from nesting not only on the mainland but also on low and accessible islands, even where these would otherwise have been suitable. In the western North Atlantic the pattern is similar. More than 70% of the 33,000 pairs breed in the Gulf of St Lawrence and the remainder on the Atlantic coast of Newfoundland (Fig. 11). Of the six Canadian colonies three (Bird Rocks, Bonaventure and Baccalieu Islands) are on isolated and precipitous islands, one (Cape St Mary's) is on a stack narrowly separated from its mother peninsula, one (Funk Island) is on a low slab of granite and the sixth (Anticosti Island) is at the tip of an island large enough to be called a 'mainland'.

Gannets may be particularly countable, but there are many pitfalls. Often, the stated accuracy is unlikely to have been achieved, or the figure claimed contains hidden assumptions which may have been wrong. The problems concern how you count, when you count and what you count.

HOW TO COUNT – DIRECT OR PHOTOGRAPHIC?

'Take the largest goose form in England and compare the space occupied with the gannets on Ailsa Craig.'[48]

Direct 'counts' are really estimates. It is difficult or impossible to count a large gannetry (over 5,000 pairs) with better than about 80% accuracy, and the bigger the colony the greater the error. By 'count' I mean merely totting up heads, regardless of whether they have nests or are members of a pair. If ledges are broad and are viewed from below (as from a boat) the inner birds are masked behind the outermost and may appear impossibly jumbled. If counted from a vantage point on the rock, either it is impossible to get near enough to the edge to see below, or bulges and overhangs screen some birds. Counts of sheer cliff faces with narrow ledges and little overspill onto the top of the island are most accurate, but few gannetries are so arranged. Even then, a calm sea is essential and commendable is he who can maintain his concentration to the end of the count. Huge colonies on flat ground (Eldey, Grassholm) present equally severe problems unless the area has first been sectioned with conspicuous markers. Direct counts are nevertheless valuable, but when it comes to deciding that a colony has increased or decreased, extreme scepticism is in order. In the case of medium small colonies, or accurately defined portions of larger ones, counts can be accurate to within 5% or less.

Recently,[51] a photograph of part of the Grassholm colony was counted by ten people and the results ranged from 2,823–3,362. The mean count was 3,170, so even the extremes were only 10% and 6% off the mean. By letting each counter count several times, the extremes were narrowed; the *mean* counts ranged from 2,949–3,359, which is 7% and 6% of the overall mean. This, it should be noted, was a reasonably good, but not brilliant, photograph, from above, of gannets nicely spread out on a fairly level surface; many photographs would be far harder to count.

Photographs have obvious advantages; they can be counted and re-counted, blocking each dot out as one goes; difficult parts can be examined under a lens or binocular microscope and the final figures can be based on the concensus of several counters. In these days of good lenses and built-in exposure meters, it is usually possible to get reasonable shots even with lenses of standard focal length. At the very least, photos should always accompany direct counts. Indeed, it is valuable to have as many cross-checks as possible, so that the range of agreement between the two methods can be delineated.

Nevertheless, photos share some of the direct count problems. It is little easier to disentangle a mass of heads from a photograph than in the flesh. In many cases (as on the Bass) a major problem is to photograph all areas of the rock. The shoulder areas are countable only from above and must then be accurately married to the appropriate section photographed from below. Artificial markers are probably essential for accuracy. Ailsa, by contrast, can be adequately covered by overlapping shots from the sea. The accuracy of a photographic count thus depends partly on the nature of the colony, but is potentially, more accurate than a direct count and may even approach to within 5% of the true figure. The Canadian colonies have recently been assessed from photographs[95] but even more recent direct counts of some of them have shown unexpectedly large differences from the photographic counts.

WHEN TO COUNT

Gannet numbers fluctuate throughout the season and also through-out the day, so that accurate counts at the same colony in the same year may well show real differences. However, for most purposes a single, representative, annual figure is enough, and so it is useful to correct for seasonal and daily factors in order to make this as good as possible.

June and July are the months in which there are most birds at gannetries, and here I refer to *birds which are clearly within the breeding ranks*. 'Club' birds are another matter (see below). In some respects, June is an especially favourable month for a count. It gives a maximum figure and chicks are not yet large enough to clog the view. But May is also a good month, because there are few transitory site-holders to confuse the issue. Later on, when these are numerous, fluctuations in their attendance can make a significant difference to the total count.

Unfortunately, gannetries do not all consist of the same *proportions* of young and old birds. And since site-holding non-breeders are generally young birds, it follows that one cannot determine a generally applicable figure for the proportion of such birds. This is relevant, because these birds (the site-holding non-breeders) show the most pronounced seasonal differences in attendance; but because their proportion varies one cannot easily allow for this. A rough rule-of-thumb is that counts taken before June and after August are likely to be down by some 20% on the June/July figure. A rapidly growing colony is likely to attract more young birds for short, mid-season periods of attendance than is a stable or slowly growing one, and is therefore likely to show a higher discrepancy between mid-season and early or late counts. Sarah Wanless[137] found that Ailsa's population fluctuated substantially from month to month even within the same year (see Table 2).

Numbers fluctuate throughout the day as well as the season. Loosely attached site-holders, especially unmated ones, are most likely to attend in the early morning and, particularly, the evening. Midday counts are likely to be down by some 30% on evening ones. A late afternoon count in June or July is thus more likely to produce a maximum figure. The main determinant of the daily attendance pattern is the birds' fishing behaviour, and since this is likely to vary from gannetry to gannetry, so, too, will attendance. The figures given here are merely a rough guide.

WHAT TO COUNT

The main difficulty in interpreting gannet counts is to know what has been counted. Many investigators, including those doyens, Fisher and Vevers, did not count what they say they did. Early counts were sometimes expressed as the number of individuals, but in the main they have been given as 'pairs' and frequently as 'breeding pairs', or 'nests'. Actually, they were site-owning individuals: *many* were breeding; *most* had nests; and the *great majority* had mates and thus did represent pairs. It is impossible in a single count, or even a few, to distinguish pairs that have a nest from those that have merely a site, for there is every gradation from a bare site to a large pedestal. Also, a good nest can be demolished in half an hour. Similarly, it is often impossible to distinguish non-breeders from failed breeders, and since the latter are nevertheless 'breeders', impossible to get a direct figure for breeders. So gannet counters, whether direct or from photographs, are in fact counting individual birds, each of which represents at least an occupied site (this assumes that a pair present on the site together, is

1 Grassholm
2 Little Skellig
3 Bull Rock
4 Great Saltee
5 Ortac
6 Les Etacs
7 Rouzic
8 Ailsa Craig
9 Scar Rocks
10 St Kilda
11 Flannans
12 Bearasay
13 Sula Sgeir
14 Sule Stack
15 Fair Isle
16 Foula
17 Noss
18 Hermaness
19 Bass Rock
20 Bempton
21 Westmann Isles
22 Eldey
23 Skrudur
24 Raudinupur
25 Stori-Karlinn
26 Mafadrang
27 Myggenaes
28 Storebranden
29 Skittenskarvholmen
30 Skarvlakken
31 Innerstauren
32 Isle of May
33 Lundy
34 Gannet Stone
35 Ingolfshofar
36 Grimsey

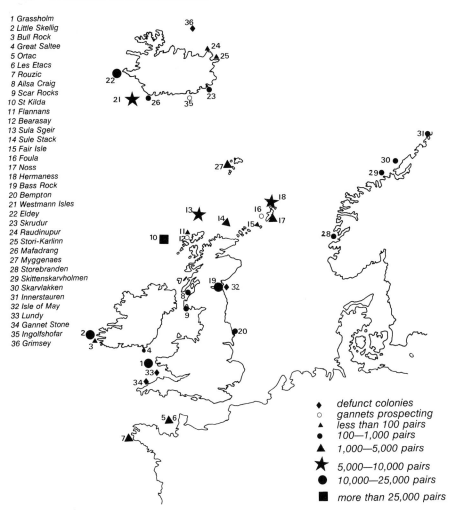

◆ defunct colonies
○ gannets prospecting
▲ less than 100 pairs
● 100—1,000 pairs
▲ 1,000—5,000 pairs
★ 5,000—10,000 pairs
⬤ 10,000—25,000 pairs
◼ more than 25,000 pairs

Fig. 6. Gannet colonies of the eastern Atlantic; sequence of numbers as in text

counted as one site, but see below). The practical implications of this can be illustrated by a hypothetical case, using rounded figures.

A medium sized gannetry counted from a boat around midday in mid-August yields, say, 5,000 individuals, mostly on nests with large chicks. Pairs, even when clearly seen, are counted as two individuals so that a correction factor can be applied to the whole colony. This is best obtained by counting pairs in an appropriately visible portion of the colony, including a slice of the fringe; or, less satisfactorily, by applying a general figure of 15% (see Fig. 12); so, 5,000 birds represent 115% of the actual sites, which thus number 4,348.

In the example, because it was mid-August some of the loosely-attached site owners will have gone for good, and because it was midday some will be away fishing. To make our count roughly comparable with, say, one in June or July, we may assume that 15–40% (let us say 20%) of the sites that were occupied when the gannetry was at its maximum that year, are now empty. 4,348 thus represents 80% of the maximum figure, which was 5,435 occupied sites. If we consider our direct count to have been potentially wrong by ±20% the count could have been anything between 4,000–6,000, which on corrected figures would be 4,345–6,521 occupied sites in June/July. The mid point of this figure, namely 5,433, is not hugely different from our original estimate of 5,000 but we would be in a better position to interpret any discrepancy between our count and others. After all, between our maximum and minimum figures there are 2,166 occupied sites, or nearly half the estimated total, to play around with.

If we wanted to know the potential recruitment rate of the colony it would be necessary to decide how many of the 5,433 pairs had tried to breed, and then to apply a figure for the number which could be expected to do so successfully. The actual number of fledged young could then be calculated. Unfortunately, the *proportion* of non-breeders varies between colonies; 25% non-breeders would be reasonable. Again, at least the basis for the eventual figure would be known, whereas a bald claim gives one nothing to work on.

In sum, counts should be expressed as 'occupied sites', or as pairs, and not as 'nests', nor (unless the necessary corrections have been made) as 'breeding pairs'. If, by 'nests', is meant 'sites' (as must often be the case), then the correct word is preferable.

Coming now to the world's individual gannetries (see Tables 3, 4 and 5), and starting with the eastern Atlantic, we may follow Fisher and Vevers in grouping them according to arbitrarily defined sections of their breeding range, at the same time recognizing that these *are* purely for convenience and bear little or no relationship to discrete 'populations'.

SOUTH-WEST BRITAIN, IRELAND, FRANCE AND CHANNEL ISLANDS

(1) *Grassholm, Pembrokeshire, Wales (latest count 20,370 nests, 1975)*

This famous colony lies 11 miles north of Milford Haven. Grassholm has the fascination of a 'difficult' and uninhabited island. You will find no lighthouse to stamp man's presence, no landing stage to receive you; not even a safe and easy natural inlet. More than likely you will have to transfer to a dinghy and pick your spot on the side which happens to be the most sheltered. The prevailing wind is from the south-west and there is a nice little crevice on the north side, the north gut, where the visitor is greeted by a small colony of kittiwakes.

Before landing you will doubtless circle the island, passing through the 'jabble' at the corner, which can be dangerous when the fierce current and wind quarrel. Despite the difficulties, Grassholm may have supported a Bronze Age settlement; faint outlines can still be discerned on aerial photographs. Apparently,[59] Grassholm appears in semi-legendary Welsh tales under the name of Gwales but was first mentioned as Grassholm in the early 17th century (in Michael Drayton's *Polyalbion*). Now, more than half of Grassholm's nine hectares of basalt are bare, and the gannetry is steadily encroaching on the remainder, but until about 1930 there was a vast puffinry here; the collapse of the undermined turf is thought to have led them to abandon the island.

Although the gannets crowd Grassholm's low cliffs, by far the greatest number carpet the top of the island on the slope facing south-west (see plates) and probably only Eldey (Iceland) presents a finer spectacle of gannets en masse. Difficult though it is to imagine, Grassholm gannetry has grown from almost nothing to its present size well within the lifetime of people still living, for the population did not exceed 300 pairs until after 1913. The history of those early years is obscure; the present gannetry had certainly been established by 1860 (possibly as early as 1820) but between 1886 and 1913 there were probably never more than 300 pairs. In most years, disturbance and exploitation by fishermen ensured that probably less than 100 young were reared. In 1922 there were 800–1,000 site-owning pairs and in 1924 nearly 2,000. Clearly, by then, the gannetry was growing rapidly.

The 1933 count by Salmon and Lockley[116] is particularly valid because each carried it out independently with both sea and land photographs. Their totals were 5,045 and 5,181 adults, which, allowing for 7% to be occupied by pairs, meant 4,750 occupied sites. They calculated the *annual* increase between 1914 and 1922 at about 16%; between 1922 and 1924 at 42%; and between 1924 and 1933 at 10%. The 1924–1933 increase was actually 2,750 pairs, which Salmon and Lockley reckoned could have been produced by their calculated 10% per annum, but even on the most generous assumptions the 2,000 pairs of 1924 could have produced only 1,167, or less than half of Salmon and Lockley's 2,750 pairs. So even over this period of relatively *slow* increase, more than half of the colony's growth must have resulted from immigration, a conclusion opposite to theirs. They recognised, however, that the more spectacular increases must have resulted from immigration. Grassholm has grown to its present size of more than 20,000 pairs in a series of uneven jumps rather than by a steady increase. Throughout, it has continued to receive immigrants, though with intervening periods, sometimes of several years, when it has scarcely held its own let alone increased. The detailed figures are given at the end of this section.

Immigrants may have come largely from Little Skellig, though it is likely that gannetries far to the north have also contributed recruits (see the end of this chapter for a fuller discussion).

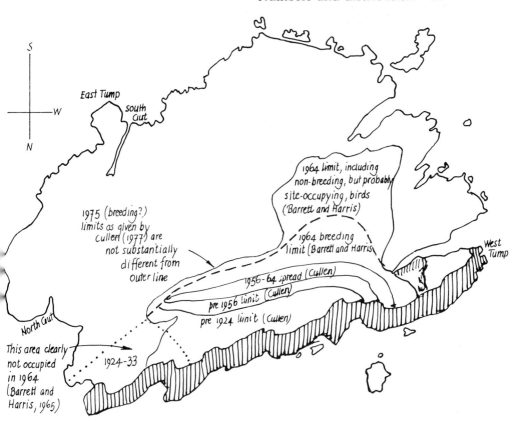

S

W

N

East Tump

south
Cut

1975 (breeding?)
limits as given by
Cullen (1977) are
not substantially
different from
outer line

1964 limit, including
non-breeding, but probably
site-occupying, birds
(Barrett and Harris)

1964 breeding
limit (Barrett and Harris)

1956-64 spread (Cullen)

pre 1956 limit (Cullen)

pre 1924 limit (Cullen)

West
Tump

North Cut

This area clearly
not occupied
in 1964
(Barrett and
Harris, 1965)

1924-33

Fig. 7. Spread of Grassholm gannetry, 1924–75. Note: boundary lines,
pre 1964, are from Cullen (1977) but are inconsistent with Plate 34
of Barrett and Harris (1965)

The Grassholm gannets started near the bottom of the northern slope
and gradually spread upwards, slanting towards the west. The 'snowfield' inched its way upwards until, in 1973, it just crossed the ridge
which bisects the island (see Fig. 7). It seems that the birds chose the
aspect that best facilitated take-off into the prevailing wind. Even so,
many birds have to travel on foot along the fringe of the colony to find a
suitable take-off point. In 1975 I saw a constant procession of adults
scrambling through the nesting ranks, to the fringe, and then making
their way to the take-off point. Cape gannets have to do the same thing.
   Summary of counts: 20 nests (1883), 250 nests (1886), *c*. 225 pairs
(1889), 200+ pairs (1890), 240 nests (1893), 300 nests (1895), 250–300
pairs (1903), 300 pairs (1905), 500+ pairs (1907), 800–1,000 pairs
(1922), 1,800–2,000 pairs (1924), 4,750 nests (1933), *c*. 5,000 nests

(1937), 5,750–6,000 nests (1939), *c.* 6,000 pairs (1946), *c.* 6,100 pairs (1947), *c.* 7,000 pairs (1948), 9,500 pairs ± 13% (1949), 10,550 pairs (1956), *c.* 15,500 pairs (1964), 16,128 pairs (1969), 20,370 pairs (1975).[25]

(2) *Little Skellig, Kerry, Ireland (latest estimate: 20,000 pairs, 1975)*

Perhaps less has been written about Skellig than about any other major gannetry. It is not too inaccessible, 12 km (7½ miles) offshore, but until the advent of air travel south-west Ireland was itself remote. Also it is a rock rather than an island with hardly a flat patch on it. It is now bare, basaltic rock, but once sustained turf and grazed sheep. Gurney[48] describes it as 'grandly pyramidal, rearing its tall head 450 feet [136 m] into the blue vault of heaven'.

It is an ancient gannetry. Birds bred there in large numbers before 1700, but by 1850 man had reduced it to about 1,000 birds, and by 1880 to some 30 pairs. An astonishing increase then began. By 1890 there were several thousands and by 1906 Barrington, who had estimated 60 birds in 1880, now reckoned 15–20,000 birds. This represents the most rapid increase ever recorded at a gannetry. The 30 pairs of 1880 could not have bred to more than a few hundred by 1906; so immigrants must have flooded into Skellig and were likely to have come from the Scottish gannetries. Skellig offered a special combination of circumstances. It was splendidly situated in rich fishing grounds, precipitous, and an ancient haunt of gannets. These factors, however, would not have been enough without two others: there must have been an ample flow of recruits and something must have channelled a disproportionately large share to Skellig (see discussion).

After the early 1900s the increase continued more slowly. The 1913 figure was 8,000 pairs and that for 1930 was 10,000. Neither of these is indisputably different from the 1906 figure, though the 1930 comment, that almost every available ledge was occupied, suggests an increase. In 1949 there was an estimated 12,000 pairs and in 1966, 17,700 pairs. A count from photographs gave 18–20,000 pairs in 1969 and 20,000 in 1970;[34] telling comment on the supposedly 'full up' house of 1930. A hasty survey in 1974 suggested a decline; some areas which had been covered with gannets in 1970 were bare, but in 1975 these patches had been filled again.

Having sucked in large numbers of recruits, Skellig has probably been exporting on a substantial scale for many years. It cannot now accommodate its own output and has probably become less attractive to birds from other colonies (see discussion).

Summary of counts: 'Incredible number' (*c.* 1748), 500 pairs (1850), *c.* 30 pairs (1880), 150–200 pairs (1882), 'several thousand' (1890), 'many thousands' (1896), 15–20,000 birds (1906), 8,000 pairs (1913), 10,000 pairs (1930), 9–10,000 pairs (1938, 1939, and 1941), *c.* 12,000 pairs (1949), 17,700 pairs (1966), 18–20,000 pairs (1969), *c.* 20,000 pairs (1970), <20,000 pairs (1974), 20,000 (?) pairs (1975).

(3) *Bull Rock, Cork, Ireland (latest count 1,500 pairs, 1969)*
Until the founding of the Saltee colony in 1929 the Bull Rock was the only Irish gannetry besides Skellig, from which it lies 27 km (17 miles) to the south-south-east. Founded, apparently, about 1856 the colony had grown to many hundreds by 1868, again through immigration, and to about 2,000 by 1884. By 1891 the population was down to about 200, a decrease plausibly attributable to blasting operations and human interference during the building of the lighthouse. By 1908 there were still only about 600. Subsequent counts remained at or below this level until a direct count in 1969 gave 1,500 pairs. It is apparently nearly full

and, like Skellig, with which it probably exchanges recruits, may now be exporting.

Summary of counts: 11 pairs (1858), 'many hundreds' (1868), up to 1,000 pairs (1884), 500 (?) pairs (1889), *c.* 100 pairs (1899), *c.* 1,000 pairs (1902), 300 pairs (1908), 250 pairs (1913), 400 pairs (1930), *c.* 450 pairs (1937), 440–500 pairs (1938), 550–600 pairs (1939), 295 (1949), 500 (1955), 1,500 pairs (1969).

(4) *Great Saltee, Wexford, Ireland (latest count 170 apparently occupied nests, 1976)*

Saltee is not really an ideal site for a gannetry. The island's cliffs, at the southern tip, are neither high nor extensive and probably cannot accommodate more than about 1,000 pairs. But it is an interesting colony because, like Bempton, its growth from an original pair or two has been well followed (see Fig. 8). In fact, these two colonies offer the best information we have. Saltee probably began, in 1929, with a single pair, in which case it is the only known case of one pair attempting to breed in complete isolation. However, the relevant records are ambiguous. The 'colony' teetered along for more than twenty years with never more than three, almost always unsuccessful, pairs. Indeed, none at all bred in 1938. Not more than a total of three young were raised in all that time. In a shorter period Skellig, in contrast, grew by many thousands from its modest 30 pairs of 1880.

Saltee began to climb rapidly from about 1954 and rose to 500 gannets on the cliffs (150 young hatched) by 1964, after which growth slackened, and in 1975 there were still only 193 nests.[114] Like Bempton, Saltee struggled ineffectually until it reached an apparent 'threshold', but having crossed the 'threshold' it grew faster by attracting immigrants. Again like Bempton, the physical limitations of the gannetry precluded massive growth of the Grassholm or Skellig type, but both colonies have achieved the normal rate of breeding success for the species, which formerly they signally failed to do. Why an increase in numbers affects breeding success is discussed in Chapter 4.

Summary of counts: 1 or 2 pairs (1929), 2 pairs (1932), 1 nest (1942), 2 pairs (1943), 2 pairs (1946), 1 nest (1947), 2 nests (1948), 4 nests (1953), at least 4 nests (1954), 9 nests (1955), 17 nests (1956), *c.* 20 pairs (1957), 22+ pairs (1958), *c.* 40+ pairs (1959), *c.* 60 nests (1960), 65 nests (1961), *c.* 55 nests (1962), 100 nests (1964), 120 nests (1965), 110 nests (1966), 125 nests (1967), 150 nests (1968), 155 nests (1969), 165 nests (1970), 175 nests (1971, 1972), *c.* 200 nests (1973), 200 nests (1974), 193 nests (1975), 170 nests (sites?) (1976).

(5), (6) *Ortac and Les Etacs, Alderney, Channel Islands (latest counts 1,000 and 2,000 pairs respectively, 1967)*

These colonies have not been well chronicled, for they grew up during the 1939–45 war years when seabird enthusiasts were otherwise occupied.

Ortac is a small sandstone rock, about 24 m (80 ft) high. The most suitable nesting areas are on the crown and eastern face. Gannets probably began nesting there in 1940 (one nest). In 1946 photographs from sea and air showed about 250 pairs.[28] In 1950 there were 570 pairs and in 1967 about 1,000 pairs, which (as with Skellig) is about twice the predicted capacity.

Les Etacs, the Garden Rocks, are two groups of igneous rock about 600 m² (720 yd²) and 39 m (130 ft) high. The gannets are mainly on the largest, most westerly islet which used to have some soil and vegetation. In 1946 there were 190 nests on the two sides of the summit ridge, about 130 on the northern slopes and 60 on the southern. A further 10 pairs occupied a pinnacle in the eastern group of rocks, some 100 m (110 yd) from the main colony. In 1960 there were about 1,000 pairs and in 1969 about 2,000 pairs, judged by direct counts from land and sea.

The Channel Islands' gannets have certainly received immigrants. The Irish colonies are about 600 km (375 miles) away and Grassholm is half as far; both were expanding rapidly whilst the Channel Islands' gannetries were growing.

(7) Rouzic, Brittany, France (latest count 4,400 nests, 1977)

Rouzic, a Nature Reserve in Les Sept Îles, is the gannet's most southerly breeding station in the East Atlantic, as it is, also, the fulmar's. Gannets became established before 1939, by which time there were 30 nests. By 1947 the number was, apparently, much the same, though this figure was probably artificial and due to disturbance. In the following year 92 eggs were counted. Milon[75] counted the number of nests for the years 1950–65, with an estimated potential error of around 10%, during which time the population rose to about 2,500 pairs.

Summary of counts: c. 30 nests (by 1939), c. 30 nests (1947), 100 nests (1950), 550 nests (1955), 690 nests (1956), 1,000 nests (1959), 1,150 nests (1960), 1,350 nests (1961), 1,650 nests (1962), 2,000 nests (1963), 2,400 nests (1964), 2,600 nests (1965), 2,500 pairs (1967), 3,000 nests (1971), 4,000 nests (1975) and 4,400 nests (1977).

MID- AND NORTH-WEST BRITAIN AND SHETLANDS

(8) Ailsa Craig, Ayrshire, Scotland (latest count 16,000 pairs, 1976)

Ailsa, St Kilda and the Bass are arguably the most famous east Atlantic colonies. All are physically awesome, have rich human histories and are large and ancient gannetries. The Bass is the most intensively studied colony, but Ailsa is unquestionably the most assiduously counted gannetry in the world. 'Elsay . . . quherin is one grate high hill, round and roughe, and one heavin (haven) and an aboundance of Soland Geise.' Ailsa's hump, 'Paddy's Milestone', dominates the outer Clyde. My first experience of nesting gannets was on Ailsa. On an afternoon in July 1952, with 200 gannet rings, a kitbag of bread and a dozen tins of pemmican left over from somebody's Greenland expedition, a friend and I landed from *Selina II*, out from Girvan.

Ian Girvan was at that time quarrying Ailsa's famous granite for curling stones, and Mrs Girvan's teashop at the top of the old jetty was in full swing. Those days on Ailsa, scrambling amongst the gannets on Kennedy's Nags, probably determined my whole future, starting with three years as a Nature Conservancy student on the Bass. Twenty years later, Sarah Wanless stepped ashore to begin a similar three year study on a NERC studentship, awarded for an Ailsa gannet project arising from the Bass work.

Ailsa and the Bass are the only readily accessible Scottish gannetries. Ailsa, a round-shouldered granite giant, 340 m (1,120 ft) high, lies 15 km (10 miles) west of Girvan. It covers some 90 hectares (220 acres), and is 4 km (6½ miles) around the base. On the east lies Foreland Point, a 12 hectare (29 acres) spit of silver boulders dominated by the light-house and merging into close-cropped sward, bright with sea-pinks and ragwort. This concession is rapidly revoked; flatness is not of Ailsa's spirit and Foreland Point soon surrenders to precipitous bracken and heath-clad slopes glistening with grey scree. Even these are severely restricted. Sheer cliffs rise from the rocky foreshore on the north, west and south sides. Barestacks, on the west, falls for more than 183 m (600 ft), reputedly the second highest sea cliff in Britain (the highest is Conachair, on Hirta, St Kilda). Ailsa's granite is fine-grained syenite.

Its soaring, cathedral columns rise in tiers, clear silver, green and ferric orange. The white crosses of wheeling gannets against granite and an azure sky are Ailsa's imprint on the mind. As Gurney remarks, 'the whole Craig is a marvel of life, and, given fine weather, one of the most enjoyable spots in the world'. But as always, there is another side. The gloomy, dripping water caves, green with slime, the blackened boulders from which the nettles and rank vegetation rise on a tide of debris, feathers and corpses till they fall back from the sheer cliffs; the broken gannets lying there, the crippled juvenile herring gulls hunching among the slippery boulders – these are also Ailsa's imprints. Seabird islands are a potent mixture of the rhapsodic and the repellent.

Ailsa's 'top' is divided by three main gulleys, two of which meet at a small summit loch, on which may be the site of a Stone Age settlement. The ruined castle on the east slope is thus not the oldest inhabitance on Ailsa. Today, in late spring, the 'top' is a riot of campion and bluebells. Rats and rabbits are common but the sheep and goats which used to inhabit the slopes are gone.

Ailsa's gannets are, and within historical times always have been, mainly inaccessible. In only a few places do they spread beyond the cliff top, and nowhere do they climb the slopes, though some of these would make fine nesting areas. Perhaps because of its size and dispersed population, Ailsa does not immediately strike one as a teeming gannetry like Grassholm and the Bass, and indeed it appears to have few early estimates. Nevertheless, it is an ancient colony, referred to in 1583 and subsequently described in phrases indicating vast numbers.

Estimates of 5,000–10,000 pairs in 1868 and 6,000 pairs in 1869 are probably untrustworthy and so, too, is the impression of one observer that, in 1871, the ledges were almost full. Gurney visited Ailsa in 1905 and counted 725 nests on a photograph, which he thought comprised a sixth of the total colony. This suggested 6,500 individuals to him, whereas it should have suggested 4,300 *pairs*.[145] Until 1940, 72 years after the 1868 guess, there is little to indicate a major change from a population of 5–7,000 pairs, except for the years between 1922 and 1924, which saw an estimated increase of 3,100 pairs. In that same period (1924) Barestacks was first colonised and Main (or East) Craigs followed in 1936, so an increase may have been afoot during this period.

There was an apparent decrease from the 6,232 of 1940 to the 3,518 of 1941. With one trivial exception, this applied to every one of the 20 areas counted; usually the number of gannets dropped by half or more. However, the count was in early April, when not all potential breeders are back, and when they are exceedingly wary; at the time, there was Naval gunnery practice in the Clyde, which probably scared off large numbers and may well have been responsible for the decrease.

Since 1936 yearly counts by J. A. Gibson[44,45] have shown remarkable apparent fluctuations. Increases and decreases of several thousands of pairs have been recorded in successive years. The decreases are particularly puzzling because they indicate that large numbers of birds which apparently held sites within the breeding areas of the colony were there one year and absent the next. But we have every reason to believe that *established* gannets do not change colonies. Nor could such numbers die between years. The only explanations are either that large numbers of transient birds were included in some counts, or that the differences were largely due to counting error. Whilst the former is not impossible, it would constitute a hitherto undocumented phenomenon, for whilst we know that 'clubs' fluctuate in numbers, we do *not* know that young birds settle among the breeding ranks and hold a site for a season, and then move elsewhere. It will be seen from the summary of counts (Table 2) that whilst Gibson's yearly direct counts indicate a *drop* of some 3,000 pairs between 1974 and 1976, Wanless' photographic counts show an *increase* of several thousands over the same period. This illustrates the colossal differences that can arise between different estimates. In my opinion, the photographic counts are likely to be much more accurate.

During the years 1974–1976, inclusive, monthly photographic counts showed some fluctuations and the population as a whole rose from 10,500 to 16,000 pairs.

Despite the problems mentioned it seems reasonably certain that, in some years, Ailsa has gained substantial numbers of immigrants. This is in full accord with the current picture[93] of a large population of young birds ('floaters') visiting gannetries other than the one in which they were born, before choosing one at which to settle down. The factors influencing that choice are discussed later.

It has been suggested that Ailsa's cliffs could accommodate 8,000 pairs. Yet the population has been as high as 16,000 pairs (1976) without causing birds to spread above the cliffs. Gannetries are repeatedly judged 'full' when they are no such thing, a point worth emphasis because it bears on the important matter of interchange between colonies.

Summary of counts: Plentiful when first recorded (1526); less abundant than at the Bass (1578), various adjectives denoting abundance up to (1837), c. 7,500 pairs (1868), c. 6,000 pairs (1869), possibly c. 3,250 pairs (1905), c. 4,900 pairs (1922), c. 8,000 pairs (1924), c. 7,000 pairs (1929), c. 7,000 pairs (1935), 4,800 (1936),* c. 5,945 (1937), c. 5,387 (1938), 5,419 (1939), 6,232 (1940), 3,518 (1941), 4,829 (1942), 5,383 (1947), 5,190 (1948), 4,947 (1949), 6,579 (1950), 7,833 (1951), 7,987 (1952), 8,249 (1953), 8,555 (1954), 10,402 (1955), 8,063 (1956), 7,742 (1957), 9,506 (1958), 9,390 (1959), 13,532 (1960), 8,504 (1961), 9,573 (1962), 11,699 (1963), 11,715 (1964), 13,273 (1965), 12,747 (1966), 10,518 (1967), 10,924 (1968), 13,054 (1969), 12,729 (1970), 14,347 (1971), 15,219 (1972), 15,892 (1973), 17,367 (1974), 12,246 (1975), 14,051 (1976), 10,500 (1974),† 11,500 (1975),† 16,000 (1976).†

(9) Scar Rocks, Wigtownshire, Scotland (latest count 482 nests, 1974)

The Scar or Scare Rocks (gaelic 'Sgeir', Old Norse Sker) lie in Luce Bay midway between Burrow Head and the Mull of Galloway, about 10 km (6 miles) from the nearest land. They are 75 km (46 miles) south of Ailsa Craig from which, one suspects, the founders came. Scar Rocks are bare, composed of a hard, blue-grey schist with some quartz which has weathered to produce good seabird ledges. Gannets attempted to establish themselves as early as 1883 and may have bred, but there are no immediately subsequent details. Possibly, the later (1939) attempt was helped by the war, which reduced disturbance, and their presence then drew in a steady trickle of recruits. Gannets nest solely on the Big Scar, 18–21 m (60–70 ft) high and 92 m (300 ft) long. The early counts show a tiny colony of between two and six pairs in 1939 rising to about 500 by 1970, since when there has been no further increase, but in fact a slight decline. The rate of growth, due to immigration, has been much faster than at Bempton, which started at roughly the same time, probably because Scar Rocks lie athwart much greater traffic, are nearer to a major gannetry, and are topographically more attractive.

Summary of counts: 2–6 pairs (1939), c. 10 pairs (1941), 20–25 nests (1942), 140–150 pairs (1943), 35–45 nests (1945), at least 28 nests (1946), 90 nests (1948), 100 nests (1949), 134 nests (1953), 158 nests (1957), 167 nests (1960), c. 200 pairs (1962), at least 240 breeding pairs, with a maximum of 300 nests (1965), 437 nests (1968), 450 nests (1969),

---

* All counts, 1936–1976 inclusive, by J. A. Gibson (numbers of pairs).
† Photographic counts by S. Wanless (numbers of pairs). But see Table 2, for it is difficult to give a single figure as representative of an entire year.

500 nests (1970), 480 nests (1971), 430 nests (1972), 471 nests (1973), 482 nests (1974)[147].

(10) *St Kilda, Outer Hebrides, Scotland (latest count 59,258 pairs, 1973)*

St Kilda is the world's greatest (Atlantic) gannetry, though only by default, for in the last century it was far exceeded by Bird Rocks (St Lawrence). The gannetry itself was never inhabited by man, but as everybody knows, the doughty St Kildans from Hirta regularly climbed freely on these precipitous faces, gathering adult gannets and gugas for their feathers, fat and meat. This was a true culture, comparable to any other in which people are fully dependent on wild animals, giving rise to the same sort of folklore, astonishingly detailed natural history, and fierce attachment in the face of obvious hardship. Probably, the impoverished St Kildans were happier than are today's affluent car workers on the production line.

Situated on the edge of the continental shelf, 72 km (45 miles) west of North Uist, these volcanic islands are the visible remnants of a broken ring of granite and gabbro, deeply sculptured. St Kilda's cliffs are the greatest in Britain. Boreray's western wall is a sheer 380 m (1,250 ft). It is attended by Stac an Armin, 191 m (625 ft), and Stac Lee, 166 m (545 ft). Not for St Kilda the choppy waters of a petty Forth, gazing across to cultivated fields and the works of man, but the measured swell of the open sea and the brute violence of ocean winds. What a place for gannets!

The difficulties of counting gannets there are formidable and estimates, prior to Boyd's[11] count from photographs, probably have a potential error of at least 30%, often much more. Perhaps, oddly, the first mention of St Kilda comes long after the Bass and Ailsa, when Sibbald (1684) noted that gannets nested on the Bass, Ailsa and Hebrides. The first reasonable estimate, quoted and accepted by Gurney, was that of 1902: 3,500–4,000 nests on Stac Lee, 3,000 on Stac an Armin, and 8,000 on Boreray, some 15,000 nests in all. This is considerably less than would be calculated from the number of gugas reputedly taken, but these were almost certainly highly exaggerated. The next estimate, from a count in 1931, was 21,300 birds (10,000 on Stac Lee, 7,000 on Armin and 4,300 on Boreray), but even its author warned that it could be far wrong. This transmutes to 18,521 pairs if one assumes they were all site-holders and that 15% were occupied by pairs at the time of the count; absent site-holders might increase the total to 19,500 occupied sites. It is interesting that Boreray held thousands *less* than the other two, whereas in 1902 it held thousands *more*. This could hardly have been an artefact and fits well with what we now know about shifts in distribution within gannetries. The 1939 and 1949 counts (16,900 pairs and 17,035 pairs) hardly differ from the previous counts back to 1902 and suggests that during the first half of the 20th century Kilda did not experience the burgeoning increases shown by Grassholm, Skellig, and Bull Rock. Gannet raids by the

islanders had virtually ceased by 1902 and any young in excess of those needed to keep Kilda's numbers up must have gone elsewhere. In 1959, however, a photographic count[11] produced a figure of 44,526 pairs. This represents an average annual increase of 10·1% since the 1949 count, which means that St Kilda must have been receiving immigrants. Ten years later, in 1969, the 'Seafarer' count gave 52,099 pairs but this difference ought to be treated with the utmost reserve, for the 1969 count came from combined photographs taken in three different months and gave only partial coverage. From photographs taken in 1973, a total of 59,258 site-occupying pairs was derived.[27] This represents a 37% increase over 1959, which is 2·1% per annum for this period, or well within the colony's own capacity for increase. On the face of it, therefore, a period of increase partly dependent on immigration was followed by one of increase which *could* have been produced by St Kilda itself. But apart from the inherent inaccuracies of the counts, interpretation depends on the period over which the yearly increase is calculated. However, it is clear that St Kilda has increased markedly since 1939, though the balance between immigration and emigration remains unknown.

Summary of counts: Up to 1902, unreliable estimates of the number of gannets taken, together with wild guesses (up to 200,000) of the number present. About 15,000 nests (1902), 21,300 *birds* (1931) (this count was transmuted to 16,500 breeding pairs), 16,900 pairs (1939), 17,035 pairs (1949), 44,526 pairs (1959), 52,099 pairs (1969), 59,258 pairs (1973).

(11) *Flannans (Roareim), Outer Hebrides (latest count 17 nests, 1973)*

There are seven main islands in this group, which lies some 27 km (17 miles) west-north-west of Gallan Head, Lewis. All are cliffbound (Roareim's are about 50 m (165 ft) high). Gannets were first noticed in June 1969 when about 16 pairs (35 birds) were counted from the sea. Nest contents could not be determined. Since then the only count (again from the sea and from photographs) yielded 17 nests (29 birds),[9] and a brief inspection from the air (1977)[56] showed around 20 pairs. From this it seems that Roareim is still very much in the throes of becoming fully established. One may wonder why it has grown so slowly, but Bempton, Saltee and Scar Rocks did much the same.

(12) *Bearasay, Hebrides*

No breeding as yet. The gannet's increase this century has taken in rather few new localities. Fair Isle is the latest, but Bearasay and Foula may soon be added. Bearasay lies off Bernera on the west coat of Lewis, within sight of that other recently founded colony, the Flannans. It has sheer cliffs, some of them with suitably broad ledges. A pair of adults has been present in 1973, 1974 and 1975.[56]

(13) *Sula Sgeir, Outer Hebrides (latest count c. 9,000 pairs, 1972)*

This remote gannetry well to the west of Sule Stack and 64 km (40 miles) north-east of the Butt of Lewis, is known by repute to everybody interested in seabirds, though trodden by few. It is a great haunt of grey seals and Leach's petrels, besides a magnificent gannetry. Within living memory, and despite the culls, gannets have increased (though by immigration) and now nest on the summit flats as well as the cliffs. Early estimates are understandably rough. In fact they vary by no more than the potential counting error. Thus the 1884 figure, which was also the highest (7,000 pairs) hardly differs from the 1949 estimate (6,200 nests), and the lowest count (1939) was 4,000 pairs. The 1969 'Seafarer' count gave 9,000 pairs, whilst a direct count and one from photographs, both in July 1972, gave 9,940 and 9,000 occupied sites respectively – an amazingly good correspondence.[34] So a real increase has occurred since 1949 and visible evidence lies in the extension of occupied ground to a point (reached in 1958) 6 m (20 ft) beyond the 1954 limits, which were marked by a cairn.

The interpretation of population trends is complicated by the practice of harvesting gugas (see plates), which still occurs here, as it has done since at least 1549, and perhaps since the 12th century or earlier. If the average breeding population between 1919 and 1958 (years chosen because the number of gannets taken is roughly known) is estimated as 6,000 pairs (a generous figure), then on reasonable assumptions of breeding success and mortality Sula Sgeir produced 180,000 young. The Noss men took at least 44,840 (assuming only 19 raids) leaving (after natural mortality) some 33,750 to survive to adulthood. Since only 27,900 adults would have died in this period the colony could have increased by its own output. However, the gannet raiders have traditionally taken both young and adults in large numbers. Killing adults has a far more serious effect than taking young and probably rules out any possibility of Sula Sgeir's increase stemming from its own output. Indeed, the increase between 1939 and 1969 was 2·7% per year, which is almost that of an *unexploited* colony. Probably many birds come from Sule Stack.

Summary of counts: c. 7,000 pairs (1884), over 5,000 pairs (1887), about 7,000 pairs (1891), c. 5,000 pairs (1932), c. 4,400 pairs (1937), c. 4,000 pairs (1939), c. 6,200 pairs (1949), 8,964 pairs (1969), c. 9,000 occupied sites (1972).

(14) *Sule Stack or Stack Skerry, Outer Hebrides (latest count 4,018 pairs, 1969)*

This eroded stack of naked hornblende gneiss about 40 m (130 ft) high and covering about 2·4 hectares (6 acres), lies 64 km (40 miles) north-north-east of Cape Wrath, and west of Orkney mainland. There is a small, south rock separated from the deeply cleft main hump by a narrow channel. The north hump is covered with gannets and gives the impression of being full. The south hump is much frequented by non-breeding birds, probably mainly young birds in immature, subadult or new-adult plumage. The south hump has held nesting birds (6 pairs in 1914 and 100 pairs in 1939) but there were no nesting birds there in 1967,[124] though the customary 3,000 or so 'non-breeders'.

Sule Stack is an ancient gannetry, established at least as early as 1710, but so inaccessible that only a handful of naturalists have visited it this last half century, though until about 1932 it was regularly 'harvested', up to 1,200 birds being taken in some years. Despite this, the population evidently remained fairly stable. In 1887 the entire summit was densely populated and it seems that between then and the present time there has been relatively little change. This is probably because the rock has been virtually full. The 1967 count (3,500 nests) divided the birds into 2,000 on the summit and sides, other than the east, and 1,500 on the east face. These figures plainly show that Sule Stack must be exporting most of its recruits; its own annual increase between 1939 and 1969 was less than 0·5%. With this in mind, the notably large number of non-breeders in the south hump, which at an estimated 3,500 in 1967[124] is proportionately the largest recorded for any gannetry, raises interesting questions. Are they Sule Stack recruits, those in adult plumage 'waiting to get in', or are they part of the large population of 'floaters', many of them born at gannetries other than Sule Stack? Probably some of each.

Summary of counts: 3,500 pairs (1890), 4,000 pairs (1904), 5,000–6,000 pairs (1914), 3,500 pairs (1937), 3,490 nests (1939), 2,010 pairs (1949), very approx. 2,800 pairs (1960), 3,500 nests (1967), 4,018 pairs (1969).

(15) *Fair Isle, Shetlands (latest count at least 34 occupied sites, 1977)*

In summer 1973, up to 300 gannets, mostly immature, spent time along the west coast of Fair Isle[13] and a few adults were noted high upon the cliffs of the main island. In 1974, birds came back to the same ledge from 26 April (or earlier) and by early June up to 100 were on the main island at Dronger, though usually there were 25–35 birds. Five nests were built on a ledge at Glimpster but no eggs were noted. In 1975, 17 nests were built of which at least five contained eggs. Four chicks were reared. The largest number of birds seen on the cliffs was 80 on 14 June. In 1976 there were 27 occupied nests, though nine were not consistently attended. Seventeen or 18 eggs were laid, 15 chicks were seen and probably 14 fledged. In 1977 at least 34 sites were occupied, of which 26 held large nests. At least 20 eggs were laid and about 15 chicks fledged. In early July, some 450 birds were on the cliffs. This is the time of year when non-breeders, many of them probably transitory, swell the numbers. Though the latest in the string of new colonies, Fair Isle almost certainly will not be the last.

(16) *Foula, Shetlands*

Although Foula's narrow and crumbling ledges are basically unsuitable for gannets, there is a heavy passage of birds off the island and the early stages of colonisation are now underway. Gannets have been showing interest in Foula for more than 10 years,[60] carrying nest material in the vicinity and landing on the stack. Since about 1973[41] there have been up to 150 birds settling on and near the flat-topped stack on the east(?) side. In 1977 about seven or eight nests were built following less active nest-building in 1976, but no eggs laid.

(17) *Noss, Shetlands (latest count 5,498 adults, 1977)*

A small island lying on the east side of the Shetlands, Noss (the nose or rocky point) was, as its brochs show, at one time inhabited. The gannetry lies on the south-east cliffs from the Noup of Noss, a 184 m (600 ft) cliff with faces to north and south, to about 1·6 km (1 mile) south of the Noup. All the gannets nest on inaccessible ledges, well down the cliff face. From Rumblewick, a cliff between the Noup and Geordies Holes, one gets an excellent view of part of the gannetry, whilst the entire north and south faces of the Noup and Rumblewick can be viewed from a distance, and the north face of the Noup from the Point of Heogatoug.

Gannets first prospected Noss in 1911 or 1912 and the first pair bred above Rumblewick in 1914, followed by four pairs the next year, five in 1919 and ten in 1920. We do not know when 'take-off point' occurred, but by 1930 there were about 200 pairs, so it is reasonable to assume that it was roughly as at Bempton and Saltee, at perhaps around 30–50 pairs. In 1934 or 1935, a very rough estimate gave 800 pairs, and by 1938 and 1939 more accurate counts gave 1,518 and 1,830 nests respectively. The increase continued, and in 1946 the estimate,[105] admittedly rough, was 2,600 to 3,775 pairs. The 'Seafarer' count of 1969 yielded about 4,300 pairs. Since then, there have been three counts, for details of which I am much indebted to M. G. Richardson of the Nature Conservancy Council. In 1970 and 1974 den Held counted 8,181 adults and 8,093 adults respectively, and in 1977 C. Fillmore counted 5,498 adults. den Held counted from the land, and Fillmore made five counts from an inflatable in calm conditions. Assuming 20% of nests occupied by pairs, the 1970 and 1974 counts represented approximately 6,700 site-occupying pairs. den Held calculated that, in 1974, Noss held 4,100 nests *with young*, which, assuming 30% empty nests (see Chapter 4), gives approximately 5,900 nest- or site-occupying pairs. It is not yet possible to judge whether the apparent decline in 1977 resulted from the different method of counting, or from the withdrawal of transitory birds which had been included in the count (see Ailsa Craig). The annual increase between 1939 and 1969 was 2·8%, which is about the rate at which it could have grown by its own output, though its earlier explosive growth must have depended on considerable immigration.

There are some possible areas still uncolonised, so presumably there is potential for further growth, though most of this would not be visible from the land. Non-breeding birds gather in several areas, including wave-cut platforms at the foot of the Noup,[65a] and there is a fringe of newly established pairs along the edges of breeding groups.

Summary of counts: 1 pair (1914), 4 pairs (1915), 5 pairs (1919), 10 pairs (1920), *c*. 200 pairs (1931), *c*. 800 pairs (1935), *c*. 900 (+?) pairs (1937), 1,518 pairs (1938), 1,830 pairs (1939), 2,600–3,775 pairs (1946), 2,100–2,300 pairs (1949), *c*. 4,000 (pairs?) (1955), 4,300 pairs (1969), 8,181 adults (1970), 8,093 adults (1974), 5,498 adults (1977).

(18) *Hermaness, Shetland (latest count 6,012 nests, 1970)*

Hermaness is a peninsula in the extreme north-west of Unst, the most northerly island in the Shetlands. The strata slope to the east and the high cliffs and stacks are on the west. The gannets nest on the offshore skerry to the north, and on the western cliffs of the Hermaness Nature Reserve. The colony was established on Vesta Skerry by 1917, and spread from there to Burra Stack (109 pairs by 1920), Humla Houl, the Neap and Neapra Stack (possibly over 600 pairs by 1934, and 1,000 in 1935) and to Humla Stack (2,045 pairs by 1938). Subsequent counts for the entire colony gave 2,611 nests (1939); nearly 4,000 nests (1945); at least 3,150 nests (1949); 3,450 (±900) sites (1965) and 5,894 pairs (1969). The 1965 count excluded the western faces of the large stacks on the west coast of part of the area. Recent counts[115] have shown that significant fluctuations are occurring at Hermaness, though an appreciation of the events requires an examination of the different parts of the colony rather than the simple total. Counts (occupied sites) for Humla, Burra Stack, and Clingra Stack, together, went from 1,200 (1965) to 1,148 (1969), 892 (1974), 618 (1975), 988 (1976), the overall decreases from 1965 to 1976 being 212 (17·6%). By contrast the population counts in the area from Neap to Saito Point were: 2,250 (1965), 2,470 (1969), 4,333 (1974), 3,692 (1975) and 3,799 (1976), the increase from 1965 to 1976 being 1,549 (68·8%). There are apparently large fluctuations in the numbers of 'club' birds (up to about 1,800) around the colony, which could indicate that 'floaters' are constantly swelling and depleting the reserves from which transitory site holders could come.

Between 1935 and 1938 immigration was definitely continuing from the early days of the colony's establishment. Between 1939 and 1969 the average rate of increase was 2·6% per year, or about the rate to be expected from Hermaness' own output, but between 1965 and 1969 the increase was 10·8% per year. The apparent unevenness of the rate of immigration thus agrees, in type, with the evidence cited above.

In 1976, five pairs bred on a large rock at Soorie Geo and almost 100 gannets were flying around in the bay near the Kame of Flouravoug, and settling on adjacent cliffs. Early in July, about 500 birds were on and around Gruney at the Ramna Stacks, at the north end of Yell Sound.[115] It will be interesting to see if these localities eventually become nesting places.

Summary of counts: Established (1917), 109+ pairs (1920), less than 1,000 pairs (1928), c. 1,000 pairs (1935), 2,045 pairs (1938), 2,611 pairs (1939), c. 4,000 pairs (1945), 3,150+ nests (1949), 3,450±900 sites (1965), 5,894 pairs (1969), 6,012 pairs (1976).

EAST BRITAIN

(19) *Bass Rock, East Lothian, Scotland (latest count 13,500 occupied sites, 1977)*

Until Bempton was founded in the 1920s or 1930s, the Bass Rock was the only colony on the east coast of Britain. This stands in marked contrast to the west, where a string of gannetries extends along the entire seaboard.

Bass Rock. What vivid associations those two words have had for centuries. For me they evoke all the feelings bound up with island living. There are grander isles, wilder rocks, but there is nowhere with quite that blend of might, history, caverns, cliffs, seabirds and – something that could detract from its appeal, but somehow doesn't – a close association with man, the beautiful Lothian plains and the Kingdom of Fife. For, on a quiet summer's evening, sounds carry clearly from the mainland, and Tantallon Castle, 3 km (2 miles) away, seems but a stone's throw. Then, the puffins gather in the worn old battlements, the gargling of guillemots swells, the eye passes easily from the green trees and fertile fields to the sparkling firth and the whitened cliffs, and it all blends. Perhaps it is because, within view, nothing man-made is yet an eyesore. The Bass remains blessedly unspoilt and industry's ugly manifestations at Prestonpans and beyond are mercifully distant. The May Isle, Craigleith, the Lamb and Fidra are 'real', and welcome to the eye.

The Bass Rock lies in the outer reaches of the Firth of Forth, 40 km (25 miles) east-south-east of Edinburgh. To the north lie rich sand-eel fishing grounds in St Andrew's Bay and the Tay estuary, whilst to the south are the highly productive fishing grounds off the Farnes, where Bass gannets often feed (sometimes in thousands) in Belhaven Bay off Dunbar. The Bass Rock is one of a series of volcanic plugs stretching across the Scottish Lowlands, matched on the mainland by North Berwick Law and Arthur's Seat. It is made of clinker basalt, black and rusty where not whitened by seabird excreta. It looks big because it is so near, but is only about 1·5 km (1 mile) round the base, 100 m (340 ft) high and with a planar area of some 2·8 ha (7 acres). The highest sheer cliffs, approaching 90 m (300 ft), are on the north-west – precipices with dark, narrow ledges. The west and south-west cliffs are more round-shouldered, and drier, with broader ledges. The east, also, is towering, in places virtually smooth, rejecting even the kittiwakes. Gloomy caverns hide in its base, alive with guillemots, whirring out, plopping into the water and diving, the silvery air bubbles fading as they go. The south side is open, descending to the lighthouse and battlements and thence to the mallow slope and the rocky spur on which are the two landing places and (since 1974) a helicopter pad.

Its surface is well vegetated, pleasantly turfed on the south and east but, increasingly since the gulls took over, unattractively lush with soft stemmed *Holcus mollis* on the north, west and summit. On the east, below the summit, there is a walled garden from the days when the garrison was occupied (primarily in the 14th–17th centuries, inclusive), and a well which is fed by seepage and provides water the colour of rich urine, to be recommended for tanning the skin but not for diluting the blood. We used to stagger down the hill carrying this stuff in a dustbin, to use for washing. Lower down, on the south face, sits the

14th century chapel, probably on the site of St Baldred's 7th century cell, though if it were me, I would cut a hole further down still, out of those blistering westerly winds that were the curse of our life. The famous garrison, never conquered throughout its long life, dominates the only landing place and its battlements look directly across to Tantallon. Those interested in the rich civil and ecclesiastical history of the Bass should read M'Crie.[69]

The Bass, or 'solangoosifera bassa', is the *locus classicus* for the gannet. It would be fascinating to know when gannets first came, but this is likely to have been before man existed. Bass gannets are first mentioned in John de Fordun's *Scotichronicon* of 1447; Hector Boece's oft-quoted account 'certes there is nothing in this rock which is not full of admiration and wonder; thereine also is great store of soland geese . . . and nowhere else but in Ailsaic and this rocke' probably drew at least in part on Major, the best of the early accounts, in which Bass gannets are described as 'a marvellous multitude'. Other 16th century descriptions, probably derivative, are equally lyrical and imprecise (see Chapter 7 for further historical notes). Harvey accompanied Charles I to the Bass in 1641 and remarked that the surface of the island was almost completely covered with nests, 'so that you can scarcely find free footing anywhere'. This tallies with other early chroniclers, such as

Slezer ('the surface of it being almost covered with their nests, eggs and young birds'), Sibbald and Mackay. Into the 19th century, apparently, they still nested on the summit, and whilst Macgillivray's estimate of 20,000 birds in 1831 may be too high, his remark that 'the nests are placed on all parts of the rock where a convenient spot occurs but are much more numerous towards the summit' is of interest. He describes, also, 300 nests on a gravelly slope near the landing place, which must refer to the slope beneath the battlements, a most improbable place and not now used. Fleming's 1847 estimate of 5,000 pairs, based on extrapolation from the 1,800 juveniles taken annually, seems likely to be the most accurate up to that time.

The subsequent decrease, which continued until at least the end of the 19th century, was partly due to the wanton shooting of nesting birds '. . . evil days came upon the gannets when their principal value was thought to be only as a mark of sportsmen . . . One year the whole west front of the rock was depopulated. This . . . must have gone on for a good many years for when I (Gurney) was at the Bass in 1876 the lessee still bitterly resented the numbers shot after the 1st of August (when therefore the close season ended) many of them even while flying with fish to their young ones', adding that he had seen the sea strewn with dead gannets which the shooters did not trouble to pick up. Nevertheless, it seems there were some on the slopes as late as 1862. This, however, need not mean more than that a few were to be found just above the cliff edge.

Actual estimates in the second half of the 19th century were c. 6,000 pairs (1869) and c. 10,000 pairs (1871). These are almost certainly unreliable figures as shooting was rife at that time and the rate at which young were being taken was dropping, which probably indicated a falling population. At any rate, the first critical estimate in the 20th century, taken from photographs in 1904, was of 7,000–8,000 individuals, which Gurney considered much too high. After this, protection, plus the cessation of culling (since 1885), began to take effect and numbers began to rise. The 1913 estimate was about 3,250 pairs; the 1929 count 4,147 nests; the 1936 estimate 4,150 nests; the nest counts of 1939 and 1949, respectively, 4,374 and 4,820. My count of June 1962 gave a maximum of 7,126 (minimum 6,690) occupied sites which, allowing for a potential error of at least 10%, gives 6,021 to 7,839, or roughly 6,000–8,000 occupied sites. Another estimate in July 1968 gave 8,977 (say 9,000) pairs which, on the same potential error, gives 8,000–10,000 pairs. In 1974 there were some 1,500–2,000 extra sites, mainly on the north-west and west slopes and to a lesser extent on the cliff top above the north face. I estimated the 1974 population to be 9,500–11,500 site-owning pairs. Counts from photographs in May 1977, gave approximately 13,500 occupied sites, which represents around 4% per annum increase since the previous estimate, which was only a rough one.

The increases in most of the colonies described so far has been due in part, or mainly, to immigration and, in view of the Bass' isolated position, it is of particular interest to know whether this applies here, too. From the figures given (and in the summary) it appears that between 1904 and 1977 the increase per annum has been about 3%, fluctuating between less than 1% and 5·5% in successive periods. Between 1939 and 1969, when the counts were probably the most accurate, the annual increase was 2·4%. Thus, the large increases and decreases recorded for Ailsa, and the large increases seen at many other west coast colonies, are conspicuously absent from the Bass, and the increase recorded fits well with that which would be expected were the Bass Rock an autonomous colony, experiencing little or no loss or gain through emigration or immigration. It is known that the Bass loses some recruits to Bempton, but so far the number has been negligible.

At present Bass Rock gannets, like the species as a whole, are, simply, climbing steadily back to their former numbers following wholesale depletion by man; they are not 'exploding' in any sense. Their most spectacular advances have been on the north-west and west slopes, and there seems no reason why this should not continue, though significantly hampered, particularly on the west, by disturbance. On the east they cannot pass the concrete path and handrail and it seems unlikely that they will ever occupy the entire summit whilst these obstacles remain – but, of course, they may not do so for ever! The disproportionately rapid growth on the north-west was initially the result of our protection, which allowed new breeders to establish themselves. This in turn created a lively area of expansion which funnelled in birds, some of which would otherwise have settled elsewhere on the rock. A similar effect has created a flourishing little group opposite the top of the lighthouse. There is a growing group above the south cliffs, west of the battlements, and although the mighty east cliffs at the south are too smooth for gannets, there is a group on a low spur just above the splash zone. Round to the north the cliffs present broader ledges and are densely occupied to the top, and continue so round into the northern and north-west sectors. The northern rim, west of the foghorn, is now attracting growth but suffers from disturbance, which can hardly be helped; visitors naturally swing west after following the path to its end. The finer features of distribution on the Bass are thus attributable to man's influence. When the Bass was completely covered, it might well have held 20 or 30,000 pairs.

No account of Bass gannets would be complete without mention of the black-browed albatross that visited the Rock between May and August in 1967 and was seen again in 1968 and possibly 1969. It consorted with the gannets[139] and attempted to display with or to them. It roosted on the Bass, and was caught and handled at least once. In the 1970s, it (for it seems likely to have been the same individual) turned up at the Hermaness gannetry and is still visiting there.

Black-browed albatrosses are the most likely member of their redoubtable family to be met in the northern hemisphere, and, once there, will naturally be attracted to gannets, which they resemble quite closely. One was shot on Myggenaes in May 1894. It was believed to have spent several summers there and apparently was known as the 'Sulkonge' or Gannet King.[48] It was shot because it was said to act as sentinel and thus to hinder the islanders from taking gannets. There have been several sightings of this species at sea, off the British Isles, in the last fifteen years and 1967 appears to have been a peak year.[139]

Summary of counts: c. 10,000 pairs (1831), c. 5,000 pairs (1847), very rough estimate c. 3,400 pairs (1850), c. 6,000 pairs (1869), guess of c. 10,000 pairs (1871), c. 3,000 pairs (1904), c. 3,250 (1913), 4,147 pairs (1929), c. 4,150 pairs (1936), 4,374 nests (1939), 4,820 nests (1949), c. 7,000 occupied sites (1962), c. 9,000 occupied sites (1968), c. 10,500 occupied sites (1974), c. 13,500 occupied sites (1977).

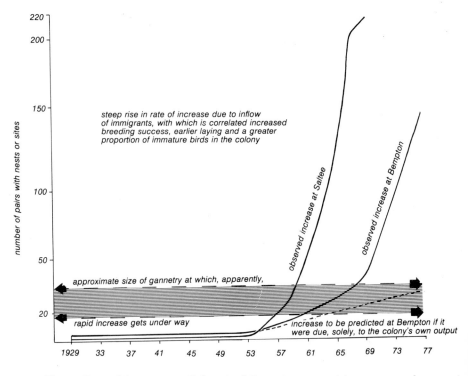

Fig. 8. *Rate of increase at Saltee and Bempton gannetries compared with the rate at which they would have grown had there been no immigration*

(20) Bempton, Yorkshire, England (latest count 169 occupied sites, 1977)

Bempton, Britain's only mainland gannetry (see plates) is growing in fame, as in size. Since 1974, it has been a reserve of the RSPB and earlier it was a renowned 'egg-climbers' cliff. The precipitous limestone cliffs of this great and ancient seabird haunt form a splendid site scenically, even though (I have been told!) a second-rate one from the gannet's viewpoint. The usable ledges are on the whole very narrow, and separated by large areas of completely impossible cliffs, so that the gannetry cannot become large and dense, as most colonies do. Gannets gained a toehold in the 1920s or 1930s, probably the former, but the early years were not documented. The gannet sites were virtually invisible from the cliff top and the 'climmers' did not keep written records. The growth of the colony is of great interest because of the way in which it suddenly began to increase fairly rapidly, after a long period of near-stagnation, and because of the changes in age-structure, timing of breeding and breeding success that accompanied the rise in numbers. These ecological aspects are described in Chapter 4. Here it may merely be said that the colony grew from its original one or two pairs, to less than 10 occupied sites throughout the 1950s, and to 21 pairs by 1969, after which it increased more rapidly: 24–30 (1970); 33 (1971); 44 or more (1972); c. 80 (1973); c. 100 (1974) and at least 120 pairs (1975). These figures refer to pairs with a definite site and usually a nest, though they have not necessarily been known to lay. The recent increase (some 25% per year between 1970 and 1974) like the earlier ones, has undoubtedly been due mainly to immigration. Bass gannets regularly pass Bempton during dispersal and feeding movements. Three of my Bass Rock colour-ringed chicks turned up as breeders on Bempton and it is likely that most if not all the immigrants are from the Bass. Now, Bempton has a dispersed 'club' of immatures and young adults, which is growing larger. Increasing numbers of young birds are being attracted by the burgeoning social activity at Bempton.

Summary of counts:[18,35] 1 or 2 pairs (1920s, 1930s), probably less than 4 pairs (1940s), less than 10 occupied sites (1950s), c. 9 occupied sites (1960), 21 occupied sites (1969), 24–30 pairs (1970), c. 33 pairs (1971), 44 or more pairs (1972), c. 80 pairs (1973), c. 100 pairs (1974), at least 120 pairs (1975), 133 pairs (1976), 169 pairs (1977).

ICELAND, FAEROES AND NORWAY

Again, this is merely a grouping of convenience until we know more about the nature of any interchange between these and other gannetries. The most recent estimates of the size of Icelandic gannetries are given in Table 3.

(21) *Westmann Islands, Iceland (latest count 5,315 pairs, 1960)*

The Vestmannaeyjar or Westmann Islands are of unequal size and importance as gannetries. Sulnasker, the largest, is about 92 m (300 ft) high and gannets nest on the cliffs and summit. Geldungur split into two stacks in 1896 (Stori- and Litli-.) and gannets nest on both. The other two Westmann gannetries are on Brandur and Hellisey.

The nineteenth century population was probably in the order of several thousand pairs. The record of 400–500 gannets taken annually from Sulnasker alone[38] means that this colony probably held well over

2,000 pairs; it was the largest of the four Westmann colonies. Gurney thought that, altogether, there were probably more than 4,000 'breeding individuals' (presumably this means 2,000 site owning pairs) in the Westmann Islands as a whole. By 1919[97] the figure was put at considerably more than 5,000 pairs, though the 1932 count of 3,900 'breeding pairs' was nevertheless considered too high by Lockley and Salmon, who modified it to 3,514 pairs. In 1935, 317 nests were counted on Brandur and about 2,600 on Hellisey, but the first accurate count of all four rocks was in 1939, and in terms of nests gave: Brandur (467); Hellisey (1,703); Geldungur (589) and Sulnasker (1,600) – a grand total of 4,359 nests. In 1949 the comparable figures were 487, 2,216, 913 and 1,918, total 5, 534 pairs. In 1960 the figures were very similar (Brandur 436, Hellisey 2,057, Geldungur 1,122 and Sulnasker 1,682, total 5,315 pairs) but the items counted were probably not strictly comparable since (presumably?) birds owning sites but not nests, were excluded from the 1939 totals.

The relative stability of this group may depend partly on the fact that the annual cull is variable, rather than fixed. It probably does receive immigrants, perhaps from Eldey, particularly, which for many years has been apparently full, but nevertheless the Westmann group has not markedly increased.

Summary of counts: *c*. 2,000 pairs (1898), *c*. 5,000 pairs (around 1919), *c*. 3,514 pairs (1932), *c*. 4,000 pairs (1935), 4,359 pairs (1939), 5,534 pairs (1949), *c*. 5,315 pairs (1960).

(22) *Eldey, Iceland (latest estimate 16,300 pairs, 1962)*

Eldey, 77 m (250 ft) high, is one of four volcanic rocks south-west of Cape Reykjanes. Eldey itself, 'the mealsack', is the most northerly rock, the only gannetry of the four and an ancient one, the first references under the name Fuglasker, the bird skerries, going back to at least 1772.

Around 1908, about 4,100 birds a year were being taken from Eldey and the population must presumably have been well over 6,000 site-occupying pairs – perhaps as high as 10,000. It is difficult to know what proportion of the total output of young was taken but, because of Eldey's topography, it was probably unusually high. A count in 1935 gave 9,328 nests. Eldey has been protected since 1940 and the population has increased. An aerial photograph in July 1942 yielded 8,840 'breeding' pairs (my commas); and in July 1953, 15,178 pairs. The 1962 total was 16,300 pairs, giving an annual increase of 3·1% between 1939 and 1962. Possibly, Eldey can accommodate at least 18,000 pairs.

Summary of counts: Possibly *c*. 10,000 pairs (1894, 1904, 1919), *c*. 9,000 pairs (1934), 9,328 pairs (1939), 9,000+ pairs (1941, 1942), 15,178 pairs (1953), 16,300 pairs (1962).

(23–26) *Skrudur, Raudinupur, Stori-Karl, Mafadrang*

These four small Icelandic colonies[31] were founded between 1940 and 1960 but none of them has grown much. Skrudur, the earliest and largest, numbered 134–150 pairs in 1949 and 314 in 1961. By then, ten

pairs had moved onto the top of the island; previously all had nested on the cliffs. Raudinupur consists of the main colony on Solvanof and (since 1959) a pair or two on Karlinn. In 1949 and 1952 there were only eight pairs on the cliffs and none on top. Since then, part of the cliff has collapsed but it still held 33 pairs in 1962. Stori-Karl held 23 pairs in 1959–62, and Mafadrang 100 pairs in 1959 and 1962, all of them on cliffs. A fifth potential colony (Drangey), which held one pair in 1949, did not persist.

The present increase in the Icelandic gannet population is within the production capacity of its own gannetries but it seems unlikely that the Icelandic population is discrete. There is probably interchange with the Westmanns and perhaps with the Faeroes and Norway. Even interchange with British and Irish colonies cannot be totally excluded.

(27) *Myggenaes (Mykines) Holm, Faeroes (latest count 1,500–2,550 occupied nests, 1972)*

The stack of basaltic columns, the Holm, lies to the west of Myggenaes. An ancient colony, probably much older than its first record (1673), it has long been culled. Most nests are on a broad ledge on the north face about 30 m (100 ft) above sea-level, with small groups above and below. Gannets nest, also, on the summits of the small neighbouring stacks of Pikarsdrangur and Flatidrangur (31·7 and 24·7 m (104 and 81 ft) respectively).

Apparently, Myggenaes has never been a huge colony and consistent culling has played a part in keeping numbers down. The 1892 estimate of 750 pairs was made when, perhaps, 300 adults and twice as many young were being taken each year, so it is hardly surprising that there were still only 750 pairs in 1928. By 1935 there were about 900 pairs, rising to 1,615 pairs in 1937 and 1,473 in 1939. The 1966 and 1972 counts gave 1,801 and 2,982 birds, representing 1,500–2,550 occupied nests depending on the correction factors used.[136]

Despite culls, Myggenaes grew at a yearly rate of 2·3% between 1909 and 1939, and must have been receiving immigrants. During this period, of course, the gannet population in general was increasing. Similarly, about 1,000 birds per year were still being taken in 1969, yet there was a marked increase between 1939 and 1972.

Summary of counts: estimated 750 pairs (1892), c. 750 pairs (1928), c. 900 pairs (1935), 1,615 pairs (1937), 1,645 pairs (1938), 1,473 pairs (1939), 1,801 birds (1,500 pairs?) (1966), 2,982 birds (2,550 pairs?) (1972).

(28) *Storebranden, Runde, Norway (latest count 494 nests, 1974)*

Norway's largest gannetry is on a rock of granitic gneiss, with cliffs rising to more than 150 m (500 ft) in the north-west, where gannets established themselves in 1946. Once again, the first decade saw relatively little progress (14 birds in 1947 and 80 in 1956) though even this was more than the colony could have produced on its own. After this period the increase was more rapid. By 1963 there were almost 200 occupied sites; by 1968 over 300 and by 1972 more than 400 occupied sites.[17] Growth has certainly been largely due to immigration.

Summary of counts: established 1946; 14 *individuals* (1947), 481 individuals (1954), 60 (1955), 80 (1956), 325 (1962), 196 *occupied sites* (1963), 214 (1966), 326 (1968), 331 (1970), 383 (1971), 422 (1972), 494 pairs (1974).

(29) *Skittenskarvholmen, Mosken, Norway (latest count 65 nests, 1974)*

This is a group of accessible bare granite islets some 2 km (1¼ miles) north-west of Mosken in the Outer Lofoten Islands. The largest, 125 m (400 ft) long, 50 m (165 ft) wide and only 5 m (17 ft) high, holds the gannetry. The nests are a mere 5–12 m (17–40 ft) above sea-level on the eastern part, among some 70 pairs of cormorants. Breeding was first confirmed in 1968 though the colony may have been established as early as 1960. There were at least 60 established pairs in 1969 and probably 100 or more in 1970 (83 nests with eggs or chicks). In 1971, 1972 and 1974, the counts for nests with contents were 77, 60 and 65, which probably reflects the considerable disturbance by man. Again, the earlier increases were due to immigration.

Summary of counts: established 1960(?), 50 nests with contents (1969), 83 nests with contents (1970), 77 nests with contents (1971), 60 pairs (1972), 64 pairs (1974).

(30) *Skarvlakken, Nordmjele, Norway (latest count 145 pairs, 1974)*

This is another tiny rock, 150 m (500 ft) long, 50 m (165 ft) wide and only 8 m (26 ft) high. The nests are 4–7 m (13–23 ft) above sea-level and the rock is shared with 150–200 pairs of cormorants and about 30

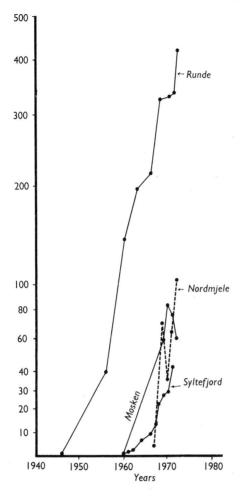

Fig. 9. *Norwegian gannet population 1940–73*

pairs of shags. Like the last rock, Skittenskarvholmen, this is most unusually low for a gannetry. Although this area possesses few cliffs, the island of Vaerøy provides a site similar to Runde (above), equally near to good fishing areas; yet the gannets chose the small, low islets of Skittenskarvholmen and Skarvlakken. As Brun suggested,[16] on both these low rocks, the cormorants may have attracted the gannets. Skarvlakken was established in 1967 (4 pairs) and, after a couple of years in which it held a high proportion of non-breeders, it increased rapidly to its 1974 total of 145 pairs. As with Skittenskarvholmen, human interference has had a marked effect. The production of young has been far below expectation. For example, between June and July, in

both 1971 and 1972, the number of occupied nests dropped substantially. Furthermore, in 1973 and 1974, a mere 35 and 39 young were
reared from 127 and 145 pairs.

The colony has been legally protected since 1969 and Brun claims
that it has been almost totally undisturbed. If so, there is something
very odd here; possibly toxics are involved.

Again, the colony has received immigrants. A chick colour-ringed on
Ailsa in 1966 was found breeding here in 1970.

Summary of counts: established 1967; 77 birds (1969), 36 occupied
nests (1970), 65 nests (1971), 103 nests (1972), 127 pairs (1973), 145
pairs (1974).

(31) *Innerstauren, Syltefjord, Norway (latest count 55 nests, 1974)*
This is a 40 m (130 ft) stack attached to the mainland towards the
western end of the seabird cliff on the north side of Syltefjorden, east
Finnmark. The gannets have chosen the edge of the flat top and some
broad ledges on the side facing the sea. The colony was established in
1961 (2 pairs). There has been a particularly high proportion of
non-breeding birds; in 1966 there were 51 birds but only 9 occupied
nests. The only other place at which records suggest the same
phenomenon is Foula.

Summary of counts: established 1961, 3 occupied nests (1962), 6
nests (1964), 9 nests (1966), 13 nests (1967) 23 nests (1968), 28 nests
(1969), 29 nests (1970), 44 nests (1971), 55 nests (1974).

The Norwegian colonies take the gannet to its most northerly
breeding point, within the Arctic circle. Runde, as the only sizeable
seabird cliff, was a natural choice for the first colony,[16] given that
gannets were attracted to the area by the rich herring fisheries.
Syltefjord is near the northern limit of the herring's distribution but is
particularly well-placed in relation to capelin, which spawns in great
numbers off east Finnmark. In 1970 and 1971, massive spawning as far
south as Andøya, is suggested to have caused gannets to move in to
Nordmjele and Syltefjord in those years.

The growth of the Norwegian gannet population (all colonies) has
certainly depended on immigration. On reasonable assumptions of
mortality and age of first breeding, it has been calculated[16] that (as I,
also, have suggested) previous figures thought to be reasonable for
intrinsic rates of increase at gannetries have been too high, and 5% or
less is more realistic. The recruits probably came from Scottish colonies. Hermaness and Noss are the nearest (430 km (267 miles)) and St
Kilda is an attractive candidate, but the only proof of origin is the Ailsa
bird at Skarvlakken (above). The bulk of recoveries of ringed gannets
from Norwegian waters is, however, of Bass Rock birds.

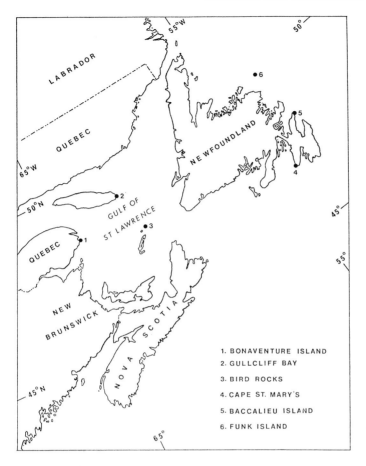

1. BONAVENTURE ISLAND

2. GULLCLIFF BAY

3. BIRD ROCKS

4. CAPE ST. MARY'S

5. BACCALIEU ISLAND

6. FUNK ISLAND

Fig. 10. Distribution of Canadian gannetries (from Nettleship 1976)

CANADA (GULF OF ST LAWRENCE AND NEWFOUNDLAND)

(32) *Bird Rocks, Magdalen Islands (latest count 4,527 pairs on Great Bird; 804 on Little Bird, 1973)*

British gannets return in late winter to cliffs which, though bleak indeed, cannot match the icy conditions of the Canadian colonies. There, ledges are untenable before April, and even incubating birds may be largely buried in snow. The season closes early and with icy finality. Only the gannet's pronounced ability to utilise the rich fishing which lies to hand enables it to rear its chick in time. Yet these icy, productive waters, often rough and misty, suit the gannet so well that the largest colony ever recorded was on Bird Rocks, Quebec, and before it was ruthlessly devastated, the North American population dominated the world figures.

Bird Rocks (see plates) lie in the twelve islands of the Magdalen Archipelago, in the Gulf of St Lawrence. Great Bird's limestone cliffs are 30 m (100 ft) high, but North or Little Bird, now two stacks, immediately north-west of Great Bird, is eroding rapidly. The earliest account is that contained in Hakluyt's story of Cartier's voyage of 1534, in which the three islands in the group were 'as full of birds as any meadow is of grasse, which there do make their nestes; and in the greatest of them there was a great and infinite number of those that we call Margaulx, that are white and bigger than any geese'. Although this vast colony continued undiminished until the 19th century there is no estimate of numbers until Bryant's visit of 1860, by which time the slaughter wreaked by the fishermen since, at least, the 1820s had taken effect. He estimated about 50,000 nests on half the summit of Great Bird, and about half that number on the sides of Great Bird and on Little Bird, together. From this it was estimated[38] that the top of the rock once held around 100,000 pairs and the whole colony 125,000 pairs. Since this was calculated using a density of a little under 1 pair per square metre (which is usually exceeded), the population may have been even greater. On the other hand, the original guess of 50,000 pairs is potentially subject to gross error. In any case it was probably by far the greatest gannetry in the world, though still as nothing compared with the piqueros of the Peruvian islands.

The decrease within the next four years, if accurately judged, was remarkable, to say the least. Fisher put the 1864 population on the plateau at 40,000 pairs, plus 25,000 on the sides, which means that 30,000 adults and presumably many young, were killed in each of the four years between 1860 and 1864. Assuming that 10,000 young were taken and that the yearly period during which the gannets were approachable lasted four months, 2,500 birds were killed each week, which taxes one's credulity. The slide continued at the same terrific pace. After the building of the lighthouse in 1869, the 1872 Plateau population was put at 2,500; by 1881 the summit, which well within a man's lifetime had held 100,000 pairs, was nearly deserted. A paltry 50 nests were there, all recently robbed. However, the cliff sites were as full as ever and Little Bird was probably full to capacity. But even this situation did not remain. Chapman's visit in 1900 suggested about 600–700 pairs for the entire rock. Little Bird, by 1900 eroded into three stacks, was evidently fairly well occupied but was shot up and robbed later the same year. An estimate in 1932 gave about 700 birds on Great Bird and 300 on Little Bird.

Summary of counts: rough estimate based on area, Great Bird 100,000–125,000 pairs (1833), rough estimate *c.* 50,000 pairs on Plateau and some on sides Great Bird, and *c.* 25,000 on Little Bird and sides of Great Bird (1860), *c.* 40,000 pairs on Plateau and some on sides Great Bird, and *c.* 25,000 on Little Bird and sides of Great Bird (1864), *c.* 2,500 pairs on Plateau Great Bird, and *c.* 25,000 on Little Bird and sides of Great Bird (1872), none (?) on Plateau Great Bird, 'thousands' Little Bird and sides Great Bird (1878), 50 pairs on Plateau Great Bird, *c.*

25,000 Little Bird and sides Great Bird (1881), *c.* 50 pairs on Plateau Great Bird, *c.* 5,000 pairs on Little Bird, now in two parts, and sides Great Bird (1887), none on Plateau, 650–700 pairs on sides Great Bird, state of Little Bird not recorded (1898), *c.* 450 pairs on sides Great Bird, Little Bird now in three pieces, over 40 pairs on one piece (Pillar) (1900), *c.* 450 pairs on sides Great Bird, *c.* 1,000 pairs on the 3 pieces of Little Bird (1919), *c.* 350 pairs on Great Bird, *c.* 150 pairs on Little Bird (1932), total *c.* 1,250 pairs (Great and Little Birds) (1934), *c.* 3,750 occupied sites Great Bird, 1,250 Little Bird (1967), 4,397 occupied sites Great Bird, 807 Little Bird (1969), 4,527 occupied sites Great Bird, 804 Little Bird (1973). The increase between 1932 and 1967 could well have depended on the colony's own output; similarly, that between 1967 and 1973 was less than 2% per annum. The shift of birds from Little Bird to Great Bird between 1967 and 1969 was perhaps due to cliff erosion.

(33) *Bonaventure Island, Quebec (latest count 17,281 pairs, 1973)*

Bonaventure (see plate) is roughly circular, about 2·7 km (3,000 yards) by 2·5 km (2,750 yards) at the widest points, about 6·4 km (4 miles) in circumference and with an area of about 730 hectares (1,800 acres), mostly covered with conifers, the predominant cover of the Gaspienne Peninsula of which it is the extremity – some 3·6 km (2¼ miles) offshore. On the east (to the north and south) there are steep cliffs, 76 to 107 m (250–350 ft) high, composed of conglomerate and red sandstone – not ideal for gannets. The gannets nest on the south-east and continue onto the tops in places, nesting beneath the dead remnants of fir trees, a most unusual, if not unique, spectacle. The first record of nesting gannets, about 1860, bears no relationship to the colony's founding date (unknown) and gives no numbers. The first estimate (1887) was merely a guess (1,500 pairs) and the next (1898), some 7,000 birds. Much the same figures were suggested in 1914, 1915 and 1918, after which the colony apparently increased, reaching a peak in 1966. The recent decline[94] is thought to be the result of extremely low breeding success, due to low hatching of eggs, which are heavily contaminated with toxic chemicals.[64,102]

Bonaventure is the site of the only comprehensive study[110] of the gannet's breeding biology in the west Atlantic, and of particular value and interest because, there, the climatic conditions are much more extreme and the season shorter. Canadian gannets have evolved several adaptations to these circumstances which illustrate, in extreme form, the species' general adaptive syndrome to arctic environmental conditions. Here, in the Canadian north, the gannet is probably working near the limits of its ability to fit a breeding cycle into the available time.

Summary of counts: *c.* 1,500 pairs (1887), *c.* 3,500 pairs (1898), *c.* 4,000 pairs (1914, 1915, 1919), *c.* 6,000 pairs (1932), *c.* 6,500 pairs (1934), *c.* 7,000 pairs (1938), 6,600–7,000 pairs (1939), *c.* 6,680 pairs (1940), *c.* 13,250 pairs (1961), 21,215 pairs (1966), 20,511 pairs (1969), 17,281 pairs (1973).

(34) *Gullcliff Bay, Anticosti Island (latest count 135 pairs, 1972)*

This small gannetry lies on the south-east tip of Anticosti, an island 225 km (140 miles) by 48 km (30 miles) in the western entrance of the St Lawrence. The birds nest in small groups of between two and 37 pairs, along 1·6 km (1 mile) of highly fractured and crumbly limestone cliffs, 45–60 m (150–200 ft) high. It is relatively new, founded no earlier than 1913, and perhaps sometime between then and 1920. In 1923 there were reputedly hundreds in at least two distinct groups: a small one south-east of Table Head and the main one at Gullcliff Bay. The latter numbered about 500 nests in 1928 and the same in 1940, at which time there was thought to be little room for increase. In fact the colony has since decreased from 200 pairs in August 1963 to 167 pairs in July 1969 and 135 in June 1972.[95] If this decrease is natural, it is of great interest. The site is obviously far from ideal and may have been colonised as a result of the terrible disturbance at traditional colonies. Now, young birds may be attracted to these traditional sites, currently underpopulated, and Anticosti may be slowly running down. This, however, is speculation.

(35) *Cape St Mary's, Newfoundland (latest count 5,260 pairs, 1972)*

Slightly separated from the south-west extremity of the Avalon Peninsula lies a stack, some 152 m (500 ft) high, called Bird Rock. It is densely covered with gannets on the seaward face. The year in which the colony was founded has been accurately judged as either 1878 or 1879, when there were no more than three pairs. This had grown to 8–10 pairs by 1883 (necessarily immigrants) whilst by 1890 there must have been hundreds; it was said to be 'literally covered with birds' and 'thick' with gannets and guillemots. In 1934,[145] by which time Bird Rock may have become full, there were about 4,000 nests covering the whole of the steep, sea-facing slope and upper-cliff. This was thought to represent a 25% increase over the population of 10 years earlier, and perhaps twice as many as were present in 1913. In about 1926, gannets first crossed the narrow gap to the mainland but did not attempt to breed until 1931, and apparently still do not nest there successfully. Up until at least 1939, mainland nests were destroyed by fishermen. The difference between the count of July 1969 (about 3,000 pairs by ground count) and 1972 (5,260 pairs by aerial photography) probably reflects the different methods used, the former being too low. This would seem to be confirmed by the low figure of 4,866 pairs obtained by direct count in 1977[79] (the counts for the other two Newfoundland gannetries were also lower than the previous photographic count). However (but see below), it is possible that the photographic counts over-estimated the number. Cape St Mary's would seem to be another colony established as a result of the persecution at traditional sites. It may well have been producing emigrants for some time, since a spread to the mainland has been frustrated. As early as 1934, Wynne-Edwards saw 500–700 adult-plumaged birds standing on the mainland slope. Probably some of them were young adults unable to acquire a site on Bird Rock.

(36) *Baccalieu Island, Newfoundland (latest count 441 pairs, 1977)*

Baccalieu is a rocky island situated off the north-east tip of the Avalon Peninsula, about 2·5 km (1½ miles) east of Split Point. It is about 6·5 km (4 miles) long but less than 1·6 km (1 mile) wide. The gannets nest on precipitous cliffs near the middle of the east coast facing the sea. The colony was not discovered until about 1941, by which time it was already about 2,000 pairs strong and, by local repute, some 40 years old. The cliffs are far from ideal for gannets; most of the horizontal surfaces are undercuts rather than ledges and, again, one suspects that it was colonised because Bird Rocks and Bonaventure gannets were so persecuted. The first proper census was in July 1960, when some 900 occupied nests were counted from land and sea. The 1969 estimate (350 pairs) may not represent a large decrease, because part of the colony may have been missed. In 1973, counts from aerial photographs yielded 673 nests, and a ground count in 1977 gave 441 pairs.[79] Perhaps the colony is, if anything, in slight decline, but the authors of the latest count do not think so. They interpret the difference as the outcome of the different methods of counting (by photography or direct).

(37) *Funk Island, Newfoundland (latest count 2,509 pairs, 1977)*

Funk Island is a slab of granite a mere 14 m (46 ft) high, 800 m (½ mile) long and 400 m (¼ mile) wide, lying some 56 km (35 miles) north-north-east of Cape Freels. Mentioned by Cartier in 1534, this colony has had an eventful history. It became extinct sometime between 1857 and 1873 and was re-established, probably in 1935 (there were no gannets in 1934 and about 7 pairs breeding in 1936). All subsequent counts have been ground counts, except that for 1972 which was from photographs, and they show a fairly rapid and consistent increase to 4,051 pairs. The difference between the 2,987 pairs of 1971 and the 4,051 of 1972 probably, in part, reflects the two counting methods but still suggests a real increase. Since this was first written, Funk Island has been counted again by the direct method and the figure obtained, 2,509 pairs, reverts to that of 1971! This is a surprisingly large difference to result from counting method, especially since photographs are often believed to underestimate.

SUMMARY OF CANADIAN GANNETRIES

Surveys in 1972–73 indicated about 32,800 pairs in the six North American gannetries. Sixty-nine per cent were in the Gulf of St Lawrence and the rest on the Atlantic coast of Newfoundland. The most recent counts, however, indicate a somewhat lower figure, there being a total of only 7,816 pairs in the three Newfoundland colonies, against 10,344 pairs according to the previous most recent counts. This means a difference of 2,528 pairs in the Canadian population, which thus becomes about 30,000 pairs. And if a pro-rata difference applies to the other three colonies, the Canadian population would be about

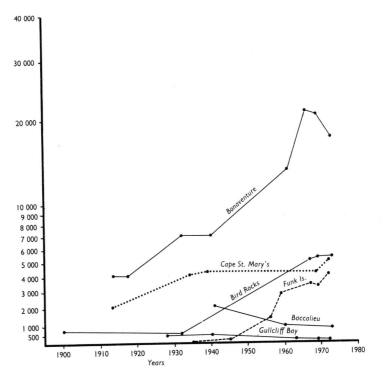

Fig. 11. *Population trends in Canadian gannetries, 1900–70*

25,000 pairs. However, it would be rash to assume this and, until the apparent anomalies have been ironed out, I have left the world totals as they stood before the 1977 series of counts. Anyone interested in doing so can readily adjust the figures on the basis of the counts given above.

Since 1966 the numbers in the St Lawrence have declined slightly, due mainly to a fall in the population of Bonaventure which may have resulted from low recruitment due to toxic chemicals. The eggs of Bonaventure gannets are much more contaminated than those of Bass birds and their shells are 17% thinner than they were in October 1915.[102] The Anticosti colony, also, appears to have declined between 1969 and 1973, and it, also, is situated in the most contaminated part of the Gulf, where the concentration of chlorinated hydrocarbons and heavy metals is greater than it is along the Atlantic coast of Newfoundland. Levels of toxics in gannet tissues are significantly higher at Bonaventure than at Funk.

Nevertheless, overall, the west Atlantic population increased by 2·6% a year between 1909–1939, and 3·2% per year between 1939–69. Since the east Atlantic population has done the same, the *world* increase has been almost at the level which one would expect from known recruitment and mortality rates. I do not think we can present such complete world figures for any other common seabird. It seems highly unlikely that there is any significant interchange between the populations on the two sides of the Atlantic; though the fact that, so far as we know, they remain indistinguishable both morphologically and in every other way is, perhaps, slightly surprising. We now know, by contrast, that the puffins on St Kilda differ even from those on the Isle of May.[49]

WORLD NUMBERS

The world statistics for the gannet (Tables 4 and 5) are thus: 34 colonies containing some 213,000 site-holding pairs. Twenty-eight colonies (163,000 pairs) are in the eastern Atlantic (Britain, Ireland and Shetland 16, Iceland, the Faeroes and Norway 11, and France 1), and six (50,000 pairs) in the western Atlantic. The eastern North Atlantic thus holds 77% of the world population and Canada holds the remainder. The most densely populated area is to the west and north of Scotland. For most of the century the world population has been growing at about 3% per year.

In addition to site-occupying pairs there are all the immature and 'club' birds. These numbered perhaps 70,000 individuals at the time the world population was some 200,000 pairs, giving a total figure of very approximately half a million gannets in the world. This is really not many compared with auks, gulls, fulmars, petrels, etc. In terms of biomass, gannets rank high in the list of seabirds breeding in Britain, though this point is of little or no practical significance, since there is not a great deal of overlap between gannets and other species in food taken, and in any case we are far from knowing whether, at the moment, density-dependent competition for food is limiting *any* seabird around Britain.

DEFUNCT COLONIES

Gannets are notably faithful to their breeding localities but, usually because of interference by man, several colonies have become defunct. The following list[38] comprises all stations at which gannets have been known or suspected to breed, but no longer do so.

(1) Gulland Rock, Cornwall. An ancient (1468) unconfirmed record.

(2) Gannet Stone, Lundy, Devon. An ancient (1274) colony, rapidly decreasing by 1871 and only about 70 nests, 1890. Extinct by 1909, possibly 1906. An attempted re-introduction by cormorant-fostered eggs (1938 and 1939) failed.

(3) Stags of Broadhaven, Mayo, Ireland. There is good reason to doubt that gannets ever bred there. Knox's 'young on the wing' were probably from Skellig and nobody claims to have actually seen nests there. In any event 1936 is the last claim that they nested here.

(4) Calf of Man, Isle of Man. Gannets bred here, possibly in consider-

able numbers, in the sixteenth and seventeenth centuries (there is still a considerable passage nearby). There is no record of their demise.

Oddly enough, further north (on the west coast), where there are so many cliff-girt islands, there is not a single sure record of a defunct gannetry. The following have tenuous claims:

(5) Islay.   (6) Eigg.   (7) Rhum.   (8) Haskeir.   (9) North Rona.

In 1925 or 1926, a pair made an unsuccessful attempt to breed on (10) Copinsay, and in 1941 on (11) a small island near Sanda, off Mull of Kintyre.

On the east there is (12) Isle of May, Fife, where gannets bred before 1850 (no record of numbers) and a pair tried to nest in 1922. Future colonisation from Bass Rock is not unlikely. (13–15) Craigleith, the Lamb and Fidra, are mentioned by Sibbald as places upon which the gannet had attempted to breed.

There are no records to add to the Iceland, Faeroes and Norway group.

In the St Lawrence, (16) Gannet Rock, Grand Manan, New Brunswick, had possibly a fair colony before the lighthouse was built in 1830 but probably became extinct before 1870.

(17) Gannet Rock, Yarmouth, Nova Scotia. Hundreds of gannets and at least 150 nests in 1856. Probably extinct soon afterwards as a result of persecution by local fishermen.

(18) Perroquet Islands, Mingans, Quebec. Up to 1857–59 gannets bred on the north-western island of the group, apparently in considerable numbers, but by 1881 it contained only robbed nests and by 1887, though a few birds remained around, none were breeding. Nor have they bred since.

From this it is clear that few major gannetries have become extinct within historical time. For many hundreds of years, at least, the gannet has stuck fairly closely to a few traditional breeding places, most of them supporting great colonies which have managed to persist despite man. On the other hand, the recent founding of several gannetries and their growth to large size shows that sites were available even when (earlier) they were not in use. This raises the intriguing matter of the adaptive significance of colony size (Chapter 4).

SOME IDEAS AND IMPLICATIONS

Especially in the 19th century, gannets were exploited in a way that can only be described as wantonly savage. The fate of Bird Rocks, formerly the world's largest colony, beggars belief. How could man manage to kill off more than 100,000 pairs in a few years? Subsequently, due to protection, the world population began a spirited recovery which is continuing at a steady pace.

These facts are simple enough, and it would be premature to drag in changes in food as possible factors in the increase. Changes there have been, and very possibly the decline of the herring, the recent upsurge

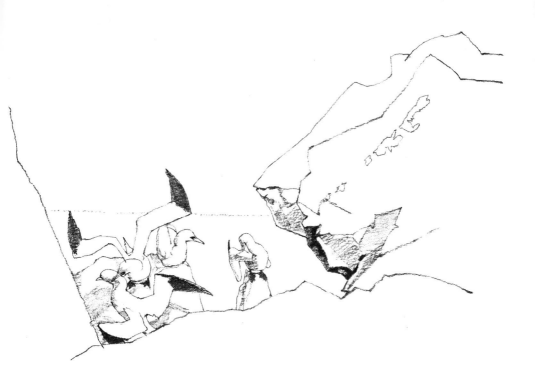

in commercial fishing of sprats, sand-eels and mackerel, and slight changes in the temperature of parts of the North Sea could exert an appreciable effect. But it would be pointless to say more.

However, the unparalleled effort put into counting and observing gannetries has raised several interesting points. First and foremost, there is the matter of interchange between colonies, unquestionably indicated by the rapid increases at many colonies. Indeed, *all* new colonies grow by attracting immigrants. Some of them, such as Grassholm in certain phases, suck in crowds of youngsters from elsewhere. Disregarding, for the moment, the wider implications of this phenomenon, there is the obvious difficulty of determining where they come from. As I mentioned earlier, we tend to divide up our colonies on the basis of simple geography, but the populations of these regions are not correspondingly discrete and we have no idea where to draw the boundaries. Skellig and Grassholm are obvious candidates for interchange; Grassholm and Ailsa Craig may be; the north-west Scottish colonies seem likely to exchange birds. But is there a vast network of interchange embracing the Scottish, Shetland, Faeroese and Icelandic colonies? Is there a limit to the distance from birth place that a gannet will settle? Is the Bass largely autonomous (we know that it contributes to Bempton but it may be independent of the colonies to west and north).

Then there is the question of mechanism. What makes a gannet choose a colony? Here, I feel, there *is* more ground for informed speculation. There are two obvious factors – physical space and social attraction. Clearly, it would be difficult to gain a site in a gannetry that was nearly full, but the matter is far from being so simple. Few colonies *are* full. Ailsa Craig, for example, has plenty of space. St Kilda gains and drops hundreds of pairs on one small face over the years; Grassholm grows fast, then more slowly, then fast again; Skellig doubles its population after observers said it was nearly full. Nor is space *within* the colony the determining factor, as it seems to be with some gulls. Gannets always nest at a very uniform density; the fringe may be 'looser' but it is so at each gannetry. So it is not mainly a matter of looking for a gannetry that has plenty of spare sites or has a

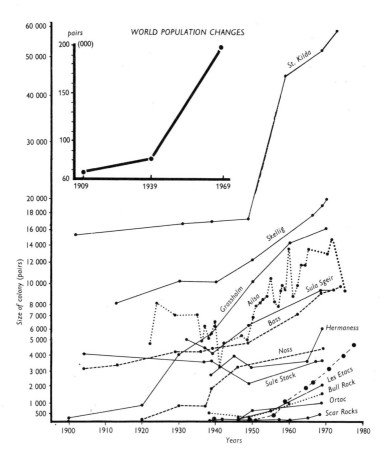

Fig. 12. *Population increases in some eastern Atlantic gannetries (Bempton, Saltee and the Norwegian gannetries excluded on grounds of small size; Iceland colonies also small or few counts available)*

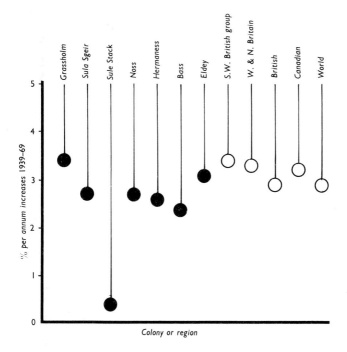

Fig. 13. *Percentage increases in some gannetries, 1939–69. New colonies which obviously depend on immigrants and, in many cases, have a highly artificial breeding success (e.g. Norway) are excluded. Ailsa Craig is omitted because figures fluctuate widely*

particular pattern of dispersion within the colony.

So far as the social factor is concerned, we now have several bits of evidence that together make a sketchy picture. First, we know that new colonies usually 'take off' after reaching a certain threshold. Also, certain areas *within* a generally growing colony increase disproportionately rapidly. Third, the tempo of activity (territorial display and sexual behaviour) is higher in a rapidly growing 'new' colony than it was before, and is higher in a rapidly *growing* part of an old one compared with a more *stable* part of the same colony. Fourth, the *proportion* (not merely the absolute number) of young, immature birds tends to rise in these active colonies or parts of a colony. The obvious implication is that young birds are attracted by the noise and excitement; they investigate, and if conditions are suitable, some of them prospect for a site.

It is easy to imagine the entire sequence of events. A third year Ailsa-born gannet wanders casually north in April. His path enters the orbit of Grassholm birds and – either because he attaches to a group returning from fishing or moves directly to the visible concourse of gannets – he approaches the colony. At this stage in his physiological development, with maturing gonads, he is beginning to feel the pull of the breeding colony. He has, remember, been in a gannetry before, even if only as a chick, and he knows what gannet behaviour 'means'. A gannetry is a stimulus to which he is both *genetically programmed* and *conditioned* to respond. He settles amongst a thousand other young adults and immature birds in the 'club'.

From this point on it is a matter of probabilities – a balance of imponderables such as the bird's internal state, the strength of his tendency to. push on to his natal colony (and this obviously varies) – and the available space at the gannetry, together with the social climate. No doubt, as in any complex vertebrate's development, the precise balance of reinforcement and 'punishment' that his early encounters at the colony mete out, have their effect, too. And it must be remembered that simply to *perform* a consumatory act such as a ritualised display, is itself a reward. The social climate, that is, the number of site-establishing birds and the frequency with which they display, may be expected to affect the likelihood that a young incomer will be stimulated to stay, encounter other birds and display. As a result of all this, he may stay on throughout June and July, perhaps foraging for days at a time. Each return will strengthen his attachment, and the next year will see him ready to establish a site. Alternatively, after a brief stay at the colony, a young bird may move on and attach himself to another colony. Somewhere or other, and particularly at his home colony, he will encounter the right 'mix' at the right time for him.

So one imagines tens of thousands of young gannets ('floaters') wandering the summer sea-lanes, fishing much of the time but responsive to the sights and sounds of gannets and gannetries which they encounter. Where, for whatever reason, a colony or a group *is* extremely active, the attractant effect may snowball: more attracting yet more (observation would seem to support this), and that particular colony or group increases rapidly.

The wider biological implications largely concern the nature of the adaptations which each 'population' (however we define its limits) may be assumed to have. Clearly, interchange on a considerable scale makes it impossible for each colony, or even each 'local' population (where this might conceivably be a group of colonies), to become genetically adapted to its particular environmental circumstances. Yet it is equally obvious that these vary enormously. It would have been 'nice' to think of Bass Rock, or Ailsa Craig, gannets as having incorporated local adaptations into their respective gene pools, so that a Bass gannet would be better able to cope with Bass Rock circumstances including foraging, than would an Ailsa bird, and vice versa. However, the prevalence of interchange merely means that the necessary adaptations are acquired by experience. It will be recalled that the fairly long period spent at the colony *before* breeding is attempted is probably for just this purpose. So interchange doesn't preclude local adaptedness; it simply determines the mechanism.

The steady increase in gannet numbers makes one wonder where it will stop. Despite the growth in total population, relatively few new colonies have been founded. Compared with species that are really breaking new ground, such as the fulmar and the herring gull, the gannet has done poorly. It seems that the gannet is simply re-filling traditional sites and, in the process, spilling over onto a few marginal sites that will not develop significantly. On the other hand, there are many islands and headlands that gannets probably could use, but at present do not. Undoubtedly, traditional gannetries could absorb many more thousands of pairs before major new ones became necessary. Obviously, we will never know how the future population, when it stabilises, compares with the one that existed before serious exploitation by man, but it is clear that, conditions having changed in the meantime, it need not be at all comparable. Finally, it bears repeating that the present increase is not an 'explosion', or a significant extension of range, or indicator of change in the availability of food, and hence of increased recruitment compared with times previous. It is simply the normal output which is refurbishing the population after a period of artificial decrease caused by man. Good luck to the gannets!

SUMMARY

1.   More is known about the world population of the gannet than about any other common seabird.

2.   The gannet's breeding distribution is tied to that of its food fish, principally herring and mackerel, and to the presence of suitable islands; its weight and wing proportions make it dependent on wind for landing and take-off and, for this and other reasons, it prefers cliffs.

3.   Nearly 40% of the world's breeding population of gannets occurs on islands west and north of Scotland, excluding the Icelandic colonies. The east coast of Britain is little favoured.

4.   Its breeding range covers 48° of latitude, from the most northerly (Syltefjord, Norway) to Rouzic (Brittany).

5.   Direct counts and counts from photographs each involve large potential errors. Ideally, counts should be given in terms of the number of occupied sites. At large gannetries it is impracticable or impossible to obtain a figure for 'nests' or 'breeding pairs'. Allowance should be made for the percentage of site-owners likely to be absent, and (if the original figure is in terms of 'heads') for the proportion of sites occupied by pairs.

6.   Each of the world's gannetries is described and a summary of previous counts given.

7.   There are currently 34 breeding colonies in the world (excluding Foula), containing some 213,000 pairs. Of these, 28 colonies (163,000 pairs) are in the eastern Atlantic and 6 colonies (50,000 pairs) in the western.

8.   For most of this century, the world gannet population has been growing at some 3% per annum, a figure which fits well with known reproduction

and mortality rates. This growth is not explosive, but simply a steady climb back towards numbers which were formerly present, before massive destruction by man reduced them.

9. There is undoubtedly considerable interchange between gannetries on the west coast of Britain and Ireland, insofar as many young settle to breed at other than their natal colony. But, once settled, adults do not change colonies. The scale of interchange and the size of the area over which it occurs, is unknown.

10. Probably, a young gannet eventually settles to breed (if not at its natal colony) for preference at a colony which shows a high level of social activity.

3: Breeding behaviour

The current overrating of quantification as a source of knowledge has very serious epistemological consequences. The first and worst is that it leads to contempt of observation pure and simple, which is the basis of all inductive science. The depreciation of observation has gone so far that the term 'naturalistic' as applied to scientific work has assumed with some behaviouristic psychologists a definitely derogatory connotation.

Konrad Lorenz: *Methods of approach to the problems of behaviour* (1958)

By cautious movement one can penetrate to the heart of a gannetry without disturbing it. There, from gannet's eye level, and without the protective capsule of space, it becomes faintly possible to imagine what it may feel like to be a site-owning gannet in a great colony. You are encircled with bayonets, steely beaks boldly outlined in black and couched between cold blue eyes. Serried ranks of birds guard their drums, snowy plumage stirring in the wind. In early July some are still neatly on top of the mound, sealing the nest-cup as they incubate stained eggs; others are brooding reptilian squabs or standing guard over fluffy chicks already approaching adult size; a few stand on empty, flattened pads or even bare sites. Rare indeed is the unguarded site, whatever its contents, and if it is evening, many nests hold pairs. If this sounds a peaceful scene, nothing could be further from the truth. The noise and activity is phenomenal. You are engulfed by waves of brassy sound. The air is thick with gannets, signalling their arrival with harsh incoming calls, or flying low over the nesting mass, stimulating outbursts of display. From single birds, sweeping movements with heraldically outspread wings and rhythmic bows, and from re-united pairs, ecstatic meeting ceremonies. Over all, the metallic clangour that, in unison, and at some distance, is the full-throated uproar of a great gannetry. Indeed, a gannet city so far as crowds and stimulus go, but in no sense chaotic. In fact, the two most prominent and thought-provoking features of a gannetry are the tempo of activity and the rigidly ordered framework within which it occurs.

The highly organised cooperation between mates, or the effective relationships between neighbours in the colony, are largely achieved by the sign language of posture and movement. Mostly, as in all the main displays, these are innate. They are as much a result of the gannet's genetic blueprint as is the pattern of diving and swimming, or indeed the gannet's shape. Despite the extraordinarily precise match, down to the finest detail, between the gannet's requirements and its behaviour, it would be basically wrong to conclude that gannets know what they are doing. There are absolutely no grounds to believe (and plenty not to) that gannets, in any ordinary sense, understand the full relationship between social act and result. They behave in particular ways, at particular times, because an unimaginably complex set of internal and external events combine to make them do so. They are indeed extraordinarily and exasperatingly stupid. If the blueprint says 'do that in this situation', they are in many instances unable to modify the plan, however modestly. A nesting gannet will menacingly dispel an approaching gull but a gannet gathering nest material can be routed by the same gull. Many people find this general concept of unthinking response to stimulus unpalatable, but I am sure that a few days of intensive watching would persuade them of its correctness. Were it otherwise, many of the things I am about to describe would be totally inexplicable.

Before my own study, which began in 1960, several people had tried to describe the gannet's behaviour at the nesting colony,[105,68,4] but only John Warham, writing about the Australasian gannet, had managed to produce a coherent, structured account.[138] This serves mainly to show that the golden rule is to watch known individuals, for long periods. Only then does it become possible to base interpretation on sound evidence. Perhaps one reason why Niko Tinbergen is held in such uniquely high esteem among many ornithologists, quite apart from ethologists, is that, first, he opened windows for us and let us really *see* how birds behave; then, and only then, did he make convincing sense of it all, in terms of what 'caused' the behaviour and what it 'meant'. To see how rare this is one need only recall that in James Fisher's monumental monograph on the fulmar[36] there is virtually nothing on fulmar behaviour. Much the same may be said of ecology. Basically, it is the approach that matters. Contrast, for instance, Tinbergen's implicit dictum that natural selection is all pervasive, and adaptations therefore infinitely subtle and complex, with the suggestion by another eminent but much less biological behaviourist[4] who wrote: 'without endangering the race, it [the gannet] may work off surplus energy in harmless posturing'. Never!

Behaviour, of course, is very much a visual thing and I have tried to capture some of its aspects by using several methods of illustration. The straightforward photographs of the main displays (see plates) capture a frozen instant of what is actually a stylised sequence of movements. The composites (see plates) show groups of birds, many of them displaying, so that the essentially social nature of the interactions can receive comment. The drawings in Fig. 15 are grouped to show the relationships between the various displays. Finally, I have included a series printed from ciné film, to illustrate the sequence of events in a complex interaction.

THE IMPORTANCE OF THE SITE

Gannets are highly unusual in that they not only attend the colony

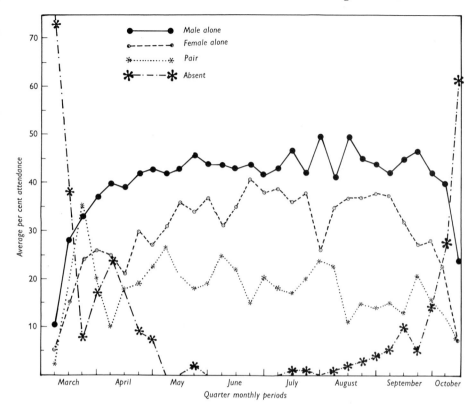

Fig. 14. *Site attendance in established pairs of gannets, Bass Rock*

for almost all of the year (Fig. 14) but are also active in display throughout. For some reason, even when there is no egg or chick, it is important for a gannet to guard and display on its nesting site, though at sea it would most probably be safer and certainly better fed. The site, furthermore, is the source of bitter competition and of quite astonishingly ferocious fighting, beside which the competitiveness of other seabirds seems tame. It is crucial to understand *why* the site is so important and I have offered an interpretation[86,87,93] in terms of the relationship between a *socially* adequate site (of which there are relatively few) and successful breeding. Here, I stress the role of the site and the competition for it because it helps one to understand why aggressive behaviour, including aggressive display, is so dominant in the gannet.

Commonly, species in which both sexes share the defence of the site look alike. Probably this is because by so doing each presents the same warning-off appearance to potential intruders. In almost all British seabirds both sexes have much the same plumage. In the gannet the sexes are often indistinguishable. Moreover, gannets take shared defence very seriously. Females fight, threaten and display just as do the males. The only difference is that the aggressive displays of the female are less intense, and less frequent, than the same displays of the male (Fig. 16). In this, again, the paramount importance of the site is evident.

The best way to describe the details of behaviour would seem to be to follow the gannet's life history in chronological sequence. This allows a more or less continuous narrative rather than a series of separate and sub-divided sections. All the displays described here can easily be seen, almost any day, at a gannetry. To help make these displays 'real', instead of lifting them from their context, as individual sketches may do, I have, as already mentioned, included annotated photographs of *groups* of gannets, in which much behaviour is going on at the same time (see plates). This is how it would be if you were there. It may add to the 'feel' of the descriptions of display to keep turning to these concrete examples. In fact, gannets are ideal material for the behaviourist. Not only are their displays conspicuous and easily recognised, but they occur frequently and, because the birds are large, they are slow, so one can recognise and measure their individual components. Besides describing behaviour, it is important to try to understand its motivation – is the bird aggressive, afraid, sexually motivated or what? Further, as Tinbergen has repeatedly stressed, we need to know its function; what does it achieve for the animal in terms of survival value? This latter is a particularly fruitful question to keep in mind when discussing gannet behaviour. Several aspects, for example its dense nesting habit and fierce site competition, seem in many ways anomalous and can be understood only if their function is understood.

A final preliminary point – the behaviour I will describe is verifiable; it is not anecdotal. In other words, it is equivalent to physical characteristics in that other observers can go to a gannetry to check, which is impossible with the one-off episode. It is typical of the species, not merely the individual. A study of the Canadian population[110] has revealed that behaviourally, they differ in no discernible way from the birds of the eastern Atlantic. Furthermore, when I make quantitative generalisations, such as 'behaviour x becomes commoner after the egg has hatched', I am basing them on actual counts.

SITE ESTABLISHMENT AND MAINTENANCE

The gannetry powerfully attracts the young bird. Having migrated south as a black juvenile between August and November of its birth year, it soon begins to feel the pull of home waters. Commonly, it begins to move back whilst in its second year (though sometimes in its first) and many reach a gannetry in April, May or June of their second year – that is, when 21, 22, or 23 months old. It spends countless hours sailing around in the busy air-traffic, peering down at the nesting birds. It cannot land right amongst them, for there is usually too little unoc-

cupied ground, but it can join a gathering of immature and non-breeding adult-plumaged birds (a 'club') or, if the gannetry permits, it might sit on a ledge near the breeders – usually below or above them. May, and particularly June and July, are peak attendance months for two and three year olds. In the 'clubs', they tend to assemble in the company of similarly-aged birds rather than scatter randomly. Mostly, they show no strong attachment to any particular spot, but they interact with each other, showing low intensity territorial and sexual behaviour (brief skirmishes; threats; display and incomplete copulation). During these first months back at the colony they gain a great deal of valuable experience. They cope with the wind conditions around the gannetry, especially important when landing and taking off; they use adjacent fishing grounds in all weathers and they employ the social signals by means of which, later, they will recognise and respond to the many situations which will face them when acquiring and maintaining a site and mate. So those early years, of which there may be two, three, or even more, are preparatory, and the activities mentioned are important enough to account for the long deferred maturity in Atlantic gannets.

Sometime during his fourth, fifth or sixth year (that is when three, four or five years old) a male begins to look seriously for a site. The exact timing is variable and a bit complicated. A male may acquire a site fairly late in the season and come back to it early the following year, or he may acquire it fairly early in the season and keep it for the remainder, often without breeding. Much depends on his age when he acquires the site; and upon his success in getting a mate and upon her maturity. In the most extreme case, a two year old male may come back to the colony in April and acquire a site. He will be three years old in

June of that year and hence in his fourth year from June onwards. Such a male would not breed. But the same sequence for an April three-year-old could lead to breeding in that year; the bird would then be four, that is in his fifth year, by the time his chick hatched.

Gannetries differ significantly in their proportion of immature birds. Moreover, a gannetry differs in this respect at different stages in its development and (though it is much the same thing) in different areas within it. Some gannetries, and some areas within a gannetry, grow faster than would be expected from their own output; these are the ones that attract a disproportionately large number of young birds, intent upon establishing themselves. There are several ways in which such areas could be recognised by a prospecting gannet: they contain a higher proportion of birds in immature plumage; in some cases nests are slightly more widely spaced; and the tempo of territorial activity is distinctly higher than in a non-expanding group.

Of course, not all prospecting birds concentrate on such areas. There is a very marked tendency for young gannets to return to the part of the colony in which they were reared. If there is no room for expansion there, and this is often so on a cliff face (see plates), they must take a vacant but established site (of which there are few, since only about 5 or 6% of males die each year, and the rest usually remain faithful to their old site) or they must squeeze in, which is difficult and leads to a number of young males attempting to establish themselves on manifestly unsuitable sites.

Whether a young male becomes attracted to the fringe of an expanding group (see plates) or returns to his native heath, he goes about it in the same way. He is already familiar with the colony from thousands of flight circuits. Now he concentrates on his chosen area, flying past or over it time after time. When he first settles there he is very unsure of himself and easily displaced. Even we can easily tell the difference between an anxious and a confident gannet, and we may be sure his neighbours can. Of course, unless he is one of the lucky ones to hit upon a vacant drum, he will have no nest, only a small patch of grass or muddy ground, or part of a ledge. One can never know how many times before he has 'played' at establishing himself nor, at first, whether he is in earnest this time, but, by watching colour ringed birds the course of events can be accurately followed in at least some cases, from the very start of the males' occupancy.

Let me describe what happens to a young male at the fringe of my observation group on the Bass in 1976. He bears a colour combination which shows that he was ringed there as a chick in 1972. When first noticed, he is guarding a site well within pecking distance of a number of other birds similarly engaged. A check with last year's annotated photograph shows that he was more or less at the same spot last autumn. It is a bright day in early April with a cold easterly wind into which he can lift off simply by opening his wings. There is brisk traffic sweeping into the air space above the group, checking and peering, with downturned tail and winnowing wings before letting the wind

take them up and away, and turning to come in again. On such a day the gannetry is incredibly active. The birds are in beautiful condition, plumage pristine, and deep buff heads and necks china-smooth. One of the over-flying birds does not sweep in silently, as the others do. He begins to call whilst some yards away and then lands, almost dives, onto the site of our young male. Battle royal is immediately joined. In many cases, where attachment to the site is loose, such an attack would lead to the immediate panic flight of the on-site bird. This saves a lot of unnecessary fighting; inevitably, some prospecting males settle on a vacant site which is unoccupied only because the owner happens to be away fishing and has no partner to guard the site. Thus, a short period of tentative, apprehensive occupation by the new male, which he readily cedes when challenged, is an advantage to all concerned. But once a male has remained in possession for a reasonable time – say two or three days – he is firmly attached. The site is 'his' and on that possession rests the weighty matter of licence to breed. If challenged now, it is quite another matter.

Really serious fights are most commonly caused by two males each acquiring, through a variety of circumstances, legitimate and initially uncontested, ownership of the same site. They are emphatically *not* caused by one bird trying to usurp another, nor by 'misunderstandings' of the kind described above. This is why newly colonised fringe areas are in a state of frequent and considerable flux, with apparent owners being displaced and brief skirmishes and frequent display the order of the day.

Our site-owning male is thus vigorously challenged by an incomer with equally good title deeds. These have been acquired, initially by mere presence on the site, then by repeated short flights from the site.

Flying in

'Flying in' is an infallible sign of ownership. It is accompanied by loud calling which is followed immediately after landing by an aggressive display. When a male has done this many times, he and the neighbours reckon the site is his. It is quite easy to say whether he is a well established owner or not, merely by observing the way in which a male flies in, lands and displays, and the way in which neighbours react.

Fighting

The fight (see plates and Fig. 15) which occurs in this case is likely to be severe and prolonged. If I were asked to give a snap judgement on what impressed me most about gannets, my mind would leap not to their plunge diving but to their fights. The most indelible impressions are from the days in 1961, 1962 and 1963, when my observation colony was growing rapidly and the stage was just in front of my hide. There, on wet days in March and April when the ground was a quagmire, erstwhile immaculate males became plastered in mud, pockmarked with stab wounds on the head, torn and bleeding about the face, with pale blue eyes crackling electrically from the mud mask. And females fought females just as fiercely.

Commonly, such encounters lasted half an hour, sometimes an hour and, rarely, up to two hours without a pause. The technique is quite different from that of, say, a herring gull. The gulls peck at each other's head (mainly), lock bills briefly, dance around with flapping wings and disengage, breathlessly, to grass-pull and long-call after a few hectic but lightweight seconds or minutes. Similarly, kittiwakes jab, lock beaks, wing flap and twist each other till one or both falls off the ledge. Probably, gannets too evolved their fighting method on cliff ledges and perhaps that is why it is so, as it were, 'unintentionally' severe on flattish ground, where contestants cannot terminate it by falling (that is, being pushed) and will not give in.

They lock bills, which are extremely powerful and to which the terminal hook and serrated edges of the mandibles impart formidable cutting power, and attempt to push each other off the site. They use their wings to thresh over the ground or, stretched right back, to brace a forward push, but never to strike with. Nor do they strike with their feet. The neck is often extended, which means that it must be exceptionally strong, since to transmit a powerful thrust through an extended neck is not conventional mechanics. Doubtless, their ability to do this is derived from the great neck-strength required for their plunge diving. In practice, and on flat ground, they do not quickly succeed in pushing their adversary far before a counter attack, delivered with galvanic fury, reverses the position. And so it goes on, with

Fig. 15. (i) *Aggressive (territorial) behaviour in the gannet (explained in text), (a) fighting, (b) jabbing, (c) threat, (d) ground biting, (e) bowing*

Fig. 15 (ii) Sexual behaviour in the gannet (explained in text), (a) male, advertising, (b) nape biting, (c) mutual fencing (greeting), (d) mutual preening (pair bonding), (e) copulation

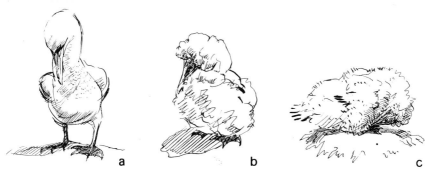

(iii) *Appeasement behaviour, (a) adult 'pelican posture', (b) chick 'pelican posture', (c) bill-hiding*

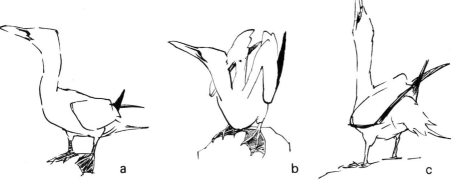

(iv) *Preparation for flight, (a) alert posture, (b) crouch, (c) skypointing*

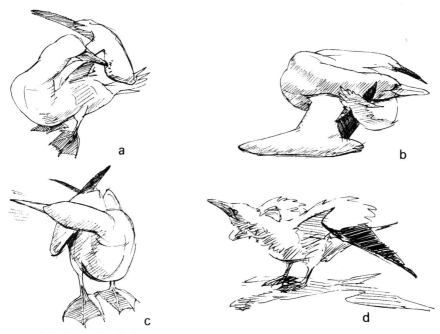

(v) *Grooming behaviour, (a) preening, (b) oiling, (c) head-fling (to clean bill), (d) rotary headshake*

lightning changes of grip, each of which lacerates any facial skin unfortunate enough to get in the way, or (sometimes) the inside of the mouth, or occasionally the eye itself.

During these exhausting surges of fighting, the combatants often have to endure furious stabs from the neighbours into whose nesting space they push each other. These 'pecks' are often harshly punishing, because they are delivered to a head that is held in the vice of the opponent's beak, and this is why they often puncture the skin. They fight without a respite, fortunes swaying back and forwards. Just when one bird has absorbed a terrific hammering, back he comes with beserk fury. It is noticeable that the winner is often not content with winning; he prevents his rival from disengaging, pursues him and renews the fight even when it could have ended. Occasionally, if the struggle is near the cliff edge, they fall over, and continue grappling in the air or on the sea, where again the winner denies easy escape to his exhausted rival. And exhausted they are. After a fight like that, a bird may sleep more or less continuously for two or three days, filthy, tattered but victorious. Before he sleeps, though, he will certainly do one thing, and that is to perform his site-ownership display. That scrap of muddy ground has been won by hard fighting and its possession is signified over and over again by this aggressive display. By contrast, never will the loser display, though he, too, may be standing on a scrap of muddy ground beyond the fringe. It is not the scrap!

As I said, this sort of prolonged fighting usually cannot occur on cliffs but, even there, fights are notably vigorous and attended by the added danger of falling and damaging a wing. On Ailsa, this may be one cause of the many adult casualties that litter the cliff base. It is difficult to get an accurate figure for the frequency of severe fighting. Not only does it vary with the type of terrain, but also with the rate at which new sites are being established. When my study group was expanding rapidly, such fights were commonplace and most sites were contested in this way. It is certainly fair to say that, even in a stable group, disputes like these are not infrequent where the ground permits. They are the trial which every aspiring breeder may well have to face. Indeed, it would be surprising if any male did not have to fight at least once or twice in his life. Strong selection pressure is thus exerted against weak males.

One must conclude that competition for a breeding site plays a very important role in the gannet's life. As I suggested earlier, this is not mainly because there is a shortage of physically suitable breeding sites. Quite clearly it is the attraction of, and thus the competition for, sites which are near to or actually among existing breeders. A lovely, windswept, spacious site, utterly uncontested, is no good to a gannet if the site is several metres from the neighbours and the space between is suitable for breeding on. Some believe that this is because semi-isolated, or even fringe sites, are open to predation, but this is not so. A breeding pair derives significant *behavioural* stimulation from neighbours, which enhances their chances of producing a chick which will survive to breed. The way in which this works is discussed later. The point, here, is that the struggle to acquire a site which provides behavioural (social) stimulation, offers a reasonable explanation for an otherwise puzzling degree of site competition, an explanation which is not supplied by any other advantage of breeding densely, yet postulated. The function of dense nesting was one of the first problems that gannets posed to me, and it remains a central one.

Jabbing

Our male, then, wins his fight and remains on his fringe site. At the moment, he is still single and is spending some three-quarters of the daylight hours guarding and displaying on his territory. Fighting is the extreme expression of aggression, but there are many other ways in which aggressive motivation may be expressed and its distance-evoking function fulfilled. The behaviour most closely akin to fighting is jabbing. Neighbouring gannets jab each other a great deal. One may define a jab as a vigorous forward lunge which makes contact with another bird, but which does not result in holding, or if it does, only fleetingly. Jabbing itself grades from silent, single and casual jabs, to vigorous and repeated striking, with strident calling. Single birds jab singles or, less often, members of a pair, and members of a pair frequently combine to harass a single neighbour. These differing expressions reflect different contexts and one can distinguish many signs of the various combinations of fear and aggression, such as the degree to which the head is withdrawn (fear), the amount of 'hesitation' preceding a lunge; the extent to which the beak is opened (very wide is usually a sign of fear and is accompanied by twitching of the mandibles and a higher pitch in the call). These and similar details are sometimes useful in interpreting interactions between known individuals and in providing references against which to assess specific encounters. Jabbing keeps neighbours in their place and dispels intruders, even if these are unintentional (as when a bird crashes during take-off). One would never see a serious dispute settled by means of a jabbing match, but it copes with less extreme situations.

Threat-gaping or menacing

Below jabbing, in the aggressive scale, comes threat-gaping or menacing (see plates and Fig. 15). In this, there is no contact, merely a forward thrust with open beak. It is interesting in that it is clearly 'ritualised', that is to say, exaggerated; modified in form from straight 'threat' and highly stereotyped. The modification lies in the conspicuous sideways twist to the head and in the immediate withdrawal of the beak. One sees a thrust-with-twist-and-withdrawal, thrust-with-twist-and-withdrawal, in a stereotyped sequence and clearly without any attempt actually to grip. Like jabbing, it grades in intensity. The version of threat-gaping just described is the typical form employed between neighbours, often in an almost 'conversational' manner immediately followed by other behaviour, such as genuine (as against pseudo-) preening or sleeping, which shows that the bird is relaxed rather than tensely aggressive. Menacing is one of the commonest behaviours in a gannetry and helps to prevent possible encroachment. Measured over the season (Fig. 38) it gives a useful index of the level of aggression. Interestingly, it is rarely seen in its typical form away from the territory, even though gannets may encroach on each other's space in other contexts, as when gathering nest material or competing for trawler offal, or when crowded on the water during fishing.

The 'bowing' display

Jabbing and menacing would be labelled 'aggressive' by anybody. The most picturesque and commonest way in which a gannet defends its site, however, is by means of a display which is not so obviously aggressive. Like all these things, it hardly matters what one calls it, though it is best to use a descriptive name which conjures up some idea of the behaviour. I call it 'bowing' because the displaying bird (*not* birds, because bowing is not performed when the *pair* is together on the nest; instead they 'mutual fence') sweeps its head down to the ground (see plates and Fig. 15). Others have called it 'solo curtseying', or 'solo bowing'. Everybody who has ever watched at a gannetry must have seen it. Typically, the bird begins by shaking its head, bill slightly below horizontal, and sweeps it forward and down, tilting the body forward as it does so. Then it raises its head, shakes it from side to side, dips forward again and so on, two, three, four or five times in quick succession. It terminates the display by pressing its bill tip against its upper breast in a pronounced 'bill-tucking' or 'pelican posture', which it holds for two, three or four seconds before relaxing and resuming a normal stance. The wings are opened at the first 'dip' and held up and out, flexed at the carpal joint but not waved, and the tail tips up as the head tips down. The bird calls loudly and repetitively throughout, at about the same tempo as in the incoming call. One could not have a better example of a highly ritualised display – the conspicuous movement, the enhancement by calling, the stereotype and the repetition. But why does the gannet do it? One can be sure that it is highly significant, if only because it occurs so often and throughout the whole of the long breeding season. A gannet bows thousands of times a year, and each performance uses energy. The fact that evolution has produced such a complex and polished display also indicates that it is an important signal. In the physical field – as for instance in a flamingo's bill – we would never doubt that such an unusual structure had evolved for a special and important job. No more should one doubt it for a display.

The first task is to establish the context, for this will tell us much about the bird's motivation (that is, the nature of the 'energy' which is driving it) and about the function of the display. After that we can see whether there are other aspects which fit with the picture thus formed. This procedure is far removed from mere speculation. The likelihood of the interpretation being true is increased by every bit of evidence that

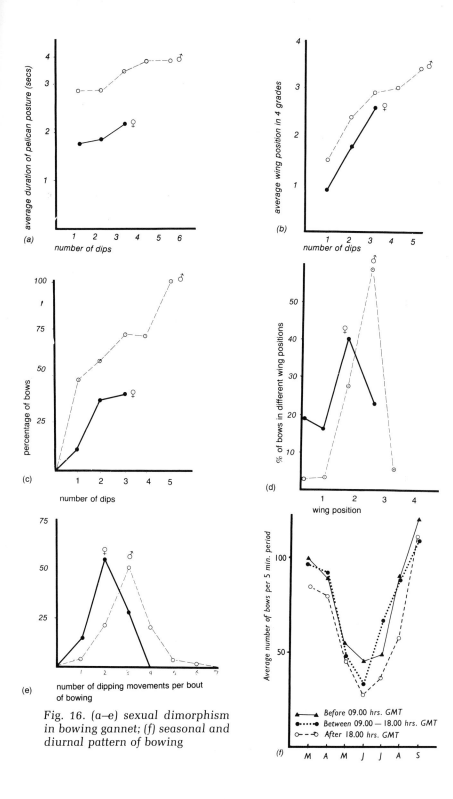

Fig. 16. (a–e) sexual dimorphism in bowing gannet; (f) seasonal and diurnal pattern of bowing

Before 09.00 hrs. GMT
Between 09.00 — 18.00 hrs. GMT
After 18.00 hrs. GMT

fits, so long as there are no, or very few, bits that do not. One gains confidence the more the picture hangs together. Remarks on scientific methods sometimes seem to imply that a hundred bits of inconclusive evidence are no more conclusive than one, which is nonsense. I make these remarks here, not because I have any doubts about the meaning of bowing, but because they apply in general to this way of looking at behaviour. Interpretations of function, at least so far as unmanipulated field observations go, are necessarily based on circumstantial evidence, but may nevertheless be extremely strong.

A gannet bows immediately before threatened intrusion (a bird showing signs of coming too near), or after actual intrusion (for instance after a fight has spilled over onto its territory, or a departing bird crashed nearby, or a bird brushed past to rejoin its mate), or after it has been threatened. It bows at high intensity after it has fought and won in defence of its site. It bows, also, apparently spontaneously. In most of these situations it is clearly either aggressive (immediately after a fight) or is dealing with a situation in which it is prepared to fight if necessary (intrusion), or has actually displaced an (albeit unintentional) intruder. In apparently spontaneous bowing one cannot, by definition, discern any external stimuli which may have elicited it. This may mean that the stimuli have been rather general (for example overflying birds representing potential intrusion), rather inconspicuous (for instance a fairly distant neighbour showing signs of moving in that direction), or that there genuinely is an internal causal factor which, if it builds up sufficiently, requires only a very slight external stimulus (or none at all) to release bowing. All the circumstantial evidence thus suggests that bowing birds are partly, probably mainly, motivated by the 'feeling' or 'emotion' of aggression. Equally clearly, the bowing display is concerned with defence of the site. It is a signal of ownership; a visual message saying that the bowing bird will repel intrusion. It is not used to communicate anything other than this general message. Other situations have their own displays and this situation-specific system is never transgressed. So one may assert, with a high degree of certainty, that bowing is an aggressively motivated display signalling ownership of the site. Armstrong's[4] analogy to a couple of Japanese friends engaging in a polite soliloquy with interminable bowing is singularly inapt!

Having got that far, all sorts of details then click into place. For example, there are sex differences in the display – and remember that bowing is *not* done to or with the mate. Males bow more often than females; they perform three or four of the downward bowing movements per display against the female's two or three and they hold their wings further out. Also their pelican postures last longer than those of the female (Fig. 16). By these four measures, all of which I have documented for many hundreds of bows, males can meaningfully be said to bow at higher intensity, and this is what one would expect if bowing is indeed an aggressive site ownership display. After all, males establish and fight for the site, and they spend much longer guarding it.

Their attachment is in these terms stronger, and so one would expect the display which expresses that attachment to be more intense than that of the female. It is usually easy to recognise the sex of a gannet by the nature of its bow. Comparably and predictably, the bowing display of tentatively established males, and of 'club' males, is shorter and less intense than that of established males. All this, incidentally, is hard to explain if one rejects the notion of aggressive motivation acting in some sense as a unitary driving force for a number of different (but all aggressive) behaviour patterns. On the above evidence, something like threshold effects are operating; females and young males have less aggression than established males and this is manifested in weaker versions of aggressive behaviour patterns. The fact that the external stimulus of the *site* is also necessary for the expression of internally-generated 'aggression' does not in the least invalidate this argument.

Like menacing, whose seasonal pattern of frequency it closely follows, bowing is a useful measure of aggression in relation to the site. It is most frequent early and late in the season, when the gonads are most active.

Another indication that bowing is aggressive is that one can convincingly show that it is a modified form of ground-biting (aggression re-directed from the opponent who elicited it to a less fear-evoking object, namely the ground). Site-owning gannets that are unusually aggressive and fearful (aggression and fear are almost always, or always, linked in different proportions according to context) characteristically incorporate ground-biting into their bow. This may be seen in newly established males, or in males that regain their site immediately after a fight; or early in the season when the desire to re-establish themselves is high but they are still fearful of land – a fear that wanes as the season advances. In these cases the ground is stabbed or seized. This is the origin of the downward reaching, or bow. The headshake then becomes a means of dispelling the dirt from the beak. In fact, gannets (like most birds) do use a sideways headshake to get rid of dirt or water on the bill or head. Such a movement is not, in *that* context, a display, any more than preening is. The bow and the headshake were thus linked from the start. Simply by modifying the actual biting into near-biting (the beak taken down to the ground) and repeating it three or four times, and retaining the (now unnecessary) headshake, we get the fully ritualised bow display. The pelican posture may be interpreted as an avoidance bill-movement, keeping the bill out of the position in which it could attack or be attacked. This would be consistent with the fact that gannets are not only aggressive towards their neighbours but also (and for good reason) afraid of them. Although a fully polished bow would not strike the uninitiated as obviously aggressive behaviour, the ground-biting version would. Even minor shifts in motivation can quickly and temporarily produce a modified bow, with the bill making biting movements as it reaches the lowest point, from a bird which, until that moment, had not shown any biting movements. Such a shift could be caused, for instance, by a sudden jab from a neighbour. So the original and derived behaviours are still closely linked.

The bow is thus tied to the site; gannets may compete (as they do for food) away from the site but they do not bow. I once saw a gannet alight on a piece of floating wood and repel others; *there* he bowed. It seemed that the wood was temporarily a site and had released the response. Gannets will even attempt to bow in the air, if for example they are hanging in the wind just above their site.

It may be objected that an interpretation like the one advanced above, namely that bowing repels potential intruders, is just a guess, since the observation that birds bow on site and subsequently are not subject to intrusion cannot meaningfully be compared with observations of birds that simply stand on site without bowing; they, too, probably will not suffer intrusion and so (the objection might run) bowing makes no difference. This argument has little weight, however. For one thing, gannets do, verifiably, bow in all the contexts just described and this act must have a function. A critic would have to advance an equally plausible interpretation for its function. For another, one does occasionally see a natural control experiment. For example, if bowing signifies ownership and thus warns off potential intruders it should, by the same argument, goad a rightful owner to furious attack, and indeed does so. Thus, if, after a fight between two 'rightful owners' (arising as described earlier) one regains the site, his opponent may endure it for a moment, until the rival actually *bows* on the disputed site. This is too much, and elicits another attack. This situation does not arise often enough for quantitative analysis, but the observation fits perfectly, despite its apparent paradox. Finally, so far as function goes, one should add that the positive evidence just given is not balanced by negative evidence. There is nothing which runs counter to these interpretations.

So, much of the noise and activity at a gannetry comes from hundreds of birds bowing and shouting stridently, endlessly maintaining their right to be there.

PAIR FORMATION AND MAINTENANCE

Sexual advertising ('headshake and reach')

An understanding of the bowing display was, for me, the key to the recognition and interpretation of another gannet display, which solved a considerable puzzle. Besides establishing a site, the male must also attract a mate and establish a strong bond with her. In many species the males have evolved a conspicuous 'advertising' display to which unattached females respond. This is presumably far more efficient than for the female to wander around, 'trying out' every male and judging by his reaction whether he wants her or not. The male gannet seemed to lack such a display though the closely related boobies have one. It was easy to see that young female gannets 'prospected' for a partner by wandering around the fringe (see Plates), or by finding a point within a group from which they could scan the neighbourhood. Their sleek, peering, long-necked posture was quite distinctive.

The male's display (Fig. 15), however, is not only inconspicuous, it is made more difficult to recognise because it is mainly headshaking, and gannets headshake a lot, so it hardly stands out. Once recognised, its relationship to bowing is obvious, for the display consists not only of an exaggerated headshake but also of a slight forward and downward movement of the head (prosaically, I called it 'headshake and reach'). Clearly, it is a highly inhibited bow. The aggressive part (the part derived from ground biting) is inhibited and shows merely as this hesitant forward reach, and the 'neutral' part (the headshake derived from a cleansing shake) is exaggerated. In addition, the wings are kept close to the body rather than held out, and the male does not call. Obviously, all the aggressive components of the bow have been greatly suppressed and the result is a display which, though oddly subdued, is nonetheless distinctive and (most importantly) clearly different from bowing. This fits beautifully with what we know about bowing; clearly a female showing every sign of imminent approach, and looking like a male (that is, bearing all the relevant 'releasers') would predictably elicit the male's 'keep off' display, which is bowing. But since this message would be totally inappropriate, it has to be modified. Although we can never know for certain what happened in a case like this, we can offer suggestions. Thus, the male approached by a female does not receive *precisely* the same stimulus as the male approached by another male. After all, he can *recognise* females from males. So his motivational balance differs in the two cases. But the key stimulus he receives is that of a male-like gannet approaching, and this is enough to trigger the neural circuit which says 'bow'. But the bowing circuitry is not independent of the bird's overall motivational state, and since, as we have said, this state has been affected by recognition that the approaching bird is female, the bow is a modified one. That is, it is what we (and the female) recognise as 'advertising'; a modified 'bow'. We should not think of the gannet, as a species, *first* developing a fully aggressive bow *both* to males and females and later modifying it when given to females. There never was a generation which could afford to miss mating. The full bow and its modified (inhibited) expression, must have developed together, each in their particular motivational framework.

Nape-biting (male): facing-away (female)

The prospecting female's response to this 'headshake and reach' is, usually, to approach. The male just stays where he is. When they meet, the result varies! Usually they make quick, tentative bill touching movements preceded or interrupted by the male biting the female's nape (see plates), presented to him by a rapid facing-away movement on her part. This may escalate into the full greeting ceremony (see below). Alternatively, the male may attack the female, and despite her prolonged facing-away and vigorous efforts to push close up to him and initiate the greeting ceremony, he may drive her right from the site. There is nothing surprising in this; after all, we know that our own moods change from minute to minute, and even though we can substantially override the effects by conscious control, they still influence our behaviour. In a bird, which has virtually no conscious control, the slight threshold shifts are reflected in rapid changes of mood and action. His occasional attacks on the female reveal how near the surface is the aggression which she elicits in him. It is very impressive that she accepts this aggression and soaks it up without retaliating. She is no weaker than him and when she is fighting another female her ferocity equals that of the male, but she is strongly inhibited from attacking a male on site. If she did, this would release full attack from the male and the fight would be completely maladaptive. By accepting his attack and facing-away (appeasing) she has some chance of switching it off, or at any rate of remaining until it wanes.

The male is not the only one who experiences mood shifts. The female, too, may approach and interact with him, only to lose interest and move away again. One male may be visited by several such females in the space of an hour or so. This, incidentally, is one reason why a male may end up with two or even three females, a situation leading to severe fights between them. The events are as follows.

When a female goes to a male, she is initially (as he was when establishing his site) very nervous. Besides greeting behaviour and (eventually) copulation, the male has another means of strengthening her attachment. He repeatedly leaves her (with the appropriate 'I am about to depart' display (see 'skypointing')), and quickly returns, maybe with nest material but often without. Every time he returns, he flies in with the customary calling, bites her nape (ritualised aggression) and fences briefly (meeting ceremony). Then he repeats the sequence. In this way he conditions the female to *expect* his return and thus to accept his absences until, eventually, she will remain on the site even whilst he is away on a long fishing trip of a day or two. At first she would soon have wandered off or nervously succumbed to displacement or threat, but after this conditioning process she is a committed partner. When *she*, in turn, is away, the male may continue to advertise to other females. There is no point at which, with a firm click, the pair bond is formed, and it is presumably advantageous for males to go on advertising to ensure pair-formation. By a process analogous to that in which one can have two rightful male owners of the same site, so one sometimes has two rightful partners of the same male, and when they meet it is war to the bone. Nor is it only newly established males that acquire two females. Established males may, early in the season before their old partner has returned, advertise to a neighbouring female. In fact, almost never does a partnership last for life, even though fidelity to the mate is high and pairs may remain together for many years (Table 17). Unless formed very early, a new pair is unlikely to breed in its first season. The full bond takes time to develop and the nest has to be built.

Once the bond is firm, the pair cooperate in guarding the site and

from then on it is rarely unguarded. Nest material can accumulate — impossible otherwise, since neighbours pilfer all unguarded nests within seconds or minutes. All firm pairs, including old breeders, have a glorious meeting display (see plates) variably termed 'fencing', 'mutual fencing', 'sparring', 'head wagging' and 'scissoring'. It takes place in full form whenever they meet after an absence of more than an hour or two; shorter absences engender no more than a perfunctory version of the ceremony. It is usually preceded by ritualised nape-biting, in which the male bites the female (never the reverse) and she faces away. Nape biting, incidentally, is a good way of sexing gannets; it is often very forceful, knocking the female off the nest.

Mutual fencing

Mutual fencing is one of the finest displays in the bird world, comparable to the mutual 'triumph ceremony' of geese or to the mutual dance of albatrosses. Together with bowing, it is the main source of noise and activity in the gannet colony. Fencing birds stand breast to breast, wings outspread as in bowing, and clash their bills against each other's, maintaining actual bill contact rather than just waggling their heads and accidentally knocking against their partner's. Intermittently they sweep their heads downwards, often over the neck of their partner. Throughout they call loudly, as in bowing. A really good performance lasts for several minutes, non-stop. The record is held by a pair in which the female had been missing for five weeks; when she returned the pair fenced at full pitch for 17 minutes! And, like the greylag's triumph ceremony, it is a display that continues undiminished for life; it is not just a way of forming the bond, but of maintaining it. Similarly, the males of old pairs nape-bite their mates virtually every time they meet, as a prelude to mutual fencing.

Mutual fencing is not confined to meeting. It occurs in all situations in which, were the male or female alone on the site, they would have bowed. These two contexts indicate strongly that aggression is a major motivational component of mutual fencing, for we know that the male is aggressive when the female joins him, and when he joins her (in both cases he attacks); and mutual fencing as a response to real or threatened intrusion is obviously an aggressively-motivated response, just as bowing is. The very strong resemblance in form between bowing and mutual fencing, and the aggressive calling in both cases, are further indications that it is aggressively motivated. Still further, the seasonal pattern of frequency and intensity shown by menacing and bowing, is matched by mutual fencing, indicating that a common causal factor (internally produced aggression) is shared by all these behaviours. So the case for considering mutual fencing to be partly aggressively-motivated behaviour seems extremely strong, and if I am right, it means that mutual fencing is a means by which the aggression between mates is given not merely harmless, but positively pair-bond-strengthening expression. I say 'pair-bond-strengthening' rather than 'harmless', because it seems that mutual fencing has acquired a sexual connotation. It is closely associated (as in nape-biting) with actual copulation, since until the egg has been laid, birds follow each meeting on the site by fencing and then mating. This means that scores, or more likely hundreds of times in the pre-laying period, mutual fencing is tied to copulation. It is thus associated with the 'satisfaction' of a consummatory act and has thereby become positively rewarding.

This could be an extremely simple and important mechanism enabling high aggressiveness (so important in site competition) to co-exist with, and indeed to facilitate, an extremely strong pair bond – equally important in the context of shared defence. At first it might seem (indeed, it did to me) that there would be a conflict of 'interest' here, in that a male whose extreme aggressiveness helped him in competition for a site would, because of it, be likely to over-attack his female and disrupt the pair bond. But if the aggression (in the form of nape biting and mutual fencing) is sexually stimulating (through its link with copulation), then the aggressive male gains both kinds of advantage and there is no weakening compromise required. And all the observations fit into place; mutual fencing is most prolonged and intense when aggression and sexual motivation are highest. Dividing the season into three blocks (March to mid-April; mid-June to the end of July; September to mid-October), bouts of mutual fencing averaged 208 seconds (39 cases) in the early season, 30 seconds (38 cases) in mid-season and 88 seconds (11 cases) late in the season. Similarly, bowing and threat behaviour are commonest early and late in the season. Thus, when birds are fighting and bowing and threatening most, they mutual fence most. Moreover its form is then explicable as a modified form of bowing; which is what an intruder – here the mate – 'should' elicit, just as it did in the pair formation context, when it gave rise to the 'headshake and reach'. Here again, the more bits of the jig-saw which fall into place the stronger the likelihood that the interpretation is correct. And all three displays (bowing, headshake-and-reach and mutual fencing) fit the same set of assumptions. A weak alternative, with no comparable consistency in relation to other behaviour, is that mutual billing is derived from the parent-young feeding behaviour, in which case its motivation could be presumed to be quite different from that just advanced, and the whole of the relationship between bowing and mutual fencing would have to be explained in quite different terms.

After their greeting ceremony, mates commonly preen each other, intently nibbling head and neck. This mutual preening is modified aggression rather than functional feather care. The idea that it removes lice from positions inaccessible to the bird's own beak is superficially plausible but it is clear from close observation of form and context that low intensity aggression is the main component. It actually grades into and out of nape-biting in certain knife-edge motivational situations, becoming rougher and rougher as the threshold of attack is approached. Furthermore, attention is extremely localised; the partner's mandibles may work away at one point and ignore the rest. No doubt the odd louse is beheaded or removed, but the main function of mutual preening, as of the mutual fencing with which it is so closely linked, is *pair-bonding via* the sublimation of aggression.

Copulation

Nape-biting and mutual fencing take care of aggression in the pair context. As mentioned, they occur before actual copulation. Copulation in the gannet is probably more than just a means of insemination; it is a prolonged source of sexual stimulation, particularly for the female. This, I think, is why it takes so much longer than in any other sulid (about three times as long) and why it entails vigorous nape-biting and foot pattering by the male – both powerful tactile stimuli. Also, it occurs over a much longer period before laying than it does in the boobies. The female solicits by vigorous headshaking, from a sitting position. The male grips her nape, mounts from the side and begins rhythmic and increasingly rapid pattering with his webs, at the same time opening and loosely waving his wings. After some 20 seconds, which is much longer than copulation lasts in most large birds, he works his tail, with side to side shuffling movements, beneath the raised tail of the female and applies his everted cloaca to hers. Ejaculation is accompanied by a brief, climactic immobility after which the male slowly relaxes his grip and dismounts, sometimes in the skypointing posture which precedes and accompanies movement from the site. Before copulation the female increases her soliciting headshake until, during the act, it may become a violent flinging movement. Immediately afterwards she may reach up and attempt to mutual fence, or reach forwards and touch or arrange nest material on the nest rim. Typically, the male, after variable behaviour (perhaps returning the threat-gape of a neighbour, or peering around myopically) leaves the site after skypointing and returns with some nest material. Several copulations and their attendant display may occur in an hour. On a quiet Spring day the colony is full of the sound of pattering feet, departure-groans and the strident calls of birds coming in with nest material. The feet marks on the female's back are useful indicators, not only of sex but of the probable absence of an egg, for with very few exceptions, copulation ceases abruptly once the egg has been laid.

Copulation may be seen between January and September but there is a well marked peak two to three weeks before the peak of egg-laying. Copulation has not been recorded at sea, but occurs in 'clubs', though there it is usually incomplete.

Adults (particularly males) sometimes mount chicks of seven weeks or more (commonest age nine weeks) but usually without ejaculation.

BEHAVIOUR ASSOCIATED WITH THE NEST

Gathering nest material and nest-building
As mentioned, nest building is closely linked with copulation. It is a most important activity for a gannet. The nest, drum or pedestal usually endures from year to year and is added to. Material is brought from the sea (seaweed, flotsam) or from the nesting island, or one nearby. There is no record of gannets collecting nest material from the mainland. An amusing note in the *Haddingtonshire Courier* of 24 February 1911 reprinted 24 February 1961, confuses gannets with real geese: 'There have been many complaints concerning the damage that is being done by solan geese on East Lothian farms and this season their depredations have been more than usually severe. They come from the Bass Rock and other natural habitats and settle in large flocks on the fields of winter wheat'.

Gannets now nest on mainland cliffs at Bempton, but do not venture onto the ground, even immediately above their colony. Gannets typically gather nest material communally, tearing out grass with great enthusiasm and making considerable local impact on the vegetation. In strong contrast to their behaviour in the colony, they do not quarrel at all during this activity, even though they are crowded together. Males are mainly responsible for gathering nest material; before the egg has been laid females rarely collect any material, though they occasionally do so afterwards. The males fly in, calling, and either surrender the nest material to the grasping female (shades of man) or deposit it and help to build it into the nest structure.

During the most active phase, much energy is spent bringing nest material and a male may come in every few minutes for two or three hours. The seasonal pattern peaks with copulation, and so there is a major peak of building activity associated with the fortnight before the main laying period, and a minor peak associated with late laying and replacement laying. Also, wet weather induces gathering on a massive scale, because a substantial nest is an advantage to the chick under these conditions, because it raises it above the general morass of mud.

Nest building is done by simple side-to-side movements of the head, varying in amplitude and vigour and ending with rapid tremoring. The mandibles release material, especially if it is sticky, by rapid and spasmodic vertical tremoring. Grass, mud and seaweed is carefully drawn up the sides of the pedestal by the sitting bird, who then places it in front or to one side of itself. Many a protracted tussle takes place over a coveted item lying in the trough, equidistant from two sitting birds. Just before the egg is laid and during incubation, nest material – especially feathers – is carefully tucked around the breast and flanks, as though to seal the gap between bird and nest rim. This behaviour may well help to prevent loss of heat from the nest cup, and even under the snowy, icy conditions of the St Lawrence gannetries, incubation temperatures are as high as in birds that have a brood patch, so the practice must be efficient.

Nest digging

Commonly, and particularly during incubation and when the chick is tiny, gannets dig and probe vigorously in the floor of the nest, picking out fragments and flinging them away with a violent sideways head-shake. Very probably, they do this to remove hard lumps, which could injure the chick or puncture the egg, for the adult weight of 3,000 g ($6\frac{1}{2}$ lb) or more, transmitted through the small area of the webs, could press an egg damagingly hard onto a sharp fragment.

BEHAVIOUR ASSOCIATED WITH THE EGG

Egg laying

The egg is laid after (usually) at least 24 hours attendance by the female, during which she often sits closely, as though incubating. She now occupies the centre of the nest (earlier, the male spent most time there, or they stood side by side). She even gets up from time to time and turns around (foot-shifting) as she does when adjusting her webs over the egg, so it is difficult to establish whether an egg is present at this time. Actual laying takes between one and two minutes. The female tips forwards, sometimes wings slightly asprawl, lifts her tail and ejects the egg, after the inevitable dilation of the cloaca. The egg emerges broad end first, though there is often little difference between ends. Usually, she immediately tucks it beneath her webs and makes sideways nest-building movements for half an hour or so. However, females laying for the first time may show highly incomplete tending behaviour. They may either stand over the egg, or mandibulate it with tremoring movements, or tuck it excitedly and too hard. Several eggs are thus lost soon after laying, and *always* such inept behaviour is by a first-time breeder. Like the comparably inept treatment of newly hatched chicks by some inexperienced females it suggests that the innate behaviour patterns concerned have failed to mature properly in time for their first usage.

Incubation

The egg is incubated beneath the webs (Fig. 17) which have an approx. area of 63 cm² (10 in²). The egg covers 40–50 cm² (6–8 in²). Early accounts treat this matter very strangely, as though it were difficult to accept. It *is* an unusual method of incubation, but so plain to see that one wonders who could have doubted it. Yet, Gurney . . . 'I was not then aware that this singular habit had been placed on record in the sixteenth century by Conrad Gesner, though subsequently it was discredited by less informed writers, and disbelieved'.[48] And even Professor Fleming[39] felt constrained to rationalise instead of to observe, and quoted Dr Walker. This gentlemen, who had not hesitated to castigate the great Willughby for lacking *first-hand* knowledge of gannets, proceeded to quote the then keeper of the Bass to the effect that gannets 'do not stand upon the egg, as is commonly reported, but sit upon it with their breast . . . like other fowls, but one of their feet is always folded under them upon the egg'. Fleming writes: 'In approaching the nest during incubation, the gannet seems usually to move off by the side, and while one foot is on the margin of the nest, the other may very frequently be observed resting on the egg. . . . It seems probable that the gannet rests on the egg in the nest as other birds do, but in preparing to move . . . does not hesitate to set its foot upon the egg, and hence it has been imagined to embrace it always throughout the whole process of incubation.' As indeed it does!

Fig. 17 The egg is incubated beneath the webs

The webs are placed in overlapping fashion over the egg, whose long axis may lie across or up and down the long axis of the gannet. They are adjusted by rocking movements whilst the bird is slightly lifted, after which it settles back into the cup. Position is changed on average once in about 10 minutes by birds which are not disturbed by the activity of a neighbour. Both sexes share incubation duties about equally, though male stints are slightly longer (Table 5). This is not surprising when one remembers that his extreme attachment to the site will play a part in keeping him there, in addition to his inclination to incubate. During the first half of the incubation period on the Bass the average stint lasted 37·2 hours (7–84) in the male and 30·8 (4–70) in the female. These shortened to 33·2 (6–62) and 29·1 (10–46) during the second half. Immediately before hatching they shorten dramatically, probably as a result of cries emitted by the chick, which begins to vocalise once it has penetrated the airspace. The length of incubation and guard spells is partly dictated by the duration of foraging trips, and thus varies from colony to colony (Table 6).

The incubating bird spends more time sleeping than does the site-attending gannet without an egg; it bows whilst still clasping the egg, though much less than formerly, and frequently threatens its neighbours. It never leaves the egg unattended, even fleetingly. Towards the end of incubation, it may transfer the egg to the top of the webs. In very warm weather it may stand over the partly exposed egg, but this is rare. Usually, on cliffs, gannets sit face in to the cliff. I think they do so to avoid abrading wing-tips and tail feathers against the rock, though it also enables them to defaecate clear of the nest. The disadvantage is that they are not facing into the wind and their skirts get blown up!

Nest relief (change-over) and skypointing
During a spell of incubation the on-duty bird may become very soiled from the excreta of neighbours. It also becomes hungry, and the arrival of its immaculate mate, fresh from foraging, would, one might think, be a welcome release. Often it seems so, and after the invariable ritual of nape-biting by the male and the ensuing mutual fencing, the incubating bird may show signs of wanting to leave. If the incomer is the female, this may suit them both. If it is the male, he may feel inclined to fetch nest material (an activity closely tied to mutual fencing through the mutual fencing, copulation, nest-building sequence). This is a situation fraught with potential danger to the egg or young chick, for if both parents were to leave, even momentarily, pilfering neighbours or egg-stealing gulls would quickly move in. This is a classical example of the need for clear communication in birds. It would be misleading to suppose that a gannet 'realises' that if it leaves its nest unattended, the egg might be stolen! That is not how gannet behaviour works. One might as well say they 'realise' that a chick which has fallen into the trough at the foot of the pedestal needs feeding, but in fact they would never feed it, and unless it regained the nest it would be allowed to starve.

The gannet, therefore, has evolved a highly distinctive display (see Plates) for which a good name is 'skypointing', whose message is 'I am about to leave', or more precisely (since they do not always do so) 'I am feeling like moving'; usually, it is movement away from the site but often a bird will preface its movement onto the site with the same display. When both partners desire to move off the site, both of them skypoint. But of course, each sees that the other is displaying and is influenced by this feedback. Eventually, one begins to posture less and less, whilst the other continues posturing at high intensity. When, and only when, the situation is clear (that is, when only *one* partner is still highly motivated to leave) he (or she) leaves. Skypointing is much in evidence at all times in a gannetry. A skypointing bird stretches its neck, points its bill vertically skywards (or even backwards of vertical), lifts its wings by a busking movement, which raises their tips but doesn't spread them out sideways, and lifts its feet with comical exaggeration, drooping them so that the green lines on the upper surfaces are fully displayed. As it moves, at first slowly, after pivoting or 'marking time', but then faster and perhaps with a hop, it brings its eyes to bear binocularly forwards and, depressing its tongue bone, it utters a peculiar 'ooh-ah' on a descending pitch – a sepulchral groan. If the bird is taking off from a cliff ledge, this groan occurs just as it departs, still in this peculiar posture. A skypointing bird thus displays to the maximum its black gape lines and throat line, green web-lines and black wing tips.

Skypointing indicates the tendency to move, and its basic function is to ensure that partners collaborate during change-over. Of course, having become tied to the 'I am about to leave' situation, it is found in all sorts of contexts where this tendency operates, and is not confined to nest-relief. Thus a male about to dismount after copulation may skypoint on the female's back; a fringe male will skypoint before moving a few steps to steal nest material; a lone bird will skypoint before stepping off its ledge and so on. In other words, the strong, simple mechanism is maintained, rather than weakened by the intro-duction of all sorts of caveats and modifications. It does no harm to skypoint on those occasions when it is *not* essential to communicate the fact that one is about to move.

Skypointing is of great interest on a number of counts. It has often caused comment, and the usual interpretation has been that it is appeasement behaviour; so-called 'excuse-me' behaviour by which a bird which wants to leave, but cannot easily reach a suitable take-off point, informs neighbours of its innocent intentions, removes its bill from any semblance of an attacking position, and thereby lessens their tendency to treat it as an intruder, when it has, perforce, to pass by them.[4] One or two authors have allowed their imagination to run riot and have embellished a nice idea by describing how well it works, and how neighbours allow unmolested passage to a skypointing bird. In fact simple observation shows, and detailed analysis confirms, that neighbours react to a skypointing individual by threatening, jabbing, seizing, or bowing; and that *after* prolonged posturing the bird often stops skypointing, lowers its head and makes a dash, which it could have done in the first place. In other words, the skypointing has not appeased anybody. Moreover, if appeasement were the function, why would a bird skypoint when about to step off a ledge, beyond anybody's reach, in just the same way as when about to pass through neighbours? The fact is that skypointing is *recognised* by neighbours as the prelude to movement (and hence, probably, intrusion) and elicits

the appropriate hostile response. The message is directed to the mate, not to the neighbour.

It seems likely that this posture has been derived from the neck lengthening and chin lifting which are among the normal preparations for flight in many birds. These and the associated foot-movements have become exaggerated. The wing-movement is rather unusual, for it differs from the normal way in which wings are lifted and spread sideways prior to flight. It is, instead, a swivelling of the upper arm bone in the shoulder socket, thus lifting the wing tips but not spreading the wing. Whether this is an adaptation to avoid sudden and dangerous displacement from cliff ledges by gusty winds, or, by restricting the spread, to reduce physical intrusion in the crowded gannetry, or something else entirely, is pure speculation – quite a different matter from interpretation of its overall function.

Whilst skypointing, gannets sometimes make swallowing movements which may help to inflate the anterior air sacs prior to flight, but this is certainly not the main function. Interestingly enough, the African

Fig. 18. African gannet skypointing sequence

gannet possesses a much more extreme form of skypointing (Fig. 18). Although it is equally ineffective in procuring an unmolested passage, its great elaboration does make one wonder whether it has a somewhat different function. It should be mentioned that, despite its apparent inefficacy as an appeasement posture, Jarvis[61] does indeed consider it to be such, and links its greater conspicuousness with the greater nesting density of the African gannet. What we lack, however, is any *evidence* for such a function.

CARE OF YOUNG

In the last few days of the incubation period the incubation stints are significantly shortened. As mentioned, this is probably cued by the calls of the chick within the egg and is adaptive in ensuring that the newly-hatched chick does not go too long without food. Normally, the adult transfers the egg to the top of the webs (see plates) once it has pipped. This simple action, it seems, is not based on awareness of the effect of pressure on the weakened shell but is purely innate; it is a series of muscle movements which do not – cannot – occur until the necessary neural mechanism has matured. This, in turn, either is not precisely timed, or the variation in the age at which birds first breed is not covered by the mechanism. Either way, the result is that a few first-time breeders fail to switch the egg from beneath the webs and thus they crush it and kill the chick. Flattened, shell-impregnated cut-outs of chicks can be prised from the bottom of the nests. This, and inadequate attention to the newly laid egg, is one of the reasons why first-time breeders are less successful than older birds.

The egg shell is not removed far from the nest; either it is placed on or over the rim, or pieces remain in the nest itself.

The newly hatched chick is carefully brooded on top of the webs and at this stage in the cycle the adult's ventral feathers seem noticeably ruffled; this may well be to allow more warmth to reach the chick, since the webs cannot transmit heat as effectively as when wrapped around the egg.

The adult's care of the chick comprises brooding, preening and feeding. Brooding is mostly continuous for the first 10–14 days, though in fine weather the chick may be partly or fully exposed. Until it is three weeks old it can still be more or less completely brooded and is thus quite safe, whatever the weather, provided the nest is a good one (a poor nest may mean that the chick is lying in mud and water). After three weeks the chick becomes increasingly impossible to protect, and between three and six weeks it is at most risk from chilling (see Chapter 4). Preening by the adult is probably not important to the chick. It is mostly perfunctory and the chick is capable of preening itself. Even so, the down often becomes filthy and matted.

The chick may be fed even before it is quite clear of the shell. When newly hatched it is too weak and wobbly to do much more than raise its head and make palsied and apparently aimless movements before collapsing again. It certainly does not attempt to peck at the parent's bill, as a young herring gull does, for example. This suggests that, in the early stages, the adult's feeding response is not regulated by the chick. Later, of course, the chick does beg for food and in this way controls (at least partly) the amount it gets. The hungrier it is the more persistently it begs. If this is correct, it would explain an otherwise puzzling aspect of the gannet twinning experiments (Chapter 4).

The adult feeds its tiny chick on semi-digested fish, which it regurgitates in small amounts. It bends its head down, opens its beak wide and engulfs the chick, which then gropes in the trough of the lower mandible. Alternatively, the parent bends its head right over so that its forehead is resting on the nest and the food falls into the upper cavity. It does not regurgitate onto the floor of the nest, nor does it place morsels into the chick's beak. There is no record of a gannet bringing water to its chick, as cormorants do. It sometimes moves the chick in the nest by placing its mandibles over it and nudging it along.

As the chick grows, it begins to beg, to pester more actively, which greatly stimulates the adult. The prelude to regurgitation is a forward movement of the head, with lengthened neck and convulsive swallowing movements. Then it leans further forwards and down, opens its beak widely and with more or less violent retching brings up a whole fish, two or three small ones, or a bolus of small fry, all in various stages of digestion. If the chick continues begging, the final feeds may be produced with great effort from the deeper regions of the gut. Food may be produced more or less immediately after return to the site or not until several hours have passed. The fish are taken by the chick in whatever position they happen to be after its vigorous digging in the adult's mouth and throat. After delivering a feed, the adult gulps back. It usually picks up large pieces which have been dropped and swallows them; smaller ones are picked up and scattered with a violent sideways fling of the head. Fish regurgitated in fright are, however, rarely or never eaten again, even though they are often in better condition than pieces dropped during transference. The motivational state of the adult is different in the two cases. The frequency of feeds, the amounts brought, and other details, are described in the chapter on ecology (see Table 7).

The adult's relationship with its chick is intriguing. It does not reject strange chicks and will accept substitutes greatly different in age from its own. But it usually repels a chick, including its own, that is *approaching* from outside the nest. Indeed, its attacks on chicks attempting to gain the nest are sometimes berserk. I have seen a small chick attempting to crawl up the side of the pedestal and being lacerated so badly, and eventually killed, that it was agonising to watch. The chick's soft down is pathetic against the steel of the adult's bill. This is why it is so essential for gannet ringers to ensure that they do not displace chicks by causing them to run. The adult gannet's reaction makes sense in that natural selection has produced a system in which, despite the vast and crowded colonies, there is an ordered distribution of chicks; nobody wanders about and no adults get strange chicks instead of or in addition to their own. This could be achieved either by individual recognition (a common phenomenon in species whose chicks wander) or by penalising wandering and so doing away with the need for recognition. Wandering is dangerous or impossible on cliffs, but could occur easily on flat ground. There are several reasons why it would be disadvantageous to exchange chicks. A major one is that a pair could lose the advantage of having laid early (see Chapter 4) which the selfish gene could never allow.

In general, the adults are remarkably free from a tendency to attack their young. This may seem an odd statement, but when one recalls the male's vigorous attacks on his mate, it is worth notice. The probable significance of the juvenile's black plumage in this respect is discussed in Chapter 1.

Parents tend their chick for about 13 weeks and it is then the chick, not the parents, that terminates the relationship. It often takes more than ten years for a finding to filter through and some authors *still* persist in propagating the myth that young gannets are forced to leave the ledge because their parents stop feeding them.* In fact, young gannets are in some cases fed right to the hour they leave, and if the *number* of feeds given to fully feathered young tapers off before they fledge (as may well be) it is because the chick itself becomes less interested in food. This can be seen plainly in chicks reared in captivity; for a variable period before they leave, they may refuse to feed. This is in itself fascinating, though of course we know nothing about the mechanism. But the fact remains that many or most young are fed right to the day they leave; and any that are not would be far from starving – they carry far too much fat for that. Even a strange juvenile that manages to gain access to a site en route to the cliff edge may be

* After I wrote this, the issue of the prestigious 'Encyclopedia of Birds' dealing with the gannet appeared, and re-told the same old tale. Oddly, whilst much of it was clearly based on my work the refutation of the starvation theory did not get through.

fed, which is not surprising in view of their lack of 'on-site' discrimination against strange young.

Their complete indifference to its going might seem surprising. After all, they have guarded it without a moment's neglect for over three months and one might have expected them, at least, to watch it go. But their failure to do so is in fact much less surprising than an obvious concern and 'interest' would be. After all, they do not go with it and do not recognise it as an individual (or, more accurately, they do not discriminate between it and a stranger). To be 'interested' would probably imply thought processes which, as numerous examples already quoted have shown, they do not possess. The departure of the chick is by no means the end of the breeding season for the parents. When it goes, they continue as before, attending their site without remiss and displaying; in fact their display is more frequent than in mid-season (Fig. 15). Not until the gales of autumn are settling into the grey November depths of approaching winter will they take a brief respite from their by then barren rock. And whilst the bitterest days of January and February are still ahead, they will be back on their ledges, which are now bleak beyond description.

BODY CARE

In dealing with the sequence of events as they occur, I bypassed several aspects of behaviour. Most of them have to do with care of the plumage or some other form of comfort behaviour. None are displays in the same sense as bowing, that is 'deliberately' transmitting information which will affect other individuals, though all of them convey information (just as doing nothing does).

The behaviour that comes nearest to a display is a complex plumage shaking and settling (see plates) which I have called 'rotary' headshake to distinguish between it and the ordinary side to side headshaking. The full sequence begins with vigorous wing-flapping, the body axis at about 45°, after which the body feathers are ruffled, especially the ventral plumage and the head and neck, and the head is rapidly rotated through 90° or more and back again. The expansion of the face feathers and the depression of the hyoid give it quite a full-faced, owl look. Finally, the tail may be waggled from side to side and the wings are re-settled. There are variants of this, the commonest being a 'dogshake', during which the wings are only partly loosened and are not flapped. The dogshake is the commonest response to sudden fouling of the feathers, as by a neighbour's excreta. The full rotary headshake sequence, too, is concerned with getting rid of loose feathers, or water or dirt, and is undoubtedly a response to tactile stimulation, whether of pressure or irritation, or tightening of the skin and thus stimulation of the feather follicles. It is extremely frequent and peaks during the moult of body feathers (Fig. 15) which begins about the time that the eggs hatch. Presumably because it is a response to skin tightening, it is highly correlated with alarm. Anything which makes gannets slightly anxious when they are in the colony (but not when they are outside it) causes an immediate and dramatic outbreak of rotary-headshaking. Gull clamour sets up a wave of rotary headshaking. In this way, the alarm shown by a few individuals is communicated to others and acts as an inadvertent signal.

It is a curious fact that fully feathered young do not perform the wingflap-rotary-headshake. They wingflap by the hour, and they headshake frequently, sometimes in a slightly rotary manner, but the normal adult sequence is not a part of their hour-by-hour comfort behaviour as it is with adults. This may be because in adults it is undoubtedly caused by (among other things) tension or conflict, which is why it is so frequent early and late in the season, when fear of land is high. Juveniles, on the other hand, have never known anything other than dry land; the colony is 'safe'. Only later will they come to associate the sea with safety and the land with danger. Why the full wingflap and rotary headshake, rather than the dogshake, should be the typical correlate of alarm is not clear. Possibly, it is because the former is the behaviour most intimately connected with preparation for flight.

Two other important feather maintenance activities are preening and oiling (see plates). Preening has not been exhaustively studied; it employs nibbling with mandible tips; stropping (a sideways application of the beak to the feathers of the underparts), and drawing wing and tail feathers through the beak. Gannets spend much time preening, and activity charts show that on site, except when sleeping, gannets rarely spend more than a few minutes without preening. Prolonged and intensive bouts of preening take up to an hour, and the same parts of the body are treated several times; whether randomly or in specific sequences has not been worked out. Preening does not show marked seasonal trends, which is in keeping with the need to maintain the plumage in tip-top condition all the time. Mutual preening, in which partners preen each other, is not a form of feather care; it is modified aggression. Gannets are heavily infected by feather lice on the head and neck, and they treat these regions by scratching with the pectinated

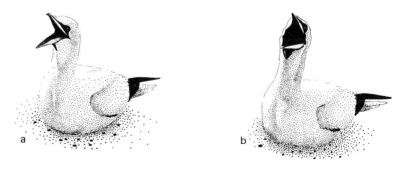

Fig. 19. (a) *Raising upper mandible*
        (b) *Distending gape, as when swallowing large fish*

Fig. 20. Temperature regulation in African (left) and Atlantic gannets: panting, gular fluttering, wings away from body, gular strip exposed (note African gannet's long gular strip, which is probably an adaptation to hot climate)

claw of the middle toe, but not very effectively, as the heavy infestations show.

Oiling is usually part of an intensive bout of preening. The gannet puts its head right back onto the oil gland at the base of the tail and rolls its crown and the sides of its head on the gland. It then rubs these oily areas of the head onto the feathers of the wings and the back. It also transfers the secretion onto tail and wing feathers by use of its beak.

Relatively minor 'comfort' behaviour patterns, though worth listing for those interested in comparative studies, are as follows. Wing stretching or limbering, one at a time and only downwards, over one leg and foot (sometimes lifted and partly clenched) most commonly follows preening; gannets never arch both wings upwards as gulls and terns do. Forward stretching with depressed hyoid is really the prelude to the rotary headshake but may occur on its own. Yawning, with the buccal cavity enlarged by sideways and downward distension is sometimes followed by raising the upper mandible, using the frontal 'hinge', in what we called a 'custard bird' gape.

Birds reap great advantages from their high metabolic rate. Where this is allied to exceptionally efficient insulation their ability to withstand the cold of the worst that the world's climates can throw against them is astonishing. Gannets have thick quilty feathers, thick skin, air-spaces and a layer of fat, so it is not surprising that 48 hours sitting on a ledge in January sleet matters no more than an icy gale in the middle of the North Sea in winter. But what about sitting on a baking-hot slope, with rocks absorbing and radiating July heat? It cannot shed its feathers or its skin, and though it could conceivably lose some fat and certainly could deflate its air spaces, the former would entail serious disadvantages. It has three ways of avoiding or mitigating heat stress (Fig. 20). The most obvious is panting; gaping slightly and fluttering or resonating the throat skin, with head tilted upwards and, usually, with eyes almost closed; this loses moisture and heat to the atmosphere, whilst the upward tilt of the head exposes the naked black throat skin, and the closed eyes similarly expose the eyelids. At the same time the wings are slightly lifted so that there is an air space, presumably to let heat from the thinly feathered axillary region escape. Thirdly, it exposes its webs. Oddly, it almost never lies down and thrusts one foot to the side, as chicks do. I am not sure whether it deliberately excretes onto them as the African gannet does, to aid heat-loss by evaporative cooling. Usually the substrate is wet anyway, which is not the case in an African gannetry.

Obviously, gannets defaecate at the colony or at sea (more rarely in flight). There is no evidence that they save up their excreta, as Peruvian boobies undoubtedly do, to use as nest material. On the other hand they do void sticky, viscous material from the vent onto the sides of the nest; their 'whitewash' they squirt clear of the site. Nor is it merely that they cannot squirt glue! Often they depress their tail which effactually guides excreta onto the nest. In fact it is undoubtedly true, as with kittiwakes, that it is only the cementing action of excreta that enables gannets to nest on the narrow ledges, knobs and sloping faces which they sometimes use. Gurney found this too much to believe!

Gannets sleep standing or sitting with their heads tucked into the scapulars which can be raised on both sides to envelop the head. They insert their bills with a dexterous snuggling movement and then the feather walls close delicately around their head. They spend about half of their time on the site, asleep, though obviously this varies inversely with their overt activity and this, in turn, with the time of year. Before they have an egg they prefer to sleep standing rather than sitting, though as laying time approaches they sleep more and more in a sitting position. Probably the preference for a sitting posture as incubation time approaches is hormonally controlled. The unusually long sleeping spells which follow severe fighting have already been mentioned.

Gannets bathe just offshore from the colony (and no doubt at sea, also). They employ the motions common to most water birds, thrashing the surface with partly loosened wings and ducking. They occasionally roll onto one side, but not as a usual part of bathing. Oiling, rotary-headshaking and sideways headshaking with drinking or false-drinking, are common whilst bathing. When landing on the surface to rest, bathe or gather nest material they commonly enter in a shallow dive, but occasionally feet-first like a duck.

I have now described all major, discrete patterns of behaviour that a gannet performs at the breeding colony and I would think it incompetence on my part if anybody, on visiting a gannetry, were to see gannets doing something that I have not described, or something that could not easily be related to such descriptions. However, it may help to clarify the relationships between various behaviours if I now group all these activities by function and motivation (see Figure 15).

Territorial behaviour comprises *fighting* and the various forms of *ritualised threat: flying-in with calling* and *bowing*. It is aggressively motivated and repels actual or potential intruders, but it has, also, a strong fear component. The *pelican posture* (bill tucking) which occurs in bowing, and also as a discrete response to aggressive behaviour from neighbours, is at least partly a fear response. **Sexual, pair-bonding and pair-maintaining behaviour** comprise sexual *advertising* (male); *prospecting* (female); *nape-biting* (male); *facing-away* (female); *copulation with biting* (male); *mutual fencing* (greeting) and *mutual preening*. Here, aggression and fear, as well as sexual motivation, are clearly evident, not only in the male's overt biting but in the advertising (derived from bowing), in the mutual fencing and mutual preening and, so far as fear is concerned, in the facing-away. *Skypointing* has to be grouped among pair-maintaining behaviours if my interpretation of its function is correct, though it is the only behaviour pattern in the list so far that has no discernible fear or aggression components, unless one considers the tendency to fly away as 'fear'. Activities functional in **making a nest and caring for egg and chick** are: *gathering nest material*; *nest building*; *nest digging*; *incubation*; *brooding* and *feeding the chick*. Nest building movements often appear in conflict (fear and aggression) situations, as displacement activities, but are likely, nonetheless, to be expressing genuine nest building motivation (via disinhibition). **Body-care activities** form another major group, comprising *bathing, preening, oiling, headshaking* (sideways and rotary), *defaecating* and *thermo-regulating*. Of these, sideways headshaking is the only one that has found its way into displays (bowing, advertising, mutual fencing) and also is common in conflict situations. Preening, so common as displacement activity in many birds, has not been deployed at all in this way by the gannet.

Finally, a word on the subject of derivation. The bow, fairly certainly, derives from ground biting and the cleansing headshake. Also, fairly certainly, the male advertising (headshake-and-reach) and the greeting ceremony (mutual fencing) are related to bowing. It would probably be incorrect, however, to say that they were *derived* from the bow. They evolved along with it; gannets have always had to cope simultaneously with territorial and sexual selection pressures. To assume that a behaviour pattern becomes perfected unilaterally (for example the bow) and then provides the material for another behaviour pattern (say mutual fencing) would clearly be incorrect, since meantime the gannet would have had to evolve some behaviour for dealing with pair relationships. *All* behaviour patterns which are motivationally and functionally related must evolve as a group, each modifying the other through the different advantages produced by the slightly different forms and intensities of the behaviours which variability, due to sexual reproduction with its re-shuffling of genes, inevitably throws up. Then one must add to the equation the effects of changing environmental pressures, whereby competition for a site, for example, may have varied during the gannet's long evolutionary history and with it the set of advantages conferred by aggressive behaviour. Some behaviour, however, such as incubation behaviour, has probably always been independent of the aggression–fear–sexual system but has evolved under an equally complex set of interacting pressures. For example, the choice of nesting site may have contributed towards the adoption of the under-foot incubation method, by providing a wet, cold surface and wet, cold material against which, often enough, the egg had to be insulated (as with penguins, also). Nesting site, in turn, has been forced on the gannet by the bird's aerodynamic qualities, which are closely linked with fishing. And so it goes on, infinitely complex.

Why it is that in some species some constituents of behaviour, such as sideways headshaking and nest building, become incorporated into displays or are common displacement activities, or both, whilst others, such as preening, do not, is a moot point. The salient fact is that even complex displays are derived from common, simple acts like intention movements, or from displacement activities.[132] This knowledge, and a broad appreciation of the role of aggression and fear in ostensibly sexual behaviour, has enabled us to understand a lot more about displays than would otherwise have been possible. Nor need we exclude humans from that!

BEHAVIOUR OF THE YOUNG GANNET

It is convenient to deal with the activities of the chick[85] and fledgling separately from those of the adult. Two important shaping factors have been cliff-nesting and adult aggressiveness.

Begging and feeding
Organised begging is first seen when the chick is about ten days old; until then, its uncoordinated movements, though they may stimulate the adult, are not directed towards it. Later, the chick pesters the adult by pointing its bill upwards, swaying its head from side to side and aiming mild lunges at the parent's beak. High intensity begging includes a repeated 'yipping' note which, alone, sometimes elicits regurgitation movements from the adult. But the main point about gannet chick begging is its relative restraint, compared with that of the booby. There are two reasons for this. First, and most important, violent begging with wing-flailing would seriously endanger the chick on cliff ledges. Also, gannet chicks are rarely starving, whereas booby chicks often are, and frenzied begging presumably enhances their chances of making the adult regurgitate.

Young gannets take fish from the mouth or throat of their parent by inserting their head, distending their gape (thus enormously dilating the adult's pharynx) and pumping hard. At the same time the adult is actively pushing food out, and as its head is dragged down by the

Fig. 21. *Restrained begging of young gannet (adaptation to cliff nesting) compared with frenzied begging of young red-footed booby*

chick, food slides easily into the chick's mouth. It then points its bill upwards and gulps repeatedly to settle the meal. It can accommodate large mackerel and can take up to at least 500 g (1 lb) in one bout of feeding. A single entry into the adult's mouth is rarely enough to transfer sufficient food; up to five successful entries, and between one and four unsuccessful, comprise a 'bout' of feeding (Table 7). A hungry chick can accommodate the offerings of both parents in fairly quick succession, though this rarely happens. Chicks may mandibulate spilt food but they seldom eat it.

Body care
    When about a week old the chick, still almost naked and with rudimentary wings, makes its first recognisable attempts at wing-flapping, rotary headshaking and sideways headshaking. Sideways wing-stretching and wing-arching, with head horizontal and stretched forwards and down, occur within the first fortnight. Interestingly, although the full adult pattern of rotary headshaking develops, the *frequency* never approaches that of adults. Even when the chicks are feathered and are shedding down in vast quantities, the incidence of rotary headshaking does not increase in the way it does in adults that are moulting. I think this is because chicks are not afraid of land as adults are and the rotary headshake is partly fear-induced. Sustained bouts of wing-flapping occur from three weeks onwards but are not regular until the flight feathers have erupted. Then, it is unfailingly

stimulated by rain. A most remarkable sight in a gannetry occurs when the young are in the black juvenile plumage, and a heavy shower begins. Myriads of black wings suddenly sprout from between the white adults and flap rhythmically, whilst the adults stand unmoved (Fig. 22). At a guess, this behaviour by the juveniles may have something to do with the fact that they have not yet been to sea, and heavy tactile stimulation with water may release bathing-flapping. Certainly, their first act upon landing in the water after fledging, is to wing flap vigorously.

Wing exercising bouts last about 30–60 seconds, usually facing the wind except on cliff ledges, where they face inwards. It is not accompanied by jumping or walking, as it is in young gulls. At first the whole wing is flapped but gradually the action of the proximal part decelerates until only the wing tip moves. Some chicks fall to their death as a result of wing exercising (see Chapter 4) but presumably it is essential for development.

Chicks begin to nibble at their down from about ten days, though until the feathers grow it is perfunctory behaviour. Gradually the time spent preening increases until it becomes a major occupation and uses all the patterns described for the adult. When fully feathered (from about ten weeks), chicks sometimes preen their parents and engage in mutual preening with them. Often they preen them on the back, which adults rarely do to each other. They do not have the adult's pre-occupation with head and nape, which is perhaps understandable in view of the ritualised nature of adult mutual preening. Oiling starts at about eight weeks, when the feathers are well grown though in places still thickly interspersed with down. Yawning, adult pattern, occurs within the first week. Gular fluttering occurs then, too.

Chicks sleep prone, often with their heads hanging limply over the nest rim, looking quite dead. Even experienced observers may be fooled. After about six weeks they begin to sleep with head in scapulars, though even fully feathered young may revert to prone sleeping, never seen in adults. Often, one foot sticks out to the side; as mentioned, this is to radiate heat from the large web.

Gannet chicks cannot regulate their own body temperature until they are about a month old, and until then they are fully or partly covered by the parent. Dry down is a good insulator but wet down is useless, which is why sodden chicks are highly vulnerable to chilling (Chapter 4). But excessive heat, as in the adult, can be a problem. Chicks use the same methods to dissipate it and in addition make much greater use of their webs. It took me some time to realise this; I often saw chicks holding a leg with a spread web out to the side; legs with rings on were particularly obvious and, at first, I assumed it was a reaction to the ring! Undoubtedly, however, it is a way of losing heat. Chicks usually have filthy webs, and whilst some of this could be accidental fouling, it may be deliberate use of evaporative cooling.

Tiny chicks cannot void clear of the nest and do not produce faecal sacs; they soil the nest. Whether adult nest digging is intended to

Fig. 22. Juveniles wing-exercising in rain; adults unaffected

remove some of this is not clear.

Chicks begin to pick up, mandibulate and 'place' nest material from about two weeks of age; later they snatch material from adults and 'build' it onto the rim. From about eight weeks they play with nest sticks, feathers, etc, juggling and tossing, catching and turning them, using the movements employed by adults in dealing with fish.

Bill-hiding

When attacked, chicks show an extreme form of bill-hiding (Fig. 15); they tuck their bill right underneath their breast, sometimes lying prone as well. From about nine weeks onward, they also face-away as the adult female does. One can easily induce bill-hiding by tapping the back of the chick's head, and it is undoubtedly effective in reducing the severity of an attack by a strange adult, though such attacks are rare because the chick is usually guarded. Attacks by its own parents are also rare, so the well developed appeasement posture might seem excessive. Again, however, *one* attack could be lethal if not deflected.

When a chick *is* attacked, the aggression provides some interesting insights for us. It grades into rough preening and then into 'proper' preening as in the mutual preening of adults. It concentrates on the nape (largely because this is presented to it) and despite the appeasement, may continue long enough to kill the chick. Appeasement postures, as one sees when females try to appease an unreceptive male, do not work like a switch. At best, they reduce the attack or increase the speed with which it wanes, and eventually stops, in enough cases to be of advantage.

It is not absolutely clear that facing-away in the chick and in the adult are homologous (that is, share the same origin) and less obvious that the chick bill-hiding and the adult pelican posture are so. Chicks occasionally use the pelican posture as well as bill-hiding (extreme form) and facing-away, and whilst they all look reasonably like versions of the same basic movement, there may be differences in motivation between the adult pelican posture and the chick bill-hiding. Adults use the pelican posture when they are simultaneously afraid and aggressive, whereas chicks are mainly afraid. This, however, may be no more than a difference of balance between the two components: Chicks do begin to use the pelican posture more when they are fully grown and, presumably, more likely to experience the physiological causes of aggression. Certainly it is tempting to derive the adult patterns from the similar ones of the chick. It is interesting to note, incidentally, that chicks do not skypoint, which further supports my rejection of this movement as an appeasement posture.

Facing-away begins to appear as the chick becomes more aggressive. Chicks menace each other when about a month old, but perfunctorily. Later they develop ritualised menacing, complete with twist and withdrawal. They attack trespassing chicks, often yapping vociferously (the equivalent of the adult's aggressive calling during fighting). Occasionally, they menace neighbouring adults but are usually ignored, and from about seven weeks they threaten and attack their parents so vigorously that the female faces away; from time to time both sexes retaliate strongly, particularly the male. This early manifestation of overt aggression is interesting in view of the prominence of aggression later, and if (as seems likely) it is necessary, in developmental terms, it makes the chick's black plumage even more adaptive as a device to blunt the male's retaliation. Chick attacks are delivered with the uncoordinated movements typical of young animals: violent and mis-timed jabs, excited yapping, contorted and perfunctory self-preening are all mixed together.

Aggressive display (bowing and mutual fencing), though rare, does occur in chicks of eleven weeks or more. The bows are ill-defined, but clearly incorporate the headshake and an incipient dip with wings partly open, and are accompanied by yapping. Fully grown chicks occasionally perform a short bout of mutual fencing with an adult. Interestingly, in view of the role of aggression in mutual fencing, these rare occurrences are stimulated not by arrival of a parent, but by some aggressive act from a neighbour. The chicks of some boobies, in which the adults are less aggressive than in the gannet, commonly show aggressive (territorial) display.

Adults of each sex, but particularly males, infrequently copulate with chicks of seven weeks or more, but chicks were never seen to mount an adult or another chick.

FLEDGING

The traumatic moment in which a juvenile gannet rushes headlong to the cliff edge (see Fig. 23 and plates) and jumps, topples or is pushed over or (if it is lucky) jumps off its ledge in its own good time, breaks a fantastically strong tie. For thirteen weeks, such an act has meant death

Fig. 23. Fledging: juvenile running the gauntlet of nesting adults, to reach the cliff edge

and the chick has countered the risk in every possible way. It is little wonder that, as the chick's conflict behaviour shows, the actual launching comes so hard; yet an irresistible force builds up and literally forces the young bird to fledge.

Before leaving the ledge, practise flight has been impossible. To begin with, the fully-feathered chick is too heavy to fly effectively, and cliff sites, once left, could not be regained. On flatter ground the aggression of neighbours deters any attempt to leave the nest site. Nevertheless, from about a month old, the young possess a visual image of their site in relation to its surroundings which enables artificially or accidentally displaced chicks to return from any angle. They are remarkably persistent in this, struggling for up to two days to regain their nest. They show a marked tendency to clamber uphill, using their beak as a lever (never to grip with) and their wings and tail to assist their scrabbling feet. Understandably they are reluctant to venture downhill, for they tend to topple forwards, but will go if they have to. Occasionally, a displaced chick will push its way onto a strange nest and if it can resist the initial attacks of the adult and rightful chick, it may stay there, either as a twin or (if bigger) as a usurper. But usually the desire to regain its nest is so powerful that it will endure terrible punishment from neighbours in order to do so.

This ability to recognise its surroundings so accurately may well be the basis for its strong tendency to return to its precise area of birth. The advantages of doing so may be several. Although rarely, the ability may save its life if it mis-fledges and has to return to its site by a route that it certainly has never traversed before, and anybody who has moved around in the heart of a big group will know that a given nest looks totally different when seen from different angles.

Fringe young are the only ones that could (and often do) wander fairly easily from their nests. Even so, only the late fringe youngsters can do so with impunity, for by then the fringe non-breeders have gone. The young of Australasian and African gannets wander, and practise flying, extensively, but they are predominantly flat-ground nesters, and the adults are less aggressive.

It is probably no coincidence that, in these other two gannets the young are much paler than the Atlantic gannet, for the appeasing function of black plumage is probably less important.

Gannets fledge[82] (that is, leave the site irrevocably) when between 84 and 97 days old (Table 8). Details of age, weight, mortality and so on are given in the next chapter; this account is solely of their behaviour. They never fledge voluntarily until completely free of down and a young bird which fledges prematurely, with down still present, will try to return to land and wait until it reaches the 'proper' threshold or dies. As remarked, there is a gradual and easily observable build-up of fledging tendency. From one to four days before departure the young spend more and more time wing-flapping and keep turning to face the sea, in a characteristically long-necked, forward-leaning posture (anxiety-posture), gazing intently seawards, oblivious to all surrounding activity, for two or three minutes before relaxing, turning away and showing the usual interest in surrounding affairs. They may do this more than thirty times in the day before fledging and I once spent thirteen hours glued to a ciné camera, thinking it was going to happen any minute. If, after facing the sea as described, the juvenile wing-flaps, it is a sign of motivational shift and the bird will not leave before going through the preliminaries again. It may then toss nest material about or preen half-heartedly for two or three minutes before resuming sea-gazing. The sequence in the few minutes before a departure is, typically, as follows though it may be shorter and, indeed, chicks knocked over the edge can fly successfully without all this preparation; it is essentially a matter of reaching the right 'mood' and if it is knocked off, this doesn't apply! The bird takes up the long-necked position, often thrusting its neck forward as though to get a better view of the sea, half lifts its wings in a flicking movement, hesitates, turns this into a bout of wing-flapping, preens perfunctorily, turns to face inland several times but always jerks back to face the sea, swallows repeatedly and conspicuously (air-sac inflation?), patters its feet and headshakes. Actual take-off occurs after two or three preparatory wing flicks and the bird then simply jumps into the air. From a cliff, they are quickly airborne, but from a cliff-top slope, they may crash amongst nesting birds, then they must flounder to the edge, violently attacked by adults and chicks. Wouldn't it be nice if they were kitted out with a perfectly effective 'excuse-me' posture! But they are not. Nor are adults 'sensible' enough to know that these are merely confused youngsters trying to get clear of the group.

Young from inland nests without a take-off point are in the worst predicament and one wonders how an early chick from the middle of Eldey, or even the southern face of Grassholm, reaches the edge at all. On the Bass, many are forced to work their way to a more favourable spot or blunder blindly through the nesting ranks. They often make two or three abortive runs towards the cliff-edge and may return to their nests from a considerable distance. Occasionally they get stuck and lie doggo for hours or days (five days in one case, after which the bird was so fouled and pecked that it had virtually no chance of survival). Yet some, on the way to the edge, are accepted, preened and even fed by strange adults. As mentioned, adults are sometimes very aggressive to their own chick if it has become separated from the nest. Parents play no part in their chick's departure and show no signs of noticing it.

Once in the air, the chick flies strongly after a shaky start. Often, it falls 15 m (50 ft) or more before levelling out, but in a fresh, onshore wind it may soar immediately. At first, its wing beats are wobbly and it yaws and side-slips erratically, making over-vigorous compensating strokes. Then its wing beats, though shallow, become regular and it flies strongly, usually in a wide curve, often soaring much higher than the cliffs and banking proficiently. It usually lands within 400–800 m ($\frac{1}{4}$–$\frac{1}{2}$ mile) of the colony but can fly much further. Several have been seen, still flying strongly, when at least 3 km (2 miles) from the rock.

It lands in the sea, feet or belly down, with a great splash and immediately begins to bathe excitedly, sometimes even waterlogging its plumage. It swims fairly low in the water, head retracted and bill slightly upwards, often with the tail awash, something which adults rarely, if ever, do. Early fledglings are liable to land in the midst of resting adults, off-duty breeders and immatures alike. Sometimes they are vigorously attacked (Fig. 24), and the fracas may attract others until up to twenty are swimming around the fledgling, hanging onto it, and

Fig. 24. Newly fledged juvenile harried at sea by adults

lunging at its head. Often it is partly submerged for seconds at a time and all its efforts to thresh clear are unavailing; the ordeal may continue for up to two hours without stopping. This rather unusual behaviour is not an important cause of mortality even around Bass Rock (though indirectly it undoubtedly causes some fatalities), and at other gannetries it may be much less common. Off Ailsa Craig, there are fewer birds on the sea and fewer non-breeders (who may be largely implicated); and off Bempton it has been looked for in vain, though there are only a few birds there.

The newly-fledged young of several species draw attacks from adults. In the gannet's case it may simply be that the neural dictum 'attack young off the nest' has not been worth modifying to read 'except at sea'. Later, the behaviour seems less common; perhaps there are then fewer non-breeders and off-duty breeders; or the motivational state of breeders has changed. However, this is guesswork; the fact is that the attacks occur and they seem (and almost certainly are) functionless.

The newly fledged juvenile swims away from the colony. Most of them go south. It is well known that it cannot, at first, raise itself from the surface[63,84] no matter how hard it tries, mainly because it has too much fat. Also, its wings are not quite fully grown. Its parents do *not* accompany it and so it is thrown entirely on its own resources. If any adult *does* feed it at sea, this can be only an exceptional piece of luck. Thus it has fuel for a limited period, perhaps 1–2 weeks depending on the circumstances (of wind, temperature, etc. which affect the rate at which it uses up energy), during which time it must acquire the extremely difficult art of catching fish by plunge diving. It has been estimated that a young Manx shearwater with 200 g (7 oz) of fat, out of the bird's total weight of 550 g (19 oz), has a flapping flight range of 3,000 km (1,900 miles) and a gliding and flapping range of perhaps 6,000 km (3,800 miles). The young gannet has proportionately about half that amount of fat but is a larger and, therefore, in this context, a more efficient flier. If it flew from the very beginning of its journey it could probably reach its winter quarters on its fuel reserves, but a few days of swimming, covering perhaps 75–150 km (50–100 miles) altogether, may use up half of its reserves, or more. The interesting matters of the selection pressures which have encouraged the gannet's unique (within the family) method of acquiring independence, and the heavy mortality it entails, is discussed later. The question here is, how does it learn to fish? The short answer is that nobody knows, but one can construct a reasonably likely scenario. Either it has innate ability to recognise a fish, or its experience at the nest has taught it to do so. As it swims, it frequently puts its head in the water. The skin which then reflexly covers the eye enables it to see clearly and it will in time see fish. It is not known whether the young gannet can submerge from the surface, like a cormorant, from the outset, but this is unlikely, though adults can do so. However, as it uses up fat, it will be able to raise itself more readily and perform a splash dive which will enhance its penetration. Each time that it gets near to a fish it will grab at it.

Eventually, either this way, or after it has become air-borne and has dived properly, it will catch one and will then be well on the way to success. But the balance is fine; once it is light enough to fly, its fat reserves will be substantially exhausted and a spell of bad weather can then be fatal. But it should be well south and presumably decreasing this likelihood as it goes, which is one reason why juveniles press on with such speed, sometimes reaching Morocco in less than a fortnight. They are on the wing from mid-August (occasionally earlier) and are commonly to be seen accompanying an adult. This has led to the suggestion that their parents may accompany them but the real explanation is that the juvenile has tagged along behind an adult (indeed an adaptive thing to do). There is no possibility that its own parents, both of whom are still in full attendance at the colony, could repeatedly fly out to sea and locate their migrating juvenile. It is a hard time for the young, but part of the price paid by the species for the advantage of a site-attachment strong enough to ensure possession of a breeding place that will fulfil all its needs.

At this crucial juncture the juvenile is on its way to warmer waters and its behaviour upon return to the colony is taken up at the beginning of this chapter. The interesting matter of its possible wanderings as an immature bird, and the signals to which it responds when choosing a colony or a group, are discussed in Chapter 2. Finally, it might be helpful to follow the gannet's fortunes diagramatically (Fig. 25), from the moment it cheeps whilst still within the egg, to full circle, when it perpetuates its own genes, in the shape of its first fledgling.

Chick vocalises in egg before hatching: switches parent to shorter absences so food will be available.

Releases internally controlled feeding behaviour from parents, independent of chick's begging behaviour.

Controls adult food-giving by its own begging, which is restrained, probably as an anti-falling device.

Fig. 25. *Schematic representation of gannet's life history, with particular reference to behaviour*

Fledges (jumps off cliff) without prior flight practice.

Swims off on first leg of migration which is later continued on wing and may take it almost to the equator. Lives off fat deposits, fasting for first week so.

Returns to home waters in 2nd or 3rd year, and is attracted to a colony usually but not necessarily its own.

Joins a 'club' of immature and adult birds, but is probably transitory in attendance, spending long periods foraging at sea and visiting other gannetries.

3rd or 4th year. Much aerial circuiting by adult male above the colony, particularly examining the section in which it intends to settle.

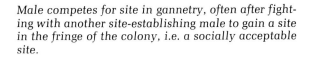

Male competes for site in gannetry, often after fighting with another site-establishing male to gain a site in the fringe of the colony, i.e. a socially acceptable site.

After establishing its site the male defends it by ritualised display — bowing derived from re-directed aggression (biting the site).

The male then 'advertises' to prospective female, using inhibited version of the site ownership display.

When the female approaches, the male often attacks, but she 'faces away' (appeasement).

They then perform the greeting ceremony (mutual fencing). Eventually such an encounter leads to the initial formation of the pair.

If all goes well, the male begins to fly off and return to the site repeatedly, to condition the female to expect his return, so that when he leaves for a foraging trip she won't desert the site.

The male brings in nest material — the female building it into the nest structure. This and the previous phase may last for a whole season without leading to laying.

Each time the male returns he bites the female and she faces away.

Return, nape biting, greeting and copulation with biting, are the usual sequence of events, leading to a strong association between these activities.

Skypointing is the way in which a bird about to depart signals its intention to its mate, and this ensures that egg and chick are not left unattended. Incubation is shared by both sexes.

SUMMARY

1. Social order is maintained in a gannetry, despite the close proximity of highly aggressive neighbours, by ritualised display.

2. There are objective grounds for asserting that gannets are more than ordinarily concerned with the acquisition and maintenance of their site.

3. The site is established by the male, usually during his fourth or fifth year, after prior experience in a 'club' and after much aerial reconnaissance. Site establishing males are particularly attracted to areas in which others, also, are establishing themselves.

4. An established male always flies in to his site calling aggressively, and usually displays on it after landing.

5. Fighting over sites is common, and contests are extremely savage and punishing.

6. The site is defended by threat and jabbing, which occurs in both ritualised and unritualised form.

7. The main territorial (site ownership) display is a complex movement (bowing) derived from re-directed aggression (nest biting), which has become highly ritualised.

8. Males attract 'prospecting' females, which are readily recognisable, by performing an inconspicuous display (headshake-and-reach) closely related to the aggressive site-ownership display.

9. The male customarily bites the female (nape-biting) when she approaches closely and she responds by averting her bill (facing-away).

10. The pair-bond is strengthened, in the first stages, by the male's practice of frequently leaving and returning to the female ('conditioning' her).

11. The pair perform a lengthy and conspicuous greeting ceremony on the nest. This is typically preceded by the male nape-biting the female and is partly aggressively motivated.

12. Commonly, after greeting, mates preen each other's head and neck (mutual preening). This is again basically aggressive behaviour rather than functional body-care.

13. Copulation, which usually follows mutual fencing early in the season, is prolonged and gives the female considerable tactile stimulation (nape-biting, and 'tramping'). Nape-biting is thus strongly associated with sexual stimulation and may be itself a 'pleasurable' stimulus.

14. Nest material is gathered communally and over the entire season. Nests are highly functional in safeguarding egg and chick. Males gather almost all the material.

15. Nest digging removes hard lumps which could damage the egg.

16. Incubation (under foot) is sometimes inept in inexperienced females and leads to loss of egg.

17. Nest relief (change-over) is co-ordinated by a conspicuous display (skypointing) which signals the bird's rising flight tendency.

18. Incubation stints shorten before the egg hatches. The newly hatched chick is brooded on top of the webs, but some inexperienced females fail to transfer the hatching egg, in which case the chick is crushed.

19. The tiny chick is fed, probably, without having to beg, but later it actively solicits food, though in a relatively restrained manner to minimise the dangers of falling from cliffs.

20. The chick is fed right up to the day, or even the hour, in which it fledges. There is *no* starvation to induce its departure. It fledges with its fat store intact.

21. Adults do not depart with their fledgling, nor show any interest in its going. They cannot, of course, feed it after it has fledged.

22. Gannets have the usual range of behaviour patterns whose function is to keep the plumage in good order. They 'oil' their plumage, using the secretion from the preen gland. Tactile stimuli (dirt, rain, feather tightening) elicit a wing-flap and rotary headshake, which is particularly common during moult.

23. Temperature regulation (dissipation of heat) is achieved by panting, gular fluttering, wing-loosening and possibly by evaporative cooling (excreting onto feet).

24. Feathered young (but not adults) are highly stimulated by rain, which causes much wing flapping.

25. The chick early develops a wide range of behaviour, amongst which is appeasement behaviour (bill-hiding). However, it only rarely shows ritualised display (aggressive) *contra* some other sulids.

26. The chick typically shows a fixed sequence of behaviour before actually jumping off the cliff. It fledges once-and-for-all.

27. Once on the water, it cannot regain the air, probably for a week or so.

28. Early fledgers are not infrequently attacked on the water by adults.

4: The breeding ecology of the gannet

There is a vitalising thrill in being amongst a multitudinous host of wild creatures; when these are big, elegant and powerful birds in the full vigour of breeding activities the experience is almost akin to exaltation.
E. A. Armstrong: *Bird display and behaviour* (1947)

As previous chapters have shown, the Atlantic gannet inhabits cold, stormy waters, often more than 150 km (100 miles) offshore; waters rich in fish and with marked seasonal differences in weather and availability of food. It is physically well adapted to exploit this feeding niche. In fact, nothing can compete with the gannet in its ability to plunge dive, to penetrate deeply, to handle large prey and to forage far from its breeding place. As always in animals, the characteristics evolved in connection with feeding are basic and impose demands and restrictions on all other activities.[88] In the gannet they have stipulated not only the type of breeding habitat and the colonial habit, but also the nature of the breeding regime, particularly its *timing* and all that goes with this. These points are of constant use in interpreting the details of the gannet's breeding ecology.

BREEDING HABITAT

Thirty-three out of the thirty-four existing gannetries are on islands, mostly mere rocks or stacks. Nearly all are entirely or mainly on cliffs or precipitous slopes, though many spill onto flattish ground and one (Eldey) is like a table top. There are three main advantages to islands, particularly offshore ones: they are safe from large mammalian predators, perhaps man, principally, which must have been important in the evolutionarily recent past; they are windy; and they are surrounded by food, whereas a mainland colony is 'dead' ground except on the seaward side. Wind is especially important to the gannet, a relatively heavy bird. Its weight is partly due to fat, which insulates and provides a fuel store, each of them feeding adaptations. Also, its long, narrow wings, again an adaptation for foraging, make landing and taking off difficult, even dangerous without wind assistance.

Cliffs are important mainly because they are easier to land on and depart from. On the mainland they are of course a safeguard against predators but there are few such mainland colonies. Land masses clearly repel gannets and though there are, around the British coast, several large islands and peninsulas with towering cliffs, they are ignored by gannets. Even on islands, cliffs are preferred and are the first areas to be colonised initially and to be re-populated each year. Seventeen out of the nineteen colonies founded this century started on cliffs. It is impossible to say whether gannets have always used both cliffs and flattish ground, or if not, which was the ancestral habitat. Certainly they now show several behavioural adaptations for cliff nesting (below) but these could have been acquired when the Atlantic gannet pushed northwards and evolved its physical characteristics as feeding devices, these latter encouraging it to take to cliffs.

INDICATIONS THAT GANNETS ARE PRIMARILY ADAPTED TO CLIFF NESTING

Behaviour or characteristic	Significance
Fighting	Intensity maladaptive on flat ground; method leads to displacement of cliff opponent; diving onto opponent effective only on ledges.
Cementing of nest with excreta	Enables utilisation of ledges which would otherwise not accumulate material. However, does not bring mud as cliff-adapted kittiwakes do.
Lacks ability to retrieve egg	Useless on cliff ledge; but some ground nesting species also lack this ability.
Does not discriminate its own from strange young	Young cannot usually wander on cliffs so discrimination superfluous; but this trait could have evolved on flat ground as result of adult aggression to young.
Extreme clinging ability of young	Anti-falling behaviour.
Passive begging of young	Anti-falling behaviour, particularly cogent compared with boobies.
Black plumage of young	The most different-from-adult plumage in entire family, possibly to eliminate features which could elicit attack from the male with displacement of young – fatal if cliff nester.

It seems likely that the ancestral sulid, and even the ancestral gannet, was a slope and/or flat-ground nester, and even today the gannet's adaptations to cliffs do not debar it from flat ground; flattish ground (on precipitous islands) poses no problems which cliff-adapted gannets cannot overcome. The reverse is not true, for cliffs hold dangers requiring special adaptations. Recent work on Ailsa[137] has provided startling evidence of the hazards associated with landing on and departing from cliffs.

The updraughts near cliffs can be spectacular. I have seen Bass gannets hurled from their nests by it, and off Ailsa Craig, Sarah Wanless saw a flying bird blown head over heels.

Even if certain flat offshore islands were windy enough to facilitate flight, cliffs could still be an advantage in protecting a large, densely nesting species like the gannet from mass destruction by early man, who must have affected the numbers and distribution of seabirds when hunting them for food.

Gannetries are almost always on igneous rocks such as basalt rather than on sedimentary sandstones and limestones. This is because, ideally, gannets like long, fairly broad, flat ledges upon which nest material easily accumulates and where several pairs may nest. But they will use narrow ledges down to less than 15 cm (6 in) wide, sloping ledges and faces, and even knobs which can support only one pair. Sometimes they try to use sites which are plainly ridiculous for anything but a kittiwake! In such cases, possibly, the male was once a chick at a nearby nest and is trying to establish himself in his home area. This seems to happen on a certain part of the Bass Rock, a distinctive, needle-like pinnacle which has suitable ledges for about 35 pairs. Every year since I began watching it in 1960, the ledges have attracted about 20 additional males, each of whom strives to build on totally unsuitable, or downright impossible, faces or points of rock. They fail, and the number and distribution always stays much the same. Probably, the unsuccessful birds eventually move elsewhere but there are always local recruits to take their place. Similarly, males occasionally try to squeeze into small gaps between established pairs in flatter areas, and sometimes they succeed.

Because of spray, the extreme bases of cliffs are avoided, though sometimes temporarily used by immature birds. The exact height of the cut-off point varies, probably according to aspect and thus to wind and swell.

Between the tiny ledges on the precipitous north-west face of the Bass Rock or the awesome precipices of St Kilda and Ailsa Craig, and the table top of Eldey or Bird Rock, there lies every intermediate, and gannets use them all. On Skellig, some birds nest densely among littered stones in gulleys; on Grassholm they carpet every type of surface from sheer rock above the splash zone, right up the variably sloping south face in a continuous snowfield; on the Bass they extend over the cliff edge and onto ground varying from flat to 60° slopes and so on. Where they move onto vegetated areas, as recently on Grassholm and the north-west slopes of the Bass they soon strip off the grass and soil. Their activities, and the erosion which they facilitate, quickly take such areas down to bed rock and substantially change the topography of the area (see plates).

Probably the main factor influencing the directions in which the birds extend at an existing gannetry, or the slope or face which they first use in the case of a new one, is the direction of the prevailing wind; they much prefer to take off into it. Thus the west and north-west slopes of the Bass have taken most of the recruits these last 20 or more years, and the direction of the dramatic spread on Grassholm has probably been influenced by wind. However, other factors are involved, also, chief among which is the behavioural 'badge' (tempo and nature of behaviour) of the area. Recruits go to areas which recently have expanded most, even where this expansion started for reasons other than wind or topography.

A final important point about nest sites is that it is useless to seek an explanation for the gannet's habit of nesting in colonies solely in terms of shortage of suitable areas. Certainly, this is the origin of the colonial habit; there would not be enough sites to go round if every gannet wanted a whole cliff, but the *degree* of crowding can never be explained on this principle.

COLONY SIZE

A seabird colony is, in a sense, a supra-organism. It has characteristics of size, density and structure which are typical for the species, and is not just a homogenous mass of birds.

In view of the enormous range of gannetries (Table 5) from a few to more than 100,000 pairs, it is clear that there are no stringent selection forces at work on this aspect. However, established gannetries are typically large (several thousand pairs). Their 34 colonies break down as follows: 1–100 pairs (6); 100–1,000 (10); 1,000–5,000 (5); 5,000–10,000 (9); 10,000–20,000 (3); 20,000–50,000 (0); more than 50,000 (1). Large colonies are brought about because the favoured nesting habitat of gannets is somewhat limited and enforces a degree of coloniality; there is little or no penalty in the form of intra-specific competition attending large colonies since gannets live in rich waters, forage widely and are not competing with other species. The limits to the size of any gannetry, where it is in fact limited, are probably set only by the amount of suitable nesting space. But few gannetries are full. Large and small colonies are equally effective in terms of breeding success, except in the cases of new, or very small, colonies (less than about 50–100 pairs). Membership of a large group probably offers the gannet important social benefits; 'large' in this context means anything from a few hundred pairs, since the individual is stimulated only by those gannets which it can see or hear. For this reason there need be no social difference between a colony of 5,000 and one of 50,000 pairs.

COLONY DENSITY

The density at which gannets nest is quite another matter; it is highly consistent, regardless of whether the nesting group is fifty pairs or whether it is the huge carpet on the main face of Grassholm. The average distance apart, nest centre to centre, is about 80 cm (32 in). The figures for various gannetries are: Bass Rock 76 (58–120) cm; Bonaventure Island 80 (61–99) cm; Ailsa Craig 78 (57–117) cm. Where the ground allows, this consistency leads to remarkably regular spacing which even rough ground does little to disrupt. On ledges, too, the distance between nests remains constant. The tendency to cohere as a group is so strong that it causes birds to tolerate highly inferior sites, so long as these are near to others. This was remarkably evident on Bempton Cliffs where, for years, new breeders established themselves on tiny ledges near to existing nests rather than accept the gaps which colonisation of broader ledges would have opened up. Obviously, pioneers will occur, and occasionally a male will voluntarily build

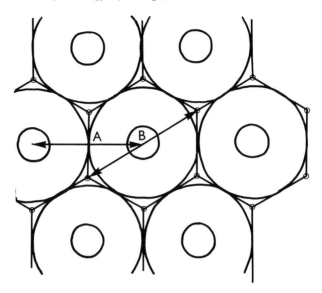

Fig. 26. Spacing of gannet nests (from Poulin 1968)

right out on his own. The size of each 'territory' is just about the minimum which is needed to accommodate two large adults, including room for mutual display, and a large chick (African gannets nest more densely, but they do not attend their large chick as Atlantic gannets do). Thus they are nesting as densely as they can. Because nests are spaced, as it were, within hexagons,[110] there is dead space between nests, and axis 'A' is shorter than 'B' (Fig. 26). Gannets tend to sit with their beak–tail axis along B, though this pattern can be overridden by other factors, such as strong wind, into which they will all face.

   The advantages which gannets gain by nesting at this density rather than half, or a quarter, or a tenth of it, have been 'explained' in quite different ways. Some have attributed it to shortage of sites, but this is clearly only a contributory factor. Not only are most gannetries less than full but there are many places which could support colonies but do not. Theoretically, gannets could once have been so numerous around Britain that every suitable site was crowded and maximum density enforced, but this would have meant an improbably vast population. A favourite suggestion is that dense nesting is an anti-predator device, but this is unlikely. Islands and cliffs are safe from mammals, and the gannet's size and strength protect it against avian predators except, perhaps, the sea-eagle. Furthermore, sea-eagles would take gannets in flight (probably rarely, at that) and could never have been the cause of the high nesting density. Except in rare circumstances gulls and skuas cannot cope unaided with the task of stealing eggs or chicks. As for man, dense nesting helps rather than hinders his depredatory habits. So far as I can see, there remains only one valid answer important enough to justify the considerable and competitive effort which gannets make to obtain a site at the standard spacing. This is, that dense nesting provides behavioural (social) stimulation which enhances reproductive success. The nature and role of social stimulation is more appropriately discussed when considering the timing of breeding, which it affects; here, it is enough to say that timing is extremely important in the gannet and social stimulation is one of the mechanisms by which optimal timing is achieved. So it is that, whether the gannetry is large or small, on a slope, cliff or flat ground, the nesting density remains about the same.

COLONY STRUCTURE

Basically, a gannetry consists of two main categories of birds – experienced breeders and newly established pairs. Equally basically, it is in one of two main states – stable in numbers, or changing (increasing or decreasing). If it is stable, the recruits are continually replacing the birds that die. Since adult mortality is low, and usually only one member of a pair dies at a time, the stable colony will tend to keep the same boundaries; bereaved males stay on their sites and re-mate; bereaved females are joined on their site by a new male, or go to a nearby bereaved male; and empty nests are quickly taken over by young males. Since, further, there is almost certainly no difference in the mortality rate of old birds near the outer edges of the colony, compared with birds nearer the centre, it follows that there will be no difference in the number of vacancies to be filled, and so none in the proportion of young birds filling these gaps. The frequent assertion that young birds occur in the fringes and old birds in the centre, is fallacious *except* when applied to an *expanding* group. This vital distinction is, however, usually ignored. A stable group consists of the same mixture of old, mixed young and old, and young pairs throughout. An expanding group, on the other hand, has a fringe of young birds, one to five ranks deep. Rarely if ever does the fringe of new breeders consist of more than five ranks, though outside these there may be further ranks of site-establishing and 'casual' birds. As mentioned earlier, certain parts of a gannetry may attract a disproportionately high number of young birds, so that it develops in bulges. Cliff faces, once they are fully colonised, of course, have no 'fringe'. This means that in a developing gannetry there may be a consistent difference between cliffs and flatter ground in the proportions of old and young breeders.

Experienced breeders are more successful than new ones (Table 12), which means that the fringes of an expanding group will breed less successfully than the central areas. This has led to the erroneous assertion that fringe sites are inferior, that they are all a young male (or pair) can get, and that they are changed for a central site when their owners can do so. None of this is true. Apart from man's influence in

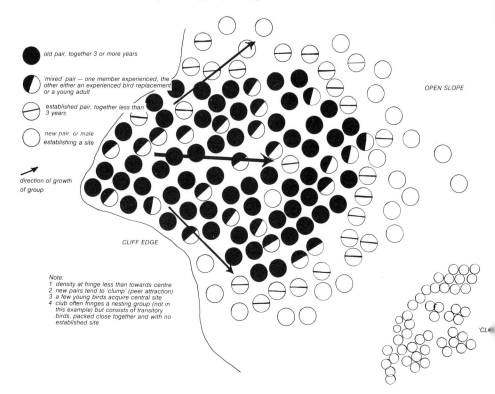

Fig. 27. *Diagrammatic representation of structure of a rapidly growing group of breeding gannets. The figure is based on an actual group on Bass Rock in 1977 (a handful of pairs, only, in 1960) and conveys the basic structure − it is not accurate in details*

disturbing fringe birds, thus opening them up to egg-stealing by herring and black-backed gulls, fringe sites are not generally inferior; nor are they less successful, once the age effect has been allowed for. Nor are they systematically changed for 'better' sites, though a negligible amount of shifting occurs. All this is perfectly consistent, once we know enough about related topics. For example, we would predict that the astonishingly fierce competition for a site, and the subsequently strong attachment to it, would predispose the male not to chop and change. Think, too, of the associated fact that either he would have to have a mechanism for taking his female with him, or else go through the whole business of pair-formation all over again. Then, why should fringe sites produce a lower breeding success when we know that failure is largely due to inept parental care? An inept bird is as bad in the centre as in the fringe.

A final point about the fringe of a group is that it creeps outwards, rank by rank, but at first with slightly wider spacing between new nests (see plates) than is found in an established area of a group. New males establish themselves near to neighbours rather than staying apart, but their level of fear at this stage is often high enough to inhibit maximum density. Later, boundaries are adjusted, often as a result of newcomers squeezing into the larger gaps, and full density is established.

REPRODUCTION

The nest

The gannet constructs a substantial nest of seaweed, grass, other vegetation and general flotsam. The structure begins as a ring of material, sometimes the loosened earth of the site itself, which becomes a mound with a nest-cup in the middle; eventually it may build up into a large pedestal or drum. Over the years it becomes an extremely durable base to which a new cup is added annually. Where nests are side by side on a steep face, this accretion may form a 'ledge'. If it disintegrates, it may be that the original nests were stuck to exceptionally difficult sites. The average nest is about 30 cm (12 in) across the top (outer measurements) and some 20 cm (8 in) high, but pedestals with a sloping side measurement of more than 100 cm (39 in) do occur, and many are at least half that height.

The seaweeds *Fucus vesiculosus, F. serratus, Pelvetia canaliculata* and *Laminaria spp.* are commonly used and, notwithstanding Gurney's incredulity, their gelatin helps them to stick to rock and form a base for the accretion of material which otherwise would not have stayed in place. Gannets may carry seaweeds some distance, perhaps 3–5 km (2–3 miles) but Macgillivray's claim that they fly up to 100 km (60 miles) for nest material is difficult to credit. Doubtless, birds occasionally pick up seaweed far from land, but that is not the same thing as going for it. Grasses are used in quantity and are pulled from the nesting island, or one nearby, but not from the mainland. Bempton gannets will not even venture onto the cliff-top ground. The St Kildans believed that gannets plucked grass on windy days because, then, they were resting from fishing. The real reason is that gannets dare not land in such spots without a strong wind, from a suitable direction, to aid take-off.

Moulted feathers are added to the nest, along with a motley assortment of rubbish, including straw; garden prunings; wood and plastic items (a plastic frog brought to a Bass Rock nest decorated our tent pole in the Galapagos for a year), and synthetic nets and lines. Among the most unusual items recorded from gannet nests are false teeth, a catheter, a gold watch, a fountain pen and golf balls. Some of these items suggest that the gannet beachcombs. Synthetic fibre lines and nets have fairly recently become a menace; at gannetries they are now an unpleasantly common cause of death, both of adults and young, and a particularly miserable death at that. Birds become tethered to the nest without a hope of breaking the cord or of pulling it loose. Up to seven chicks have been found roped together on the Bass Rock, whilst adults (both there and at Bempton) have died lingering deaths from a length of net on the cliff face. In 1977 two of the breeding adults in the new colony on Fair Isle died as a result of becoming entangled in their nests. Sometimes the birds can still fly, but their beaks are jammed with fluffed-out cord in the serrations, or at the angle of the gape, or their mandibles lashed together at the tip. Others have pieces of netting over their heads or around their legs. At many gannetries between a half and two thirds of nests contain this material (actual figures: Bass Rock 50%, Bempton 75%, Grassholm 49%, Ailsa Craig 1%). The reasons for Ailsa Craig's low count[137] are not known. The only practical measure rests in the hands of fishermen – this is to *avoid throwing any waste material of this kind into the sea.*

The cup is not systematically lined with finer materials but large, lumpy items are selectively removed, and feathers placed there. Adults do not defaecate into the nest and chicks tend to void clear at first, so that it remains fairly clean until the chick is about three weeks old. After that it becomes progressively fouler and more flattened. The nest is important to the gannet; obviously it is almost essential for incubation, partly because it keeps in heat and prevents contact between the egg and a cold wet substrate, and also because an egg incubated underfoot on a bare ledge would probably crack. Later, the chick needs the nest to keep itself clear of the water and mud that accumulate in the flatter parts of a gannetry.

The egg

The egg is long, sub-eliptical to oval; pale blue or greenish in appearance, and translucent when newly laid but becoming white and opaque, with a thick chalky outer layer – 'the egg casts a thick scurf'.[73] This outer layer soon chips and roughens, and becomes heavily stained; it may be partly protective and may help the adult's webs to get a grip. The shell is about 0·6 mm (0·025 in) thick, which is well above average for this size of egg, but apparently there is nothing unusual about the cross-sectional structure of the shell. If it requires extra strength to withstand incubation underfoot, this must come from its thickness. The average shell weight of 100 eggs was 11·59 g (10·8–12·9 g) which is 11·1% of the fresh weight – an unusually high proportion. The egg can usually be aged fairly reliably up to at least a week, by the amount of dirt, but it is dangerous to try to give a detailed guide, for much depends on the weather. Nevertheless, a clean, blood-stained egg is almost certainly fresh.

The average measurements of 100 British eggs were 78·06 × 49·1 mm (max. 78·6×53·7 mm and 87·5×49·0 mm; min. 62·5×43·1 mm); of 20 from Canada 82·27×49·66 mm and of another 44 also from Canada, 77·6×47·0 mm. This is not significantly larger than those of the African and Australasian gannets, even though these are smaller birds. The average weight of 393 fresh Bass Rock eggs was 104·6 g (81–130 g) and of 57 Bonaventure Island eggs (corrected for weight loss due to part

Fig. 28. Adult and juvenile gannets caught in netting

incubation) 103·2 g. About 9–13% of the egg's weight is lost during incubation. The weight as a percentage of the female's weight is 3·4 (Bass) and 3·2 (Bonaventure) which, for a bird, is very little. The corresponding figure for the African and Australasian gannets is 3·9% which is significantly more. The foraging trips of the two latter gannets are also significantly longer, which suggests that the smaller egg of the Atlantic gannet is viable because the new chick has (on average) less time to wait for its food and can manage on smaller reserves. If this is so, it fits with all the other evidence about the respective food situations (see Chapter 6).

Earlier eggs are heavier than later ones,[87] probably because they come from older females, which, in birds in general, lay heavier eggs and/or larger clutches. Nobody has yet studied breeding success in relation to egg weight, but the gannet's generally favourable food supply suggests that there would be little if any correlation.

Clutch size
Occasionally (in less than one case in a thousand) two eggs are found

in the same nest, but where this happened in my observation colony there had been two females involved, so it seems likely that the same applied on cliffs, where I twice saw 'twins'. On Grassholm, many nests were observed to hold two eggs or two chicks[67] but there was no obvious explanation. Possibly one of the influxes of new breeders which Grassholm experienced had led to a number of triangular associations (two females and one male) that year. These would have been concentrated in the fringe, which is likely to have been the area investigated. On Bonaventure, Poulin examined 1,112 nests without finding a two egg clutch. Bewick[7] says 'she lays three eggs although ornithologists assert that she will lay only one egg if . . . undisturbed' but he was probably referring to *replacement* laying. Since Atlantic gannets are able to rear artificially doubled broods with apparent ease it is interesting that the one egg clutch is so nearly invariable. If two egg clutches were common (and heritable) one might expect at least part of the population to evolve them. If they rarely or never occur, the question does not arise. Similarly, in the Australasian gannet they are extremely rare or absent. They have been claimed[62] to occur more commonly in the African gannet but the evidence is not unequivocal.

Replacement laying

Gannets readily replace their egg if it is lost before about 25 days from laying. On Bass Rock the interval between loss and replacement was 6–32 days, most eggs being replaced within 18 days. Four females re-laid a second time, making three eggs in all. Poulin recorded 15 cases of third eggs and two of fourths, never before recorded. Experienced females are more likely to re-lay than are birds breeding for the first time (26/34 compared with 2/16), at least partly because the former lay earlier anyway, and the tendency to lay again wanes as the season advances, when there would no longer be time to get the chick away with a reasonable chance of surviving. On Bonaventure[109] 27·3% of lost eggs were replaced (1966, 21%; 1967, 32·3%). In 52·8% of such cases the first egg had survived less than four days; in 75·5% less than seven days, in 87·4% less than 14 days and in 95% less than 28 days, which agrees closely with my Bass Rock figure. The mean interval between loss and replacement was a fortnight (1–39 days) which is a little less than on Bass Rock, presumably for the same reason that laying is more compressed in the first place; 17% re-laid in five days or less; 61·6% in 15 days or less; 74·8% in 20 days or less; 89·9% in 25 days or less and 96·2% in 30 days or less. Poulin's finding that 29·2% of 'centre' birds re-laid, against 21·2 of 'fringe' birds, probably reflects the fact that there are more young females in the fringe.

Replacement eggs are less successful than first eggs. On the Bass Rock, 10 out of 27 replacement eggs, or 37%, against 152/192 first eggs, or 79%, gave rise to fledged young in 1962, all in the same group. This was mainly because a higher proportion of replacement eggs (37% against 10%) failed to hatch. Poulin, too, found that on Bonaventure Island only 16·9% of replacement eggs hatched. The reason for this apparently higher infertility is unknown but well worth investigating.

INCUBATION

On Bass Rock, the egg takes, on average, 43·6 days to hatch (42 days (9); 43 (25); 44 (38); 45 (9); 46 (1), the figures in brackets being the number of cases in each category). Poulin's figure of 43·9 days is an interestingly exact parallel in view of the much lower ambient temperature on Bonaventure Island. Incubation underfoot would seem to be extremely efficient (see Chapter 3 for behaviour details).

Both sexes incubate. On Bass Rock, during the first half of incubation, the male's average stint was 37·2 hours (7–84) against the female's 30·8 hours (4–40). During the second half these shortened to 33·2 hours (6–62) in the male and 29·1 hours (10–46) in the female. This indicates considerable flexibility in the gannet's foraging behaviour, and a very large foraging range. Stints at other gannetries may be significantly different (see Table 6). As mentioned elsewhere, stints shorten markedly a few days before hatching (Table 6) and an unusually high proportion of nests with chicks a day old, or less, have the pair in attendance. This ensures that they are fed soon after they hatch.

THE CHICK

The new born chick (Fig. 29) is about 11 cm (4½ in) long and weighs 70–80 g (2½–3 oz). Its skin is loose, especially in the gular area, blackish and looks almost naked, though in fact it is very sparsely clothed with tracts of the first generation of white down (neossoptiles). The eyes (dark bluish) are partly or entirely closed until the second or third day. The bill is dull or dark, paler towards the tip and with a whitish egg tooth. The legs and feet are deep grey.

The first generation of down is replaced by fluffy, snow-white down (Fig. 1) varying in length and thickness. It is very long and dense on the sides and underparts but often short and sparse on the forehead, around the eyes and on the throat and chin. This second generation is shed as the juvenile feathers grow, but is not replaced by them, nor is it replaced directly, in continuous growth, by the under-down of the feathered stage,[141] though the under-down succeeds it.

It is fairly easy to age chicks by eye and, even on a short visit, this can be useful in determining the timing of laying in a colony. A chronology is given below, and the photographs also help.

Week 1. By the end of the week, the chick is still fairly black though the white down has become noticeable. Movements still wobbly.

Week 2. Down thickens over the body; by the end of the week, chicks look considerably larger than their parents' webs. The head and neck are often bare, and the radio-ulna and 'hand' still blackish. Down scrubby; movements vigorous and well co-ordinated.

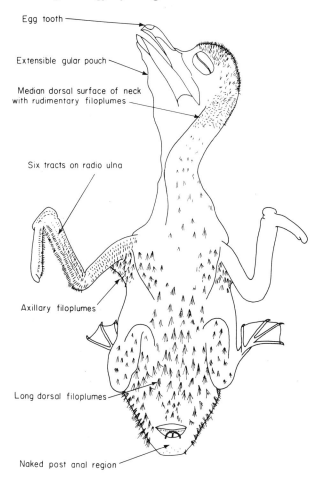

Egg tooth

Extensible gular pouch

Median dorsal surface of neck
with rudimentary filoplumes

Six tracts on radio ulna

Axillary filoplumes

Long dorsal filoplumes

Naked post anal region

Fig. 29. Distribution of down on newly hatched gannet

Week 3. Chick fully covered in white down, but lacks the luxuriantly fluffy look of the month old. Head down usually well grown and wings covered. Becoming too big to be fully covered by parent.

Week 4. By the end of week, the down is notably long and fluffy and the chick is now large and fat (about 2 kg (4½ lb)); takes up most of the nest and looks perhaps two-thirds of adult size.

Week 5. This is perhaps the difficult week, grading both ways. By the end, in early birds, some wing and tail feathers have erupted and are just beginning to show black, through the down. The chick is approaching adult size.

Week 6. Down long and the black of scapulars, wing and tail feathers becoming conspicuous. Looks bigger than parent.

Week 7. Black on wings, back and tail steadily expanding and chick now covered in long white down beneath and on head and neck. Mixed black (feathers) and white (down) on back.

Week 8. Advanced chicks are losing down from feathered forehead, back and tail. Now mainly black above.

Week 9. Down is beginning to thin on parts of ventral surface though still thick on flanks, belly and parts of neck. Perhaps the 'raggedest' time.

Week 10. Rapid clearance of down, but some remains on nape, flanks and back.

Week 11. Early in week, advanced chicks retain only wisps on nape and flank. By the end of week they may be clear. Retarded birds may not reach this stage until 93 days old.

Growth

Thirteen weeks may seem a long time to be growing, but it is remarkably little in comparison with the rest of the family. Atlantic gannets enjoy an abundant and dependable supply of rich food, which enables them to produce a large chick with substantial reserves of fat in just over half the time it takes some tropical red-footed boobies to produce a small chick with no fat. Moreover, there is virtually no starvation and parents can afford to guard their chick continuously throughout its growth, and even to spend a fair part of daylight hours resting together on the site. The Galapagos red-footed booby referred to above loses many, sometimes most, of its young through starvation and does not guard the chick at all once the latter can control its own body temperature. The gannet is even able to cope with an extra chick without much disrupting its normal pattern of attending the nest. All this is worth emphasising because it focuses attention on food, to which so much of a seabird's breeding biology is geared.

Bass Rock gannet chicks were fed on average 2·7 times each day (daylight hours), counting all the times a chick entered its parents throat during a bout of feeding as merely one feed (Table 7). Ailsa Craig and Bempton chicks were fed about once and three times a day, respectively. The apparent difference in feeding rate between the Bass Rock and Ailsa Craig, though probably genuine, correlated with Ailsa birds' longer foraging trips, may be less than these figures suggest. One 48-hour watch for each colony is too brief a period for accuracy, and the proportions of the different age-classes of young in each of the two colonies may have been different. Since foraging trips are related to age of young, this would influence the results. Indeed, since Ailsa birds grew as fast as Bass young, it seems unlikely that they were fed much less frequently, unless each feed was bigger. Fourteen per cent of feeds were given between 04·00 and 08·00 hours when the parents returned after a night at sea, but the main influx of adults was between 14.00 and 20.00 hours (40% of feeds were delivered in this period), many of them being birds that had been relieved from guard duty in the early morning. It is possible that chicks are fed during the hours of darkness, even though adults do not come in to the colony; birds already there can regurgitate after several hours.

The most feeds given in a day to a single chick (only three weeks old) totalled five, with 21 possible transfers of food; and to twins, nine feeds with at least 37, and possibly 45, transfers of food. The weight delivered per feed was not studied directly, but by calculation from weight increases, and taking account of the probable loss of body weight between feeds, it varied (for a large chick) between about 150–500 g (5–18 oz) and probably averaged around 250 g (9 oz). Much depends on the species of fish. Three good mackerel, brought back whilst still fairly fresh, can easily weigh 500 g (18 oz) whilst a packet of small sand-eels containing more than 100 items, partly digested, will probably weigh less than 200 g (7 oz).

The commonest food fish are mackerel, herrings and sand-eels. Booth[8] describes the many parcels of fish (herring and mackerel) that are spilled during feeding and lie in stinking heaps among the nests. Similar observations have been made on Grassholm. I have never found this on the Bass Rock, despite numerous careful forays into the heart of the colony, nor have I seen it on Ailsa Craig or Grassholm, and I can only guess that these other reports were the result of massive disturbances, preceding the visits of the observers concerned. Gannets readily vomit fish when alarmed.

The frequency with which the chicks are fed obviously depends on how long it takes their parents to forage, which in turn will probably depend on how far they go. This can be gauged only indirectly, based on the length of the periods spent away from the nest. I do not think there is much chance that an off-duty bird spends a long time elsewhere in the colony. Over the entire period that the chick is in the nest, the sexes take about equal shares of guard spells and foraging, though the males' guard spells are longer than the females' during the second half of the chicks' growth. During a continuous 48 hour check on the Bass Rock, 65% of absences were between seven and thirteen hours long. Ailsa Craig gannets took significantly longer foraging trips than Bass birds, whilst Bempton gannets took much shorter ones (Table 6). It is likely that breeding gannets, whatever their colony, have specific fishing grounds suited to the season, and to the weather at any one time. The Farnes, for example, are certainly favoured by Bass Rock gannets. The return journey would take about five hours, which leaves plenty of fishing time during a foraging period of ten or twelve hours. The situation could be exceedingly complex for the west coast gannetries, whose foraging areas probably overlap.

Bass Rock parents spent about 15% of daylight hours together at the nest, four pairs spending about half the day (9–12 hours) together. This

applied even to pairs with well-grown young; indeed, parents with chicks less than a fortnight old spent *less* time together than those with chicks aged a month or more, possibly because small chicks demand more frequent feeding, though little at a time, and parents are unable to hold up assimilation of food in their own stomachs. This deployment of time suggests that gannets are not forced to seek food to the limits of their capacity, a conclusion supported by their ability to feed twins. There were two remarkable cases, at Bempton,[137] in which the females disappeared when the chicks were part grown (nine and five weeks) and, in both instances, the chick fledged successfully. In one case it undoubtedly was underfed; the male's absences were usually less than 20 minutes and intruders were common. In the other, the chick fledged when 12–13 weeks old and it, too, was rarely left for more than an hour, and was attacked frequently and severely by neighbouring adults. The male fished mainly between 10.00–11.00 and 16.00–17.00 hours. Apart from chicks which lose a parent or are in some way abnormal (for instance with deformed beak) there are, remarkably, no known instances of gannet chicks starving.

The rate at which a bird grows can be assessed by measuring several parts (bill, wing, tail, tarsus, toes, total length or total weight) and all these increase at different rates. Each part grows at the rate, or in the manner, which is most adaptive. Selection pressures in these matters are probably substantial, for it is likely to make a great deal of difference to chances of survival if, for instance, wings are fully grown at fledging age, or only partly grown.

Weight, in particular, is a sensitive indicator of food supply. Compared with the rest of the family, and even by comparison with the other two gannets, Atlantic gannet chicks grow very rapidly[93] (Fig. 30). Not only do they reach a weight (over 4 kg (9 lb)) which is large in absolute terms, but they reach it quickly. Of course, the adults have only a single chick to feed, and they produce less biomass (as a proportion of their own weight) than, for example, a shag does. But a shag fishes much nearer to its nest and so can return with food more frequently. The young gannet increases its weight, between hatching and fledging by a maximum of some 75 times. The rate of growth is fastest between two and eight weeks, after which the curve flattens. This is partly because, by then, the growth of feathers, and the energy required for various activities, takes up most of the energy provided by the food. By the time it is six weeks old it has reached adult weight and has already deposited a great deal of fat. After a further six weeks, it weighs up to 30% more than an adult and may have packed well over 1,000 g (35 oz) of fat around its viscera and beneath its skin. Once it has fledged this is all that stands between the young gannet and starvation.

One of the most striking things about a gannetry in late July is the vast crop of thriving, fat young. Not a sign of starvation is to be seen, whereas some tropical booby colonies are littered with starved young. It would not be a significant exaggeration to say that young gannets never starve in the nest. However, they do show considerable fluctuations in weight. Individuals may jump from a weight far below average, to one far above it, in the space of a week. Much depends on how recently they had been fed when weighed, but some fluctuations no doubt depend on temporary reductions in food.

All this strongly supports the suggestion that young gannets grow at a time when food is abundant. However, there is little or no difference in growth between early and relatively late chicks, so the period of abundance is not highly restricted. Very late juveniles do in fact weigh and measure less than those fledging in the main period, but we do not know whether this is because food is less available to the adults or merely because they are by then less eager to spend time at the nest. Probably both factors operate; mackerel move back out to deeper water in October.

Twinning in gannets

Because it seemed likely that birds rear as many young as they can feed, adequately,[66] and that this applied, perhaps particularly, to single-chick species, I did not expect that those gannets to which I gave an extra egg or chick[83] would easily cope. Surprisingly, they did (Fig. 30). The twins lived amicably together only if they were the same age and were together from hatching; otherwise, the larger dominated the smaller. By the time they reached maximum weight they weighed almost as much as singletons of the same age, and although I did not continue to weight the twins up to fledging (because this would have endangered them), it seems unlikely that they would reach the age of

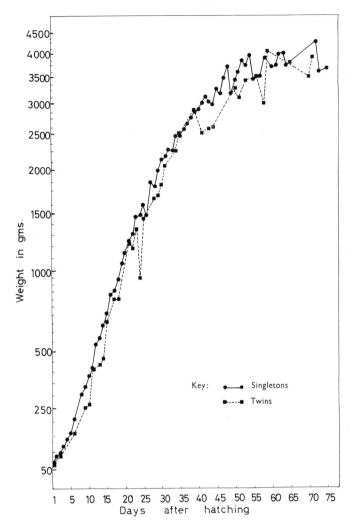

Fig. 30. Comparison of growth (by weight) of young singleton gannet
with artificially produced twins

70–74 days (covering the period of maximum weight increase) without
dropping significantly behind, only to do so in the last three weeks. In
fact, at several ages (up to 60 days) and averaging the weights of at least
seven pairs of twins for the age in question, they actually *exceeded* the
average weight of singles. It seems unlikely that twins fledged at more
than about 5% underweight, and since they took four days longer to
fledge, perhaps not so much. Certainly it is hard to believe that the little
by which they may have been underweight could have meant that they
would virtually all die. Given the huge variability in the fledging

weight of normal chicks, and the large part played by chance weather conditions in affecting survival, I cannot believe that the adults sending off twins could fail to gain a large reproductive advantage over those with only one. If they did gain an advantage, it would be interesting to know why some gannets do not rear twins (see below). I repeated the experiments another year with similar results, but workers who have done the same with African[61] and Australasian[113] gannets found that twins were much less successful than in the Atlantic gannet. However, other factors (see Chapter 6) indicate that these two species do not enjoy quite such abundant food as the Atlantic gannet.

Growth of wings, tail, feet, bill

Returning to the subject of growth: it has been found for the Canadian gannet[109] that the different parts grow at different rates (Fig. 31). The bill (culmen length) grows at a relatively constant rate. This

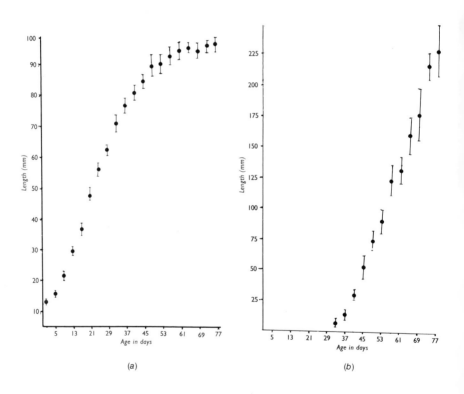

(a)   (b)

Fig. 31. (a) *Growth of young gannet's bill (culmen), Bonaventure*
Island, Canada (from Poulin 1968)
(b) *Growth of young gannet's tenth primary, Bonaventure*
Island (from Poulin 1968)

(top) North Atlantic gannet: late first-year plumage. (centre) Early second-year plumage: white epaulettes on wings; dark back beginning to break up. (bottom) Advanced second-year plumage.

2 (top) Early third-year plumage: occasion-ally, very advanced second-year birds may reach this stage. (bottom left) Late third-year plumage. (bottom right) Early-to-mid-fourth-year plumage: by this stage, highly variable.

3 (top left) Advanced first-year plumage: the brown on head and neck (usually the first to go) has already broken up; the bill is becoming blue and the iris lighter-coloured; the ventral surface is already white. (top right) Fairly typical late-ish second-year plumage. (bottom) Late third-year plumage.

4   (top) The precipes of Little Skellig, Co. Kerry, Ireland. Photo: D Cabot. (centre) Grassholm, June 1976. (bottom) Sula Sgeir, 1969. The thinly scattered birds, extreme right, are gulls. Photo: Operation Seafarer.

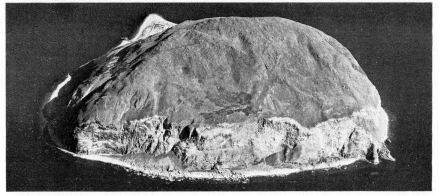

5 (top) Ailsa Craig, showing mainly the west side. Photo: Aerofilms Ltd. (centre) A general view of the Bass Rock showing the west side and (below the deep shadow left of centre) the author's main study group which has increased from less than 100 pairs (1960) to almost 1000 (1977). The spread up the western slope (centre and to right) has been held back by visitors, but is continuing. Photo: Aerofilms Ltd. (bottom left) The limestone cliffs at Bempton, Yorkshire, the only mainland gannetry. The narrow ledges are not ideal for gannets. (bottom right) Part of the main Bempton group, June 1973, from the south. Photo: R Vaughan.

6   (top) Sule Stack (Stack Skerry). The separate rock on the left is the site of a large club. Photo: Operation Seafarer. (centre and bottom) Bird Rocks (Magdalen Islands), Gulf of St Lawrence, Canada. Great Bird; North Bird. Photo: D N Nettleship.

7   South-west face of the Bass Rock. Notice that tiny projections and ledges, as well as larger ones, are used. Sloping ledges are often difficult to build on, but nevertheless are used. The gannet's excreta helps to cement the nest to the ledge.

8 (top) Bass Rock gannets nesting on the slope above the north-west face. The islands of the Forth in the background. Note the traffic of birds – prospective males or females looking for potential sites and mates, respectively. (bottom) Gannets nesting on the columns of Ailsa Craig, with broad ledges beneath. Dislodged gannets often strike the column or ledge below instead of falling sheer and this may be one reason why Ailsa gannets seem to have an unusually high mortality rate. Photo: S Wanless.

9   (top) Grassholm, August 1975, looking south. This an example of nesting on flatter ground. The birds on the separate rock are members of the 'club', not breeding birds. (bottom) A rapidly expanding group at the top of the north-west cliffs, Bass Rock. Sites on the fringe are more widely spaced than in the centre. Compaction then occurs. If the gannets are undisturbed, fringe sites are not inferior to central ones.

10　(top) Part of the fringe of a rapidly expanding group, Bass Rock. Notice the wider spacing of sites and the high proportion of birds with immature plumage, also the large number of pairs in attendance. (bottom) Club birds, Bass Rock, showing the high proportion of two and three-year-olds.

1 (top left) On Sula Sgeir. After plucking, the birds are singed over a peat fire to remove the last of the down and feathers. The wings and tail will then be chopped off before the bird is split and salted. Photo: Jas MacGeoch. (top right) Sula Sgeir gannet hunt; 2,000 salted gannets ('gugas') piled high before being flung from man to man (chain fashion) down the gully to the relief boat. Photo: Jas MacGeoch. (bottom left) Gannets being lightly salted to keep them until they can be more thoroughly treated for winter storing. (bottom right) Placing the 'gugas' in barrels for winter supplies. Photo: Jas MacGeoch.

12 *(top) 5-day-old chick. (bottom left) Gannet with 10-day-old chick. (bottom right) Gannet wi chick between 3 and 4 weeks old.*

3 (top) Gannet with chick about 4 weeks old. Note the energy-conserving sleeping posture and the temperature regulating exposed web. (bottom) Gannet with chick about 5 weeks old. The forehead down often rubs off.

14 (top) Gannet with chick 6-7 weeks old. Wing and tail feathers have erupted and black feathe
are increasingly evident, especially on the back. The chick is approaching maximum weight. (bottor
Chicks aged 8-9 weeks, gaining the black plumage of the juvenile.

15   (top) Adult gannet with 10-week-old chick. The wispy down will have disappeared in about a week. Photo: John Barlee. (bottom) Fully feathered juvenile about to fledge. Photo: John Barlee.

16 (top) Gannets seeking sites (males) or sites-with-males (females) overfly the colony repeatedly or prospect from vantage points within or at the edge of the group. (bottom) Territorial fighting is fierce and fighting birds often violate the space of others. They are then vigorously attacked and, unable to defend themselves, may suffer appreciable damage.

17 (top) Ritualised threat (menacing) between neighbours prevents encroachment and maintains regular spacing in the colony. (bottom) High intensity bowing and headshaking; bill is raised almost vertically and wings held far out.

18 (left) Bowing, the territorial (site ownership) display; here, the downward sweep of the head is beginning, the bird calling loudly. (right) The termination of the bow; the pelican posture. (centre) Overflying gannets cause a site-owning bird to assume the bill-tucked position (ambivalent fear/aggression). (bottom) The male gannet's inconspicuous 'advertising' display by which he indicates his sexual receptivity to a female. Bird 1 is 'reaching' towards the female (out of the picture) and bird 2 is headshaking. The display may be called 'headshake and reach'. The bill may be opened (bird 1) but vocalisation is inhibited (see text).

19 (top) A returning male bites his mate on the nape; she faces-away (appeasement gesture). This ritual occurs each time they re-unite, throughout life. (bottom) Greeting behaviour (mutual fencing): bills are open and the birds calling loudly.

20   (top) Ordinary (auto-) preening and mutual (allo-) preening; the latter often follows the greeting ceremony. (bottom) During copulation the male bites the female vigorously on the nape; she headshakes violently (a continuation of soliciting behaviour).

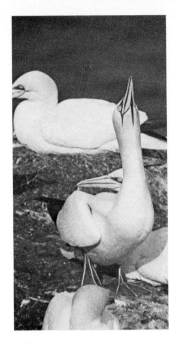

21 (top left) Typical intensity skypointing (ritualised behaviour which co-ordinates change-over at nest) with on-the-spot foot-raising and wings loosened but hardly raised at tips. (top right) Gannet taking flight in skypointing posture. At this juncture, it utters a soft groan. (bottom) Slight alarm elicits this stereotyped behaviour, probably via tactile stimulation (tightening of skin stimulating feather follicles), which shakes, cleanses and re-adjusts plumage; main components are wing-flapping at increased speed and rapid swings of the head from side to side.

22 (top) Foot-settling movements by incubating gannet to adjust the position of its web on the egg. (bottom) The web is placed over the egg; the ruffled plumage of belly and lower breast presumably aids transfer of heat to the webs and egg.

23 (top) Adult with newly hatched chick on top of webs; failure to transfer hatching egg to the top of the webs is a common cause of chick mortality for first-time breeders. (bottom left) Gannet coming in to land on nest; incoming gannets call loudly and their voices are recognised by mates and neighbours. Photo: J Barlee. (bottom right) The gannet's method of feeding its chick: the chick, about a month old, is evidently peering into its parent's throat, aiming for the bolus of food.

24   (top left) Diving gannet. Photo: A & E Bomford. (top right) Just after entry; the old Celtic name for the gannet stems from 'seth', an arrow. Photo: A & E Bomford. (bottom) Gannets usually do not surface with a fish, unless they need to disable it before they can swallow it. Photo: A & E Bomford.

25 (top) Shallow slant-dive by which a gannet usually alights on water, rather than feet first. Photo: R Reinsch. (bottom) Competing for trawler spoils. Photo: R Reinsch.

26 Cine record of a male gannet returning to the nest, nape-biting the female with such force that he knocks her off the nest pedestal, subsequently performing the greeting ceremony with her when she has struggled back onto the nest.

27 This is a photograph of the fringe of the author's study colony on the Bass Rock in early spring, 1962. Bird Number 1, a site-owning male, is showing interest in bird 4, a female. She is anxious (head withdrawn). Pair 3 and bird 2 are reacting to her obvious intention to pass between them to reach bird 1. Pair 3 are making threat movements towards her and bird 2 is in a deep bill-tucking posture indicating ambivalent aggression/fear. Birds 5 and 6 are performing the aggressive territorial (site-ownership) display.

28   The author's study group on the Bass Rock in early spring. A fight (5) is in progress, attracting the hostile attention of birds 2, 3 and 4. Bird number 1, a male, is skypointing, the display which precedes movement, and is about to join the female immediately in front of him. Pair 6 are interested in a piece of nest material at the base of their pedestal. Bird 7 is bowing because bird 19 is about to move towards him on its way to the empty site. Birds 8, 11, 12 and 13 are all males performing high intensity territorial display (bowing). Commonly, bowing occurs simultaneously or successively in close neighbours, the asser-tion of one stimulating others to proclaim site ownership. Number 16, also, is bowing. Bird 14 is about to move, but it is difficult to say where. The bird is just about to fly in early. Bird 15 wing-flapping and rotary headshaking (a plumage settling movement). Birds 17, 18 and 19 are long-necked and alert.

29   This is the same group as plate 28 a few seconds later. The fight is rampaging on (number 1). Bird 2 is about to wing-flap and rotary-headshake, usually a response to some form of tactile stimulation and here, probably, a slight alarm response to the fighting birds. Bird 3 is threatening an individual passing too close on its way to the fringe. Bird 4 is bowing (site-ownership display): the stance indicates that it is a male, whereas bird 5, also bowing, is a female. Females bow at lower intensity and appear more cramped. Bird 7 has just bowed and is in the bill-tucking posture which terminates a bow. Bird 6 is stealing nest material from the site which the fighting birds are disputing and bird 8 (bird 19 of the previous plate) is about to do the same, which is why bird 7 (in previous plate) was bowing! Pair 9 are engaged in low-intensity greeting (mutual fencing), the male (1 of previous plate) having joined her on the site.

30 (top) Australasian gannets, mutual preening, exactly as in the Atlantic gannet. Note white outer tail feathers. Photo: John Warham. (bottom) Juvenile plumage of Cat Island Australasian gannets. Note pale underparts compared with Atlantic gannet, and also marked pectoral band (a feature common to many juvenile sulids). Note size of spilled fish (right foreground). Photo: John Warham.

31 (top left) Australasian gannet, male, 1-year old. Photo: C J Robertson. (top right) Australasian gannet, female, 1-year old. As in Atlantic gannet, female is later than male in development. Photo: C J Robertson. (bottom) Australasian gannet, 2-years old. Photo: C J Robertson.

32   (top) Nesting group of African gannets, showing flat habitat. Note long gular strip, diagnostic of this species, and all-black tail. Photo: M F Jarvis. (bottom) Juvenile African gannet, stretching. Plumage is similar to Atlantic gannet, in contrast with Australasian. Photo: M F Jarvis.

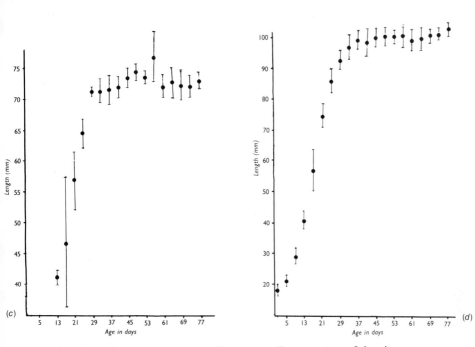

(c) Growth of young gannet's tarsus, Bonaventure Island
(from Poulin 1968)

(d) Growth of young gannet's middle toe, Bonaventure Island
(from Poulin 1968)

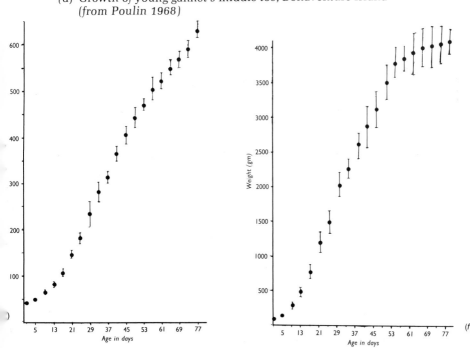

(e) Growth of young gannet's wing, Bonaventure Island (from
Poulin 1968)

(f) Growth of young gannet by weight, Bonaventure Island
(after Poulin 1968)

means that it is not much affected by temporary food shortages; it continues to grow at about the 'right' rate. The period of maximum bill growth, averaging 2·7 mm ($\frac{1}{10}$ in) per day, is between 9 and 33 days, but after day 49 the difference between consecutive mean measurements is no longer significant; which indicates that it is no longer a reliable method of estimating the chick's age. The curve flattens and becomes asymptotic at 96 mm ($3\frac{3}{4}$ in). The bill is an important tool for feeding in the chick, and it might be distinctly disadvantageous for a chick to have a bill short for its age. This applies only up to a point; in severely starved boobies, bill length suffers. However, we do not know whether adult gannets match size of prey to age of chick; tropical boobies almost certainly could not.

The total wing length is a good indicator of age; between 1–77 days each mean point is statistically different from the preceding and following one. The growth of the wing from wrist to tip (tenth primary excepted) is slightly more variable; between days 49 and 57 the difference between successive lengths is not significant.

By day 29, wing and tail feathers have appeared and thereafter grow rapidly (5·5 mm ($\frac{1}{4}$ in) per day during the period of quickest growth), but with marked variability in length of tail and of tenth primary. For example, at 33 days, the tenth primary may be only half as long in one bird as in another. The tenth (outer) primary measures 228 mm (9 in) at 77 days, whereas in the adult it measures 296 mm ($11\frac{1}{2}$ in). Since it grows relatively little between day 77 and fledging, the remainder of the growth must occur after fledging, probably whilst the juvenile is swimming southwards.

The middle toe grows rapidly immediately after hatching, from 18 mm ($\frac{3}{4}$ in) at day 1, to 97 mm ($3\frac{3}{4}$ in) at day 33. Between these days it is a reliable indicator of age, but later it is not. Its length is proportional to the whole foot and its rapid growth in the first month means that, just when the chick has become too large to be covered by its parent, it has a web big enough to be an effective structure for losing heat (see Chapter 3).

Tarsi show considerable variation in rate of growth and are not good indicators of age. This makes the relatively invariable web growth even more significant, for if one part of the limb grows so irregularly, the fact that another does not implies adaptive significance.

Fledging period

The young gannet grows from about 60 g (2 oz) to more than 4 kg (9 lb) in about 90 days (range 84–97 days on Bass Rock), which, incidentally, is virtually the same age (94 days) at which Booth's captive young gannets stopped accepting food from their parents. There is no significant difference in time taken to fledge at different gannetries. Actual Bass Rock fledging ages were 84 days (3% of 111 cases); 85 (5%); 86 (4%); 87 (5%); 88 (12%); 89 (17%); 90 (13%); 91 (12%); 92 (6%); 93 (12%); 94 (5%); 95 (3%); 96 (2%); 97 (1%). Chicks from cliff-edge nests fledged at 88·8 days (84–95) and from inland fringes at 88·9 days (83–96), so that the trauma of reaching the edge apparently does not inhibit fledging. When it is time to go, they go! Birds breeding for the first time produced young that fledged at 90·1 days (83–96), which was exactly the same as young from experienced breeders. This proves that young parents are not at any significant disadvantage in catching enough fish to satisfy their young – a conclusion which bears on the subject of competition for food. Obviously, even young adults are thoroughly competent foragers before they breed; to achieve this may be one reason for the long period which they require before breeding.

On the Bass Rock, chicks which fledged in September took significantly longer than those fledging in August or October; the figures were 87·8 days (83–90) in August; 91·5 days (86–97) first half September; 90 days (83–96) second half of September and 86·4 (85–88) in October. This probably means that early chicks grew best, and so took less time, and late ones fledged slightly prematurely. Premature fledging could be caused by general unease (the colony is deserted by substantial numbers of adults by then); also, although birds with late chicks still in the nest do not desert them, they may feed them less regularly.

On Bonaventure Island, gannet chicks fledged at 90·6 days (82–99), which indicates that these west Atlantic birds are just as well off for food as those of the east Atlantic. This has important implications for breeding success and so for population dynamics; both populations seem to have a rate of increase of about 3% per year. As on the Bass Rock, late Bonaventure young took less time to fledge (87·4 days), which was attributed to rapidly deteriorating weather in late September; the late young were not underweight. On Ailsa Craig (mean fledging period 91 days, ranged 80–100, extremes accurate only to within 3 days) late young *were* underweight,[137] because they were fed less frequently than 'mainstream' young, but Ailsa (and the Bass) has a much longer tail to the season than does Bonaventure Island.

Fledging season

The time of year at which the young gannet finds itself thrown abruptly onto its own resources is likely to be a very important factor in its chances of survival – which, for all, are none too good! Although the time taken to *grow* (the fledging-period) is the same at different colonies, the time of.year at which they *fledge* varies with area. This, of course, means that the time at which gannets lay their eggs also varies with area – a subject to be discussed later.

On Bass Rock, in 1961–63, two-thirds of the young in my study area fledged in the first half of September and about a fifth in August. However, these dates are misleading, for they came from a rapidly expanding group in which the mean laying date was later than for the rock as a whole. In fact, as later years have shown, the bulk of Bass Rock young fledge in late August or very early September, though a sizeable proportion fall on either side of this period. Bempton birds fledge at about the same time, and Ailsa Craig birds some two weeks later (Table

8). Grassholm gannets fledge at dates somewhere between the Bass and Ailsa Craig. Bass and Bempton birds fledge at the time which, on average, gives them the maximum chance of avoiding North Sea gales. Early September gales are relatively rare, though they do occur; just after mid-September the probability increases sharply, whilst from late September onwards they are highly probable. By laying from late March onwards, with a marked and annually consistent peak around mid-April (but also with considerable spread), gannets are hitting the most favourable time for fledging, but are also 'allowing' for the unpredictable variation in weather which marks the North Sea in late summer. Obviously it might be even better for their newly-fledged young if they laid earlier still, but other factors probably prevent this – such as a less propitious matching of the period of maximum growth of the young with peak availability of (particularly) mackerel.

It is possible that the main southward passage of young gannets, at least in the North Sea, coincides with an especial abundance of herring. In September and October, herring catches into Yarmouth used to be enormous. In one day, in October 1907, 79,200,000 herrings were brought in.

West coast gannets fledge later than those on the east coast of Britain. If their mean laying date is fixed, by, for example, the amount of food which is available to them in the critical period before egg-laying, and we do not know if this is so, the later fledging on the west coast is inevitable. But it is possible, also, that west coast fledglings face a different pattern of weather and different availability of food than their counterparts on the east coast. Some credence is given to this possibility by the fact that young shags from Lundy show a notably different mortality pattern, in time, from those on the Farnes.

On Bonaventure Island, 75% of young fledged between 2 and 20 September with a peak between 18 and 22 September (39% in 1966; 26% in 1967). By the end of September about 98% had fledged.[109] In this instance it is abundantly clear that sharply worsening weather is the spur and, despite a much later start to the season than in the Eastern Atlantic, the Canadian gannets manage to catch up until they are less than two weeks later than our west coast birds. They save time, not by shortening the fledging period, which is exactly the same, but by compressing the pre-laying period, probably by means of enhanced social stimulation.

The earliest and latest recorded fledging dates are from the Bass Rock (13 July 1976 and 25 November 1963).

As I have already said, early fledgers are at a great advantage, and this is one of the two main selection pressures which have determined the gannet's pattern of laying. The other determining factor is the incidence of maximum abundance of their main food fish, to which the growth of gannet chicks is tied. The way in which late fledgers are penalised is obvious: the additional handicap of bad weather (high winds, low temperatures) is too much for them. They are already stretched to survive, for they receive no parental help and have to acquire, or perfect, what must be an extraordinarily difficult method of catching fish. Many, perhaps more than half, soon starve. If their fuel reserve is expended against wind and cold, and their fishing attempts thwarted by too-rough seas, they are in desperate straits.

Ringed birds should give some information on this, but unfortunately gannet ringers have not categorised their chicks by age, so that the date on which they fledge cannot be estimated. It is little use counting up the numbers of recoveries at different times of year, since far too many factors influence these figures. And the knowledge that very late (October and November) fledglings survive less well than August ones tells us little. We need to know whether two or three weeks the wrong side of the mean confers a disadvantage. Since one should, presumably, exclude artificial deaths by oiling, shooting and drowning in nets (though they account for most recoveries), on the grounds that these are unlikely to relate to the seasonal time of fledging, it leaves rather few 'natural causes' to supply the answers. However, in Table 9 there is suggestive evidence that, even well within the main spread of fledging, early birds survive better than later ones. The factors that, nevertheless, maintain the spread of laying are discussed later.

This general thesis is important, too, in trying to decide why gannets nest so densely and compete so fiercely for nest sites, for laying date is much affected by social stimulation, and this, in turn, by density.

Breeding success

We have now followed the chick from hatching until the great moment when it hits the water and begins the long paddle south. Its progress is followed in Chapter 5. Here, there are several areas of breeding ecology still to explore.

Breeding success is an obvious term for a subtle and complex equation. It is not only that there are so many factors influencing the success of the individual pair over its lifetime (which is what matters) but that any attempt to relate 'success' to wider criteria, such as total numbers, puts one straight up against most basic and difficult problems. However, one can make a modest start by considering how successful gannets are at hatching their eggs (hatching success), and in raising those chicks that hatch (fledging success), and what causes the failures.

Hatching success is high, around 85% (Table 10), and in some groups, over 95%, though on Bonaventure Island it was much lower. If we assume that all eggs which are incubated beyond the maximum incubation period are infertile (which need not be so – some may be chilled, or the embryo killed in other ways), then 7·3% of 500 Bass Rock eggs were infertile and around 10% were lost before they could have hatched.

Predation by the large gulls is completely insignificant. Indeed, in my experience it never occurs unless aided by some degree of human disturbance. This need not be blatant intrusion by man, leading to unattended eggs; a partly uncovered egg beneath an anxious adult can fall to the opportunist gulls. This needs to be stressed, not only because of its practical aspects but also because in some colonial species predation is important, and adaptations against it can partly account for the density at which the species nests. This does not apply to gannets and, since physical shortage of sites does not, either, determine nesting density, one has to look elsewhere for the explanation. In the same vein, comments on the supposed inferiority of fringe sites should be more critically examined, for although they do lose more eggs to predators, this is due to human disturbance, and not to any 'natural' factor.

Natural egg loss seems mainly due to inadequate parental care, particularly by inexperienced adults. On several occasions I have seen such birds, with recently laid eggs, standing over them instead of incubating, and mandibulating or moving them with exaggerated actions which shifted them near to the rim. This, and similarly inept care of the new chick, acounts for the lower breeding success of birds breeding for the first time, compared with experienced nesters. So far as hatching goes, inexperienced Bass Rock pairs hatched 62·5% of eggs laid compared with 86% from experienced birds in the same group. A few eggs will be lost as a result of a fracas nearby, for even if they are not knocked over the ledge, they are still not retrieved; gannets cannot roll eggs and never pick them up in their mandibles. Freak weather can cause egg loss on cliffs. A severe north-westerly gale in May 1962 completely cleared a broad, flat ledge on top of the north-west face, and also emptied nests on ledges part-way down, due to terrific updraughts sweeping the birds off their nests.

On Bonaventure Island only 39·9% of eggs hatched in 1966, and 36·5% in 1967.[110] These are by far the lowest figures recorded for a large colony (small new colonies are a different case) and seemed to be due mainly to egg loss for unknown reasons; but 16·5% failed to hatch, probably due to a combination of chilling and a high concentration of toxic chemicals. An even higher egg mortality has been recorded for the Australasian gannet,[143] at Cape Kidnappers in 1945–46, apparently due mainly to infertility for unknown reasons.

Poulin has obtained details of egg loss at Bonaventure Island in relation to the length of time for which they had been incubated. In 81 out of 537 cases, the egg was lost around hatching time due, I suspect, to inadequate parental response as already described. 312 had been incubated for less than 40 days and 144 for more than 50 days. A proportion of the latter presumably became chilled, a distinct hazard at a mean temperature of 6·7°C in April and 4·4°C in May, high rainfall and snow-soaked nests. In addition, alarmed fringe birds left their nests and then lost their eggs. A useful illustration of the effect of weather lay in the observation that in the very severe (snowy) spring of 1967 the nests protected by trees hatched more than unprotected groups.

Fledging success

Gannets lose even fewer chicks than eggs (Table 10). Over 92% of eggs hatched on Bass Rock in 1961–63 gave rise to fledged young, and since then, on less exhaustive evidence in the years 1965, 1966, 1968, and 1970–77 inclusive, around 85% of nests that held eggs in April and May held large chicks in July. In no year was success significantly poorer, despite inevitable variations in the weather. Thus, over a run of 14 years, starvation has never been in the least evident among young in the nest. Other colonies (Table 10) tell much the same story over shorter spans. Even at Bonaventure Island, where hatching success was so much lower, fledging success was 78·3%, and this despite known losses of chicks due to disturbance by man.

The causes of chick loss, apart from disturbance and inept parental care already mentioned are weather, attacks by neighbours, falling and accidents during the fledging descent.

High winds with prolonged rain or sleet and low temperatures killed some Bass Rock chicks between 3–5 weeks old in late June and early July. Although such severe weather occurs fairly infrequently and the overall mortality thus caused is insignificant, it is possible that, now and again, a much more significant proportion of the chicks might be killed if all were at the vulnerable age together. It has been claimed[144] that 10% of Australasian gannet chicks may die in bad weather at Cape Kidnappers, despite a spread of ages about the same as in the Atlantic gannet. On the whole, though, it is impossible to disentangle the importance of this factor from that of variable weather at fledging; each could favour a spread in laying.

Neighbours attack and may kill unguarded chicks (we recorded five such deaths), but since chicks are never unattended except when one parent dies, or there is some other special cause, such occurrences are mainly of interest in showing that it is highly dangerous to leave chicks unguarded, rather than demonstrating that such attacks cause significant mortality.

The importance of falling as a cause of chick mortality was evident from our preliminary visit to Ailsa Craig in 1973, and has since been fully documented by Sarah Wanless. Obviously it can be important only on cliff sites, and even there, some cliffs may be much more dangerous than others. I was interested in this aspect because I had noticed that a cliff face on Bass Rock held a much higher proportion of empty nests in July than did a group on flatter ground, and the obvious suggestion (though one I did not think was responsible for the difference) was that chicks died by falling from the cliff. In fact, my figures over four years showed that, though a few undoubtedly fell, there was no really significant difference in the number of chicks lost from this cliff compared with the flatter area. Nor did Joan Fairhurst find that many young fell from the ledges at Bempton, even though they are very narrow. But on Ailsa Craig the situation appears to be quite different. There, the scale of chick mortality is extremely depressing to whoever must comb the base of the cliffs each day and put the injured young out of their misery before the rats get them. In three years, Sarah picked up no fewer than 1,326 young from the base of the cliffs. Their ages, in weeks, were as follows: 1 week (1·06%), 2 (2·26%), 3 (5·28%), 4 (6·33%), 5 (7·92%), 6 (6·86%), 7 (7·54%), 8 (7·24%), 9 (7·77%), 10 (8·45%), 11 (6·49%), 11+ (32·50%).

Thus it seems that (apart from those that fall whilst actually fledging) the most vulnerable age is when the chicks can no longer be (even partly) brooded; and especially when they begin to exercise those heavy and unwieldy wings, with the blood-filled quills – an age at which they are distinctly unstable. Later, the time just before or at fledging produces many casualties. At first sight it would appear that the chicks are either knocked off by clumsily departing adults (which Sarah Wanless and I have actually seen) or fall whilst wing exercising. Possibly, the former is unusually common on Ailsa Craig because the nature of the nesting sites (see plates) makes an adult, landing awkwardly, liable to fall onto another nest before it can gain enough lift to fly. On the Bass Rock an awkward landing (of which there are inevitably many) usually means that the bird falls into space and straight into flight, but on round-shouldered Ailsa Craig, a falling bird has a good chance of finding its free fall quickly blocked by the top of a hexagonal column, or another ledge. Any chick knocked aside in this way is likely to fall. As one would expect, there are lots of damaged adults as well as chicks at the base of the cliffs. Sarah Wanless picked up 102, 156 and 129 in 1974, 1975 and 1976 respectively. No comparable figures can be gained for the Bass Rock, since any injured birds fall into the sea, whereas on Ailsa Craig they hit the rocky slopes and foreshore. Of course, theoretically the extra loss thus sustained by Ailsa Craig birds should be reflected in lower breeding success and greater adult mortality, but this is extremely hard to demonstrate, for it must be remembered that the figures quoted are from the whole 'of a very large colony, and it is particularly difficult to find a demarcated group which can be scanned from above for chick loss and missing adults, and from below for the corresponding dead young and adults.

However, the story does not quite end there, for another intriguing finding has been that the young which fall (but not the adults) are below average weight for their age (this is not due to starvation on the ground; they were checked daily). It is not clear what this signifies. Are lighter chicks more likely to be knocked off; when wing exercising are they more vulnerable to 'lift' from the wind; do they beg more vigorously and thus fall (unlikely), or what?

Accidents during fledging do occur. I estimated that considerably fewer than 4% of fledglings from Bass Rock made a faulty descent, though some were not so much faulty as catastrophic! The wind conditions around cliffs are notoriously tricky and for a heavy bird on large, untried wings, the initial encounter must be bewildering. I have seen a bird blown completely round until it faced into the cliff, whereupon it simply plummeted onto the rocks 75 m (250 ft) below. On Ailsa Craig, 431 fully feathered young, more than 11 weeks old, were found over three seasons, either injured or merely stranded on the slopes below the cliffs.[137] Apparently they had foundered during descent.

Clearly, gannetries differ in the dangers they pose, but since Ailsa Craig is an ancient and large gannetry, as are Bird Rocks and Eldey (which are flat topped and afford maximum difficulties for getting to the edge) there seems little ground for suggesting that this is why gannets ignore so many apparently suitable islands and congregate densely on others.

Breeding success

Overall breeding success (young fledged from eggs laid) has been at least 75% over 14 years on Bass Rock, and other colonies seem similar (Table 10), except for the low figure of 29·6% from Bonaventure Island, due to low hatching success (see above).

This generally high figure should be interpreted in the light of the heavy post-fledging mortality, for the important figure, so far as population is concerned, is the number of young that survive to breed. What the gannet gains on the swings it loses on the roundabouts, for whilst some tropical boobies suffer heavy loss of eggs and chicks, their habit of feeding their free-flying young means that a much higher proportion of these survive. And gannets could not feed their free-flying young without totally disrupting the whole of their elaborate adaptive breeding biology based on the (quite different) food and weather conditions. As it is, their reproductive success and adult mortality rates at present permit an annual increase of about 3% in the world's gannet population.

Breeding success in large and small groups

Although most (or all?) large colonies show similar breeding success, small colonies and, possibly, small groups within large colonies, may do less well. This is a most interesting phenomenon because it is not susceptible to any simple explanation, such as, that small groups are more vulnerable to predation.

In practice, the comparison between large and small colonies is not easily made because (as ever) there is the matter of human interference to contend with. A meaningful difference could be swamped by a single disruptive visit. The small Norwegian colonies are difficult to interpret for this reason. However, the Bass Rock and Bempton are excellent for comparison since both are on the east coast (and indeed probably share the same gene pool), and Bempton is totally inaccessible to disturbance, whilst the Bass Rock is protected. In any case, disturbance would lower the latter's success, and since the thesis is that large colonies are *more* successful, it would be even more significant than it would otherwise have been if, despite disturbance, the Bass gannets bred more successfully than those from Bempton.

An examination of Bempton's success in relation to its size shows that, as it grew from a few pairs to a group, of 20 or 30 pairs or more, breeding success rose until it equalled that of Bass Rock. This cannot be the result of an increase in the mean age of the population, since in the early days the few pairs were all old. The recent increases have brought in many young birds (some, even, with immature plumage) *despite* which, breeding success has risen. Almost certainly, the explanation lies in the enhanced social stimulation which birds experience in a larger group, particularly one that is thriving and expanding. This affects breeding behaviour in several ways; for example, it stimulates attachment to the site; it enhances pair-bonding behaviour and it brings forward the laying date. All of these have a direct bearing on breeding success. A related but different phenomenon is the small colony which may grow very slowly until it reaches a certain size, whereupon its rate of growth accelerates rapidly. Again, social factors are responsible, this time by attracting recruits from outside. Great Saltee has been similar to Bempton, both in that its breeding success has increased as it has grown, and its growth rate suddenly accelerated after an initial long, slow haul (Fig. 8).

Breeding in relation to topography and age-structures

As I have mentioned, a gannetry is not a homogeneous mass; different parts have different topographies and different age structures. Any attempt to compare the breeding success of one part of the colony with another must explore many possible causes of divergence.

To begin with, there are cliff or cliff-edge sites compared with slope or flat ground sites. There seems no large difference in their comparative success measured 'straight', but measured in terms of output *per number of occupied sites*, there may be a considerable difference. This is because, whilst 80% of eggs laid on flat ground may produce a fledgling, and 78% of cliff eggs may do so, 75% of site-occupying pairs on flat ground may produce an egg, whereas only 50% of site occupying pairs on cliffs may do so. The actual figures for two such areas on Bass Rock are given in Fig. 32 and Table 11. Topography may affect age-structure, which in turn affects breeding effort. The full details[93] tend to be a bit boring and my interpretation of them is in any case speculative. In brief, however, it became clear that the south-west cliff face of the Bass (see plates) held a much higher proportion of empty sites and nests than did my main observation colony on the north-west slope, and that this was emphatically not due to greater loss of eggs and chicks in the former. In a nutshell, I consider that the difference is due to proportionately more of the flat group birds 'bothering' to breed. More breed because the flat group is open-ended, expanding rapidly, and is therefore subject to a higher level of social stimulation (more fights, more agonistic display, more arrivals and departures, more mutual fencing and so on). The cliff is 'closed'; it is almost full so far as good sites are concerned, but because of the tendency of young birds to return to their natal group it is constantly subject to attempts, by young adults, to establish themselves on the inferior sites. However, they often fail to do so, and presumably move elsewhere, as obviously

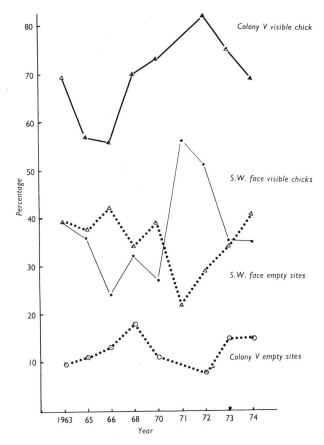

Fig. 32. *The proportions of non-breeding pairs in two topographically different areas of Bass Rock, 1963–74. The SW face is a cliff; colony V is a group on a slope*

happens on the 'needle' (see Chapter 3). Meantime, those birds which are successful in obtaining a usable site tend to have a longer pre-breeding period on it (because they receive less stimulus to breed) and thus, in my counts, they appear as site or nest owners with no contents. If this is correct, the explanation is thus primarily a social one, albeit based on topography. On Bonaventure Island, too, the cliff areas are largely full and parts of the plateau expanding rapidly. Correspondingly, Poulin[110] found that 79·4% of cliff nests received an egg in 1966, and 78% in 1967, whereas the figures for the plateau were significantly higher at 90% and 82·4% respectively.

Somewhat comparably, the undoubtedly lower success of fringe breeders in an expanding colony is not because fringe sites, as such, are inferior. They tend to be occupied by younger birds, which are less successful whether on the fringe or in the centre. Thus it is an age-effect (Table 12). Poulin, indeed, showed a conspicuous difference in the hatching success of fringe plateau birds (21·5%) and centre birds (42%) but the fringe was expanding rapidly and contained a high proportion of young birds. Also, as mentioned earlier, fringe birds are more prone to disturbance.

Also in relation to breeding success, the lower success of re-layings (37%) than of first eggs (79%), in the same group, should be mentioned. This may be due to loss-proneness (a bird losing one egg may be likely to lose another) and/or age, young birds being disproportionately represented.

When considering breeding success in terms of productivity and the replacement of adults, we may ask how many young a bird produces in its lifetime. This calculation is complicated because life spans vary in length, partners die, and new pairs form with one old and one new partner, all of which affects success, but if we simplify matters by taking only pairs that remain together over several years (and note that the criterion is merely *remaining* together, and thus being potentially capable of breeding), their success can be observed (Table 17). These figures are derived from 22 actual cases. How do they conform to the overall figure for breeding success in the gannet? An overall breeding success figure of 75% means 0·75 chicks per pair per year. As shown in Table 17, over several years (a minimum of five years) the most successful pairs had a breeding success of 100% and the least successful 66%. Altogether, 137 pairs/years gave 127 chicks, an overall breeding success of 92·7%, or almost 0·93 chicks per pair per year. This far exceeds the general figure, reflecting the extremely high success of *old, stable pairs*. One pair, for example, reared 11 chicks in 11 years. Even if 75% of these died before breeding, this pair would still have reared almost twice as many young as would be needed to replace themselves, in addition to which they were still alive and well, and capable of producing several more young. The lower overall success of the gannet is due to the failure of young birds, disrupted pairs, etc.

BREEDING REGIME

Seasonal attendance

So far, several references to the timing of the gannet's breeding season have been made. It is now appropriate to discuss its breeding strategy further.

The most striking aspect of the gannet's breeding season is its duration, if we consider 'breeding' to include the pre- and post-breeding activities. Presumably these activities are necessary, or the gannet wouldn't carry them out. Winter is little hardship to a gannet, and it returns to the colony in fat condition (St Kildans knew this well). Later they become leaner. The return date (Table 13) may be very early in the year, when daylight hours are short. We do not really know *why* some Bass Rock gannets, for instance, are always back in January, but three points are pertinent. First, the seas around east Atlantic gannetries, including Icelandic and Norwegian, contain plenty of fish in January, February and March.[112] The gannet's ability to catch them in cold and stormy seas, and to take temporary food withdrawal in its stride, may be crucial here. Second, despite the short time available for fishing, gannets spend so much time on their site that they lose weight during this early part of the season and *not*, be it noted, when feeding their voracious young; so it must be important for them to be there. Third, the return dates vary with the colony, which suggests that they are determined by local fishing conditions. An early return is more probable to those colonies near to which food is plentiful. In the extreme case of the Canadian colonies they may return four months later than some British and Icelandic gannets.

Presumably, an earlier return date usually means an earlier laying date, though certainly not on a pro rata basis (some time can be made up). If early laying is an advantage, in that the young are reared at the time when they can best be fed and will fledge most safely, then the parent birds should return to the colony as early in the season as possible, and the dates upon which they actually do so must be set mainly by day length in relation to fishing effort required. In fact, I suspect that the really critical period is the six weeks or so before laying. At this time attendance by the male is extremely high (Fig. 14) and display, copulation, egg production and nest building are all requiring energy. Thus, the period from late February onwards is important in allowing Bass Rock birds to achieve their mean laying date of mid-April; before that, more flexibility is possible. However, the earlier the return to the site the less the chances that it will have been usurped, so that the return will become as early as possible. In especially bad winters everybody may be away longer than usual, but *never* beyond mid or late February. Bad winters, incidentally, means bad by gannet standards! The weather may be atrocious for us without much affecting them.

The return of breeding adults to Bass Rock is correlated with age and sex; experienced males return first, often in a spectacular huge procession, usually in January. There is some evidence[8] that it used to be later, perhaps late February or early March, but, nonetheless, January returns were noted over a hundred years ago.

Little of worth is known about the reasons for the differing return dates at different colonies. Birds from large colonies return earlier than those from small ones; Bempton's return date has advanced as the colony has grown and now, not only are the first birds six weeks or more earlier than they were in 1960–68, but proportionately more birds have returned by a given date. This is probably because large colonies have a stronger 'pull', partly because of the greater social activity experienced there.

So far as the difference between west and east coasts of Britain is concerned, Ailsa Craig birds may lack access to a really early food supply. Bass Rock birds feed much on sand-eels early in the year, and there may be no north-west coast areas equivalent to the Tay Estuary, St

Andrews Bay, Tentsmuir and southern North Sea areas (see Fig. 6). Also, there are tremendous concentrations of sprats within foraging distance, for example in the Moray Firth. Further, it has been noted that in years when gannets have remained all winter on Bass Rock, herrings have been particularly plentiful. But this sort of claim is difficult to evaluate. Early in the year Ailsa Craig birds feed by the thousands on Ballantrae Bank herring shoals, and these appear in February or even March, rather later than the return date of Bass Rock birds. Grassholm birds are often back in January and may depend on Irish Sea herring. Also there are vast sprat shoals in the English Channel in December, well attended by adult and sub-adult gannets.[8] Gannets in the Gulf of St Lawrence are restricted by ice and snow on the ledges until April or even May.

At the other end of the season, gannets leave their colonies more or less precipitately, the colony virtually emptying within a day or two, from October to mid November. Even the Bass Rock may be very thinly attended by late September. Canadian birds leave in September or early October.

Mean laying date

At any given colony, gannets show an extremely consistent mean laying date (Table 14). For Bass Rock birds, it falls within a day or two of mid April and on Ailsa Craig between two and three weeks later. This need not mean that laying is highly synchronised; it could be greatly spread, but by the same extent and over the same period each year. However, it *is* also fairly highly synchronised. For example, three quarters of Bass Rock eggs are laid within a period of about three weeks, and on Bonaventure Island within about two weeks. Gannets are thus annual, seasonal and synchronised breeders.

The earliest recorded laying date is 10 March 1971 (Bass Rock), though in 1976 there was an egg within the first week and possibly even in February (the record depends on ageing a feathered young bird). Possibly, Bass Rock birds tend to lay slightly earlier now than formerly, although Booth[8] recorded an egg on 27 March 1867. His comments indicate that peak laying was in late April. However, much depends on whether his remarks resulted from observations on a disturbed part of the colony. Since 1961, the first Bass Rock eggs have been: 1961, 31 March; 1962, 5 April; 1963, 3 April; 1965, 28 March; 1966, 26 March; 1968, 29 March; 1970, 19 March; 1971, 10 March; 1972, 23 March; 1973, 13 March; 1974, 20 March; 1975, 2 March or earlier; 1976, 7 March or earlier. The last egg, also, is later than it used to be and falls a little after mid July. The only gannetries for which there are comparable data are Ailsa Craig, Bempton and Bonaventure Island (Table 14).

The facts just given mean that the population, made up of birds which are physiologically variable and of different ages, has arrived at an adaptive state in which the *distribution* of laying, over a long run of years, is most effective in countering the various destructive forces

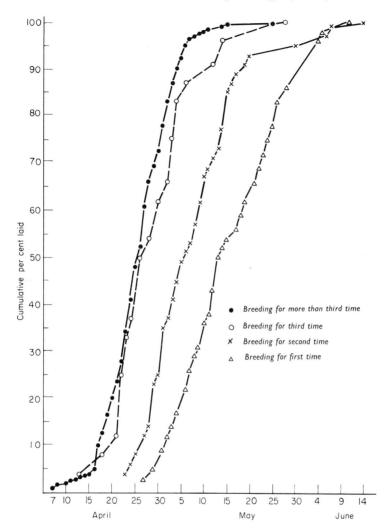

Cumulative per cent laid

- Breeding for more than third time
- Breeding for third time
- Breeding for second time
- Breeding for first time

April May June

Fig. 33. *Relationship between age of female gannet and laying date, Bass Rock, 1961–63*

which are pitted against survival of eggs and young. And these forces (mainly weather and food) vary from year to year, thus encouraging a measure of variability in those features of the gannet's breeding biology which cope with them. Our task is to make what sense we can out of the observations, on the premiss that natural selection has ensured that none of them is arbitrary.

By and large, gannets which lay early almost certainly are more successful. One factor affecting laying date is age; older females lay earlier (Fig. 33 and Table 15). Another influential factor is social stimulation.[87] There can now be no doubt whatsoever that most, if not all, colonial seabirds are affected by the excitement and interactions of colonial life. Their endocrine state responds to these stimuli and hence their gonads and the gonad-dependent reproductive processes. The changes in breeding regime which have accompanied the growth of Bempton (see later) are probably to be explained in these terms. This means that, within a group, there is finite, but significant, scope for some of its members to be 'brought on' by social stimulation; without it, or with less of it, they would lay later. This means that social stimulation is inducing a further measure of synchrony in the group, additional to that imposed by individual responses to external timers, such as daylight and temperature, and inevitable maturation processes. Of course, so far as gannets are concerned, it probably is not the synchrony, as such, that is most important (though it may help by reducing the probability of interference by conspecifics, since if most birds are doing the same thing at the same time there is less chance for damaging interactions). Instead, it is the enhanced earliness of *each pair*, which (together with a fixed starting point, of course) means enhanced synchrony of the group. The advantage accrues to the *individual breeding pair*. If all the factors which affect the survival of the egg and chick were constant and predictable, one would expect natural selection to eliminate most of the variability in the gannet's breeding regime. The mean laying date would become fixed, and there would be such synchrony that almost every bird would lay within a day or two. That this is not so depends, as mentioned already, on the variability in the environment, which in some years favours particularly early, or slightly late, breeders. Very late eggs are those of young females laying for the first time, or replacement eggs of birds whose first was already fairly late. Of course, no population can ever achieve, in *any one year*, the theoretically perfect distribution of laying if this is defined purely in terms of that which would have produced the most young, but it is always striving towards the distribution which on average does best, within the constraints imposed by the heterogeneity of the group.

Clearly, behavioural stimulation could be very important in the gannet, by influencing the timing of laying, and I tried to show, directly, that it does so by comparing a group of birds subject to relatively little stimulation (they were isolated from any large mass of birds) with two groups from the middle of a large nesting mass. The three groups were the same size and, so far as possible, contained birds of the same age and experience. This criterion is impossible to meet fully, but each group was at least composed, largely, of experienced pairs. As one would predict, I found that the isolated group began laying later and showed a greater spread of laying than the other two.

Similar results were obtained by comparing large and small groups. Thus, in 1962, the only year in which I obtained dates for the first and median eggs in several groups, the association with group-size was as follows:

First egg	Median egg	Number of nests in 'group'
4 April	27 April	200
6	28	150
8	1 May	135
10	1	125
19	2	20
16	5	59

The 'groups' were not totally satisfactory, since not all were discrete, but they were mainly or almost completely demarcated, physically, from other parts of the colony. The large groups not only produce an earlier first egg (as one would expect simply because there are more to choose from) but a higher proportion lay near to the mean; that is the big groups are more highly synchronised, and the agent is social stimulation. The moral for a gannet is: join a large group!

The precise timing and degree of synchronisation found in a group of gannets depends on many factors and may be expected to vary with locality and with the size and age structure of the group. The effects of age structure can be fairly subtle; not only do young females lay later, but the laying date of a female is influenced by the male (Table 15), so that a change of partner affects her. This type of phenomenon has been demonstrated far more elegantly for several other colonial seabirds than for the gannet.[22,74]

Once mature, a female gannet shows a strong tendency to lay at the same time each year – usually within a day or two (Table 16); but even a mature female is adversely affected by change of partner. Also, there are a few records of mature females who, over three years, gradually laid *later* instead of earlier, and these females then changed mates, even though their old partner remained alive. It is tempting to believe that these pairs may have been incompatible and that this led eventually to the dissolution of the bond. Inexperienced females lay significantly earlier when partnered by an experienced, compared with an inexperienced, male.

Regional variation in breeding regime
One might expect that, in the eastern Atlantic, northern colonies would lay later than southern, but in fact there is no simple north–south gradation. Icelandic gannets begin laying at the end of March,[47] with a peak in April and many birds laying in May, which is very similar to the situation on the Bass Rock, some 800 miles south. Yet Grassholm, 400 miles further south, is not earlier than the Bass Rock though it is earlier than Ailsa Craig. There seems more difference east–west (still confining discussion to the eastern Atlantic) than north–south; Ailsa Craig, at about the same latitude as the Bass, has its peak laying two or three weeks later. There is no detailed information about the timing of laying in other west coast colonies; Saltee certainly

has some March eggs and Skellig may be suspected to be at least as early as Grassholm. St Kilda is probably as late as Ailsa Craig. Hermaness has its first egg around late March in some years. As I mentioned in the general preamble on breeding regimes, it is as yet mere guesswork to link these differences to differences in feeding, but it is worth noting that saithe and herring are abundant off Iceland in winter, and that whilst Bass gannets gorge on sand-eels and possibly sprats, in their pre-laying period, Ailsa Craig birds do not. Sarah Wanless rarely found sand-eels in the stomachs of adult Ailsa Craig gannets which had died (by falling) in the pre-laying period. However, this is an incomplete and one-sided presentation, and a thorough evaluation of all relevant fishing data would be most welcome. Further, it would be interesting to know more about the weather conditions facing migrating juvenile gannets from the west coast, compared to the east. The selection pressures at that end, too, might be different. Certainly, west coast juveniles arrive in southern waters well before Bass birds,[130] but that is presumably because they have a more immediate exit to Biscay.

The Canadian colonies lay about a month later than Bass Rock. On Bonaventure Island the first egg is laid in late April or early May and the last egg by about the third week of June.[110] However, as mentioned earlier, laying proceeds so rapidly that much ground is recovered. Thus, peak laying is in the second week of May, only two or three weeks behind Bass Rock despite a start six weeks later. By mid May,

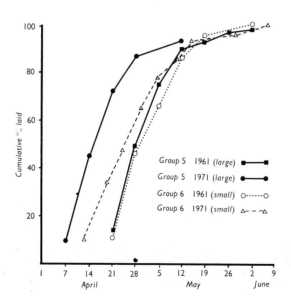

Fig. 34. *Advancement of laying in large and small groups of gannets expanding rapidly over ten years (Bass Rock, 1961–71)*

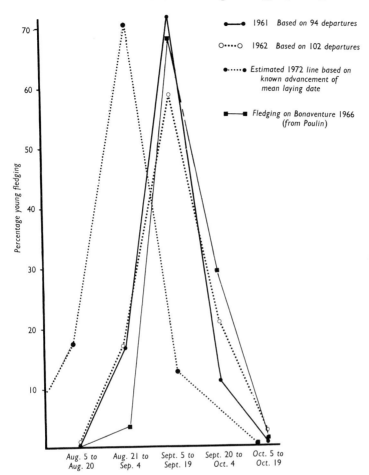

Fig. 35. *Timing of fledging on Bass Rock and Bonaventure Island showing (i) earlier fledging in 1972 than 1962, probably due to increase in social stimulation leading to earlier laying, and (ii) the relatively small period by which Bonaventure is later than Bass Rock*

more than half the eggs have been laid. Poulin's figures for 1966 and 1967 were that by 15 May 1967, 71% of eggs had been laid, and by 30 May 95%. The equivalent percentages were attained by 28 May and 4 June 1966. Taken together, the modal laying point occurs a mere five days after the beginning of laying. In my view this highly adaptive – indeed essential – speeding-up is achieved, at least partly, by the greater intensity of social stimulation which the Bonaventure Island birds experience right from the outset; for whereas at our gannetries the birds return fairly gradually, they flood back en masse to the Canadian colonies. Similar compression of the breeding cycle at higher latitude has been recorded for several other seabirds, for example the kittiwake.[24]

The Canadian regime is adaptive on two counts: first, weather is commonly appalling in the second half of May, so that it may be an advantage to have laid by then; second, and probably more important, the breeding cycle must be completed before late September, when weather deteriorates rapidly.

The role of social stimulation in the timing of breeding in the gannet thus implies that a breeding pair gains advantage by nesting where it is exposed to maximum social or behavioural stimuli (fighting, display and sexual behaviour). The amount of such stimulation depends partly on how near nesting pairs are to one another, and on the size of the colony. Nesting density, as we have seen, is consistent, at about the maximum possible. *Absolute* colony size becomes irrelevant once there are enough birds to provide the most effective amount of social stimulation (hence one reason for the variability in colony size). Competition for a site thus becomes competition for a *socially* adequate site and accounts for the observation that gannets fight so fiercely to get in amongst, or near to, established birds.

The reader may well ask, at the end of this section, for evidence that there really is an advantage in laying earlier than would have been the case *without* social stimulation. I have already mentioned the evidence in the contexts of growth (young grow more rapidly and better, especially early in the season), and of fledging (early fledgers more likely to survive). It is up to the critic who rejects the role of social stimulation in this context to explain, not only the competition for a socially adequate site, but also how it could be that a mechanism which clearly advances laying could, in the gannet's circumstances, be neutral.

Frequency of breeding

A pair of gannets, having bred once, attempts to breed every year thereafter. I have found nothing to refute this generalisation; 'deliberate' rest years apparently do not occur. In all the years I have been following the fortunes of colour-ringed pairs, only *one* pair has stayed together and, without any apparent untoward circumstances, failed to lay, and even then, in only one year out of ten. This is far from saying that any individual gannet produces a chick every year of its life. This must indeed be a rare occurrence (Table 17), for not only are eggs and chicks occasionally lost and not replaced, but partners die and a year may well be lost in establishing a new relationship. Some bereaved individuals go two or three seasons in succession before they get going properly again. So, most gannets enjoy an involuntary respite once every few years. We do not know whether breeding is, in any case, a significant stress; they do not lose weight as a result of feeding their young, and in the shag, those adults which rear most young also survive better than their less productive fellows in the succeeding winters. Probably they are better quality individuals.[108]

The empty but attended nests which occur in every gannetry at the height of the breeding season belong to pairs establishing themselves, or to failed breeders, and *not to 'non-breeders' in the sense of established pairs taking a rest.* Of course, the proportion of sites that contain an actual nest, or a nest plus contents, will vary from group to group in a gannetry (see Table 11), from gannetry to gannetry, and from year to year. All will be affected by the proportion of site-establishing birds. Some figures for the number of empty nests or sites estimated, are: Bass Rock 10–40% (according to area); Bonaventure Island about 15% overall; Grassholm about 20%; Ailsa Craig about 20% on the steeply sloping cliff-tops and up to 55% on cliff faces.[137]

Pairs that fail, but remain together, are as likely to lay the next year as are pairs that succeed; but they tend to dissolve the partnership more often than do successful pairs. Thus, a nest that fails one year is less likely to hold an egg the next year than is a nest that succeeds, for the former is more likely to belong to a new partnership, and these do not always breed in their first year together.

Age of first breeding

Gannets usually do not breed until they are in at least their fifth year. Generally, males acquire a site during April or May of their fourth or fifth year, though whether they breed depends on circumstances. Indeed, there is a markedly different picture at a rapidly expanding group compared to a stable or slowly expanding one. From 1961 to 1963 my observation group on Bass Rock held few birds with even a trace of immature plumage, but after protection for a few years had led (by immigration) to a roaring increase, the proportion of immature birds on the fringe rose dramatically. In 1965 there were about 20 three-year-olds, of both sexes, on territories in the fringe, and about 25 four-year-olds. A high proportion of both age classes bred the following year. Subsequently the proportion of three- and four-year-olds increased, until by 1974 a broad belt, some three or four ranks deep on the outer fringe, consisted predominantly of birds in immature plumage. The approximate proportions of the different age classes (both sexes) attending sites in the fringe, but not necessarily breeding, were: adult plumaged 45%; fifth and fourth year 35%; third year 15%, and second year 5%. The analysis was made at the beginning of July, which means that the second year birds would be just on, or over, their second birthday, and therefore just into their third year, and so on for the other age classes. A similar increase in the proportion of immature birds occurred at Bempton, as the colony grew; there, also, two-year-olds began to appear.

From ringed birds it is now known that both sexes can breed successfully in their fourth year; that is, they are just four years old in June or July and so are in their fourth year when they begin breeding, but in their fifth year by the time they are rearing their chick. Such birds may still possess one or two black tail feathers and secondaries. Fourth year birds can lay even without having spent more than a small part of the previous season in attendance. So far, there is no record of a bird breeding earlier than this.

Sex difference in age of breeding

Why, then, do so many three- and four-year-olds remain outside the breeding population? A clue may lie in the different ages of first breeding for male and female. Where the exact ages of pair members were known from colour rings, *males were generally one year older than females*, never the reverse. Furthermore, where one partner had more immature plumage than the other, the female was the immature bird in 49% of 153 cases, the male in 19% and the sexes looked equally mature in 32%. This line of evidence is somewhat dangerous, however, since in five pairs *known* to be of equal age (four years) and compared on the same day, the female nevertheless possessed more immature plumage. Records of individuals (rather than pairs) of known age and sex further confirmed that, age for age, females *look* younger than males. Shags resemble gannets in that males acquire fully mature plumage before females.

The conclusion must be that females take longer to gain adult plumage than males and, in addition, breed when chronologically younger. I think the latter phenomenon is because males face greater stress, in acquiring their site, than females do in acquiring their mate (see Chapter 3). Further, at a given age, it may be more useful, in territorial defence, for a male to have adult plumage than for a female, and this may partly explain the disparity in attaining adult plumage. In gulls, by contrast, males breed at a younger age than females.[23]

Factors responsible for deferred maturity

Indeed, I would go further and suggest that the actual length of the deferred maturity period, long though it appears to be, can be explained in terms of the skills and experience the male must acquire in that time. Thus, the first two years are spent in southern waters (the reasons why are discussed later). If a further year (or even two) is spent becoming familiar with the colony and with the local fishing areas (none too long in view of annual and seasonal variations in weather and food fish), and a year or part of one in acquiring a site and forming a pair bond, the full time is used up (Fig. 36). This is quite different from the suggestion, which to me is utterly unconvincing, that it takes four or five years to acquire the *physical* skills of plunge-diving. Thus there may be no need to postulate that deferred maturity is a way of regulating population size, by regulating the number of new breeders admitted.

However, there is the question of adult plumaged non-breeders at a colony. How old are they? Are they in some way unfit? Are they merely off-duty birds? We have no means of telling how old they are, nor how fit they are! Nevertheless (and it must be remembered that we are talking, now, about birds *within the breeding ranks* and clearly owning a nest or site, rather than about the quite different matter of adult

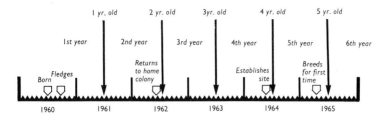

Fig. 36. Sequence from birth to first breeding of typical Atlantic gannet

plumaged birds in the clubs), such birds may be bereaved or divorced, and be with or without a new partner. The new partner may be in its fifth year and in adult plumage but may be spending a preparatory year on its site. Alternatively, they may be new pairs, both partners in their fifth or sixth years. Or they may be failed breeders or adults with sites too difficult to breed on (see earlier).

As mentioned before, at many gannetries there is no question of space shortage, but the birds may be unable to use the *physical* space because there may be a *social* limit to the number of ranks that can be established in a year. For example, the large group on the north-west face of Bass Rock has crept upwards by two to five rows per year (such blanketing of the ground by a steady expansion is typical). These ranks are less dense and regular and, particularly on the outer fringes, are contagiously wary, lacking the strong ties of eggs and young. For a gannet, the further one is from the outermost breeding rank (the rank with eggs or young) the weaker becomes the attraction of such a site regardless of its physical characters. In this way, the area of attractive ground is limited and some individuals may have too little stimulus to establish themselves outside it. In addition, human disturbance may effectively render some physically adequate areas unattractive. In any case, whether for this and/or other reasons, gannetries often do not expand evenly around the edges, but in bulges, within which they may conceivably run into the rank-number limitations just postulated. Thus, even the adult plumaged birds in the clubs could be birds unable to find a physically and socially attractive site (they almost certainly are not off-duty breeding birds).

This socially limiting mechanism could, of course, operate without any form of exclusion being imposed by pairs within the colony.

Fourth-year pairs which have a site but do not breed for a season, may have been relatively late in returning to, or establishing, the site, and this leaves them insufficient time to breed that year. The suggestion that such young birds would suffer too much strain, is, to my mind, implausible. The ease with which inexperienced fifth year birds rear chicks belies any suggestion of inferior *food-catching* ability.

In sum, gannets probably need their long deferred maturity to gain the necessary lore around the colony and in foraging. The latter will be especially important in males because they have to assign so much time to territorial activities. Some adult-plumaged birds may be unable to find a socially attractive site, and some immature site holders may have too little time to breed in their first reasonably full season. I do not see deferred maturity as a homeostatic device regulating recruitment and thus reproductive output. Nor, at present, do I see direct competition inhibiting younger birds from breeding; the circumstantial evidence is against this.

I am aware that competition for food *within the foraging area near to the colony*, has been plausibly suggested to operate in rendering young (and that means anything less than eight years old) royal penguins incapable of feeding well enough to reach the fat condition necessary for breeding.[19] But that case is quite different from the gannet's, for it depends on a dominant–subordinate relationship between old and young penguins when feeding, to the disadvantage of the younger birds, whereas in gannets, communal feeding benefits all and certainly does not involve dominance relationships.

FIDELITY TO GROUP, SITE AND MATE

All that has gone before would lead one to expect that gannets remain faithful to their site and mate, as many long lived seabirds do, and this is so. Until I came to analyse the population trends in the world's gannetries I would have guessed, also, that they bred in the colony in which they were born; but it is now clear that, though many do so, there is much interchange between colonies; that is, birds born in one colony, breed in another (there is no evidence that adults change breeding colonies and a great deal to show that they do not). However, this topic is discussed in Chapter 2. Here, it can be said that on Bass Rock, at least, colour ringed chicks returned in 95% of cases to the very group in which they were born, and in one or two cases to the very ledge (incidentally, we had cases of birds reared on flat ground establishing their site on cliffs and vice-versa). On the other hand, as remarked earlier, rapidly expanding groups sucked in recruits from outside their own area. Site fidelity (Table 19) is very strong, particularly in males, about 95% of which return to their site of the previous year. Taking site/mate attachment as theoretically indivisible where both partners remain alive (we cannot know whether it is to the site or the mate that each returns), the males were faithful in 94% of cases and the females in 88%. The female's weaker site attachment is adaptive since, after bereavements, she has to respond to advertising males, whereas he can remain where he is. Usually, she returns to her site or remains on it, and acquires a new male there, but she may move a short distance, or be ejected by a new male. Bereaved males usually stay on their sites or move merely to the next site or so (thus often creating 'threesomes' which cause fights). As mentioned earlier, failure in breeding predisposes partners to split up, and as other workers have stressed, the tendency to do so is adaptive and in a long-lived bird helps to increase the chances of achieving compatibility.

MORTALITY

Probably less than 6% of adults die between one year and the next (Tables 18 and 20). This gives an average life expectancy of at least 16·2 years*, and suggests that some gannets must live for more than forty years, for, although our oldest ringed bird is not *known* to be more than 25, a few birds must live more than twice as long as the average. If (due to error brought in by loss of rings, etc) average annual adult mortality should be found to be only 4%, the average life expectancy would be 24 years (a very small difference in annual adult mortality rate makes a large difference in potential breeding life). This would be a very low death rate, beaten, slightly, only by some large albatrosses and penguins. Were it not for man, I do not doubt that on average, gannets would in fact live that long, but man kills so many adults that he probably does affect average life expectancy.

Adult mortality can be gauged directly from colour ringed birds but mortality of younger birds bears no directly calculable relation to recovery rate. However, pre-breeding mortality can be calculated from known adult mortality and breeding success. Taking 16·2 years as the average life expectancy, after the death rate has become independent of age (probably by the third year), means that in its lifetime each pair rears on average $16·2 \times 0·75 = 12·2$ chicks (breeding success is about 75%). If the population were stable only two chicks would be required to survive to replace the parents, leaving 83% to die. But the Bass Rock (and world) population is expanding at about 3% per year so the pre-breeding mortality must be slightly less. Undoubtedly, most of this occurs in the first year of life. Thus, of 1,600 *recoveries* of birds ringed as chicks, 54·2% were in the first year (Table 25). Thereafter (correcting for the recoveries already taken into account), they are proportionately the same (second year 34·8%; third year 34·6; fourth year 33·5 and fifth year 33·1%). This of course does not imply *actual* mortality at these rates, only that the mortality levels can be compared. In the Australasian gannet a direct check of the proportion of birds ringed as chicks and returning to breed as adults gave a pre-breeding mortality of about 70%, though of course there is no guarantee that emigration had not accounted for some of it. The recoveries of gannets on the west side of the Atlantic[78] confirm this general picture. As shown by Table 25, birds ringed as adults are less likely to be recovered than are birds which were ringed as chicks, even *after* the latter's high initial recovery rate. This may reflect a greater wariness in older birds but, unless direct killing by man is a significant cause of overall mortality, need not imply that young birds, aged three, four and five, continue to show greater mortality than adults.

* Based on the simplest formula, which is $2 - m/2m$ where $m =$ percentage annual mortality.[66]

Causes of mortality

One wonders how long gannets used to live and incidentally, how many there used to be. Nowadays, man is the chief agent of death at sea, through netting and drowning, hooking, shooting or killing (by hand) gannets that are so excited by fish that they land heedlessly near or on his fishing boats. On land, he does his best by shooting or clubbing nesting birds or by providing, as waste, ensnaring cordage to throttle or immobilise them, whilst inbetween he adds toxic chemicals to the seas, so that fish poison gannets, which can then choose either the land or the sea upon which to die. Even today, gannets are not only killed by fishermen, whom they often distract and annoy, but are sometimes treated with revolting cruelty, for example by being released with a leg tied to a wing, or with their mandible secured by a rubber band. Gannets often drown in nets, into which they dive as the fish are being raised. They used to perish spectacularly on lines, taking the bait as the line was being paid out; up to 200 at a time were hauled on deck, dead. Nowadays, however, line fishing is hardly practised, at least around the British Isles, though it used to be common in the north-east.

Gannets suffer relatively little from oiling. It has been estimated that they form between one and two per cent of the seabird bodies washed up on north-west European beaches.[10] About half the gannet corpses are oiled. In the west coast and Irish Sea oil disaster of autumn 1969, 35 gannets were collected from a total kill estimated at 15,000–30,000 seabirds, mainly auks; and in the east coast oil kill of winter 1970, 45 oiled gannets were picked up compared with 7,757 auks out of a total kill conservatively estimated at 50,000. Their relative immunity can be put down to their fishing methods; they probably do not see fish beneath oil and so do not dive into it. Nor do they swim far enough on or under water to enter, or come up in, an oil-slick, as auks and ducks do. This, unfortunately, by no means precludes the possibility of a large scale kill if a massive oil spill occurred near to the great concentrations of breeding birds to the west and north of Scotland, for, near the colonies, they sit on the water in thousands. The young of the year are particularly vulnerable in the first two weeks at sea, during which time they are unable to fly. An unusual case of gannets polluted by oil occurred when birds from Rouzic picked up oily nest material after the Torrey Canyon disaster.

The toxic chemicals known as chlorinated hydrocarbons or organochlorines, manufactured as pesticides, etc, are now famous (or infamous) for their damaging effects on wildlife. Predators such as raptors and fish-eating birds at the apex of the food pyramid, are particularly at risk because these substances are concentrated with each step up the food chain. The figures for the levels of the organochlorines are difficult to interpret. Muscles are usually the tissue tested, but nervous tissue, meaning mainly the brain, is probably a better source because its fat level tends to fluctuate less, and organochlorine levels vary with fat.

Because large fish contain more organochlorine residues, both in absolute and relative terms, than small ones, and because gannets feed extensively on large fish, they tend to contain larger residues of organochlorine than do other seabirds.[101] The concentrations in their livers, after a period of starvation, are higher than in most other seabirds. Parslow and Jeffries cite 200 ppm (wet weight) in the livers of partly-starved gannets found dead or dying on the shore, with many guillemots, in Lancashire (see Table 22). This compares with 116 ppm in guillemots which died in the famous Irish Sea wreck of 1969. The total body loads were probably five to ten times higher. Furthermore, the extremely toxic mercury is present in greater amounts in gannets than in any other marine or estuarine fish-eater with the exceptions of the shag, cormorant, common scoter and red-breasted merganser. However, gannets contain less cadmium than more pelagic feeders such as fulmars, or than some inshore birds which feed on molluscs, such as eiders.

The actual toll due to toxics (PCBs and DDEs, are the main ones,

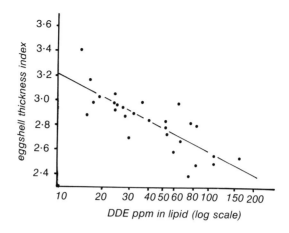

Fig. 37. Correlation between decreasing index of eggshell thickness and increasing DDE concentration in the fat of eggs of gannets in Britain (from Parslow and Jeffries 1977)

principally the latter) is impossible to estimate. First, birds may not feel the effects until stressed, whereupon lethal concentrations may be released into the blood from fat reserves and carried to glands and muscles. They may then contribute to death without actually causing it. Again, minor imperfections in co-ordination may account for landing accidents. There are several colonies at which high concentrations of DDT derivatives and/or PCBs have been found in either eggs or birds (Bonaventure Island, Ailsa Craig and Grassholm (see Table 22)), but other colonies are less affected.

Bass Rock birds have about half as much DDT in their eggs as Ailsa Craig birds (Table 21), and the shells are correspondingly thicker (Fig. 30). The high concentration of DDT in eggs from Bonaventure[96,64] (mainly due to run-off from the sprayed forests of New Brunswick) probably has lowered breeding success; many more nests fail there than elsewhere. Of course, shell thinning and consequent egg breakage, is well known to have severely affected several species, among them the brown pelicans of Florida,[118] and has reduced the thickness of gannet egg-shells in the Gulf of St Lawrence by about 17%.

White pelican and double-crested cormorant eggs in Canada showed a similar picture of shell-thinning as a correlate of concentrations of DDE and PCBs,[2] the former probably having the greater effect. They exert their effects by raising the level of steroids which in turn affects calcium metabolism. The steroids, estrogen and androgen, are essential for the deposition of bone, which is a major source of eggshell calcium. The toxics may also create an artificial deficiency of vitamin D, which is essential for calcium absorption from the small intestine. Finally, DDT inhibits the enzyme which is found in the cells of the shell gland,

and is responsible for the formation of the carbonate which combines with the calcium to form the shell.

Figures for the levels of some toxics in gannets and their eggs are given in Tables 21–22.

The extremely high, indeed lethal, concentrations of PCBs found in one or two individuals at certain colonies, may reflect individual preferences for fishing in specific areas. Such areas may vary in the amount of toxics carried to them by currents. It is not even possible to be quite sure that the 'obvious' areas for pollution, such as Liverpool Bay, the Severn Estuary and the Clyde, are receiving their toxics from local sources rather than from continental Europe.

Predators, at sea, are probably totally insignificant except to the odd gannet unfortunate enough to be snatched by a large fish or possibly a seal. Great skuas cause a few gannets to damage a wing; they often attack and upend them. In several recorded instances, gannets have choked to death on unsuitable fish, chiefly gurnards.[46]

Turning to the causes of mortality on land, deaths at the breeding colony stem from bad landings (broken wings), fighting (falling and jamming, or damaging a wing) and, nowadays, from entanglement in synthetic cordage brought to the nest. Predators are virtually non-existent. There are red foxes on Bonaventure Island but apparently they do not molest the gannets,[110] and extremely few gannetries are accessible to them.

The surprisingly massive mortality of adults on Ailsa Craig, due to falling, has already been mentioned. In 1974, 1975 and 1976 Sarah Wanless collected 102, 156 and 129 dead or injured adults at the base of the cliffs. This, at 0·5% of the adult gannet population per year, constitutes almost an eighth of the total annual mortality, a figure so high that Ailsa Craig may well be abnormal in this respect. That this scale of mortality has been going on for a long time is shown by Gurney's account, in which he mentions the remains of 73 gannets below the West Craigs in June 1905. All of them were adult or sub-adult birds.

Occasionally gannets are driven onshore by gales, and reach the central areas of Britain and equivalent distances into the continents of Europe and North America. It seems hardly worth presenting the individual records, for the fact is that the odd gannet can be picked up anywhere in Britain, on rivers and reservoirs, in fields, streets and gardens. They occur mainly between October and January and are mainly juveniles, but often adults. Usually they are single birds and never more than a few. Nothing comparable to the wrecks of petrels or auks has ever occurred. Presumably most gannets, even if driven inland, can easily cross Britain, for their strength and resistance to exhaustion must far surpass that of the smaller birds.

Death from starvation seems totally insignificant except in newly independent juveniles, where it is the major cause of death. There are one or two records of gannet 'wrecks', mainly young birds. Recently (May and June 1972) many gannets were washed up on the Lancashire coast, in an incident which mainly involved auks. They were light, but contained more than the average amounts of toxics.[101] It is impossible to say with complete confidence that healthy adults *never* starve, or even that starvation does not account for a significant part of the species' low adult mortality, but it seems unlikely to do so. Adults can fish in strong winds (up to at least force 8), have substantial reserves of fat and, judging from their excellent condition after the winter period spent away from the colony, do not go short of food at that time. The juveniles are a special case, and their long migration may be, chiefly, because they cannot yet cope with the kind of fishing that adults find so rewarding. The food is there, but only for those who can get it, and juveniles generally may be unable to do so. As mentioned, most recoveries of ringed gannets are of young birds, and although many are caught in nets etc, or are found dead and too decomposed to determine the cause, many are recovered thin and weak on shorelines. The same applies to Cape and Australasian gannets.

Disease seems to play a very minor role. No widespread occurrences have ever been found among gannets, though salmonella has been isolated from wild birds and the same bacterium (*S. typhimurium*) has also been obtained from herring meal. The bacterium *Escherichia coli* is common in shags, and might be expected in gannets, but would not cause disease unless the individual's resistance was lowered. Newcastle disease has been isolated from a dead (wild) gannet and from shags and the virus–caused puffinosis has been recorded in the shag, though not, so far as I know, in the gannet. Fungal disease (*Aspergillosis*) has been found in the African gannet. Nematode and tapeworm infections are common in gannets killed in other ways and are probably present to some extent in almost all birds, usually without becoming a significant hazard. Comparably, the mite *Neottialges evansi*, in sub-cutaneous form, often infests shags but probably does little harm under normal circumstances. As a cause (even occasionally) of mass mortality in the gannet, disease, it seems, can be ruled out, though an old reference[77] claims that gannets are sometimes attacked by an infectious disease, destroying 'countless numbers' which drift, dead, onto the shore. Gurney supposed this really referred to starvation, but even this is a rare occurrence.

THE GROWTH OF A GANNETRY

At several points I have mentioned the interesting gannetry at Bempton, which has grown from two pairs (possibly only one) in the 1920s and 30s, to 169 nest-owning pairs in 1977. Bempton has the unique distinction of being the only gannetry which has been intensively studied[35] throughout the most significant period of its growth, and monitored, more generally, in terms of numbers and productivity[18] for over 16 years. These studies fortunately coincided with my own on the Bass Rock, and support many of my predictions. So the growth of Bempton, and attendant phenomena, is a most interesting story.

There is too little space to document the details, which are in any case better suited to a scientific journal, but the points of general interest are as follows. The colony was, almost certainly, founded by birds from Bass Rock, whose members regularly pass Bempton on their migratory, dispersal and, even, foraging journeys. At least three Bass Rock birds, colour ringed as chicks, are breeding on Bempton, which proves that at least *some* are so derived. It is, remember, not only a mainland cliff, but also one composed of sedimentary rock (limestone), hence with very narrow ledges, quite different from the metamorphic rocks which characterise most of the gannet's breeding places. In these senses, Bempton is physically only marginally attractive and suitable for gannets, which may be why it went for so long without them. Some of the sites used would do credit to a kittiwake!

When they did gain a foothold, it was a precarious one. By 1951 there were still only two pairs occupying sites. Between 1951 and the mid sixties, Bempton tottered along, recruiting a few adults. Without these immigrants it could not have survived and would never have shown the exceedingly modest increase that it did (Fig. 10), for simple calculation shows that output would have been too low. Numbers then began to rise, and it is now clear that by the late sixties a threshold had been reached. Between 1967 and 1972 the rise in numbers was equal to the whole of the previous 30 or 40 years' growth of the colony. In the 1970s, numbers increased dramatically. Largely, this has been due to immigration (Fig. 10) rather than to the colony's own output, though the latter is now increasingly capable of fuelling further expansion. Of course one cannot say, from this, that *all* new gannetries depend heavily on immigration, though I consider that they do.

The main effects of increased numbers are increased breeding success; earlier return to the colony and earlier mean laying, and thus fledging, date; increased proportion of immature birds at the colony and increased tempo of activity. These are interesting and worth considering in turn.

Success in the early days at Bempton is hard to interpret, partly because when there are only one or two pairs, the loss of one egg can constitute 50 or 100% failure, and partly because visits in the early years were too infrequent to allow safe conclusions. But in round figures between about 1963, when there were less than twelve pairs, and 1969, by which time the colony had grown to 21 occupied sites, breeding success rose from about 45% to a steady 70–85%. Interestingly, 75% is about the same as that of large, well established groups on Bass Rock. So it seems that as Bempton grew in size it became more successful, until it was comparable with a large and thriving colony. Why should this happen? I do not think it is really mysterious. Put at its simplest, the social (behavioural) stimuli provided by a flourishing colony make each pair 'keener' to breed. All the many behavioural roles that have to be acted-out for successful breeding (site defence, pair co-operation, parental care) are facilitated by the social excitement engendered at a thriving colony. Therefore, pairs in such a colony are more efficient. Although this has not been demonstrated, even the frequency with which the young are fed is probably greater than in a tiny, low-key colony.

The earlier return to the colony, which means more time spent there each season, and earlier mean laying date are susceptible to the same explanation. The attraction of a vigorous, busy colony is bound to be greater and, therefore, return to it earlier than at a small colony. Nowadays, at Bempton, birds are back in January (see Table 13). Once there, exposure to intense territorial and sexual behaviour will affect gonads and thus the date of laying. The mean laying date has advanced from, roughly, early May to about mid April, although recently it has become a little later due to the influx of young breeders. The earlier laying date means that fledging has become progressively earlier. As late as 1970, 61% of chicks fledged in September or October. In 1971 this became 34%, in 1972 37% and in 1973 36%; the majority fledging in the second half of August. The same advance occurred in a small, semi-isolated group on Bass Rock, which, also, grew larger over the same period; and the same reversal of the trend towards earlier laying and fledging occurred, again, due to an increasing proportion of young breeders.

Similarly, too, the dramatic rise in the *proportion* (not just the *number*) of immature-plumaged birds, as the colony grows, probably depends on the twin phenomena of noise and conspicuous display attracting more young recruits, and these in turn attracting their peers. There seems little doubt that immature gannets *are* attracted to their own age groups, so that if the thriving colony attracts a few to start the process, it can thereafter snowball. This, too, is discussed in Chapter 2 when considering the phenomenon of interchange.

If the suggestion that the tempo of activity varies in 'thriving' as against small colonies seems vague, one can offer evidence. Thus, the frequency of specified agonistic behaviour patterns at Bempton was lower than Bass Rock, when Bempton was small, but rose to equal Bass Rock, and even exceed it, as Bempton grew larger (Fig. 38). The surpassing of the Bass Rock level is interesting in that it reflects the rise in the proportion of young site-establishing pairs at Bempton. Such pairs typically are more active in display than are old-established pairs.

CLUBS

The influx of young birds, including immature ones, to a colony, is a suitable point at which to introduce clubs. Probably every gannetry has one, but not by any means in fixed ratio to colony size. Typically, clubs (see plates) are gatherings of adult-plumaged and immature birds, including some one-year-olds, on the outskirts of the breeding colony or, perhaps, on a separate rock nearby. They are characteristically densely packed, though somewhat irregular in spacing, unlike the regularly spaced rows of nesting birds. They are essentially transitory, in that their location may move according to wind direction, but at

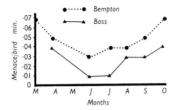

Fig. 38. Seasonal pattern of threat behaviour (menacing) at Bass Rock and Bempton

some gannetries favoured localities always hold some birds, in season. Perhaps the main questions which they raise concern the status of the adult-plumaged birds (are they non-breeders or breeders); the functions of clubs; the factors controlling their size, composition and location. I will take these in turn. To me, it has always seemed highly improbable that 'clubs' could contain off-duty breeders. Gannets are so exceptionally, indeed uniquely, site-attached (as witness their faithful attendance for months before and after breeding, their intense competition for a site and their protracted and frequent territorial display), that it seems almost incongruous to imagine a mature, site-owning gannet spending his time at the gannetry in a club rather than 'on-site'. I say 'imagine' because, as might be expected, I have never seen one of my ringed, breeding birds in a club. More concretely, though, an analysis of the time-spending budget leaves virtually nothing to spare for lounging in a club. After taking into account the time, per day, spent incubating or guarding the site or chick, and the time spent foraging, there is nothing left. Furthermore, if one compares the number of adult plumaged club-birds, even in a large club like that of Bass Rock, with the number of off-duty breeders, it is abundantly clear that only a tiny fraction could possibly be in the club. So one may safely assume that the vast majority, if not all, club birds are not breeding. A few may be young birds with a loose attachment to a new site on which they have not yet bred, but that is about as far as it goes.

Since I have shown that established birds do not take 'rest' years, it follows that adult club birds cannot be breeders taking a year off. I suspect, therefore, that club adults are young birds that are not quite ready to undertake the arduous task of breeding. Lest this should be mis-interpreted may I hasten to add that I do not mean to imply that feeding a chick imposes stress. However, prolonged site attendance reduces foraging time and, in the case of birds that are marginally unfit, or not fully in command of local fishing lore, may be postponed. Or, slight physiological immaturity may have the same effect.

Clubs are far from being just daytime roosts of resting and preening birds. They are often intensely active congregations in which birds establish temporary sites and go through the whole gamut of territorial and sexual behaviour. There is no gannet behaviour that can be seen in a breeding colony that cannot also be seen in a club, with the obvious exceptions of incubation and chick care. It seems fair to conclude that the performance of these social activities is adaptive, and one can easily see how. For example, frequent interaction with 'rivals' and 'mates' perfects the reception of, and response to, the communicative behaviour patterns concerned, as well as 'polishing' their actual motor expression. Probably, too, these activities hasten physiological maturation.

Finally, whilst using the colony outskirts as a 'club', birds find out, from experience, how long it takes to forage in all the local fishing areas; and learn local topography, likewise, and air-currents and the skills of landing under different wind conditions.

As mentioned, the locality, size and composition of 'clubs' varies from colony to colony. Usually, clubs gather where they can take off into the wind, which often means favoured patches on the top of the island or rock, as on Bass Rock, where 2,000–3,000 birds pack densely onto the west and north-west slopes, or if the wind dictates, on the north and east cliff tops. They have been observed to do so from the time records begin, and for at least the last hundred years the size of the club has apparently been of much the same order, which could imply that the colony is autonomous (see below).

Grassholm club, now in the region of 2,000 birds (and as many as 1,500 in 1930 when the colony numbered less than 4,000 pairs), often gathers on the outlying rock to the south of the main island. At Sule Stack, over 3,000 club birds frequent the southern (non-breeding) hump, and the St Kilda club was neatly epigrammed by Martin Martin as the 'barren tribe of Solan geese that never mix among the rest that build and hatch'. Its size is not on record. Canadian gannetries have their club, and sizeable ones have been recorded from the mainland slope of Cape St Mary's, and from Bonaventure Island. Even small colonies, such as Scar Rocks and Bempton, have a few club birds.

Some club birds frequent ledges *below* the main nesting mass, where building would be impracticable on account of occasional surge and spray; there are often some on Bass Rock. Ailsa Craig furnishes an example of a colony in which club birds are relatively few in relation to the size of the colony, and one where they are rarely gathered in a single congregation, but occur in groups on broad grassy ledges at mid-cliff level. In some years the total number of club birds on Ailsa Craig is less than 500.[137] Similarly, Bempton club birds have never gathered in one group, but have used ledges amongst the nesting ledges. The Bempton club has shown rather unusual features, probably because the nature of the cliff is itself unusual for gannets. For many years it was almost impossible to decide whether there *was* one, since mature-plumaged club birds could be distinguished from site-holders only by their more desultory attendance and somewhat shifting locale, both of which are not easy to document. Then, as the colony grew, and many more immature-plumaged birds arrived, the club became more easily recognisable and eventually favoured two broad ledges below the nesting birds. So both Ailsa Craig and Bempton show that the typical club, massed on the fringes or apart from the breeders, is not invariable, though it is easy to see why these two colonies depart from the normal pattern. Thus, Ailsa Craig is exceptional in that the top of the island is virtually unused by nesting gannets; club birds would, therefore, be extremely apprehensive on such ground; they are wary at all times, lacking the strong ties of nesting birds, and to be isolated on top of Ailsa Craig would certainly alarm them. Ailsa Craig is exceptional, too, in having some broad empty ledges amongst nesters. Bempton's unusual circumstances have already been mentioned. I give these details because I think it is important not to confuse the issue by implying that clubs may often be scattered amongst breeders.

Finally, the composition of clubs in terms of the proportions of age classes is rarely known in detail, and may well vary between gannetries and years, but on Bass Rock, in June and July, the club consists of birds in their first, second, joint third and fourth, joint fifth and more than fifth years, roughly in the percentages of 1, 5, 68 and 26. I specify June and July because the first, second and some third year birds are late in coming and early in going. It would be fascinating to have a detailed analysis of the exact proportions, and of the pattern of variation within and between years, for on this much could be built. For example, knowing the productivity of a colony and the mortality rates of the age classes, it would be possible to say whether the club could be made up of that colony's recruits or whether, and at which times, it must contain immigrants. From the discussion of colony interchange (Chapter 2) it will be clear that clubs may be expected to vary substantially between and within years at those colonies subject to influxes of foot-loose 'floaters'. Since birds seem to be attracted to their own year-classes, it may be that two or three-year-olds will peak in certain years or at certain times. Finally, over the long term, it would be enormously interesting to relate the pattern of growth (or decline) in a colony to the preceding pattern of club numbers and composition, on the premiss that 'clubs' feed recruits into the breeding population.

SUMMARY

1. The link between the gannet's exceptionally favourable food situation, and its breeding ecology, is made.

2. Breeding places, overwhelmingly islands and preferably cliffs, are (a) windy (which the gannet's shape and weight requires), (b) well-situated

with regard to food, (c) probably less importantly, safe from some (past) mammalian predators.

3. Gannetries are hugely variable in size but highly consistent in density. Size (above a certain minimum) does not matter, but density does.

4. The advantages of nesting at high density have little to do with economy of space or with predation, and much to do with social stimulation.

5. In a *stable* colony, the mixture of experienced and young birds is the same throughout; the idea that fringes contain more young birds which later try to move to the centre is fallacious, though in an *expanding* colony the fringes do hold proportionately more young birds.

6. The idea that fringe pairs have a lower breeding success than centre pairs is also fallacious, *once the effect of age has been taken into account*, for young birds are less successful than older ones.

7. The gannet's nest is undoubtedly important for the survival of egg and young and much effort goes into maintaining it.

8. The egg is small since large yolk reserves are not required. Those laid earlier in the season are larger than later ones because they come from older females. Two eggs are never, or virtually never, laid, except as replacements.

9. Eggs lost early in the season are usually replaced, sometimes twice. Replacement eggs are less successful than first-time eggs.

10. The chick can be aged with reasonable accuracy by its appearance. It is fed about 2·7 times per day, both parents giving equal shares.

11. Despite guarding the chick unremittingly during its 90 days in the nest, parents manage to spend some 15% of daylight hours together on the nest.

12. The chick rapidly reaches a maximum weight of 4,500 g and fledges with around 1,000 g of fat reserves. *It is not starved before fledging*, though this fact is taking a long time to appear, generally, in the literature.

13. Virtually no gannet chicks die from starvation. Even twins (artificially donated) are well fed and fledge only four days later than singletons.

14. The various parts of the body (bill, wings, tail, feet) grow at different rates and in some cases the adaptive significance can be suggested.

15. The chick spends on average about 90 days (84–97) in the nest and this holds true for young of first time breeders too, showing that their growth is probably equal to that of young from experienced parents. Canadian gannets grow at the same rate as British ones.

16. The peak of fledging (as, of course, laying) varies by two or three weeks at different gannetries, being probably earliest on the Bass Rock (last quarter of August). This may be related to early-season food which determines the time of laying.

17. Breeding success is uniformly and consistently high in the gannet (around 75% fledged from laid), though, probably due to toxic chemicals, Bonaventure has a very low hatching success. First-time breeders have a lower success than experienced ones because they treat the egg and the

newly-hatched chick ineptly, not because they cannot gather enough food for it.

18. Breeding success is influenced by the age (experience) of the female and the size of group (amount of social stimulation), but not by position (fringe or centre) as such. At least on Bass Rock the proportion of birds in 'closed' cliff groups, which attempt to breed in any one year, is lower than in 'open' flatter groups, when these are expanding.

19. Despite being markedly compressed in the time taken to rear young, the gannet's breeding cycle is highly unusual among seabirds in that it is extremely long, due mainly to the pre-laying and post-fledging attendance by parents. The probable reason for early attendance is that it pre-disposes early laying, which in turn gives the young a better chance of survival. The post-fledging attendance cements site-attachment and may pre-dispose an early return the following year.

20. The mean laying date is apparently consistent at a given colony, though varying between colonies. It may be related to the nature of the food supply around the colony and in general is as early as possible. This enhances survival of young.

21. Social (behavioural) stimulation is one of the factors which, by enhancing maturation of gonads, helps to make laying early. Social stimulation is facilitated by dense nesting and is suggested to be the main reason why gannets compete so strenuously for a site in or near others, when there is (often) ample space nearby. Direct reproductive advantage thus attends the acquisition of a *socially* adequate site.

22. Laying date is affected by several other factors, amongst which are: the experience of the male; the length of the partnership; the genome of the female.

23. Canadian colonies compress the pre-laying part of the cycle and the spread of laying, because the high latitude restricts the length of the breeding season. Despite a much later return, they lay comparatively little later than British birds. Social stimulation is suggested to play a part here, too.

24. Gannets, having bred, do not have non-breeding years; though bereavement, egg-loss, etc, imposes inadvertent 'rest' years.

25. They usually do not breed until their fifth or sixth year, having acquired a site the previous year. Males are generally older than females when they enter the colony, and even if the partners are the same age, but slightly immature, the male's plumage is more mature than the female's.

26. The pre-breeding period is probably necessary to acquire local wind and fishing lore and to establish a site, rather than to perfect the physical skills of diving.

27. Gannets usually return to the site and mate of the previous year. Chicks usually return as adults (or sub-adults) to their natal group.

28. Adult annual mortality is about 6% and life expectancy more than 16 years. Some individuals undoubtedly reach 40 years or more.

29. Mortality in the first year of life is over 60% and possibly over 70%.

Much of this is due to starvation. The avoidance of unfavourable weather conditions during the critical two to four weeks after fledging is probably the main factor determining laying dates.

30.   The main causes of adult mortality are accidents at sea (usually man-induced), accidents at the colony and (possibly) the effects of toxic chemicals. Disease and starvation are probably unimportant.

31.   The growth of Bempton is discussed and it is shown that as the numbers rose, breeding success rose, laying became earlier and more immature birds were attracted to the colony. Social stimulation is again implicated.

32.   Gannet 'clubs' are a practically universal feature of gannetries. The adult members are not off-duty breeders. Clubs help individuals to develop their social behaviour.

5: The gannet at sea

I've chased the shouting wind along, and flung
My eager craft through footless halls of air.

Anon

Nowadays, as studies of seabirds at their breeding colonies become increasingly sophisticated and mathematical, the gap between our knowledge of seabirds on land and seabirds at sea becomes wider. Indeed, we know little more than we did 20 or 30 years ago. The reasons are obvious: it is exceptionally difficult to follow or, even, observe them quantitatively, and prohibitively expensive to mount the sort of concomitant studies that are needed. It is easy to say what should be done, but not how to do it. We need details about numbers, distribution and movements in relation to food, weather, moult and the age of the birds. New or improving techniques that might help include radio-telemetry, for following individuals (batteries now last two years or more), refined radar, and computer modelling, but so far as the most basic issue – namely food – is concerned, there can be no substitute for direct and complex knowledge of fish populations and of what the birds are actually taking. So, less should be expected of this chapter than of others.

MIGRATION

The sea lanes around Britain and Ireland are always more or less busy with gannets, and to separate the migration of the newly-fledged youngster, though useful, is to some extent artificial. Nevertheless, I will deal first with this, and later with the distribution and movements of gannets as a whole, throughout the year.

The chapters on ecology and behaviour more or less converge at the point where the fat, black fledgling throws itself precipitately from the cliffs or slopes upon which it has squatted so immovably for three months. As mentioned, its unpractised wings, though a few millimetres short of their full length, can carry it for 4–5 km (2 or 3 miles) on its first flight, but once down on the sea, cannot raise it again. So in August and September, the seas around our gannetries become peppered with swimming juveniles, making their way south in response to an urge as insistent as the migratory one of the swallow. This is *the* critical period in their lives, for the fuel they carry as fat cannot sustain them for long in the face of cruel weather. They are on their own, and simply must become efficient hunters before they weaken.

Most juveniles head south immediately, but some head north then west or east around the top of Britain, or east towards the continental coasts of the North Sea, before going south on a journey which may take them some 5,000 km (3,000 miles), almost to the Equator off West Africa (Fig. 39), where, incidentally, they may overlap with African gannets which have migrated north; ringed African gannets have been recovered north of the Equator in Rio Muni, Cameroun and Nigeria and African gannets have been seen off Ghana.[14] Once they have returned to home waters, few Atlantic gannets will go so far south again. For a brief discussion of the possible advantages of this migration, see Chapter 6.

The first gannets to be ringed were marked on the Bass Rock by Gurney, 40 young and 52 adults, in 1904. Up to and including 1975, on the east side of the Atlantic, 39,392 gannets had been ringed and 2,299 or 6·83% recovered.[123] The recovery rate has increased, incidentally, from 3·2% (up to 1937), 5·4% (up to 1968), 5·65% (up to 1973) to the present 5·78%. This is considerably higher than for the Canadian population (3·8%) or the African and Australasian gannets, probably because the North Sea is a particularly favourable catchment area for the many Bass-ringed birds and because more end up on inhabited stretches of coast, or fall into European hands; both these factors increase the likelihood that the find will be reported. These recoveries can be broken down in many different ways, but the main facts have been fairly clear for a long time and additional recoveries have embellished rather than altered them. The general picture is of a dispersal (in more than one direction) followed by the well known migration down the Atlantic seaboard, as far as Morocco (commonly) and Sénégal, the southernmost recovery being 11° 52' N in Guinea-Bissau. On the way, a few filter into the Mediterranean and penetrate to its eastern limits. After this migration, most young birds stay in waters at least south of Biscay for a year or two before reappearing in home waters. Subsequently, they tend to stay nearer home, though many do move south again, as do many adults. Sir Landsborough Thomson,[128,130,131] who wrote the pioneer papers on gannet migration, divided the areas from which recoveries have been made into four zones, starting with home waters (N) and continuing with successively more distant ones (W and A), to the tropics (T), and these zones will be used here, too. I have myself ringed several thousands of gannets on the Bass Rock, and have made my own analysis of recoveries, which, with Thomson's papers, forms the basis of the present account. There is no reason to think that this bias towards Bass Rock records affects the main conclusions. Nevertheless, as one would expect, the Bass Rock birds provide many more records from the North Sea and its continental coasts, and arrive later in west European waters (Biscay) and presumably, therefore, off North Africa, than Ailsa Craig and (particularly) Grassholm birds, which have a more immediate exit. At any rate, recoveries of birds ringed on Skellig show the same pattern as Bass Rock birds.

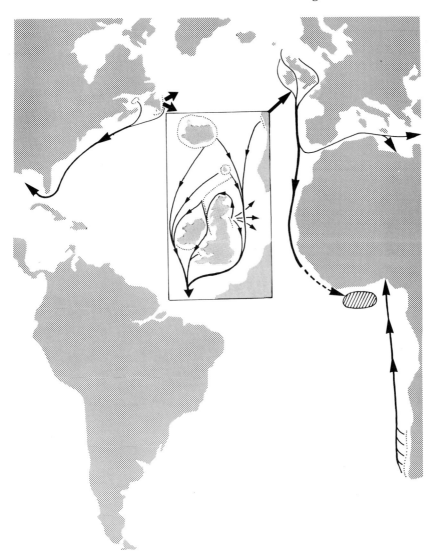

Fig. 39. *General features of migration of juvenile Atlantic gannet; inset shows main routes from breeding areas in eastern Atlantic (indicated by dotted lines). Arrow off southern African coast indicates route of African gannet and hatched area shows possible overlap with Atlantic gannet*

Beginning, then, with Bass birds ringed as chicks in July and recovered during their first year, the records (Figs. 40, 41 and Table 23) show most recoveries in September and October, when many young can be expected to fail in the first stages of their migration. The recovery figures, mine first, followed by all recoveries of Bass Rock birds between July and December of their first year, are: July 0 (8); August 8 (49); September 52 (101); October 100 (194); November 34 (81); and December 9 (33). Many had moved north, including one to the Shetlands, before migrating down the western side of Britain, mainly west of Ireland, to waters in Biscay and off Iberia. Many more had moved across the North Sea. This general picture is the same as that drawn from all Bass Rock recoveries, which show 38 on the continental coasts of the North Sea, from Belgium to southern Norway, and including the approaches to the Baltic.

Most gannets leave the North Sea via the English Channel. Few have reached Iberia by September (Grassholm birds are common there in August) but many by October. Some (I suspect, most) birds continue rapidly south to North African waters just as African and Australasian juveniles carry out their migrations at speed. A juvenile ringed on Ailsa Craig in August was recovered in Morocco 14 days later.[137]

Some birds remain in north European waters throughout their first winter (several are to be seen fishing off the north-east of Scotland in December and January) and the odd first-year bird that turns up at the breeding colony early in the season may well be such. Probably very few return from tropical West Africa in their first year, though they may wander some way back, and large numbers of second-year birds are recovered in zones A and T (Table 24). However, good numbers of second-year birds are recovered in zone W and in home waters between July and November, and most of these, just over a year old, probably *have* returned. Insofar as sight records at Bass Rock are concerned, relatively few such two-year-olds are seen. Most (appearing in May) are late second-year birds which presumably spent a second winter in southern waters. Bass Rock birds in their second year are recovered overwhelmingly (90%) to the east of Britain, but a few mingle with the west coast traffic.

Third-year birds are mostly recovered in home waters from June to October (more than a third of all recoveries). They have probably moved north from mainly west European waters, or from further south, where they may have remained during their second winter. Alternatively they may have moved north twice. More third- than second-year birds stay in northern waters between December and March, although after October some (perhaps most) return some way south, as indeed do a number of adults.

By the time they enter their fourth year almost all gannets are back in home waters and, indeed, some are already established in the breeding colony. Of 105 fourth-year recoveries all but two were in zones N and W, and of 77 recoveries in home waters, 63 fell between April and October, mainly at breeding colonies.

In their fifth year, gannets usually lose all traces of immature plumage. Fifth-year and adult recoveries are almost all made at breeding colonies, but one of my colour-ringed adult males, an experienced breeder, was recovered off Sénégal. Comparably, birds ringed as

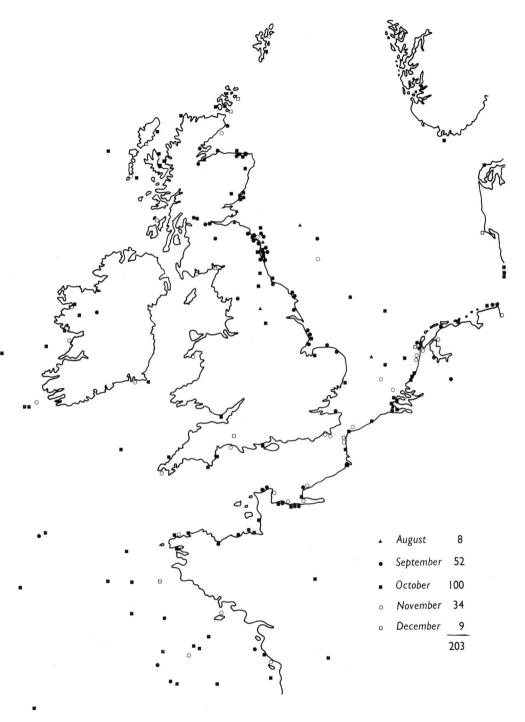

▲	*August*	8
●	*September*	52
■	*October*	100
○	*November*	34
□	*December*	9
		203

Fig. 40. Recoveries August–December of first year gannets ringed as chicks on Bass Rock

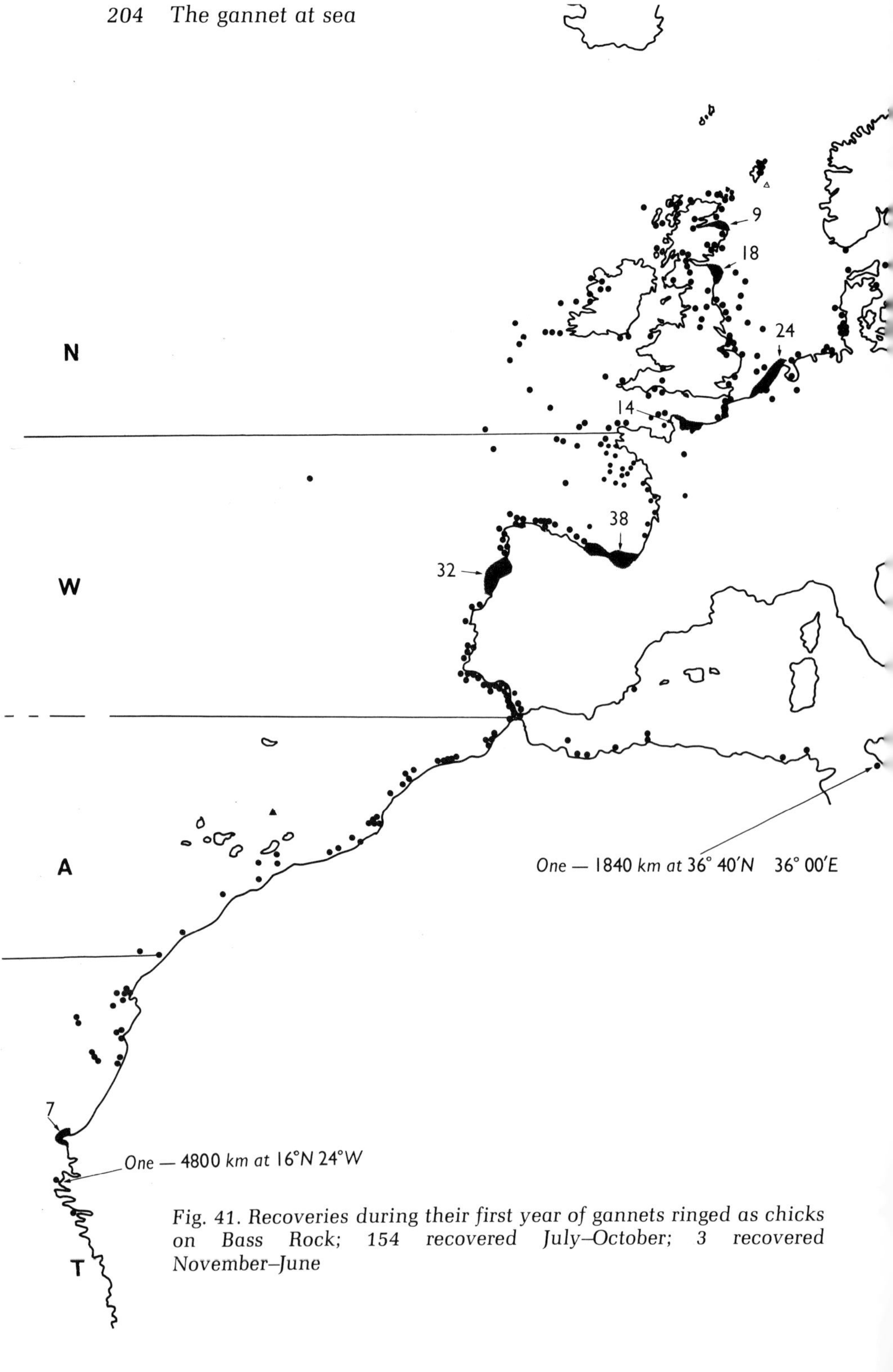

N

W

A

T

One — 1840 km at 36° 40′N   36° 00′E

9

18

24

14

38

32

7

One — 4800 km at 16°N 24°W

Fig. 41. Recoveries during their first year of gannets ringed as chicks on Bass Rock; 154 recovered July–October; 3 recovered November–June

Fig. 42. Recoveries during their second year of gannets ringed as chicks on Bass Rock

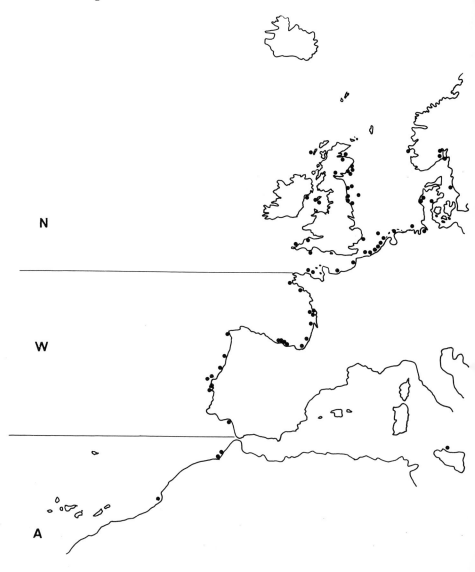

Fig. 43. *Recoveries during their third year of gannets ringed as chicks on Bass Rock*

adults and therefore probably breeding, have been recovered in zone A in winter. Thus some of the many adult-plumaged gannets seen far south of Britain (see below) may be mature, breeding birds. However, most recoveries of birds ringed as adults, and of adult birds ringed as chicks, are within zones N and W (see Table 23).

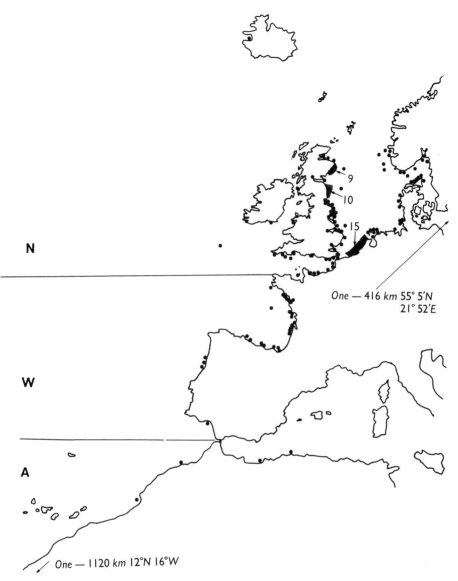

Fig. 44. *Recoveries during their fourth year of gannets ringed as chicks on Bass Rock*

The movement of gannets into the Mediterranean, Baltic and far northern waters deserves special mention. The Mediterranean recoveries, of which there are more than fifty (all except one coming from birds ringed as chicks), indicate merely a trickle from the main southward flow. Numbers in this impoverished sea fall off rapidly with distance, and birds occur on both north and south coasts. There are exceptional records from the Levant, Turkey (Gulf of Iskenderun) and Israel. The ratio of birds recovered in their second rather than their first year is about twice as high as for all birds recovered south of Ushant, which suggests that many of the first-year birds that penetrate the Mediterranean remain there into their second year.

Gannets are uncommon in the Baltic Sea, especially in winter, and most recoveries are in the approaches, although a Bass Rock bird was found in June of its fifth year in Lithuania at about 55°N, 23°E.

Recoveries north of the most northerly British breeding station (Hermaness) (Fig. 45) include birds from Bass Rock, Skellig, Grassholm, Ailsa Craig and Hermaness. They are all within the foraging ambit of Icelandic, Norwegian and Faeroese gannetries; and since all of the recoveries except one were in summer, and most were immature, the birds concerned may have been on extensive foraging trips. Such birds, whether or not attached to a colony, probably spend long periods at sea. Indeed, even breeding adults from Scottish colonies may conceivably forage that far afield.

The migration of Canadian gannets (Fig. 46) follows much the same general pattern, in that the juveniles move south-west (after first

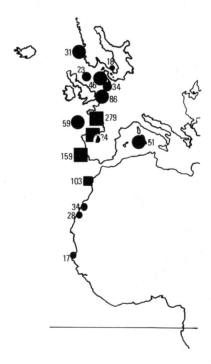

Fig. 45. *Recoveries of gannets in European and NW African waters, from data in Spencer and Hudson (1972, 1973, 1974, 1975). Numbers indicate number recovered in locality of symbols*

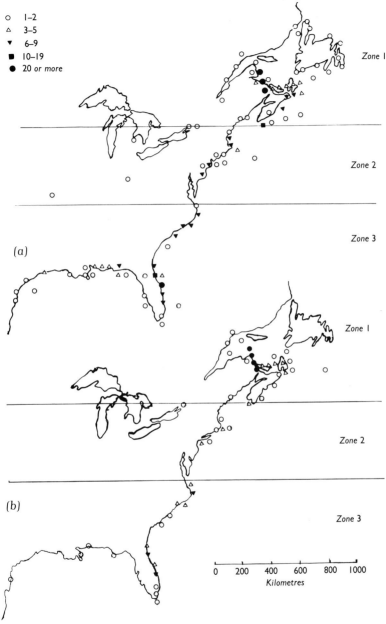

Fig. 46. (a) Recoveries of juvenile gannets ringed as chicks on
Bonaventure Island (from Moison and Scherrer 1973)
(b) Recoveries of adult or sub-adult gannets ringed mainly as
chicks on Bonaventure Island (from Moison and Scherrer
1973)

travelling south-east) to warm waters about as far south as the Mexican border at 26°N, a journey of over 5,000 km (3,000 miles). The general target area appears to be off Florida and it is there, and in the area immediately south of the colonies, that most recoveries have been made. The southward movement gets underway in late September and is very marked by the second quarter of October,[78] there being much less scope than with British gannets for a wide spread in the time of year at which birds fledge; summer closes down decisively at the end of September. By November most juveniles are in the region of Massachusetts, Long Island and New Jersey, and Florida is reached by December. In January, juveniles are common in the Gulf of Mexico and 40% of recoveries are from there, compared with 13% for immature birds and 8% for adults (Table 26).

Canadian sub-adult and adult gannets also move up to 4,000 km (2,500 miles) south each autumn; they are probably forced to vacate home waters more than are eastern Atlantic birds because of the extremely severe winters. Just before the main movement south, adults and immatures are more likely than juveniles, to be recovered to the north-east of Bonaventure Island, presumably due to feeding trips.

First-year birds remain further south than older, but still immature, birds. In February adults are on their way north, reaching home waters by April. The first birds arrive at Bonaventure Island in mid-April and sometimes, by early May, are incubating, up to their necks in snow! Immatures leave wintering areas in March and arrive at Bonaventure Island in May; and, by June, first-year birds are spread out along the coast from Gaspé to the Gulf of St Lawrence. When they arrive at the breeding area, conditions are mild and fish plentiful. The return journey, it seems, is considerably faster than the southward movement (estimated at 4–100 km (3–60 miles) compared with 25–35 km (15–20 miles) per day). Once back in the region of the breeding colony, over 93% of adult recoveries are made within the foraging range of about 60 km (38 miles). Immatures wander more widely (only 27% so recovered), and first-year birds are rarely (6%) found within this distance.

It is a fascinating fact that the two southern hemisphere gannets match the general features of the North Atlantic gannet's migration with uncanny precision, though moving north (African gannet) and west (Australasian), and some possible implications of this are discussed in a brief comparison of the three gannets. The juveniles' intriguing tendency, at first, to move in several directions rather than immediately in the main one, reflects the fact that gannet migration has evolved from sulid dispersal, which typically is in several directions. The mechanism by which they all three cease their purposeful movement at around 4,000 km (2,500 miles) may be the attainment of a particular fish spectrum and climate, or a more precisely programmed tendency to cover a given distance, the means by which this is judged being physiological rather than external.

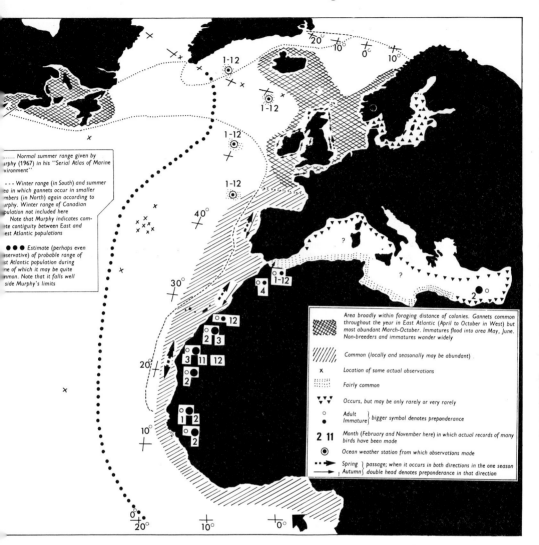

Fig. 47. Main features of distribution of gannets in the eastern North Atlantic

DISTRIBUTION AND MOVEMENTS AT SEA

Gannet migration is not clearly separable from dispersal, nor this in turn from more or less extensive foraging with a seasonal bias. Therefore, the following section, which brings together some observations on the movements of gannets, cannot be neatly analysed in terms of one type or the other. It serves merely to illustrate the scale and complexity of gannet wanderings and their main seasonal features. The complexity is partly because there are several major components (Fig. 47): seasonal movements of adult and immature birds, foraging movements of breeding adults, foraging movements of non-breeding adult and immature birds; and, finally, weather-induced movements. When they overlap, as they often do, the picture can be very confusing.

We may start with a few generalities. At sea, gannets rarely range out over deep water. They are essentially birds of continental shelves, observing the sharp boundary between pelagic and offshore waters. Nevertheless, they have been encountered in mid-Atlantic. They can live at sea indefinitely, roosting on the water in the wildest of winter weather. There is no time of the year at which adults, and every stage of immature gannet, cannot be seen in the North Sea, Irish Sea, off the west and north of Scotland, and off Iceland, although this is not to say that they are equally common in all these areas. They show conspicuous and large scale foraging and migratory movements in the offshore belt around our coasts and off the Atlantic seaboard of western Europe and Africa, which have been recorded from many observation points. Finally, non-breeding birds pursue extensive and probably haphazard summer foraging which can take them almost anywhere within their total range, except, perhaps, to the far south of it. During their movements at sea, it seems that they fly low (in common with most if not all seabirds but in contrast to land birds). A final point concerns the reliability of the observations about to be offered. When struggling to make sense of records which are of different quality and quantity it is well to remember that apparent paradoxes may stem from observer bias and from samples which are simply too small. One should not be too discouraged if the picture, whilst generally coherent, is untidy in places. The St John's Head contribution (see below) is one such. It is worth illustrating some of these points.

Breeding adults begin to forsake their ledges from September onwards, most of them having seen their youngsters depart several weeks earlier. September, October and November are busy times for the sea-watching ornithologist. The sea lanes on calm, autumn days are thronged with traffic. The gleaming, soaring, banking and diving gannet is merely one among many. Skuas, gulls, fulmars, shearwaters, sea-duck, waders, auks, shags and cormorants criss-cross, their shape, flight, and group features providing many a challenge. The really expert sea-watcher, among whose company, sadly, I do not belong, is a testimony to the excellence of the human eye and, even more, to the integrative and interpretive power of the visual cortex. But to return to gannets. Adult birds (including, no doubt, Icelandic, Norwegian and Faeroese) certainly depart in large numbers from the North Sea, and from waters north and west of Scotland and Ireland, to areas south of Ushant, but they do not do so precipitately. Not only is the actual departure spread over many weeks, but the journey is in all probability a leisurely one, with many a digression and backtrack. There are surges, when particular weather conditions stimulate mass movements, but in general it is long-drawn out, incomplete, and merged with the feeding movements of birds that have not yet forsaken their colonies. It is worth repeating that we do *not* know what proportion of adults remain in home waters all winter, nor the 'normal' winter movements and habits of those that go south. However, adults are scarcest in home waters between December and February, and at that time probably well over half or three quarters are south of Ushant, having followed the immatures and non-breeders (more strictly, non-site-holders).

Autumn movements

It will be recalled that these latter groups spend, according to age, May, June and (especially) July, at and around breeding colonies, although they wander extensively. They are the first to go south, even preceding the main movement of juveniles. The flood of juveniles and some adult breeders then follows and finally, after adults have predominated for a period, the movement slackens and dies into the December–February period which, in home waters is quiet. These movements have been logged from many observation points and the results are too complex to be neatly sewn up. Considering observation points clockwise around Britain, we may start with Buchan's out-thrust into the North Sea at Rattray Head, Aberdeenshire, an excellent place from which to monitor passage, since it mostly avoids the feeding movements of birds from west-coast colonies and Bass Rock alike. There, the autumn movement is mainly to the north, peaking in the third week of October and presumably representing Bass Rock birds moving out of the North Sea via the Pentland Firth. Of the birds seen moving north between 27 August and 21 October 1974, 56·5% of 3,540 birds were adult, 23·8% sub-adult and 15·2% first-year.[54] There was also a southerly movement of which 41·9% of 227 birds were first year. This presumably means that relatively few Bass juveniles go north but quite a lot of west coast juveniles move east and then south, or that they were Icelandic and/or Faeroese juveniles. Probably, large numbers of gannets and other seabirds from Atlantic areas north of Scotland move into the rich feeding grounds of the North Sea and thence south in spells of favourable.weather. Of the birds moving south, three-quarters were journeying as individuals, whereas the figure for northward moving birds was only 38·5%, a highly significant difference. Seven per cent of northward movers were in groups of 11–20 birds, and 0·7% in bigger groups still, whereas no southward movers fell into either of these two categories.[54] The meaning of these interesting observations is obscure; possibly more of the southward movers were migrating and more of the northward movers were in fishing (foraging) groups.

Further south, watches from Spurn Head in Yorkshire contrast with those from Aberdeenshire in showing a slightly predominant southerly movement with a strong northerly component. Over five years, between 1 August and 22 October, 7,361 moved south and 5,108 north, a ratio of 1·44:1, though in 1974 (the year best covered) the ratio was 1:2. In August the southerly movement barely predominated (1·3:1) but in September it was 1·97:1. The difference between Spurn and Rattray is probably because more Bass Rock birds feed south of Spurn than north of Rattray. This, added to the passage movement (which involves gannets from elsewhere as well as the Bass), causes the predominance of the southerly trend. The difference between August and September confirms this; in August more birds are seen on feeding movements, and their northward return movement thus diminishes the proportionate preponderance of the southerly movement. Thus, between August and October, Bass Rock birds forage north and south and, at the same time, some disperse or migrate for the winter. The latter are hardly evident in August but become so in September and October. Probably more birds move out of the North Sea southwards than northwards, but both routes are followed.

The only somewhat unexpected feature at Spurn is an apparently strong northerly movement in October, when the return of foraging birds to Bass Rock should be less evident. This may be due simply to the large number of adult birds that remain late (or all winter) in the North Sea. Observations in December and January are too few to show whether this could be so.

Undoubtedly, there is much to be learnt about gannet movements in relation to availability of their main prey species in winter. There is, for example, a vast sprat concentration off north-east Scotland in January, and the movements and availability of other important fish such as mackerel and herring are complex, involving several distinct stocks and pronounced migrations.

Further south, passage off the south-east English coast is notably poor, probably because the birds are out of range of observers.

Continuing around mainland Britain before tackling the (naturally!) complex Irish situation; heavy south-west passage has been seen off Cornwall and off Strumble Head (Wales) in September, and seems totally unexceptional. Off Bradda Head, Isle of Man, gannets can be seen all year. A fairly heavy southward flow, mainly adults, has been noted in late July/early August.[57] Probably, these were the early-leaving non-breeders. No doubt further watches would show that a strong flow continues throughout August, September and October.

The situation becomes complex and over-dominated by foraging and (possibly) variable dispersal movements when one enters the topographically tortured west coast and islands of Scotland, with their concentration of large gannetries. Probably there are few new lessons to be learnt there, but fine illustrations of some old ones. Vast numbers of gannets ply the Minch, rounding the Butt of Lewis both ways, sometimes at the rate of thousands per hour, and tracing a web of routes to and from the great outlying colonies of St Kilda and, to the north, Sula Sgeir and Sule Stack. Undoubtedly, superimposed on these movements are passages north and east, and thus through the Pentland Firth, and

Fig. 48. Simplified scheme of movements around Ireland in 1965. Arrows represent movement of at least 40 birds per hour. The basic trends shown are maintained between March and October (after Hounsome 1967)

south to contribute to the Atlantic flow west of Ireland and through the Irish Sea. Indeed, fairly recent observations off the east coast of Ireland,[57] at Clogher and (a little to the north) at St John's Head, reveal that seabird passage occurs on a larger scale than had been thought; traditionally, it had been asserted that whilst heavy southward passage occurred off the west coast, movements off the east coast were light in autumn, though more marked (northwards) in spring. At St John's Point, though on fairly low figures, passage in August and September was in fact heavier than in spring. Oddly, however, it was predominantly northward.

Again proceeding clockwise, to Carnsore Point and Hook Head on the south-east point of Ireland, the August passage was heavily westwards, containing many immature (including juvenile) birds. Doubtless these were birds about to leave the Irish Sea and join the

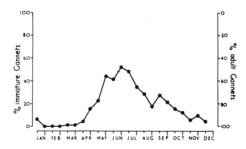

Fig. 49. Proportions of adult and immature gannets passing Cape Clear, Ireland (from Sharrock 1973)

main flow south-south-westwards to Iberia and beyond.

The next, and major, observation point is Cape Clear Island, Co. Cork, from which the densest movements seen anywhere have been recorded, consistently westwards throughout the year.[119] From August to mid-October it averages 279 birds per hour, with peak numbers up to the astonishing figure of 4,000 per hour. The largest numbers of immatures are seen in early August and of adults in early October, which is what one would expect. The immatures (including juveniles) are presumably part of the main stream of Scottish birds leaving the Irish Sea and include an unknown (but potentially large) number of Icelandic and other northern birds. The post-breeding adults, as we have seen, follow later. A minor puzzle is the apparently excessive amount of westing that they seem to make.

The west coast observation points are Brandon Point, Kerry Head, Inishshark, Annagh Head, Erris Head, Aranmore and Tory Island. Here, Little Skellig, the major Irish gannetry, may inject some confusion. Basically, however, the autumn movement is overwhelmingly south down the west coast, tending west at the bottom, both for adults and immatures. This emerges most clearly from the Annagh Head figures (August and September) with the odd twist that the southward pre-dominance of adults was apparently more marked in August than September, but of immatures, more marked in September. At Inish-shark, too, there seemed an unexpected twist in that, whilst adults moved mainly south (though many went north), the immatures moved mainly north (but many went south). I suspect both categories included a lot of fishing birds moving back and forth.

Finally, at Malin Head on the north coast, the very heavy October passage of adults was mainly west,[57] though in August and September it had been equally east and west. Thus, earlier feeding movements had given way to the exit of Scottish birds. The immatures moved mainly west in August, September and October, passage being especially heavy in September. Again, there seems nothing difficult to understand here. Scottish (and other juveniles) were pursuing the Atlantic route to the south-west of Ireland.

Once clear of Ushant, the passage to Biscay and beyond occurs on a wide front. Autumn watches from Cherbourg showed a heavy westward passage, with the proportion of immatures peaking in September and October. Off north-west Spain (Estaca de Bares, Galicia) autumn passage increased steadily from early September to early October. The bulk of early September birds were juveniles, which shows how rapidly they migrate once they can fly. Adults appeared later and the passage built up to impressive proportions. On 5 October, 3,279 gannets were counted in 11 hours, of which nearly a third were apparent adults, and one must remember that, despite their undoubted tendency to follow guiding coastlines, a very large number, probably the bulk, migrate out of sight of land. It was calculated[106] that in 1968 some 29,000 juveniles countable from land passed south off north-west Spain. But in the Bay of Biscay, about 1,000 birds, 80% of them adults, were counted on one mid-October day and there are many more records of very large numbers in Biscay and off Iberia and North Africa. It may not be wild to suggest that more than half of the breeding population, in addition to the younger birds, move right out of home waters in autumn. Adults reach the Straits of Gibraltar in the second half of October and in November, and gatherings may number more than 100, though the wintering population in the Mediterranean is probably hundreds rather than thousands.

On the eastern side of the North Sea, at Blåvand, the westernmost point of Jutland, a heavy passage of gannets occurs every autumn (August to October), two-thirds of them moving south.[73] In May, June and July the movement is mainly north. As elsewhere, immatures are much in evidence from May to July – no doubt part of the large numbers of 'floaters' foraging extensively in the North Sea, Irish Sea and Atlantic.

It is not worth pursuing the return journey in the same detail, and in any case it is not as well documented. Adults are already moving back in January, and it is not surprising that of 1,477 birds moving north off Morocco between April and June, and similarly off Cape Verde in April, a negligible proportion were adult. At Cape Clear considerable numbers of adults are moving in January, representing a distinct increase over December, and passage peaks from March to mid-May (immatures are virtually absent until mid-April). These are almost certainly adults returning, probably rather leisurely, to northern colonies after a relatively brief spell south. Immature birds then flood through in May and June, which accords well with the timing of their appearance and increase at breeding colonies.

It may well be that the many adults which take up their territories early in the year are birds which have remained nearer to home since their dispersal the previous autumn. The alternating north and south movements of gannets off Aberdeenshire between January and May[32] could have been partly foraging movements of Bass Rock birds, but a predominantly northerly passage in April could represent birds returning to colonies to the north and west.

When gannets are back at the breeding colonies, local feeding movements can obscure everything else. As an example of the scale involved, an hourly passage of 2,646 birds, two-thirds going north and one-third south, has been recorded off Unst in June; the traffic around the Hebrides, and that through the Pentland Firth (for example 2,300, mainly east-moving, in one August day) are others.

At sea, gannets may move singly or in loose groups. It is common to see groups of up to 100, and up to 1,000 have been seen off Cape Clear, though to what extent this was part of a fishing flock is not clear. There may be patterns of grouping characteristic of birds on passage; off Aberdeenshire, as mentioned, birds moving north did so in significantly larger groups than those moving south. Naturally enough, they appear to use their normal foraging behaviour at all times, rather than having a distinctive, more direct, or higher passage flight. They will sometimes check and dive, or double back for some distance, whilst nevertheless maintaining a general direction. But they do not usually move in skeins when outward bound or on passage; this distinctive mode seems to be practised mainly by laden birds returning to their colonies.

Gannets are powerful birds and seem little affected by weather, though there is some indication that juveniles are more strongly affected by wind than are adults; for instance, off north-west Spain, north-westerly winds drifted juveniles inshore more than they did adults. They move in winds up to force 8, or in calm anticyclonic conditions. Several authors correlate southerly movements with brisk north-westerly winds, and peak northerly migration off Morocco and Brittany has been associated with strong north-easterly and south-easterly winds respectively. In autumn, North Sea movement is often associated with calms between depressions or with clearing, frontal conditions. Almost everywhere, gannets tend to move mainly in the early morning, though passage continues all day and may be heavy in the evening.

Canadian waters

There are several records of gannets in mid-Atlantic (Fig. 47), and sightings off Greenland and north Labrador that provide possible stepping stones between west and east. Nevertheless, it is probably safe to assume that there is no significant interchange between the two populations. However, as mentioned earlier, it is impossible to distinguish a Canadian gannet from a European one and I suggest that selection pressures are so similar on both sides of the Atlantic that no differentiation is possible, rather than that there is considerable gene flow between the two populations.

Canadian gannet movements have been little watched, but recently their distribution and abundance at sea, in the area of Nova Scotia, St Lawrence, Newfoundland and Labrador, has been investigated.[15] From distribution maps covering March and December it is clear that, outside foraging distance from the colonies, there are extremely few gannets to be seen in the north-west Atlantic. The transects extended to 40° W but the extremes at which *any* gannets were seen, and then usually less than one bird per hour, were: March 53°W; April 48°W; May 48°W; June 48°W; July 46°W (probably nomadic non-breeders as in the eastern Atlantic); August 48°W; September, none east of Newfoundland; October 47°W; November and December, none east of Newfoundland. Northwards the transects ranged from 40°N to 58°N and gave the following results: March 43°–47°N; April 42°–47°N; May 42½°–52°N; June 43°–53°N; July 43°–52½°N; August 44°–54°N; September 44°–49°N; October 42½°–49°N; November/December 44°–47½°N. Birds were seen mainly in the Gulf of St Lawrence, off the east coast of Newfoundland, off Cape Breton (where they have previously been seen in abundance) and around the Bay of Fundy. Other, more casual observations, indicate the area around the confluence of the Gulf and Labrador streams (around 41°N, 66°W) as a good one for gannets. The offshore waters used for the southward migration extends merely to about 300 km (185 miles).

That just about sums up present understanding of Atlantic gannet movements, and despite local and seasonal complexities, the picture is reasonably clear. It is a bird specialised for existence in the cold and stormy waters of the north, but retaining, particularly in the case of the unpractised young birds, the need to retreat southwards for the most challenging months of winter. First the wandering immatures and non-breeders, then the newly fledged young, and finally the post-breeding adults disperse and then migrate south. Southward bound birds from the most northerly stations move west of Ireland, through the Irish Sea and probably through the North Sea also. Scottish birds do likewise, reaching the North Sea via the Pentland Firth. Some east coast birds move north, before gaining the west coast routes. Superimposed on these basic movements are substantial and seasonally protracted foraging movements, some of them extensive and ill-defined, others quite simple north–south or east–west return journeys.

FORAGING AND FEEDING

We have not, however, quite finished with the gannet's maritime activities, for we must discuss its foraging and fishing behaviour.

The ways in which a seabird relates to its food supply basically determine its breeding ecology and I hope Chapter 4 has traced these relationships. Four aspects of the gannet's feeding biology are worth recalling as an introduction to this section.

(a) It is a specialist sulid, having penetrated the cold and often stormy waters of the sub-arctic and northern seas where it is now the *sole occupant of a rich feeding niche*.

(b) Its food is exceptionally abundant and nutritious (large, oil-rich, shoaling fish) but is sometimes unavailable for fairly long periods and often has to be sought and caught under rigorous conditions (short days, strong icy winds, sleet, snow and rain).

(c) To cope with these features, gannets have evolved their unique combination of weight, size and shape.

(d) The important ways in which the gannet's food impinges on its breeding ecology are: (i) it determines the length of the breeding cycle – perhaps especially the time of year at which it can begin; (ii) it determines the timing of egg-laying and the rate at which the chick can grow (and indirectly, by allowing rapid deposition of extensive fat, it permits the unique lack of post-fledging feeding of the young by its parents); (iii) thus it determines fledging dates; (iv) it probably determines the length of the pre-breeding period. One cannot really understand gannet foraging and fishing without taking these factors into account.

Foraging behaviour comprises the actual hunting method and the logistics of hunting. The former we may describe in conjunction with the diving which consummates it, but the latter deserves a brief mention first. By comparison with most other British seabirds, the gannet takes rather lengthy foraging stints, anything from around three hours to between two and three days. The length varies between sexes, between individuals, between colonies and between the different phases of the breeding cycle (see Table 6). Males spend much longer than females at the nest, before the egg is laid, take longer spells of incubation and slightly longer spells guarding the chick. Correspondingly, their time away foraging is less than the female's. Before the egg is laid, males guard the empty nest for about 40 hours at a time (females 28 hours) but these stints become significantly shorter just before the egg hatches. On Bass Rock, the chick is guarded for spells of about 21 hours by the male and 19 hours by the female. All these points are important bits of the feeding/breeding jigsaw puzzle.

In the most seasonally forward colonies (Bass Rock and Bempton among them) the pre-laying spells of attendance at the nest are taken early in the year, during the dark and stormy days of late winter. At this time gannets are to some extent living on the fat deposited during their nomadic wanderings of the preceding months, when they had all day to forage and rest. Obviously, they could not afford to spend a great deal of time in energy-consuming display on site (which they do), if they had also to spend most of their time searching for food. So they must know where to go. This, I think, is the basis of the differences in the timing of breeding at different colonies. The early-season food is not the same for all colonies. For Bass Rock birds, as mentioned, it is, importantly (if not predominantly), sand-eels and perhaps sprats, which are abundant in mid-North Sea; for Ailsa birds, the Ballantrae Bank herrings; for Icelandic birds perhaps the capelin or saithe and also herrings. Later, incubation is more peaceful and stints are shorter. Then, when the young hatch, comes the great mackerel feast, important to all gannets.

Thus one can see the possibility that each colony demands of its residents a considerable experience and knowledge of seasonal food sources, which is probably why gannets require two or three years as pre-breeders in the area.

As to actual foraging, we know that gannets can fly at 65–80 km/h (40–50 mph). This, at a conservative estimate, gives breeders a range of 320–480 km (200–300 miles) from the colony, and non-breeders much more. They leave and return at all times of day except during the hours of darkness; landing and taking off is too dangerous then, and if they arrive too late, they sit on the sea and come in with the dawn. How they organise their foraging time we do not know. Probably, they will often fly more or less directly to a known locality (say, for Bass Rock birds, Belhaven Bay, St Andrews Bay, the Farne Deeps, the Dogger Bank, or other North Sea fishing grounds), though always ready to use opportunities for feeding on the way, signalled by the diving of other gannets. Thus they blend experience of known localities with opportunism, in which their dazzling plumage plays a key role by advertis-

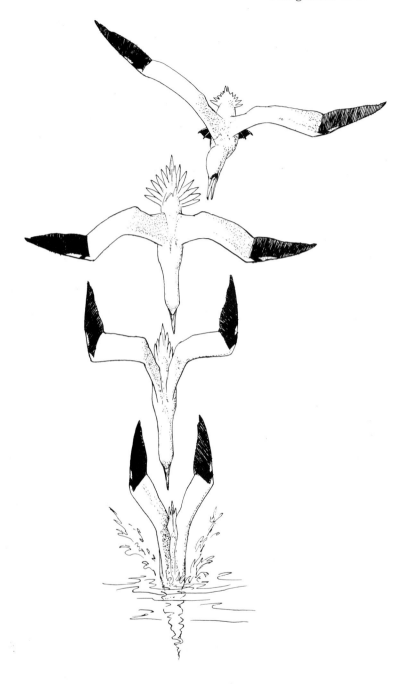

Fig. 50. Wing positions of diving gannet

ing from afar the presence of fish. It would be useless to try to pin-point the preferred feeding localities of each major gannetry. The west coast ones must greatly overlap, and the extensive wanderings of non-breeders blur the picture. Furthermore, there have been no studies using marked individuals identifiable at sea.

Fishing techniques

When flying to cover distance, rather than searching, gannets fly low, with fairly continuous wing-beats of between 170–190 a minute, gliding now and then and frequently angling and banking. They may, even when flying in this manner, suddenly check and dive, but their hunting behaviour when fishing seriously is rather different. In the presence of a shoal they beat up-wind with downward pointing beak, before either diving, or circling to repeat the process. They do this from just above the surface or from as much as an estimated 27 m (90 ft), though 9–15 m (30–50 ft) is probably the usual range.

The gannet's dive (Fig. 50 and plates) like the peregrine's stoop, is a marvel of co-ordination that automatically induces naturalists to reach for the purple ink. One dive is impressive enough; the massed diving of excited gannets can be appreciated only in the flesh, or on film. Starting from the normal height of about 9 m (30 ft) they tip steeply, or gradually, into a gravity-plunge. Sometimes they will accelerate with power-strokes. They may fall into a long, straight plunge at a constant angle, sometimes vertical; or, more spectacularly, manoeuvre on the way down, angling, adjusting, half-turning, even cork-screwing or angling beyond the vertical before striking the water. Just before entry, the wings are extended backwards, close to the body, wing tips beyond the tail, and the bird penetrates the water like an arrow head. The neck, which is enormously strong, may be shortened or extended during these manoeuvres.

A gannet may be travelling at more than 100 km/h (60 mph) when it hits the water, often with a leaden thump that resounds for hundreds of metres on a calm day and speaks volumes for the efficacy of the bird's cushioning of air-sacs. Its passage through the water churns up a milky wake through which the bird is seen as a pale green blob fizzing into the depths. They probably do not penetrate much more than 3·5 m (15 ft) as a result of the unaided dive, but perhaps occasionally descend as far as 12 to 15 metres (40 or 50 ft) by swimming, using wings and feet. Reports of gannets diving to 30 m (100 ft) and more are probably due to mistaken interpretation of the evidence. Gannets brought up in nets may have been trapped when the nets were already on the way up. Nevertheless one must allow the possibility that (though rarely) they dive deeper than I have suggested, for it seems likely that those who relate the stories are well aware of all the possibilities and have reason, still, to make their claims.

Most submergences, though, are surprisingly brief, lasting usually between 5 and 7 seconds, sometimes 10 seconds and occasionally as long as 20 seconds.[112] This does not allow much time for underwater pursuit by swimming, though this does occur; cormorants, by contrast, sometimes remain submerged for more than a minute and emperor penguins for more than 10 minutes. Gannets often emerge facing in a direction different from the one in which they entered, mainly because they emerge facing into the wind; due to manoeuvring in the dive they may have entered the water cross-wind or down-wind. They may rise immediately from the surface, gaining a metre or two before diving again, the whole making a perfect arc. The wings are not used when rising to the surface. Birds that take flight immediately after surfacing probably have not been successful, whereas those that shuffle-bathe excitedly, dip their beaks (drinking or false-drinking) and head shake, probably have swallowed a fish underwater. Sometimes, the fish is brought to the surface, shaken vigorously, tossed, juggled and swallowed, usually, but not always, head-first. Very rarely, a gannet actually takes flight whilst holding the captured fish in its beak.[20]

We know little about the actual mechanics of prey capture. First, the gannet obviously does see its quarry before it plunges, and tracks it all the way down. The exquisite manoeuvrings are evidence of this. Most likely, the gannet takes its deeper prey on the way down, by which time it will have re-oriented and begun pursuit; or on the way up if its prey is near the surface. Gannets do not dive with their beaks open and it would hardly be possible to open them whilst still under the full impetus of a powerful plunge, in other words whilst still near the surface. Shallow dives may be of this kind, a plunge being followed by a rapid turn and an attempted capture. Sometimes gannets undoubtedly spear large fish, and indeed a gannet was recovered with the carcase of a puffin round its neck! It has been suggested[6] that the terrific impact of a full-blooded dive stuns fish which are just below the surface, the blow being transmitted by the water rather than absorbed, and Barlee has himself stunned a large pike by hitting the water with an oar.

In addition to plunging, gannets have been recorded swimming among fry and scooping them up; fishing on foot in shallow, sandy bays, presumably for sand-eels; and diving from the surface and pursuing fish by swimming with strokes of half-opened wings, as does the brown booby. Booth's captive gannets dived from the surface 'in a manner closely resembling the plunge made by a coot'.

Although gannets often hunt singly, they are undoubtedly communal feeders, congregating in masses, up to a thousand or more, typically above shoals of herring or mackerel. Contrary to what one might suppose, the conspicuous white plumage of the gannet is not merely an inadvertent 'marker'. A gannet does not give the show away, and attract others, because it cannot hide its plunges. On the contrary, the dazzling plumage, as Darwin remarked, is a positive attractant. Gannet plumage has evolved because it is an *advantage* to the diving bird to attract others to the spot, and attract them it certainly does. Many observers relate the dramatic way in which a fishing flock crystallises and grows, with birds streaming in from every side. The signaller, as well as the responder, derives benefit from communal fishing. Shoals of fish that are subjected to a continuous hailstorm of diving gannets probably become fragmented, disoriented, confused, and greatly fatigued by frequent use of their rapid-swim muscles, thus falling an easier prey to each gannet than if the latter were hunting on its own. It is a question of helping oneself by helping one's neighbour; the latter is not acting as a competitor in the ultimate sense, even if he is going for the same shoal. It is understandable, therefore, that selection pressure has favoured the evolution of the most advertant plumage (as indeed the gannet's is) and the response of conspecifics to it. Furthermore, it is not surprising that under these circumstances gannets often have the chance to 'gorge themselves silly'. It is 'fortunate' that this is exactly what they are morphologically equipped to do, with fat-banks to replenish against lean days, and greatly demanding young to feed in record time!

When in full cry, they become hysterically active. The splash of a lobbed stone will precipitate simultaneous plunges from several birds and as the frenzy grows, the living projectiles rain down within inches of each other, or of boats. Nor do they always miss the boats. They may dive into nets full of fish, into scuppers, onto decks, into holds – even, it is recorded, into a fish-curing shed in Penzance. Most ringing recoveries at sea are from birds handled by fishermen. In full spate, it is no wonder that some will be fooled by a fish tied to a board, and break their necks, as fisherman traditionally relate since before Martin Martin visited the St Kildans. In fiction, L. A. G. Strong, in *The Brothers*, caused one brother to murder the other by having him towed along in the water with a fish tied to his forehead, tempting gannets to do the rest. There is even a recent record of a gannet following a plough, with a cloud of gulls, near Lochgilphead. Doubtless the sight of the gulls and the beat of a diesel engine triggered trawler-scavenging behaviour in the gannet. They quickly become conditioned to the noise of lifting gear on boats and will join a boat in response to this before there are any fish to be seen.

Trawler scavenging, for whole fish and offal, is common, though gannets tend to stream out to boats operating nearby rather than to follow them for long periods as gulls will. They are said to dominate gulls, skuas and fulmars in competition for offal, and in sheer swallowing power they would be hard to equal. Here, too, they lose all caution, and swallow anything that comes their way, including bread, rubbish, and anything that glints like a fish. A 60 cm (2 ft) brass welding rod, and a long loop of iron wire, among other objects, have been taken from gannets which mysteriously sickened and died. At night, gannets will dive amongst boats which are gutting their catch by artificial light, and, in their eagerness, a few birds have been seen to shear off a wing against wire hawsers.[50]

Gannets continue diving even in extremely strong winds when sheets of spray are being blown from the surface, but they do not fish, nor even fly much, in winds stronger than Beaufort force eight.[112] It is possible that they prefer some wind to a flat calm, not only because it helps their flight; a disturbed surface may, by refraction, obscure the fishes' view whilst still allowing the bird to discern enough to dive accurately (it is even possible that gannet lenses have polarising powers). It has been reported that they successfully caught pollack in rough seas off Eddystone but not in calm waters.

Except when gathered at a shoal it is rare to see gannets flying at sea in groups of more than 10–30 birds. Usually, they return to the colony in conspicuous skeins most commonly of 10–20 birds, though sometimes up to 70–80 and, very rarely, more. Interestingly, these skeins often contain immature birds of any age, but rarely if ever consist solely of immatures. It is as though the visual stimulus of an adult is required to initiate skein-formation; an immature will tag onto an adult, and an adult to another adult, but not an immature to an immature. The same is apparently true of boobies. The red-foot, incidentally, often flies out from its colony in groups which sometimes approach skein-formation, but I have not seen gannets do so. One simply does not see gannets set off fishing. They slip away in ones or twos, sometimes after gaining height in a thermal. By contrast, the orderly skeins of returning birds are immediately recognisable, even among a mass of circling birds.

Naturally, fishermen have developed considerable feeling for gannets and if some of it is hostile, leading to the perpetration of miserable cruelties such as tying heads to legs and releasing the birds to starve, much of it is sympathetic, admiring and, in pre-technology days, highly practical, as the following lovely excerpts about Clyde fishermen, collected by Angus Martin, illustrate. Martin's interpolations are marked 'A.M.'.

A.M.: 'That imperial fish-hunter, the gannet, unwittingly led many fishermen to great catches. His presence was always investigated if his behaviour suggested that he might be working on herring. Indeed, summer daylight fisheries were periodically based on the presence of great concentrations of the birds. The warm summer sun would bring to the surface banks of *Calanus*, to which the herring, too, rose and "fed in the sun". Over the shoals ranged the gannets, and constantly watchful of these industrious birds the fishermen ranged, too, on the bright sea. Daylight fishing was uncertain work, however, as the herring were able to see the nets set around them, and might evade capture by "dooking" below the soles before the net was closed. "Ye missed them of'ner than ye got them," John McWhirter remarked ruefully.'

But not always; David Maclean: 'We owe a great lot tae the gannet. I've got a thousan' poun' for a shot [of nets] on a gannet. A gannet strikin ... it's no' an infallible thing ... Ye know perfectly well he must be strikin on somethin other than herrin, but if ye see him comin down straight, nine times out o' ten he's on herrin. An if ye see him in on the shore-head, it's mostly in on scaffas an wee cudainns an things lik that ... My Father shot one day at a place they caal Whitefarland an got a grand shot o' herrin, an there wis boats passin where the gannet struck – They could've got the shot before him. I don' know whoot made him shot there, but he shot, an a big fishin we got.'

A.M.: 'A gannet prowling in the sky with a peculiar persistence was an almost sure indication that a shoal of herring was below it. "When ye see them hingin' yon wey, cockin' their nebs," said Donald McIntosh, "that's when the herrin' wir right thick." Explanations of the phenomenon of the uncertain bird were offered by Robert MacGowan and James Reid. The former remarked: "We always knew when a gannet circles round and round [that] it's on a spot. It must just be waitin' to get the edge o' the herrin'." The latter remembered: "We used tae say about a gannet comin' along an' seein' herrin' – if he made a dive an' then turned back: 'Oh, they're too thick'. And we'd ring on that sign." A high vertical plummet was an almost infallible indication. If the bird was working on sile close to the surface, his dive was shallow and angled, though I have heard of gannets fishing, with that technique, on herring feeding close to the surface; but it was evidently not a frequent phenomenon.'

The herring gull did it, too: Henry Martin: 'The proper herrin gull at wan time in the fisherman's life wis a sure sign at certain times o' the year, when there'd be nae gannets or anythin else in it. The proper kinna gull wis a sure sign o' herrin. Jeest the wey ye'll see a gannet prowlin roon ae roon an no strikin intae the watter at aal. That's another sure sign. There's maybe an obstruction that's keepin it fae strikin.'

The winter 'spawny herring' on the Ballantrae Banks attracted tens of thousands of gannets from the nearby colony of Ailsa Craig. John McWhirter recalled the spectacle: 'I could safely say that [there] wis a solid mass o' herrin' on these banks for aboot five miles. Ye could hardly see the sky wi' gannets. Ye wir almost afraid tae sail on it. No' an odd gannet hittin' here an' there – they wir comin' pourin' oot the sky lik' shrapnel the whole blessed day fae mornin' until night. A skyfu' o' gannets pourin' down . . .' The Ayrshire fishermen called the formations of fishing gannets rallies. 'They'd gather, just a few,' said John Turner McCrindle, 'an' they'd go round an' round till the sky wis white. Ye could hear the noise a mile away, them goin' down plop, an' the odd time ye saw the unfortunate one that had been het by some o' the others.'

And it is by no means only the gannet that tells a tale to the fisherman. They know how to interpret the herring's mood; is it jumping, then it's likely there are millions more below it, and they're steady, unlikely to 'dook'. Sometimes they 'just mak' a spleeter wi' thir tail; . . . we used taw say "aye, that's gleshans aal right". If they're playing, they're in 'dookin' mood, hard to catch, or maybe they're shifting grounds'. Donald McIntosh: 'On a dark night, if you hear herrin playin, they're shiftin. But they'll never shift wi' the moon'. The banks of 'red-feed' [*Calanus*] that used to concentrate herrings are apparently now much scarcer. Then, too, the fishermen listened for herring on calm nights, felt for them with long poles, watched for the streaming clusters of bubbles ('putting up' or 'belling') or, at night, for 'the burning' or phosphorescence. And they looked for 'buckers' (porpoises), whales and basking sharks. 'It was all eyes an' ears ... Every fish has a distinctive noise as it leaves the water an' goes back in.' ('Ginger' Reid). The fishermen even smelled herring.

When fishermen came into an area where gannets were resting full-bellied on the surface after intensive feeding, they would prod one with an oar or otherwise alarm it, so that it regurgitated the content of its stomach to lighten itself and take off. In that way, they discovered whether or not the birds had been feeding on herring. Eight or nine herrings were frequently 'bouked' up by a disturbed bird.

There was a belief among some of the fishermen that gannets were prone to blindness. 'The lenses o' his eyes, wi' so much divin' intae the waater, get hardened, an' he loses his sight,' said John Turner McCrindle. Fishermen occasionally saw 'blind' birds, flapping unseeingly away from the boats. This is not likely to be the correct interpretation. It may be that such birds are merely overladen and their floundering flight gives an impression of blindness. Natural selection would hardly produce a specialist plunge diver with such a weakness, and it is certain that gannets can endure at least 40 years of diving. Not many live beyond that. Getting tangled in nets is much more of a danger; many times, over 100 birds have been drowned in a Ballantrae net, and earlier I cited a similar figure for gannets hooked on lines.

It is a remarkable fact, which Booth noticed and I and others have many times confirmed, that gannets 'know' the boats in the area around the colony and stream in scores to 'investigate' a strange one. They are similarly attracted to a wounded gannet, or one behaving oddly, as for example with netting attached.

It may be of interest to note, briefly, the ways in which other sulids feed. All are plunge divers, but show a great range of sizes, weights and proportions (bill length, depth, wing length in relation to body size, tail length and so on). These differences undoubtedly relate to differences in foraging, fishing and food characteristics though the details are totally obscure. In general, though, the pan-tropical boobies, which are always much lighter and usually smaller and with less powerful bills than gannets, have to cope with more dispersed and scarcer food, probably nearer the surface, smaller and less powerful than (say) a large mackerel. It is better for pan-tropical boobies to forage singly, and typically they do so. One booby, the blue-foot, has evolved apparently genuine collaborative hunting. This is more than simple communal diving. It is plunging, co-ordinated by a special signal (a vocalisation) which perfectly synchronises the dives of several birds (Fig. 51). The male blue-foot (and also the brown booby) has specialised in inshore fishing, often diving into water 60 cm (2 ft) deep, or less. The males, in particular, possess unusually long tails (presumably to help them pull out of a dive so that they do not impale themselves on the bottom) and are particularly small, the sex-difference in weight being some 10 times greater than in the gannet. On a broader canvas it may be remarked that

Fig. 51. Group diving by blue-footed boobies

plunge diving is found in remarkably few seabirds. Outside the diving members of the Pelecaniformes (gannets and boobies, tropicbirds and brown pelican) only one or two shearwaters and terns really plunge. The commonest feeding methods are surface dipping and pursuit swimming after diving from the surface.

Food

'As greedy as a gannet' is no empty phrase. A gannet can swallow four large mackerel in succession, ten herrings or a codling 45 cm (18 in) long and thicker than a man's forearm at the head. It will stuff itself so full that it cannot rise from the surface. On one occasion, becalmed and satiated gannets were drifted inshore and killed by the cartload at Sennen Cove in Cornwall. Captive gannets take up to 1,000 g (36 oz) in a meal and up to seven large herrings per day. My birds accepted, also, whole or cut-up flatfish (Pleuronectids) and often refused food for a day or two after a heavy meal, but they were of course inactive.

Herring and mackerel are undoubtedly the gannet's main food fish, though I suspect that in some localities they depend heavily on other species, at least at certain times of year (for instance, capelin off

Norway, coalfish off Iceland, sand-eels off the Bass Rock).

Gannets will take almost anything they can get, and the list of recorded prey species is a long one: In the east Atlantic, recorded prey species are: coalfish or saithe *Gadus virens*; cod *Gadus morrhua*; codling *Trisopterus minutus*; haddock *Melanogrammus aeglefinus*; whiting *Merlangus merlangus*; herring *Clupea harengus*; sprat *Sprattus sprattus*; pilchard *Clupea pilcharda*; mackerel *Scomber scombrus*; hake *Merluccius* spp.; gurnard *Trigla* spp.; sand-eels *Ammodytes ammodytes*; garfish *Belone belone*; capelin *Mallotus cillosus*; pollack *Pollachius pollachius*; anchovy *Engraulis encrasicolus*; and salmonids *Salmo* spp. (Witherby *et al.* 1948; pers. obs.). Reinsch saw gannets taking the following: *Arengus minor*; anchovy *Engraulis encrasicolus*; shads *Alosa* spp.; smelt *Osmerus eperlanus*; garfish *Belone belone*; cod *Gadus morrhua*; haddock *Melanogrammus aeglefinus*; saithe *Pollachius virens*; pollack *Pollachius pollachius*; pout *Trisopterus luscus*; codling *Trisopterus minutus*; whiting *Gadus merlangus*; *Boreogadus esmarki*; horse mackerel *Trachurus trachurus*; red mullets *Mullus* spp.; sea bream *Pegallus* spp.; grey mullets *Mugil* spp.; sand-eels *Ammodytes* spp.; blue whiting *Micromesisteus pontassou*; dolphin fish *Coryphaena* spp.; ling *Molva byrkelange*; *Lycodes* spp.; cat-fish *Anarhichas* spp.; lemon sole *Microstomus kitt*; dab *Limanda limanda*; rough dab *Hippoglossoides platessoides* and plaice *Pleuronectes platessa*. Perry[104] records them gorged with eels off Lindisfarne (in October up to 60 vomited). Palmer[100] adds capelin *Mallotus villosus*; menhaden *Brevoortia* spp. and squid *Loligo* spp. from the western Atlantic. Dogfish *Squalus* spp. apparently are not eaten but probably all other fish will be accepted. Reinsch states that gannets will not take 'free' crustacea or echinoderms but ingest them with fish. Offal from fishing boats is greedily devoured and even bread and other waste food has reportedly been taken. As mentioned previously, lethal metal rubbish is sometimes swallowed, presumably because it glints like a fish. Little is known about preferred size of prey. Gannets will take up to 70 small sand-eels or one huge codling, and it would be surprising if their bio-energetics dictated a precise system of reward-per-unit effort, though in small passerines this probably is the case. Gannets have too much lee-way in time, and a too-wide range of prey, for such a balance to be critical. Nonetheless, we have everything to learn about the effects of a changed prey-spectrum on seabirds. Since the demise of the herring, the commercial fishing pressure on mackerel is intensifying massively. Sprats and sand-eels, also, are being fished much more than ever before. Overfishing in the North Sea, and possibly off the west coast of Britain, is leading to changes in the proportions of the various species and in the year-classes represented at any time. This could conceivably exert a powerful long-term effect on the breeding biology of gannets and other seabirds, by altering the nutritional equation in terms of catch composition and the time needed to gather food. This, in turn, could affect reproductive success. All of which is interesting, but beset with so many unknowns that Heisenberg's uncertainty principle is simple by comparison. Nevertheless, man-induced changes in the food of gannets, and other seabirds, could be the most potent factor in future changes in their numbers and breeding biology.

SUMMARY

1.   Little is known about the gannet's life at sea and the marine factors underlying it.

2.   The juvenile's southward migration begins 'on foot'. It carries enough fat to sustain it for perhaps a little more than a week.

3.   By 1975, 38,805 gannets, mainly chicks, had been ringed on the east side of the Atlantic and the recovery rate had increased from 3·2% (up to 1937) to 5·8% (up to 1975). The figure for Canadian recoveries is 3·8%.

4.   Most recoveries of birds in their first year occur in September and October, and are of birds that fail in their southward migration, probably mainly due to weather-induced starvation.

5.   They move south rapidly, and some reach African waters in less than a fortnight.

6.   Some birds, however, remain in north European waters throughout their first winter.

7.   But most birds remain in southern waters for at least two winters. Even some breeding adults move as far as Sénégal.

8.   Some late first-year, many second-year, probably most third-year and virtually all fourth-year birds return all or part of the way to home waters and some early fourth-year birds are already established in a breeding colony.

9.   A number of birds penetrate the length of the Mediterranean and some go north to the Baltic approaches.

10. Canadian gannets go south to the Gulf of Mexico and there are no records of young birds remaining in home waters in winter. Adults show a greater tendency to move south for winter than in the eastern Atlantic.

11. The distances moved by Atlantic gannets (up to some 5,000 km (3,000 miles)) is matched by those moved north and west by African and Australasian gannets respectively.

12. Gannet movements around Britain are massive and complex, the picture confused by the merging of foraging birds of different status with dispersing and migrating birds. Gannets may be seen off the entire British coast in any month of the year.

13. The autumn movement is first of sub- and young (non-breeding) adults from the breeding colonies, then of the year's crop of juveniles, and thirdly of breeding adults.

14. The gannet's feeding behaviour is discussed in relation to its breeding ecology.

15. Breeding gannets probably forage up to 500 km (300 miles) from the colony, and non-breeders much more.

16. They dive from as much as 30 m (100 ft), reaching 100 km/h (60 mph) or more and penetrating usually, perhaps, 3·5 m (15 ft); exceptionally, this may be extended to 12–15 m (40–50 ft) by swimming. Most submergences are 5–7 seconds, maximum 20 seconds. Fish are sometimes brought to the surface but usually swallowed first. A variety of other hunting methods are used. They continue diving in winds up to about Beaufort 8.

17. They return to the colony in skeins of up to 80 birds, usually 10–20.

18. Fishermen use gannets as indicators of the presence of fish, especially herring, and have built up an extensive lore.

6: The gannet family and the order

God created; Linnaeus arranged.

Linnaeus

The order (Pelecaniformes), an ancient and diverse one to which gannets and boobies (family Sulidae) belong, includes also the pelicans (seven species, Pelecanidae), cormorants and shags (29 species, Phalacrocoracidae), darters or snake birds (two species, Anhingidae), frigates (five species, Fregatidae) and tropicbirds or bosunbirds (three species, Phaethontidae). They are all web-footed (totipalmate) fish eaters, partly, or usually wholly marine, and between them have evolved a wide range of fishing methods. The gannets and boobies are the most powerful plunge divers, though the tropicbirds also plunge heavily. Pelicans merely splash-dive and scoop, presumably the forerunner of deep plunging, and frigatebirds snatch from the surface. Darters, cormorants and shags swim-dive and pursue fish underwater, using mainly their huge webs for propulsion. This sort of division of the feeding habitat is usually considered to enhance the chances of successful foraging for each 'specialist' group, by reducing competition. Whilst, in my view, this concept rather easily breaks down when pushed far, it is probably basically valid.

However this may be, there can be no doubt that the species' foraging and hunting technique does underlie its entire breeding strategy, and this is well seen in the Pelecaniformes.[91,92] In each species, an adaptive web has evolved, in which the main strand is food. We will explore this theme for the gannets and boobies shortly, but a sketch of the pelecaniform strategies comes first.

Distribution

The order is cosmopolitan, ranging from the Antarctic-breeding shags to the Arctic-breeding cormorants and gannets. Several of the main concentrations, also, are in higher latitudes, because that is usually where fish are most plentiful, but in terms of families and species, the order is undoubtedly tropical and sub-tropical in distribution and (probably) origin. All six boobies, all seven pelicans, all five frigatebirds, all three tropicbirds, the darters and several shags or cormorants breed, usually wholly, within the tropics, and two of the three gannets migrate there whilst the third (the Australasian) occasionally penetrates them.

It would be inappropriate to digress far into the comparative morphology of the Sulidae, but since it is often useful to have the basic measurements of a complete family I have included them in Table 27.

Colony size and density

All are colonial breeders to some extent (Table 28), as indeed are all seabirds. Pelecaniform colonies cover the entire range, from virtually dispersed (Abbott's booby) to huge, maximally dense concentrations of several million pairs at four per square metre (guanay cormorants). The biggest colonies are also the densest; which is hardly surprising since, where huge numbers occur, there is always abundant food and not-so-abundant nesting space. However, as already stated it is dangerous to assume that limited space is always the cause of large dense colonies,

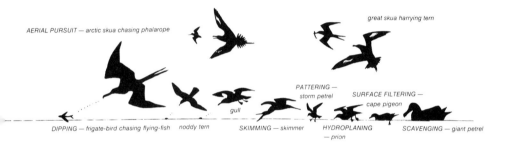

AERIAL PURSUIT — arctic skua chasing phalarope

great skua harrying tern

PATTERING — storm petrel

SURFACE FILTERING — cape pigeon

DIPPING — frigate-bird chasing flying-fish   noddy tern

SKIMMING — skimmer

HYDROPLANING — prion

SCAVENGING — giant petrel

gull

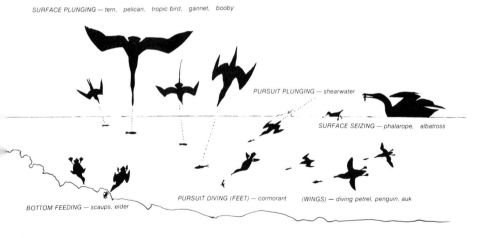

SURFACE PLUNGING — tern, pelican, tropic bird, gannet, booby

PURSUIT PLUNGING — shearwater

SURFACE SEIZING — phalarope, albatross

BOTTOM FEEDING — scaups, eider

PURSUIT DIVING (FEET) — cormorant

(WINGS) — diving petrel, penguin, auk

Fig. 52. Seabird feeding methods (after Ashmole 1971)

and fallacious to assume that the *precise* density is fixed in this way. Density, which for any species is infinitely more constant than colony size, depends on the amount of physical space relative to demand *and* on the social function(s) of density. Clearly, several widely different combinations of both these factors can determine colony size and density. Generalising within the order one may say:

(1) Extremely large and dense colonies (100,000 pairs or more) occur only in areas where food is abundant and nesting sites somewhat limited. They may consist either of inshore or relatively offshore foragers and often contain several species, as in the colonies of Peruvian guano birds (cormorants, pelicans, boobies, penguins and burrowing petrels) and their equivalents on the South African and Californian guano islands. *Inshore* foragers could not possibly exist in such large concentrations without an exceptionally rich food source, such as that in the Humboldt, Benguela and California 'currents' (really cold water upwellings). Imagine a million shags fishing off Bass Rock!

(2) Large and dense colonies (20,000 pairs or more) *may* occur relatively independently of physical shortage of sites, but only in areas where food is fairly plentiful, or where the species concerned forage at some distance from the colony, rather than close inshore. Atlantic gannets illustrate both of these aspects. The great white pelican of the African Rift Valley forms colonies up to 40,000 pairs, but these are dependent on abundant food in highly productive lakes.[134] Also, in their case, predator-free nesting areas are in short supply.

(3) Large, but not necessarily dense colonies may occur in impoverished tropical waters where islands are scarce. Islands in the empty waters of the tropical Eastern Pacific, or the tropical Atlantic, hold scores of thousands of boobies, and perhaps millions of terns, as well as frigatebirds, tropicbirds, and pelicans (and other non-pelecaniform seabirds). However, they are all, typically, capable of foraging far from base, and in many cases their whole breeding strategy is highly adapted towards coping with frequent food scarcities. Theirs are real siege economies.

(4) Small colonies typify seabirds which *must* feed locally or inshore, whether in fairly rich or impoverished waters. Most cormorants and shags, and some pelicans, are of this kind. Colonies of offshore feeders may be small if sites are limited, as in the hole-nesting tropicbirds, none of which nests in colonies of much more than 1,000–2,000 pairs. In sum, density, more than colony size, is usually typical for any species and its role is often a social one, for example in the local synchronisation of laying (which may have survival value) and in pair-formation. This is the main reason for its consistency where space is *not* limiting.

Brood size and breeding success

The biggest clutch commonly laid by any pelecaniform is four, and this applies only to the inshore feeding shags and cormorants and to one booby, the Peruvian (piquéro), which has a uniquely rich food source in the Humboldt current. Then come the pelicans, with clutches of two or three, and another booby, the blue-foot (again exceptional for reasons discussed below). The rest – frigatebirds, tropicbirds and boobies – rear only a single chick. Brood size is correlated with the frequency with which the young are fed, those foraging furthest (usually in the most impoverished areas) having the smallest broods. Not unexpectedly, these are the species (frigatebirds, tropicbirds and some boobies) whose young more often suffer retarded development (and linked to this, extremely long dependency on adults even after they can fly) and death due to starvation. In the extreme case of the frigatebirds, probably none of the five species manages to rear to independence more than about fifteen chicks from every hundred eggs laid. The adaptations which species subjected to these severe selection pressures evolve, are extremely complex, and may involve the entire social structure as well as more obvious behaviour such as energy-conserving habits. The boobies, discussed below, are good examples, as are the frigatebirds. Between these far-foragers and the inshore-feeding shags and cormorants, which occasionally rear broods of six, are the pelicans, whose foraging habits are in general intermediate. Pelicans may feed near at hand or up to 150 km (90 miles) away from the breeding colony. Moreover, food is usually plentiful; if it fails many pelicans simply abandon their breeding effort. So broods not only contain two or even three chicks, but, despite their mass, these grow much more quickly than those of the far-foragers.

The cormorants and shags, most widespread and numerous of the Pelecaniformes, rear large broods; and even the large species, such as the common cormorant, takes only half as long as the gannet to produce its chick, and only a tenth as long as a frigatebird, if the period of post-fledging parental care be included. Breeding success is high; in large broods of shags, up to 95% of those born, fledged successfully.[121] This is broadly typical of the family, and depends on the much larger amount of food, per adult, brought by shags and cormorants compared with frigatebirds or tropical boobies. This, in turn, is possible only because they feed very near to their breeding sites. Shags breeding on the Farnes spent only 4–8% of daylight hours on fishing activities, and foraging trips lasted on average about three-quarters of an hour.[103]

Equally as important as clutch size and associated adaptations in coping with the exigencies of food, is the *timing* of breeding. Few if any environments are strictly uniform throughout the year, so there is always pressure on birds to evolve an efficient breeding strategy, to make the most of the time when food or other factors are favourable. Moreover, even if the environment *was* uniform, the composition of the breeding cycle, that is the absolute and relative lengths of its parts (incubation, chick-rearing, and breeding activities before egg-laying and after chick-rearing), would give plenty of scope for natural selection, since they all depend on energy-budgeting. As we know, there is usually more than one way of budgeting, and none painless.

Without entering into too much detail, one may relate pelecaniform breeding cycles to environment as follows:

(1) *Strictly annual, highly seasonal breeders*. These have adapted to predictably seasonal climate and food, and this is found chiefly in the northern Palaearctic, for example around Britain, North America, Iceland and Scandinavia, though to a lesser extent in the southern hemisphere equivalent. Gannets, particularly in Canada, are an excellent example.

(2) *Strictly annual, losely seasonal breeders*. Where seasonal pressures are relatively imprecise the mean laying date of a population may vary in different years by weeks or even months. Though it grades into seasonal breeding, this category embraces most of the Pelecaniformes, particularly those in the higher tropical latitudes, and north and south of these, where seasons differ sufficiently in day length, temperature, wind systems and oceanographic features, to affect food, even though only broadly. At the 'tighter' end of this category are the African and Australasian gannets; then, progressively 'looser', the Peruvian booby, many pantropical boobies, probably all the pelicans (though for some of these 'loose' becomes 'almost continuous' in some areas), some two-thirds of the cormorants and some populations of (probably all three) tropicbirds; other populations, in extremely tropical and impoverished areas such as the Galapagos and Ascension, breed continuously. Similarly, the Galapagos masked booby lays in many months of the year, though each pair breeds annually.

(3) *Less-than-annual, seasonal breeders*. Besides the five frigate-birds, only Abbott's booby[89] consistently lays once every two years. In all six cases, beyond doubt, the reason is to be found in the extremely slow growth of the young and the astonishingly long time for which parents feed their *free-flying* young (up to 14 months in some frigatebirds). In turn, these characteristics turn on the specialised feeding techniques of the adults and the fact that, at one time or another during development, food is likely to be extremely scarce. Indeed, Galapagos greater frigatebirds commonly forage for a fortnight or more at a stretch, leaving their partner sitting on the egg, though they manage to reduce this when the egg hatches. Despite their unusually long cycles, the frigatebirds lay loosely seasonally, and Abbott's booby quite markedly so.

(4) *More-than-annual, non-seasonal breeders*. The only pelecaniforms which are known to have shortened their cycles to consistently less than 12 months are two boobies (the blue-foot in the Galapagos and the brown booby on Ascension[120]) and the Galapagos yellow-billed tropicbird[126] *all* of them in impoverished zones. It might seem surprising that such species should attempt *more* than the normal amount of breeding in a year, but this may well increase their success measured over a *lifetime*, by maximising the number of chances of hitting upon favourable periods. Naturally, this strategy requires spe-

cial underpinning, one component of which is the ability to raise chicks reasonably quickly by special feeding methods. This would rule it out for frigatebirds. To some extent, in this sketchy survey of the Pelecaniformes we have touched on ideas which are helpful in understanding the central role of food in the lives of seabirds – and indeed birds in general. It seems clear that pelecaniform strategies have evolved to maximise reproductive rates in relation to food. Breeding infrequently or frequently, laying many or few eggs, nesting in large, dense colonies or smaller, sparser ones, seems to rest, ultimately, on the nature of the food supply and the associated foraging techniques, the 'aim' being to rear as many young as possible. That this number is often small, and the evolved strategies weak in parts, need surprise nobody who believes, as I do, that for all its marvellous details, evolution often produces merely a means of surviving and reproducing, rather than *the perfect* means of doing so.

THE FAMILY SULIDAE

Moving, now, to the more restricted subject of sulids, adaptations of our own gannet can best be seen by comparing it with the rest of its family (Tables 17 and 29). The differences between them have come about because gannets and boobies have each moved into their own feeding and nesting 'niches' (the two are closely linked) to which they have become intimately suited, physically and in their ecology and behaviour. Nothing, for instance, shows the structure of the Atlantic gannet's adaptiveness so well as comparison with its close relative, yet diametric opposite, the red-footed booby. The exploration of family characteristics is best taken in two steps – first a comparison of the three gannets and then of the gannets and the six boobies. Tables 27–30 give the physical and ecological characteristics of the whole family, and Tables 31 and 32 the population details for the African and Australasian gannets.

The African and Australasian gannets
The Atlantic, Australasian and African (or Cape) gannets are so alike that even adults of the two latter can be almost indistinguishable, and both can, in immature stages, be difficult to identify from Atlantic gannets. Nevertheless, they are more than mere 'races', for they differ importantly in numerous aspects of ecology and behaviour. This is why I, for one, prefer to treat them as allospecies. In all that follows, it will be apparent that the two southern gannets resemble each other very closely, and far more than either of them resemble the Atlantic gannet, and that the changes which have occurred are economically interpretable by assuming that the African gannet is a modified Australasian, and (like man!) the Atlantic a modified African. It seems useful to have this in mind from the outset.

ATLANTIC AND AFRICAN GANNETS COMPARED FOR THE EFFECTS OF CERTAIN
ENVIRONMENTAL FACTORS ON BEHAVIOUR AND ECOLOGY

Atlantic gannet

large shoaling fish irregularly found	→	extensive foraging, deep penetration, powerful bill, resistance to starvation, high growth rate, etc
cold climate	→	fat advantageous (penetration, resistance to starvation) heat loss no problem
cliff-girt islands	→	permits heaviness and high aspect ratio wings
seasonal environment, predictable autumnal deterioration	→	selectively encourages optimally timed breeding; uses social facilitation, which favours evolution of aggression; largeness favoured

African gannet
(and perhaps to a lesser extent, Australasian)

smaller prey items	→	smaller size and weight, slower growth
warmer climate	→	less fat, more bare skin
fewer (and flatter) islands	→	greater density, larger colonies (does not apply to Australasian); lightness aids take off
autumnal deterioration less predictable and marked	→	breeding more seasonally variable; less social competition; less aggression

The Australasian and African are smaller and lighter than the Atlantic gannet. The latter is adapted by weight, much of it fat, to low temperatures, icy waters and large shoaling prey. With its weight goes cliff-nesting. The African, by contrast, lives in warmer seas and climes, and nests on hot, flat islands. Too much fat would be a positive hindrance so far as temperature-regulation and take-off are concerned. Indeed, it has evolved special temperature-regulation devices, amongst them distending its uniquely enlarged throat strip of naked black skin and excreting onto its own feet, thus losing heat by evaporating the excreta against the hot ground. The throat skin is some $2\frac{1}{2}$ times as long as that of the Atlantic bird and $1\frac{1}{2}$ times that of the Australasian. At take-off, a most laborious process is required. The bird has to make its way to the run-way area and boost itself into the air after hopping and bounding in suicidal fashion, at ever increasing speed. Apart from its longer throat strip, the adult African gannet closely resembles the Australasian, and differs from the Atlantic in its black secondaries and black tail feathers. Typically, the tail of the African gannet is all black whereas that of the Australasian is white except for four black central tail feathers; but there is a great deal of variation, particularly in the African gannet, and some tails are indistinguishable from those of the Australasian, though this is unlikely to pose any problems in view of their respective distributions. The juveniles, also, are similar, though the Australasian is markedly paler beneath.

Both southern gannets have a more restricted distribution than the Atlantic gannet. The African, breeds only between 25° 43′S and 33° 50′S. This span of 8° latitude compares with 14° for the Australasian

Fig. 53. African gannets taking flight down the runway

(32° 12'S to 46° 36'S, though more than 99% breed between 34°S and 40°S) and 22° for the Atlantic (48°N to 70°N). However, the actual range is probably of less significance than the fact that all three breed within foraging range of cool waters, rich in fish, and are adapted to exploit this. The main difference is that, in this respect, the Atlantic gannet has gone markedly further than the other two. The only case of any gannet species straying into the breeding area of another is that of an African gannet apparently collected (in 1831) on the Bass Rock but overlooked until now (see Chapter 1).

The number and size of colonies (see Tables 25 and 26) partly reflects available sites. The Atlantic leads, with 34 colonies against 25 for the Australasian and six for the African. The order is reversed, as between the African and Atlantic gannets, with regard to maximum colony size (roughly 100,000 pairs for the African gannet on Ichaboe and 50,000 for the Atlantic on St Kilda) and even more markedly with regard to mean colony size. This, however, is merely because islands are scarce off the Cape in the region of the Benguela to which area African gannets are adapted. For the same reason, African gannets nest more densely than their Atlantic and Australasian counterparts. The Australasian gannet clearly favours smaller colonies, though the reason is not abundantly clear, and nests, if anything, slightly less densely than the Atlantic gannet. However, the two southern gannets agree in preferring flat ground to cliffs, and in this differ from the Atlantic. As mentioned, they are lighter.

In most essentials the three gannets have similar breeding regimes. The Atlantic gannet is undoubtedly more consistent than the other two in its pattern of attendance and laying. Thus, although the Australasian gannet spends six to eight months at its breeding colony this is less than the Atlantic birds' attendance period. Moreover, it is prone to considerable yearly fluctuations, as is the mean laying date.

This is equally marked in the African gannet,[61] which varies substantially from year to year in its return and departure dates, rarely spends as long as eight months in continuous attendance, and typically does not attend its site after completing its breeding although it may roost on the island. All this suggests that the Atlantic gannet pays considerably more attention to its site, which presumably means that it is in more danger of losing it if it neglects to do so, which is tantamount to saying that competition is keener. It means, also, that the *timing* of breeding is more important in the Atlantic gannet, otherwise it would not stick so closely to its attendance pattern and mean laying date. I have already given evidence for the Atlantic gannet supporting both these propositions.

Nevertheless, both of the southern gannets are clearly seasonal breeders. The African lays from early October to late December, with a peak around the first half of November. There is, normally, a total laying period of around three months, though eggs *can* be laid considerably outside these dates, for example as late as April. The Australasian gannet lays between August and December, a five-month span. The earliest egg on record was laid on 12 July (1959), at Horuhoru,[125] which appears to be about a month ahead of the more southerly Cape Kidnappers colony. However, the *mean* laying date apparently varies by up to three weeks in the same colony in different years. This may be due to variation in the weather (and thus food supply) in the pre-laying period. The corollary is that mean fledging dates also vary. Presumably (though not necessarily) the survival of the fledglings is not highly dependent on a fixed mean fledging date, and may indeed be less so than in the Atlantic gannet.

The facts and suppositions given above mean that behavioural factors which affect the timing of laying may well be *less* important in the two southern gannets than in the Atlantic. If this is so, we have a possible explanation for the observation that, in the former, site competition is less keen, and display less frequent and intense (see below), than in the site-obsessed Atlantic bird.

The young of the two southern gannets grow more slowly than those of the Atlantic. Though relatively slight, the difference is enough to suggest *some* difference in the nature of their respective food, whether in nutritive value per food item, crude availability or whatever. Thus, young African and Australasian gannets are about 97 and 107 days old, respectively, when they fledge, compared with 91 for the Atlantic, and this despite reaching a much lower absolute weight. Also, the southern birds were fairly incapable of rearing twins when an extra chick was donated; Australasians didn't manage it at all and African gannets produced about 46% more fledglings but these were uneven in weight, one being markedly starved, and were thought to have poorer survival than normals.[62] Atlantic birds managed much better.[83,93] Though these indicators are admittedly less dramatic than the occasional violent poverty of the tropical boobies, they are consistent with, for instance, the proportionately heavier egg of Cape and Australasian gannets, the occasional mass starvations in the Australasian,[125] and the relative imprecision of seasonal timing in breeding in African and Australasian gannets. All these show that their food is not quite as rich and dependable as is the Atlantic bird's.

There is an interesting corollary of this. The southern gannet fledglings do not leave their nests in the same once-and-for-all way as the Atlantic young. Instead, they practise hop-flying around the fringes of the colony and may indeed be reasonably competent fliers when they leave the colony. This could mean a somewhat different pattern in their subsequent migration (which the Atlantic gannet begins by swimming) and post-fledging survival, though it must be said that there are no signs that African and Australasian young do in fact survive any better than those of the Atlantic gannets. However this may be, the southern gannets are clearly nearer to the normal sulid procedure, in which young practise flying and are fed by their parents for some time after they are competent fliers. Indeed, young African and Australasian gannets sometimes do return to their nest after practising on the fringe, and are fed. It is the Atlantic gannet which has cut the apron strings in the most decisive manner.

Another way in which the southern gannets, and especially the African, resemble boobies more than does the Atlantic gannet, is in the age at which they first breed. Some African gannets reach adult plumage in their third year and may breed late in their third or early in their fourth year. The Australasian gannet is a little behind this; it may, at the earliest, lay late in its fourth year, but often not until its sixth or even seventh year. So on this count, too, the Australasian seems slightly less well-off, in food, than the African gannet (the slower growth of its young suggested the same thing). If this is so, the reader may well ask why the Atlantic gannet, which I suppose to be so well-off for food, is as late or later than either of the other two in first breeding. An explanation is offered in terms of acquisition of feeding lore and attainment of ability to compete adequately for a breeding site (Chapter 4).

One of the most intriguing parallels in the three gannets is the similar migrations of the newly fledged young. Just as the Atlantic gannet (British and Canadian) moves some 4,000 km (2,500 miles) south, so the African moves almost as far north, to reach the same broad equatorial zone as the eastern Atlantic gannets where, indeed, the two allo-species overlap. Similarly, the Australasian migrates up to 5,000 km (3,000 miles) westward,[142] across the Tasman Sea to the southern and eastern coasts of Australia. In all cases the young move from cooler to warmer waters. Precisely why they do so, one can only conjecture. It costs energy and lives, and is undertaken at considerable speeds. Distances of almost 3,000 km (1,850 miles) may be covered in a week or so. Presumably, in the areas to which they move so urgently, they have a better chance of becoming proficient hunters. Probably, this is partly bound up with the size and distribution of fish. This has never been critically examined, and all we know is that at least some of the areas in which young (and old) gannets are commonest, are rich fishing grounds. The seas off Rio de Oro are a good example for the Atlantic gannet, and the Gulf of Guinea for the African. Presumably it is easier for an inexperienced gannet to scrape a living where fish are fairly thickly and uniformly spread, and not too large and powerful, even if the reverse is true for an experienced gannet with larger energy reserves. The lower energy costs of maintaining body temperature in warmer seas may also play a part, especially since the black plumage of the juvenile is a less efficient overcoat than the white plumage of the adult.[111]

The movements of the young suggest that the African gannet has arisen from over-shooting westward-moving Australasian birds; and the Atlantic from over-shooting northward-moving African gannets. The closer similarity between the two southern gannets is because their habitats have more in common than either has with the Atlantic gannet's habitat. Put another way, the Atlantic gannet has had to adapt to the stormy, arctic and near-arctic seas of the north. The prize has been considerable, in the form of large, shoaling fish; and to make the most of these, as well as to combat the cold and the periods of enforced starvation due to stormy weather, the Atlantic bird has evolved its particular features (Chapters 1 and 4). The phenomenon of gannet migration, in general, probably arose from the less directional post-breeding dispersal of sulids which was, and is, adaptive by allowing young birds to forage continuously without the energy cost of periodically returning to base.

The behaviour of the three gannets is almost identical insofar as the form of the various patterns is concerned, but there are important differences nonetheless, and fortunately (!) they are consistent with the predictions of the ecological adaptations. One factor above all, though with many ramifications, appears to be important. The Atlantic gannet is more *territorially competitive* than the other two. This means that it is *more aggressive*, which affects the interactions of mates as well as neighbours, and of parents and their young. Underlying this is the food situation, which enables Atlantic gannets to spend such an astonishing proportion of their time at the nest, guarding it and the young, but denies the African and Australasian gannets the chance to do so. One might say 'isn't it fortunate that they don't need to do so, since neighbours are unlikely to usurp the site or attack unguarded young'. But the point is, of course, that had it not been for the Atlantic gannet's food situation it would never have evolved its particular breeding strategy in which site-competition plays a vital part.

With this essential point in mind, the actual differences in behaviour between the three gannets[93] may be simply summarised: African and Australasian gannets fight less frequently and severely, and perform aggressive (territorial) displays (bowing and menacing) at lower inten-

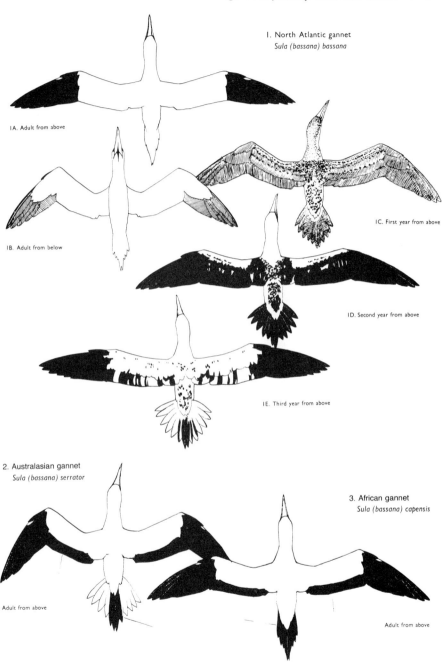

1. North Atlantic gannet
Sula (bassana) bassana

1A. Adult from above

1B. Adult from below

1C. First year from above

1D. Second year from above

1E. Third year from above

2. Australasian gannet
Sula (bassana) serrator

3. African gannet
Sula (bassana) capensis

Adult from above

Adult from above

(Leaders indicate diagnostic features)

Fig. 54 External features of gannets and boobies

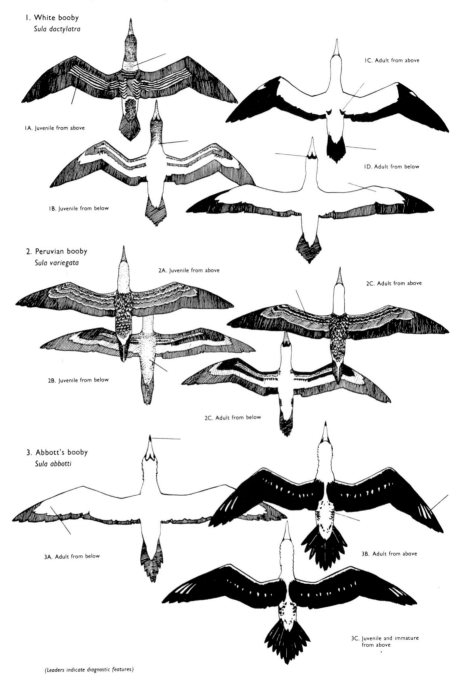

1. White booby
Sula dactylatra

1A. Juvenile from above

1B. Juvenile from below

1C. Adult from above

1D. Adult from below

2. Peruvian booby
Sula variegata

2A. Juvenile from above

2B. Juvenile from below

2C. Adult from above

2C. Adult from below

3. Abbott's booby
Sula abbotti

3A. Adult from below

3B. Adult from above

3C. Juvenile and immature
from above

(Leaders indicate diagnostic features)

Fig. 54 (contd.) External features of gannets and boobies

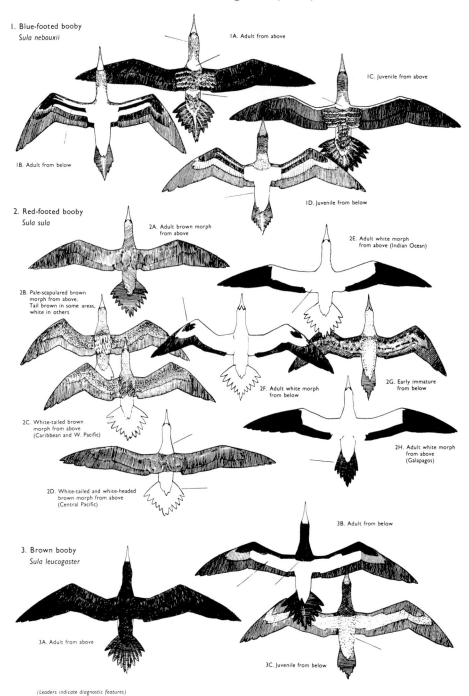

1. Blue-footed booby
   Sula nebouxii

1A. Adult from above

1C. Juvenile from above

1B. Adult from below

1D. Juvenile from below

2. Red-footed booby
   Sula sula

2A. Adult brown morph
from above

2E. Adult white morph
from above (Indian Ocean)

2B. Pale-scapulared brown
morph from above.
Tail brown in some areas,
white in others

2F. Adult white morph
from below

2G. Early immature
from below

2C. White-tailed brown
morph from above
(Caribbean and W. Pacific)

2D. White-tailed and white-headed
brown morph from above
(Central Pacific)

2H. Adult white morph
from above
(Galapagos)

3B. Adult from below

3. Brown booby
   Sula leucogaster

3A. Adult from above

3C. Juvenile from below

(Leaders indicate diagnostic features)

Fig. 54 (contd.) External features of gannets and boobies

sity and less frequently; males are less aggressive to their mates (that is, they nape-bite and attack her less) and, correspondingly, the partly-aggressive pair-bonding display, mutual-fencing, is less intense and of shorter duration; adults attack chicks less. All this hangs together in a satisfactory manner providing we can see *why* Atlantic gannets should be more site-competitive and hence more aggressive, and this I tried to explain earlier. Incidentally, it seems, also, to argue convincingly for the existence of 'aggression' as a meaningful motivational entity, causally common to many behaviour patterns. Some ethologists are apparently highly averse to this idea. Within the trio, African gannets are demonstrably more aggressive than Australasian. I would link this with the shortage of nesting islands which this allospecies (though not the others) faces. It is indeed remarkable that even in the face of this shortage, the African is less site-competitive than the Atlantic gannet. Apparently the social benefits conferred by getting the 'right' site generate fiercer competition than a straight struggle for physical space, though this could only hold true up to a certain saturation point.

The fact that Atlantic gannets, particularly males, are so aggressive means, amongst many other things, that the young are prohibited from wandering before they fledge. As we have seen, young African and Australasians wander more freely, with possibly important effects. It may not be too fanciful to link, in particular, the juvenile Australasian gannet's noticeably whiter underparts with this allospecies' lesser aggression (the lowest of the three), since it is probable that black plumage is mainly functional in appeasing adults and has in fact some disadvantages in other ways (Chapter 1).

It should be clear that the three gannets are very similar, and indeed they differ from the rest of the family enough to persuade many ornithologists to place them in a separate genus. I do not, myself, consider that the differences are more marked than those between some of the boobies, and since I would not wish to split the boobies into two or three genera, I do not see the logic of separating the gannets from the boobies, either. So I put them all in *Sula* and indicate the special relationship of the gannets by putting them in one superspecies.

I want to complete this chapter by sketching the rest of the genus *Sula* – the boobies, all of which are portrayed in the plates.

In overall sizes and weight, the nine species of sulid (counting each gannet separately) cover a considerable range, from the tiny male red-foot and brown booby, of well under a thousand grammes, to the Atlantic gannet of four times that weight. Whilst all sulids have high aspect ratio wings and a fairly high, or high, wing loading, they vary considerably in these respects, as, also, in the size and shape of bill (Figs. 54–57). The details are complex but the salient point is that despite sharing far-foraging and plunge-diving as their method of feeding (and sharing, too, many of the basic features that go with it – streamlining, pointed tail, high aspect wings, closed nostrils, etc) there has been room for considerable morphological differentiation, fitting each of the different species to the *specific* combination of environmen-

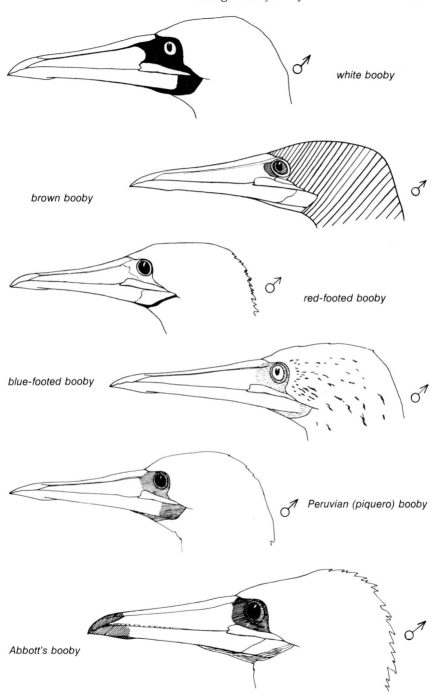

white booby

brown booby

red-footed booby

blue-footed booby

Peruvian (piquero) booby

Abbott's booby

Fig. 55 Heads of sulids

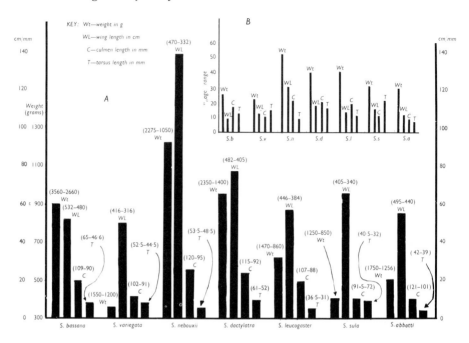

Fig. 56. *The range in morphological features in the Sulidae, expressed for each species, A in absolute terms, and B in proportionate terms. Figures in brackets are the absolute measurements and weights – the difference between them (the range) is plotted here. In B the difference between the greatest and least of the features concerned is expressed as a percentage of the greatest, for each species. It can be seen, for example, that (in B) the range in weight is, in all species, greater than the range in other features; but that wing length has, in some, a wider range than beak length; whilst in others the reverse is true. In A, the relatively huge difference in wing length between the largest and smallest blue-footed booby is evident compared with any other sulid*

tal features with which it must cope. It seems, too, that where two or more species are sympatric, each has become different enough to exploit different feeding niches, just as in so many groups of birds. Indeed (again as in many groups, notably raptors and some king-fishers), not only has this differentiation occurred *between* species, but also *within* them, in the form of marked sexual dimorphism in some. The least sexually dimorphic members of the genus are the gannets and the Peruvian boobies, which have the richest food supplies.

There are six booby species. Three are widely distributed throughout the tropics (the masked, blue-faced or white booby, *Sula dactylatra*; the brown booby, *S. leucogaster*; the red-footed booby, *S. sula*). One (the blue-footed, *S. nebouxii*) has three foci, the Gulf of California and islands off Mexico, the Galapagos Islands and the west coast of South

America from northern Peru to the Gulf of Panama. The fifth, the Peruvian booby or piquero (*S. variegata*) is restricted to the extreme north coast of Chile and islands off Peru; and the sixth, Abbott's booby (*S. abbotti*) breeds only on the Indian Ocean Christmas Island.

The boobies (Sulidae)

In the early part of this Chapter, when considering the order Pelecaniformes, food was the main theme. Again, food dominated the discussion of the three gannets. So, too, in the genus *Sula*, the major differences can be interpreted in relation to food.

I have space only for the broad outlines of the strategies adopted, but enough to show the complexities of the adaptations which each sulid has evolved. The pan-tropical belts of the three major oceans embrace

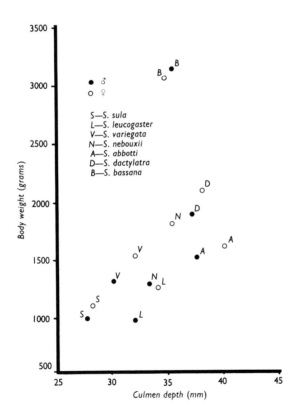

Fig. 57. *An example of the way in which physical features (here body weight and bill depth, each of which is strongly correlated with gripping power) separate the various members of the Sulidae, thus widening the spectrum of food exploited by the family*

vast areas of sea. Tropical seas are characterised by a constant temperature of about 23° C (73° F); there is relatively little upwelling and
typically little mineral, plankton and fish. This generalisation is by no
means completely valid, for there *are* areas of convergence and
upwelling, but, dominantly, tropical seas are seasonless and
impoverished. North and south of the boundaries of the equatorial
current, a more varied oceanographic pattern is common, with localised areas of abundance. Throughout these huge tracts, the masked,
brown and red-footed boobies are almost the only sulids. They wrest a
living from the sea's desert areas as well as from its pastures and it is to
be expected that, according to their particular circumstances, different
populations, even of the same species, will show very different
'profiles'. In general, however, these three species are adapted to life in
warm and impoverished seas, and therefore contrast markedly with the
Atlantic gannet.

They nest in small or moderate-sized colonies, usually at no great
density. Where islands are few, colonies may reach sizeable proportions (15 or 20,000 pairs) and a reasonable density, but never anything
like the gannet's. Also where (as often) these are sympatric, they divide
the habitat rather nicely. Masked boobies prefer flat, open ground,
brown boobies steep, broken ground or cliffs, and red-footed boobies
are tree and bush-nesters. The scarcity of food and the extreme heat of
exposed nesting sites in the tropics, favour lightweight birds rather
than fat ones, and so the masked and brown boobies, though almost as
big as gannets, are much lighter and can cope with flat, relatively
windless nesting sites which the gannet would be unable to use. This is
another example of inter-relation, since oceanic islands in these
latitudes are typically low and the windy cliffs which gannets would
require would not be available.

Each of the three boobies has evolved a cluster of characteristics
which allows it to produce the maximum number of young under these
demanding conditions. Table 30 gives the productivity figures for all
sulids. In essence, this 'cluster' involves *brood size, composition of
breeding cycle* and *timing of breeding*. Taking these three features for
each in turn, the masked booby always rears a single chick, and it has
enhanced its chances of doing so by laying two eggs, five days apart.
This gives the adults a second chance, should the first chick be unlucky
enough to hatch (and die) during a period of food shortage. If all goes
well, however, the second chick is evicted by its older sibling soon
after birth and left to die. In this way, the larger clutch size is seen to be
an adaptation to help rear *one*, not two chicks. The breeding cycle is
relatively prolonged; all young seabirds that are fed relatively infrequently and on small amounts can grow only slowly. In the masked
booby's case, the young take about 120 days to become free-flying and,
although some aspects of growth vary considerably with locality, this
period of 120 days does not. Again, this may be seen as an adaptation,
since it is obviously an advantage for the young bird to fly as soon as
possible, so that it can learn to fish and thus add to the food its parents

THE RELATIONSHIP BETWEEN FOOD AND FORAGING HABITS AND BREEDING ECOLOGY IN THE SULIDAE

Far foraging (food scarce and/or difficult to locate; fishing trips long, up to 300 miles (500 km) or more)	Red-footed booby	Clutch of one relatively large egg; slow growth; high starvation rate of young in some areas; breeding cycle may take more than a year; laying may be a-seasonal.
	White booby	Clutch of two but obligatory brood reduction; slow growth in some areas; may be high starvation rate of young; laying may be only loosely seasonal.
	Abbott's booby	Clutch of one relatively large egg; extremely slow growth; breeding cycle takes more than a year; laying fairly seasonal and thus, because of length of cycle, can breed only once in two years.
Near foraging (food relatively rich, rich, or abundant, or special feeding mechanisms not used by far foragers)	Atlantic gannet	Clutch of one small egg; rapid growth with deposition of large fat reserves; no starvation of young; laying annual and highly seasonal.
	Peruvian booby	Clutch of 2–4 (average 3); young grow quickly. No starvation except in catastrophic years; laying annual but only loosely seasonal.
	Blue-footed booby	Clutch of 1–3 (average 2); facultative brood reduction; young grow fairly quickly; starvation rate variable but mainly low; special feeding mechanism; laying seasonal or a-seasonal, annual or less than annual, depending on area.
	Brown booby	Clutch of 1 or 2 but obligatory brood reduction; young grow fairly quickly; starvation rate variable but mainly low; special feeding mechanism; laying seasonal or a-seasonal, annual or less than annual depending on area.

provide. To this end, the *wings* grow normally even though body weight, bill size and other parts of the body may vary widely according to locality. After becoming free-flying, young masked boobies continue to be fed by their parents for up to nine weeks, though six to eight weeks is probably the overall average. Thus, a juvenile masked booby of little more than half the weight of a juvenile gannet takes nearly twice as long to produce, though this comparison is not entirely fair, since at the end of it the masked booby is proficient and independent, whereas the gannet is merely independent! As mentioned in the general classification of the timing of breeding in Pelecaniformes, the masked booby breeds annually, but with such an enormous spread of laying in impoverished areas, such as the Galapagos and Ascension, that eggs can be found in almost every month. Seasonal breeding in a non-seasonal and unpredictable environment is presumably of no benefit. The proximate stimulus for laying may be food, as it is in the Galapagos red-foot (see below), though obviously there can be no guarantee that by so reacting they will ensure that there is food when the chicks are growing. Again, this is in complete contrast with the gannet.

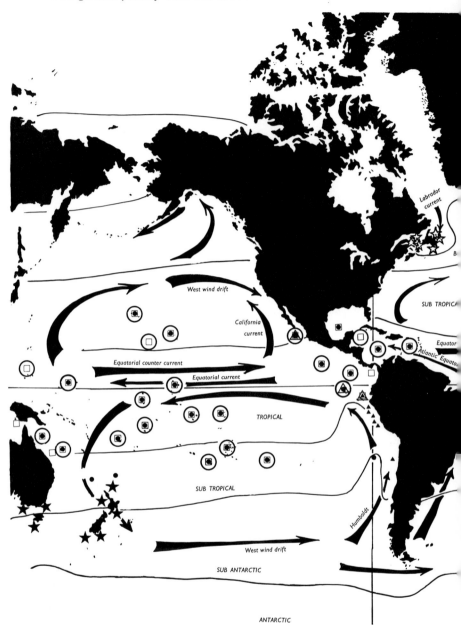

Fig. 58. World distribution of gannets and sulids

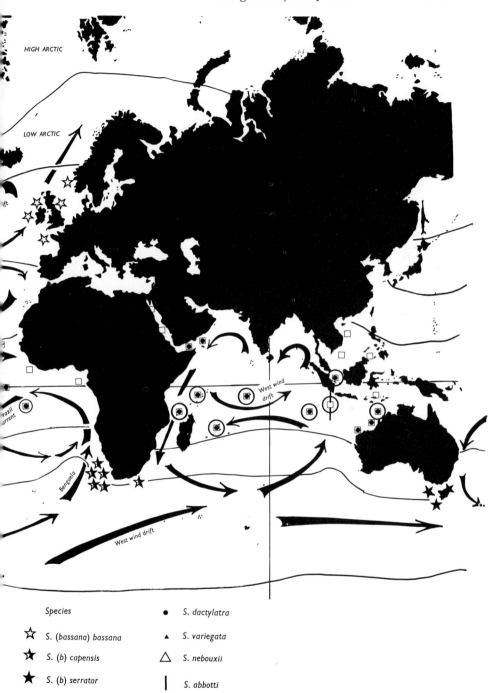

Species

☆ S. (bassana) bassana

★ S. (b) capensis

★ S. (b) serrator

□ S. leucogaster

● S. dactylatra

▲ S. variegata

△ S. nebouxii

| S. abbotti

◯ S. sula

So far as behaviour goes, the main points are that masked boobies nest well spaced out and, as just mentioned, do not depend much on social stimulation as a help in timing breeding (though group-synchrony could still be adaptive). So they are markedly less violent in defence of their territories, fighting little and briefly, and depending (for territorial defence) on ritualised display. Correspondingly, there is little overt aggression between mates and a rather poorly developed 'meeting' or appeasing ceremony. The pair bond is much looser than in the gannet and, so, fidelity to site is weaker. The whole system thus has reasonable internal consistency.

The brown booby often nests on the same island as the larger masked booby. Like the latter, it lays two eggs but rears a single chick, using the same mechanism of obligatory 'sibling murder'. It has been conclusively demonstrated that, in both species, parents of two-egg clutches rear more young than those of single eggs, yet *without* ever rearing twins. The chicks first fly when about 95 days old but may be fed for a long time after that. In 'good' areas, post-fledging feeding may last as little as six weeks, as on the Indian Ocean Christmas Island, whilst on Ascension it ranged from seven to no less than 59 weeks.[120] It is on Ascension, too, that the brown booby has achieved a beautifully adaptive breeding regime which, so far as we know, is not paralleled

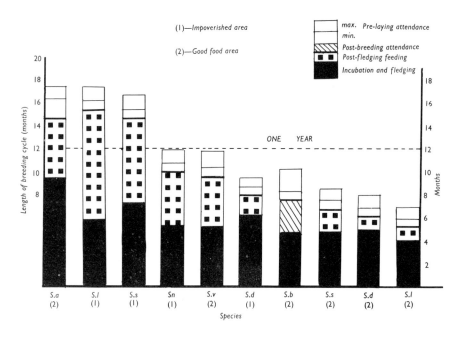

Fig. 59. Composition of the breeding cycle in the Sulidae. Note that the gannet is the only member which lacks post-fledging feeding of young

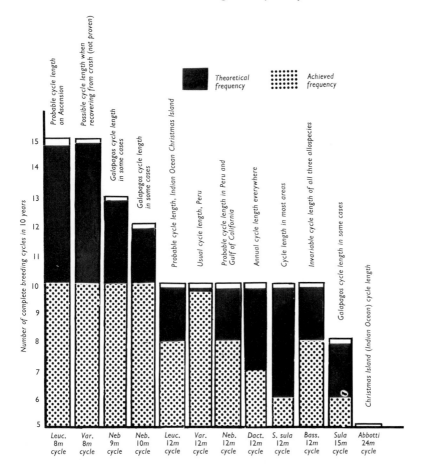

Fig. 60. Breeding frequency in the Sulidae. A breeding cycle encompasses all the events necessary for breeding, including pre-laying attendance at the site

anywhere else. The female maintains continuous occupation of the nest site and continuous readiness to breed. If one attempt fails, whether at the egg or chick stage, she begins another when food becomes adequate again. This may be almost immediately, since food shortages in this tropical environment are unpredictable in timing and duration, or it may be weeks or months later. As in the case of the variable period of post-fledging care of young, the non-seasonal environment allows this sort of flexibility. Even if a breeding attempt is successful another one starts approximately eight months after the beginning of the first, instead of twelve months, as in less exacting parts of its range. Thus, on Ascension, the brown booby fits more than the normal quota of breeding *attempts* into its life, to compensate for the large proportion that fail. If it tried to breed every year for ten years, with 80% failure, it would raise two young. If it tried to breed twenty times, and the same proportion failed, it would rear twice as many. So this device, too, is part of the attempt to maximise output in the face of a hostile environment.

The brown booby's behaviour does not differ much, in essentials, from the masked booby's except that in keeping with its steeper breeding habitat and smaller size (the male is considerably smaller than the female, too) there is greater emphasis on aerial display. There is perhaps more strenuous fighting than in the masked booby, possibly depending on whether they are breeding on steep or flat terrain (the latter producing least fighting) which is interesting in view of the demonstration[120] that steep sites vary in 'quality' and, with this, breeding success. The main pair-interaction is a ritualised jabbing comparable to that of the masked booby's and much less elaborate than the gannet's mutual fencing.

Like the masked booby, but unlike the gannet, the brown booby usually has enough space to allow it to walk about, and this provides the context for an odd-looking posture, associated with the tendency to move away from the partner. When it does so, it is particularly liable to be attacked and the posture adopted (bill-up-face-away) not only signals its intention, and so allows time for the shifting 'moods' of both birds to reach the appropriate balance, but enables it to keep an eye on its partner whilst so doing. It can then react appropriately to its mate's ongoing behaviour.

When a gannet moves off its site it skypoints and one may well ask why the related booby has a different display for this situation. The booby in fact *does* skypoint, but in quite a different context. It skypoints (a display undoubtedly homologous and not merely analogous to the gannet's) when attempting to attract the female to close quarters. My interpretation is that, way back in evolutionary time, after the ancestral gannet/booby stock had diverged, the boobies changed the context and function of skypointing from its original signal '*I am about to move away*' to its new sexual signal '*You may approach, I am sexually receptive*'. The gannets kept to the older usage. Having changed in this way, the boobies required a *new* 'I am about to depart' signal and they evolved the 'bill-up-face-away' described above. It is interesting that this new signal, like the old, is derived from the intention movements of flight – chin lifting, neck lengthening and turning away. Now, all the boobies (except, for some obscure reason, Abbott's) have acquired a modified form of skypointing as a sexual signal, and all the ground nesters (but not the two tree species) have acquired the bill-up-face-away as the pre-leaving posture! Thus the ancestral *booby* (not the ancestral sulid which gave rise both to boobies and gannets) probably had a 'sexual' skypointing and a 'departing' bill-up-face-away. This booby split into new species, which took these displays and modified them according to the dictates of their new habitats, etc, so now we find in the boobies a series of nicely different forms of skypoint, all clearly homologous. On the form of their displays, the most closely related booby trio are the brown, blue-footed and Peruvian boobies, with the masked a little more distant, and the red-footed booby more difficult to relate, presumably because of obscurities introduced by its arboreal habit. I am treating it next to the masked and brown boobies, because I chose the occupancy of the tropical belt, and its effects, as the linking theme.

Turning, then, to the red-footed booby, and starting as before, with brood size, one finds that the red-foot, throughout its vast range, is single-mindedly uniparous. One egg is quite enough, and often too much. Perhaps even more than the masked, the red-foot is a far-forager and in particularly impoverished seas, such as parts of the tropical eastern Pacific, it sometimes finds it so difficult to locate flying fish and squids, its main food, that it cannot sustain its breeding effort. So, if it is just beginning to court and build, it abruptly ceases to do so, whilst if it has a new egg, it deserts. Even a well-incubated egg may be deserted if the partner has to wait more than six or seven days for its mate to return. Young chicks starve, older ones may hang on by their eyelids until things improve and then, though greatly emaciated, make a good recovery. Under these conditions, by laying a single egg instead of two, the red-foot forfeits the masked booby's insurance policy but is enabled to put more yolk into the one egg. Presumably this is just another way of tackling the problem and maximising productivity, and it is impossible to say that one method is better than the other. Each of them works. Where, as over much of its range, conditions are better than this, starvation is rare; growth is quicker and breeding success higher. Under these conditions, eggs are smaller.

In impoverished areas the red-footed booby's breeding cycle is extremely long, due mainly to the chick's slow growth and (especially) to the long period during which the free-flying juvenile continues to be fed by its parents. Indeed, in the Galapagos, some pairs take at least fifteen months to complete a successful breeding effort; but, because there is no really seasonal weather or food supply, such pairs need not wait for the next laying season to come round. They can lay at intervals of a year-plus-a-fraction. This poses the question: what triggers breeding, if changes in daylength, temperature, etc, do not? It seem that under such conditions the red-footed booby courts, builds and lays when food is reasonably plentiful, necessarily regardless of the fact that by the time the chick hatches food may be very scarce. I say 'necessarily' because, apparently, these scarce periods are irregular and unpredictable, so that there is no way in which breeding could be timed to miss them. By courting and laying when food allows, the red-foot at least carries out these time and energy consuming activities at a favourable time. Where the climate is seasonal, breeding is annual and seasonal, too. I need hardly mention the utter contrast of this regime compared with that of the gannet.

Behaviourally, the red-footed booby conforms to the sulid pattern in that it has a ritualised territorial display, a greeting ceremony (here, very simple), sexual advertising (here, skypointing) and female 'appeasement' (a pronounced 'facing-away'). Perhaps the only special points are that the tree habitat precludes 'parading' and the associated postures and, perhaps linked with this, the pair have not evolved well-differentiated close-range greeting. Indeed, it is noticeable that the female seems much more obviously 'uneasy' in the male's presence; she flinches, tremors, ruffs her neck feathers and faces away. Often, she copes by withdrawal, simply hopping away, which is easy among twigs. The main puzzle, to me, is the function of those tomato-red feet. They are not flaunted in ritualised walking or hopping, nor 'presented' in a landing-salute as are those of the blue-foot. Yet one can hardly imagine that they 'just came'. Conceivably, they are genetically associ-ated (linked) with some other, adaptive, feature.

There remain three species of which the blue-footed booby and the Peruvian booby form a closely related pair. The blue-foot benefits from its proximity to the fringes of productive ocean areas, though the price is a more limited distribution. Consequently, it fares rather better than the 'blue water three', and its clutch size is usually two, sometimes three. Admittedly, starvation sometimes (in the Galapagos, often) leads to the death of the younger chick, but this by no means always happens. Productivity, on average, is therefore significantly higher than in the others (Table 26). Moreover, the young grow more quickly and the Galapagos blue-foot breeds at nine-monthly intervals. Proxim-ity to cold water is not the sole reason for its larger brood; even on Hood in the Galapagos, where the masked booby breeds also, it can rear two whilst the masked cannot. A second reason is the blue-footed booby's tendency (especially in the male) to fish close inshore. This largely removes the danger of the long gaps between feeds which can kill small young.

The shortened cycle found in the Galapagos depends, of course, on a relatively a-seasonal environment, and elsewhere in its range it seems that the blue-footed booby is a normal, annual and seasonal breeder.

Behaviourally, the blue-foot is the clown of a family not renowned for its dignity. Because it favours flat ground and usually has quite a large territory, it can parade around as much as it likes. Furthermore, because the male, in particular, is exceptionally light and agile, it lands and takes-off without difficulty. It exploits both of these opportunities to the full and in so doing makes extensive use of its gaudy blue feet. On its territory, it flaunts them in ritualised walking (parading) whilst collecting symbolic nest material, and flashes them in an athletic landing 'salute' after courtship flights above its territory. It has an unimpressive meeting ceremony but makes up for it by an outlandish development of the sexual skypointing, which mates perform in unison. Like the other ground nesters, it uses bill-up-face-away a great deal when leaving and entering the site.

The Peruvian booby (piquéro) is (I was about to say 'merely', but nothing is ever 'mere') a blue-foot modified for eating anchovies and

Fig. 61. *Mutual display (sexual, pair-bonding) in blue-footed booby*

nesting densely on cliffs. The anchovies are central to the piquéro's ecology. They are unimaginably prolific. In about seven months in 1969/70 Peruvian fishermen caught more than 14 million* tons[117] of anchovies which is roughly 13 trillion (13,000,000,000,000,000,000) fish. Other predators combined may have accounted for a further six or seven million tons. Sea-lions, boobies, cormorants, pelicans, penguins loll in a soup of fish; the limits to their catch are imposed only by the time it takes to grab their prey which, moreover, is on their very doorstep. Thick black skeins of seabirds snake everywhere through the mist, above the oily swell; rafts of them mat the sea and, here and there, hailstorms of diving piquéros lance the water, so densely that it appears miraculous that they avoid spearing each other.

The proof of the pudding is in the eating. Piquéros lay clutches of three eggs, sometimes four, and raise all their youngsters in record time. Such recruitment leads to explosive growth of the population, but periodic disasters repeatedly bring it low. These are the well-known Niños, which are incursions of warm water during which the anchovies virtually disappear, probably to deeper, colder layers. They are then inaccessible to the seabirds, which die by the tens of millions, adults and young alike. It is less well known that these abnormal conditions are merely an extreme manifestation of a regular, normal event which, usually, does not affect the birds. Although it gives the

* The official figure was 11 million tons but this in fact represents about 14 million tons fresh weight.

phenomenon its name, the main cause of the disasters is not the warm and strictly coastal counter current, flowing southwards from the Gulf of Guayaquil, usually around Christmas time (the height of the southern summer), hence the name 'El Nino', the child. Rather, it is a massive movement of warm oceanic water from the north and west, which is 'allowed in' whenever the cold upwelling, which normally bathes coastal Peru and is misleadingly called the Humboldt Current, weakens.[58] This may happen in two or three successive years, and to different extents, but, overall, a periodicity of about seven years seems to have some limited validity, and may be another manifestation of sunspot activity, which is known to affect many natural cycles.

For the piquéro, the combination of superabundant food and periodic disasters have been mighty selection pressures. The former makes possible the extraordinarily rapid breeding, leading to increases of some 20% per annum, and the latter ensures both that the breeding potential is realised (extinction could be the penalty for failure) and removes any danger of direct competition for food. Because the anchovies are relatively inaccessible in July/August, the piquéro's breeding is markedly seasonal. Laying occurs principally in November and December and young are most demanding from February to May. Anchovies spawn all year, but have their major spawning peak around September. A mature female anchovy may lay 20,000 eggs and the young fish are recruited when about five months old, which means that around February the shoals are massively augmented.

Despite the piquéro's riches and fecundity and the red-footed booby's poverty, it is worth recalling that the red-foot outnumbers the piquéro, simply because there are hundreds of millions of square miles of tropical ocean but only a small strip of anchovy-rich water off Peru.

The piquéro's behaviour is easily described. It is simply a blue-foot in a habitat which, whether cliffs or densely crowded flatter ground, inhibits parading and acrobatic 'saluting' in flight. Consequently the piquéro performs these in reduced form and has lost (or never acquired) brightly coloured feet. It uses skypointing in much the same way as the blue-footed booby, and indeed the two have exactly comparable ethograms; the components simply vary in speed, amplitude and frequency.

There remains but one booby, the rarest and in many ways the most intriguing. In my view it is also the most soul-stirring. Abbott's booby, an almost solitary nester in the high jungle of Christmas Island. Specialist, archaic, relic – however it is described, it is indisputably set apart from its congeners.

Abbott's booby is by far the least productive of all sulids. It lays a single egg and its chick remains dependent for more than a year after hatching. Nor can it lay at intervals of, say, eighteen months, because it is essentially a seasonal breeder. So, if successful, it is restricted to one egg every two years. However, in most years it is not successful; in such years it lays in May or June and loses its fully feathered chick in the following December/January/February. This dramatic failure (more than 90% fail) comes about largely because Abbott's booby has elected to tackle the monsoon period head-on. Instead of fitting its breeding cycle into the period between March and November, it extends the period during which the chick-cum-juvenile remains fully dependent, through the wet and windy months of November–March. The youngster has to sit stoically on a branch, waiting for parental visits which may become painfully few and far between. In some years, probably in most, it finally succumbs and falls to the jungle floor. During these critical months, the adults may hardly visit the island; alternatively, some of them may come in quite regularly. Probably, it all depends on the weather. High winds and rain keep them away, either because such conditions affect their fishing or because they make it dangerous to land and take-off from the tree canopy, probably both.

The intriguing point is that Christmas Island is not in an impoverished zone. The brown and red-footed boobies grow rapidly and, by and large, are independent when the weather breaks. But Abbott's grows extraordinarily slowly. The explanation is that Abbott's booby has *acquired* slow growth because this is linked with the ability to withstand prolonged starvation, and although the youngster may not be required to starve during its first stages of growth (July–October), it most certainly will be in its later stages. And the reason why it cannot finish growing and become independent in the favourable season (as the other boobies do) may be because its parents (i.e. the species) have become tied to a special mode of foraging and to the jungle-top habitat, both of which mean that the development can only be slow. We know next to nothing about the former, except that *abbotti* seems to favour a distant upwelling area off Java. We do, however, know that Christmas Island has moved several hundreds of miles over many millions of years, which may mean that *abbotti* has had to 'stretch' ever further to reach its feeding area. And the habit of nesting in high jungle trees, through which it is easy but fatal to fall (grounded Abbott's cannot rise in jungle), means that premature practice flights are not a good idea. Finally, there is little flexibility in the system. Once development overran into the monsoon period, it had to go the whole hog, and the chick had to sit it out. There would be little point in fledging and trying to become independent at the worst time of year. It will be clear that *abbotti* walks an evolutionary knife-edge and it may be, simply, that its low numbers result from a breathlessly close struggle against environmental forces.

Behaviourally, it is clear that the main selection pressure has shaped interactions between *abbotti* so as to minimise the risk of falling. To this end, contact behaviour is either absent or restrained. *Abbotti* do not fight; rivals and mates rarely jab; territorial display and the wonderful, protracted greeting ceremony between mates, is performed at a distance; the chick, even if it is starving, begs passively, though its desperate hunger may cause it to continue head swaying and calling for hours on end. Under similar circumstances, any other booby would decapitate its parent in its frenzy.

This concludes my brief survey of the family. I hope the similarities and differences have been made equally clear. All sulids are built alike; they all plunge; they nest in colonies; they feed their young directly from the throat; their behaviour patterns (territorial, between mates and between parents and their offspring) are often similar and homologous. Yet each species has its own morphology, its own degree of sexual dimorphism; each forages and hunts slightly differently; forms colonies with particular characteristics of spacing; lays clutches of different size; has evolved breeding strategies to suit its particular area and

Fig. 62. (a) *Flying over the colony*

(b) *Ritualised in-flying is not greatly different from ordinary landing. Saluting is most highly developed in the blue-footed booby and is undoubtedly a conspicuous and highly ritualised form of landing*

behaviour which is built on the physique dictated by its fishing needs, on the nature of its breeding habitat and on the complex interactions between its various social needs. When you have seen one, you certainly haven't seen them all.

Perhaps their displays lend themselves, better than any other aspect, to visual representation of the similarities and differences within the family, and the following stylised drawings attempt to convey this. But in principle, the same sort of analysis can be applied to, for example, morphology or ecology.

(c) *Fighting is solely by gripping, stabbing and pushing. Only in the three gannets and the Peruvian booby is it common, and only in the former is it prolonged and severe. These four sulids are the only ones to nest densely*

Gannet

Peruvian

(d) Ritualised, close range threat is highly developed only in the gannet. It is common but less highly ritualised in the Peruvian booby and is absent in the other (more widely spaced) boobies

White

Peruvian

Blue-foot

Brown

Red-foot

Abbott's

Gannet

(e) Meeting ceremonies: jabbing is a common form of aggressive interaction between sulids (between mates and rivals), as one might expect in a species which uses its beak for hunting. In most sulids, jabbing forms the only meeting ceremony and as such is variably ritualised. However, gannets and Abbott's booby have evolved elaborate meeting ceremonies. The former retains jabbing (ritualised) between rivals but not between mates, whilst the latter does not show it either between rivals or mates

Brown
(Forward head-wave)

Red-foot
(Forward head-wave)

White
(Yes/No head-shake)

Blue-foot
(Yes head-shake, rapid)

Peruvian
(Yes head-shake, slow)

Abbott's
(Head-jerk)

Gannet
(Bowing)

(f) Territorial display. All sulids possess an aggressively
motivated display whose function is to repel intruders.
Possibly all are derived from re-directed aggression (substitute biting) though this is not certain for all species. The
display is most frequent and most highly stylised in the
gannets, which are by other measures the most strongly
territorial

White. Sky-pointing,
male to female only

Brown. Sky-pointing, male to female;
also performed in flight

Male
to female

Female to male

(g) Sexual advertising displays in the Sulidae. In the boobies,
the skypointing displays are homologous. The gannet's
sexual advertising display is merely analogous. Gannets
use the homologue of skypointing for another communication function

Red-foot. Sky-pointing; unilateral and
reciprocal but not mutual

Peruvian. Sky-pointing; unilateral
reciprocal and mutual

Blue-foot. Sky-pointing; unilateral
reciprocal and mutual

Gannet. Head-shake and reach,
mainly male to female

(a) Peruvian. Bill-up-face-away

(b) Blue-foot. Bill-up-face-away

(c) White. Bill-up-face-away

(d) Brown. Bill-up-face-away

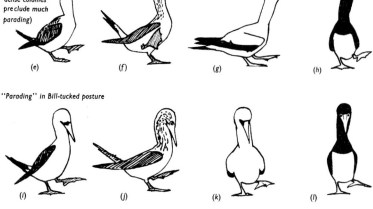

"Parading" in Bill-up-face-away

Peruvian parades "on the spot" (cliff nesting and dense colonies preclude much parading)

Blue-foot shows the most exaggerated parading (feet brightest)

White

Brown

(e)   (f)   (g)   (h)

"Parading" in Bill-tucked posture

(i)   (j)   (k)   (l)

(h) Ritualised locomotion and associated postures. Bill-up-facing-away typically precedes movement away from partner; such movement often uses web-flaunting (parading) and may be accompanied by bill-tucking. All the ground nesting boobies show these behaviour patterns; the red-footed and Abbott's boobies do not, nor are they found in the gannets, which typically use skypointing when moving away from site or partners

(i) Display used in collecting, 'showing', and building-in nest material

Collecting symbolic fragment and returning to site, often using web-flaunting

'Showing' (in an arc) the fragment (or in the case of the brown and Abbott's boobies, the functional piece) of nest material

(j) Mutual nest building. In the blue-footed, white and some brown boobies, the nest is merely symbolic but the building of it is an important pair interaction. In the other sulids the nest is functional in the obvious sense, too

Mutual

Gannet   Peruvian   White

Unilateral

Blue-foot   Brown   Red-foot

(k) *Allo-preening is basically aggressive behaviour which*
    serves to maintain the pair bond, or at least to facilitate
    harmonised proximity between mates. It is absent in
    Abbott's boobies

ANATOMY

It may be useful to append a summary of the principal characteristics
of the order and family[141,129] and of their fossil history, though I have
nothing original to offer.

The Pelecaniformes or Steganopodes, some 53 species altogether, are
globally distributed fish-eaters distinguished mainly by having webs
between all four toes (three complete webs), the hallux (lower and
turned forwards) being connected to the inner toe. In all except the
frigatebirds, the webs are efficient structures for swimming. The
external nostrils are slit-like (tropicbirds), nearly closed (cormorants
and darters) or obsolete (pelicans, frigates, gannets and boobies). The
palate is customarily defined as largely desmognathous (vomers small
or absent, maxilla palatines broad and meeting each other or the
vomers in the mid-line) but this condition is not a clearly demarcated
type of neognathous palate, which in turn is now known not to be a
valid major category, being imperfectly distinguishable from the major
alternative condition (palaeognathous). The basipterygoid process is
missing. The sternum usually has a single sternal notch (rarely, two or
none) and the furcula is largely fixed (ankylosed) to the keel. The
posterior margin of the *bony* aperture of the nares (as against the
aperture in the external covering of the bill) is rounded (holorhinal).
There are 14–20 cervical vertebrae. The tongue is small. The carotids

(a) White booby, "parallel standing" in which bills are ostentatiously not pointed at the partner; not as clearly found in the other ground nesters but some instances of incipient Bill-up-face-away look similar

(b) Female gannet Faces away from male; never vice-versa

Female red-foot Faces away from male. Not as clearly shown in other boobies

(c) Pelican posture (bill tucking), found in all sulids but in two rather different forms; motivation complex and function not clear

Gannet   Peruvian   Blue-foot   White

Red-foot

(1) Appeasement behaviour in adult sulids

may be paired or single. The leg muscle formulae (though, apparently, Garrod's notation is now inadequate) are AXY (tropicbirds), AX (cormorants, darters, pelicans and sulids) and A (frigatebirds). (A = caudifemoralis, part of caud-ilio-femoralis; B = accessory = pars-iliofemoralis; X = semitendinosus = caud-ilio-flexorius; Y = accessory part of semitendinosus = flexor cruris lateralis). ABXY, all four muscles present, represents a primitive condition; ABX, AXY and BXY are derived conditions, whilst AX, BX and XY represent further reductions. A (as in frigates) is highly specialised.

There are eleven primaries, the outermost minute; the aftershaft is vestigial or absent; the fifth secondary remex is apparently absent (diastataxis). The oil (or preen) gland weighs 5,572·5 mg (0·139% of the body weight) which is perhaps less than one might expect. Those of ducks weigh proportionately more. Indeed, the eider's gland weighs 6,108·5 mg.[65] The gland is tufted and there is down on the apteria and pterylae (pterylae are tracts of skin from which feathers grow and apteria are the areas between). The naked skin between the rami of the lower mandibles and on the throat is variably developed, most markedly in pelicans and frigatebirds. Subcutaneous air-sacs are best developed in the heavy plunge-divers (pelicans and particularly gannets and boobies). Chicks are born blind and naked, except those of tropicbirds, which are downy.

Skeletally, the sulids are particularly characterised by their strong, fairly long and pointed bill, tapered but only slightly curved at the tip and never hooked, and with even the apertures of the nostril chambers blocked in the bone of the bill; a linear groove on each side of the culmen; tomia (cutting edges) of the beak serrated; mouth rictus large, extending beyond the eye; upper mandible movable via naso-frontal hinge; bones of the lower jaw incompletely fused in the region of the os spleniale and with special articulation with the quadrate, permitting wide opening of the mouth (the three last-named features are adaptations for swallowing large prey); palatines fused in mid-line, with slight median keel; post-orbital process emarginate; greater part of the carina sterni and the region of the sternum bearing the coracoid grooves extending far beyond the anterior lateral process of the sternum; the keel of the sternum extending slightly more than half the sternum's length; outer and middle toes longer than inner; claws broad, flat and somewhat curved with serrations on the inner edge of the middle toe; 18 cervical vertebrae. Notable external features are the opening of the preen (oil) gland via five apertures; bare skin of the face and gular region; long pointed wings with emarginated outer primary; long variably cuneate tail (12–18 feathers) with middle rectrices longest; tarsus medium-short (shorter than the foot) with reticulated surface, that of the upper toes continuing up the tarsus as rows of small scale-like plates (scutes). The facial skin, bill, eyes and feet are usually brightly coloured.

FOSSIL SULIDS

The evolution of aquatic lines started early. By the late cretaceous, well over 60 million years ago, the Anseriformes, Phoenicopteriformes and Pelecaniformes (ancestral forms of geese, flamingos and pelican types) had made their appearance. At this time, the last of the dinosaurs were still abroad and the toothed divers, Hesperonithes, flourished. *Hesperornis* is the only bird of cretaceous age that we know had teeth. It was a foot-propelled fish-eater. The most recent account of fossil gannets and boobies,[52] upon which the following paragraphs are closely based, dismisses two of the oldest 'sulid' fossils (*Sula ronzoni* and *Sula pygmaea*). Harrison suggests that the first named is part of a cormorant and that the second, an upper arm bone, is too generalised to be identified with confidence. The earliest sulid thus becomes one which has been assigned to a separate genus, and named *Empheresula arvernensis* (Milne-Edwards), and comes from the Upper Oligocene of France (the Oligocene ran from 36 to 25 million years ago). It may be tentatively inferred that *Empheresula* was somewhat more aquatic than modern sulids. This French fossil is the only one from Europe; all others are from North America and (recently) Australia.

The main evolutionary radiation of the Sulidae appears to have occurred in the Miocene (25–13 million years ago), in which epoch the two genera, *Sula* and *Morus*, could already be distinguished, though whether the differences merit generic status is of course a matter of judgement, not of fact (see earlier). At this time, sulids already ranged considerably in size, from *Microsula* to a giant, long-legged sulid recently uncovered on Norfolk Island[135] Australia. *Miosula media*, another Upper Miocene sulid, had a body slightly bigger than a gannet's, with stouter legs and feet, shorter wings and a humerus which would effectively have made them rather less straight than those of the modern gannet; it probably relied more on swimming and less on flying. Its denser bones, like those of *Microsula*, tend to agree with this interpretation. *Miosula* persisted until at least the middle Pliocene (the Pliocene ran from 13 to 1 million years ago). *Palaeosula stocktoni* of the Upper Miocene appears to have been even more aquatic than *Miosula*, than which it was also bigger though shorter-winged. If these aquatic-tending sulids came into competition with the cormorant line, they might well have been beaten; they were on the wrong road.

Apart from these aquatic-tending forms, other fossil sulids do not diverge much from the typical *Sula/Morus* stock. Of the boobies (*Sula*), the earliest is *Sula universitatis*, of the Lower Miocene in Florida. The bird was about the size of the brown booby. Like another Miocene *Sula* (*Sula willetti*), it had an upper arm bone which was longer in relation to the lower arm than in modern boobies and in this was more like modern gannets, in which the relatively long humerus is a feature (but note that Abbott's booby also has the long humerus and may be older than other living boobies). *Sula pohli* (also of the Upper Miocene) had got away from this condition, and had a lower arm bone (ulna) longer than the humerus, as in modern boobies.

The most recent fossil *Sula*, prior to modern birds, is *Sula humeralis* of the Middle Pliocene. It had no obviously special features. The earliest gannets (if one goes along with the separation of gannets and boobies at generic level) occur later than the earliest sula species. Two were found in the Middle Miocene; *Morus loxostyla* was a little smaller than the modern gannet; and *Morus vagabundus* was smaller still (about the size of a red-footed booby). *Morus lompocanus* occurred in California's Upper Miocene together with *Sula willetti* and *Miosula media*.

The Bone Valley formation, California (lower Miocene), contains numerous seabird remains and also deposits of phosphate, and obviously seabirds were breeding colonially on guano-covered islands at this time. Among the fossils are *Morus peninsularis*, *Sula guano* and *Sula phosphata*, and a cormorant, *Phalacrocorax wetmorei*. *Morus peninsularis* appears to have been smaller than *M. lompocanus* but larger and more heavily built that *M. loxostyla* and *M. vagabundus*.

A fossil (*Morus reyanus*) similar to the modern gannet turns up in the Upper Pleistocene on the Pacific coast of North America, where there are now no gannets (but plenty of boobies).

The above account will probably be modified in the light of fairly radical re-assessments currently in preparation, based on several recent finds. I am far too poorly versed in avian palaeontology to venture any original comments but would again draw attention to the implications of accepting an early *Morus/Sula* dichotomy based on wing proportions. Quite apart from any difficulty there may be in accommodating recent finds, there is the problem of *Sula abbotti*, which does not show the *Sula*-type wing.

SUMMARY

1. The composition and distribution of the ancient and diverse order Pelecaniformes is briefly described.

2. All are colonial, though hugely variable in this. The major 'categories' of colony, in terms of size and density, can be related to food (mainly) and in some cases, available nesting sites.

3. Pelecaniforms lay clutches of between one and four eggs, and clutch size can be related to food and foraging techniques. Similarly, the timing of breeding can be related mainly to the seasonal (or non-seasonal) nature of food.

4. The three gannets (Atlantic, African and Australasian) are treated as allospecies. They differ substantially in breeding strategies. The Atlantic apparently has the richest and most seasonal food supply and the strongest tendency towards seasonal breeding. It is the heaviest, the quickest-growing and apparently the most site-competitive. It also takes longest to reach breeding age. Interpretations are offered for these (and other) features.

5. The migrations of the young of the three gannets offer remarkable parallels.

6. The boobies differ greatly in size and shape and these may be related to food and foraging techniques.

7. The breeding strategies of all the boobies, from the brown booby which may breed every nine months to Abbott's which lays only once every two years, are discussed in relation to food, which is held to determine their nature.

8. The different sulids strongly resemble one another in several aspects of their behaviour, but have each evolved their distinctive 'sets' of behaviour patterns which relate to habitat and other factors. These similarities and differences are discussed and summarised diagrammatically.

9. A summary of the principal anatomical characteristics of the order is given.

10. A brief account of some fossil sulids is given.

7: The gannet and man

Then too was driven
Oslac beloved
An exile far
from his native land
over the rolling waves,
over the ganet-bath

Poem of Beowulf

Gannets have lived on this earth much longer than man. Maybe, even before *Homo sapiens* ousted *neanderthalensis*, gannets were part of his lore. The relationship, as usual when we are a partner, has been woefully lop-sided, for whilst gannets have been eaten by man, have helped him find fish and have excited interest, legend and admiration, man has wantonly destroyed the gannet and, latterly, polluted its seas. Still, it has been a relationship and this chapter is about man and the gannet.

EARLY ACCOUNTS

The ways in which man views animals changes continuously. It is with this evolution of understanding in mind, that I approach earlier accounts of the gannet's natural history. It is not an ego trip at the expense of the past, but rather a look at the sort of things that were written. If they sound odd, the reason why they do so should be of interest. A detailed historical account of the gannet is to be found nearly half a century before Gurney wrote. Robert Cunningham, in his article 'On the Solan Goose, or Gannet (*Sula bassana*, Linn.)' in *The Ibis* for January 1866, gives an extraordinarily fine summary, with many quotations of all the important early writings. Gurney, in his turn, lists the early contributors as: Fordun (and his continuator, Walter Bower) 1448, John Major (by far the best) 1521, Hector Boece 1526, Peter Swave 1535, Conrad Gesner 1555, Bishop Leslie 1578, Sir W. Brereton 1634, John Blaeu 1649 and John Ray 1661. I have listed Gurney's references, with annotations, in the bibliography.

The barnacle goose (or as some think, the solan goose) myth (not mentioned by Gurney) is well known: 'So rotten sides of broken shipps do change to Barnacles; O, Transformation strange! 'Twas first a greene Tree; then a gallant Hull, Lately a mushroom, now a flying Gull' (Guillame de Saluste 1578). The goose barnacle (*Lepas anatifera*) which attaches itself to underwater wood by means of a stalk (the head) and contains feather-like appendages (legs) within plates of shell, was believed to give rise to birds which became detached and flew away. An important element in the myth was the coincidence in the timing of the autumn arrival of barnacle geese and the barnacle-infested timber thrown ashore by the equinoctial gales. The sequence of writings, culminating in the possibility that the myth may have been applied to the gannet, is broken by long gaps. The origin of the tale may have been Aristotle (as ever!) who wrote about a creature which he called 'Ephemerus' which arose by transformation from 'small pouches ... from which four-footed creatures burst, a sort of animal which lives and flies until the afternoon of the same day, but presently at the sun's going down withers and languishes, and finally at the sun's setting, dies, lasting no longer than a single day, whence it is called ephemerus ...'.

Turner's[33] account of the 'bernicle' goose's origin (which he clearly distinguished from and favoured over the solan goose as being the bird concerned in the myth) runs: 'No one has seen the Bernicle's nest or egg, nor is this wonderful, since Bernicles without a parent's aid are said to have spontaneous generation in this way: when after a certain time the firwood masts or planks or yard-arms of a ship have rotted on the sea, their fungi, as it were, break out upon them first, in which in course of time one may discern evident forms of birds, which afterwards are clothed with feathers and at last become alive and fly'. He then cites the authority of the historian Gyraldus (Giraldus Cambrensis) and the theologian Octavian, the latter as an eye-witness. He does not cite Boece, though the latter's account pre-dates his own by 18 years. He concludes ... 'the chenerotes (that is, the birds of the myth) are either bernicles, or the geese of the Bass [that is, gannets], or are decidedly unknown to me'.

Armstrong[5] delves into the mythology of this 'bird-fish' tradition. Bernicle (or more likely brent) geese were until recently, and in parts may still be, considered by Irish folk, where the tradition has always been strong, to be more 'fish' than fowl and hence legitimate fare for Catholics on Fridays and during Lent. He discusses Jewish Rabbinic literature as a source of the fish-fowl controversy and carries the legend back, first to the 10th century, when the muslim, Ibrahim ibn Ahmad at-Tortushi, describes it and then, two centuries further still, to the *Exeter Riddle Book*:

> In a narrow was my net, and beneath the wave I lived
> Underflowen by the flood; in the mountain billows
> Low was I besunken; in the sea I waxed
> Over-covered with the waves, clinging with my body
> To a wandering wood.
> Quick the life I had, when I from the clasping came
> Of the billows, of the beam-wood, in my black array;
> White in part were then my pranked garments fair,
> When the lift unheaved me, me a living creature,
> Wind from wave upblowing; and as wide as far
> Bore me o'er the bath of seals — say what is my name?

Notwithstanding the specific mention of the solan goose in some references to the phenomenon, Armstrong plumps solidly for the little auk, *Plautus alle*, as the real bird to which the legend refers. The bird's blackness, he thinks, fits the auk well; but in fact it fits the juvenile gannet better. His quote from Mouffet (1655) that 'Barnacles both breed unnaturally, by corruption, and taste very unsavoury. Poor men eat them, rich men hate them, wise men reject them when they have other meat', fits the gannet perfectly (compare the account later in this chapter).

The fact that it was taken and eaten off France, which is further south than the barnacle goose goes (at least nowadays), is perfectly consistent with the gannet, whose southward migration as a juvenile takes it past that coast in huge numbers. Admittedly, auks are subject to 'wrecks', which Armstrong suggests is consistent with the origin of the myth as due to the discovery of corpses washed up by the sea; but so, to some extent, are young gannets, hundreds of which are sometimes driven ashore, starving. The only thing that fits the little auk but not the gannet is a remark that nobody has seen the eggs and nest of the bernicle goose. If the bernicle *were* the solan goose, that of course would not be true, but Turner may have meant his remark *for* the bernicle (which he distinguished from the solan), since he made it with specific reference to the bernicle, which he favoured as 'the goose' of the legend and to which it did in fact apply. Giraldus, earlier making the same point, again referred to the bernicle. How and when the legend became applied to the solan goose is obscure but that it did so seems clear.

The origin of the story is not hard to imagine, since goose barnacles are odd, curiously feathery creatures with a beak-like shell and marine habit, and the metamorphosis would not seem incredible in the days when spontaneous generation of life was widely believed. The supposed eyewitness testimony is not unknown in respect of modern tall-stories.

It might seem more surprising that observation of simple behaviour, requiring nothing but a pair of eyes and some patience, took so long to develop. The Dane, Peter Swave, who gives an account of his 1535 visit to Bass Rock, was apparently the first to note the gannet's habit of incubating underfoot. Gesner mentions it soon after, but it still seemed to surprise Gurney, 350 years later. The latter, incidentally, would not believe that gannet excreta helps to cement nest material to the ledge ('nor can I for a moment credit the idea that the gannet's white secretions assist in binding the seaweed to the rock'), though anybody who has climbed amongst them knows that it hardens into an effective crust. In this case, his scepticism may have been a simple extension of that which rightly caused him to reject the report that gannets solder their eggs to the ledge. This in turn probably referred, in any case, to the guillemot: 'Among the many different kinds of birds which seek the Bass Island . . . one bird was pointed out to me which lays but one egg, and this it places upon the point of a rock, with nothing like a nest or bed beneath it, yet so firmly that the mother can go and return without injury to it; but if anyone move it from its place, by no art can it be fixed or balanced again, . . . The place, as I have said, is crusted over with a white cement, and the egg, when laid, is bedewed with a thick and viscid moisture, which setting speedily, the egg is soldered as it were, or agglutinated, to the subjacent rock'.[53] Another belief, again an extension of the truth (in this case, that gannets incubate underfoot) was that 'these solem-geese . . . when their eggs are sufficiently sitten, they stamp upon them with their feet and break them'.[12]

When one reflects that insight into the nature of animal behaviour barely pre-dates the European ethologists, notably Lorenz and Tin-bergen, it is not surprising that, even as late as Gurney, there is no hint of understanding, in terms of the motivation and function, of gannet behaviour. Gurney, indeed, was so fond of gannets that he seems to have mused human thoughts into them: 'Their struggles are quickly forgotten; the gannets which were fighting before, being very soon good friends again' is pure projection. Neighbouring gannets never cease to treat each other as potential rivals, to be threatened, bitten and displayed against. Similarly, 'two adult gannets which looked old and solemn enough to be patriarchs of their clan'. And he, who made a special point of remarking that 'every note, every attitude, every change in flight or gait . . . must have its reason and accordingly be worthy of study,' was apparently never struck by the magnitude of gannet display, nor moved to ponder its significance. Thus, of court-ship, he says 'it is not so noticeable in the gannet as in many species of bird'. The difficulty here, perhaps, was to appreciate that courtship display is more than simply the behaviour *immediately* before copula-tion. It includes the very conspicuous mutual-fencing display. It is not clear, incidentally, where he got the mistaken idea that males feed their sitting females (footnote, p. 279), though courtship feeding does occur in some seabirds, notably *Laridae*.

On the other hand, he happily ascribed to gannets intelligence which they certainly do not possess; '. . . the gannet is a bird which in some ways is a marvel of intelligence'. Perhaps, here, intelligence was used loosely to mean 'adaptive behaviour', as indeed it still is by not a few. And he was equally ready to give credence to a story of one 'deliber-ately killing itself against a lighthouse,' and to cite as 'extreme stupidity' the case of a bird which crashed against the wall of a lighthouse yard!

Obvious behaviour, particularly if it has practical significance, such as the evident wariness of gannets early in the year, did not escape notice. Thus Caius in Turner:[133] 'now when, at a certain season of the year, the [Bass] geese are about to return to this precipitous Island rock – not so big on the top as a kite could hover over . . . it would be too long to recount what spying, what circumspection (scouts having been sent ahead) they use before they alight: at what time of year they do this, the solitary state of the isle, when the inhabitants shut themselves up for several days, until the geese have settled down, lest they should

drive them off.' This is probably derived from Major's earlier account
(1521) '. . . these geese, in the spring of every year return from the south
to the rock of the Bass in flocks, and for two or three days, during which
the dwellers on the rock are careful to make no disturbing noise, the
birds fly round the rock.' Martin Martin ascribes the same habit to the
St Kildans: 'the inhabitants likewise say, that in these fowls there first
come over some spies or harbingers, especially of the solan geese,
towr'ing about the islands where their nests are, and that when they
have made a review thereof they fly away and in two or three days after,
the whole tribe are seen coming.'

Possibly an extension of this observation is the belief, held by the St
Kildans, that gannets post sentinels which have first to be taken
unawares before the others can be approached. The simple fact is that
any thoroughly alarmed gannet utters a call which communicates its
panic, and the others react strongly. There is no such thing as a sentinel
watching for danger, but only individuals who wake more easily and
whose startled calls set off contagious alarm.

The extraordinarily devoted attendance of the gannet at its site
impressed early observers, though nobody expressed surprise that
although it returns in January it does not lay until April. The contrast
between the solicitous attendance of the parents throughout the long
period of the chick's growth and their unconcern at its departure, did
not pass unnoticed, and may have given rise to the starvation theory
which has lived so long and is still far from dead. Thus, those respected
gannetologists, Fisher and Lockley,[37] not too long ago: 'it does not
seem surprising therefore that the adults give up this uncomfortable
feeding process gradually, and about the eleventh week, or a few days
later, the parents cease altogether to feed their chick. In its turn, the
chick appears to show no further interest in the adults.' The truth is
quite the opposite. It seems odd that, although Gurney had observed
that the parents remain behind and do *not* feed the young at sea, it
should nevertheless be thought likely that the young gannet would
waste any of its hard-won fat stores *before* fledging, when an arduous
and solitary struggle awaits it. The fact, known to the St Kildans, that in
some years young gannets are lean and 'comparatively worthless' for
eating, is interesting evidence for fluctuation in food supplies, but is
not to be put down to parents' losing interest in feeding their young.
Shearwaters, in which the young *do* fledge after a period of fasting, are
a different case because they have to be capable of sustained flight and,
furthermore, it is an advantage for the adults to be able to leave the
breeding area early. They do not hang around as gannets do. Gurney
pointed out that most juvenile gannets die between September and
December, at sea, and that in view of the difficulties facing them, they
should find it an advantage to fledge at a tranquil time. As we have
seen, this has important implications for the gannet's breeding
strategy.

Longevity has always interested people, and Gurney realised that the
gannet's low productivity meant that it must live quite a long time, but

he rather went overboard with his suggestion that 'there is nothing preposterous that there may be gannets living on the Bass Rock now, which were there in Ray's time'. This would have made them 252 years old! The record for a free-living seabird (a Laysan albatross) is about 56 years, and our own fulmar is not far behind at over 40.[30] In fact, a few gannets must certainly reach 40 or 50 years of age.

THE GANNET AS FOOD

Perhaps naturally, people were for long interested in the gannet mainly as an article of commerce:

> The Scout, the scart, the Cattiwake,
> The Soland goose sits on the lack,
> Yearly in the Spring

was but a prelude to:

> Winter cheer of sea-fowl dried, and soland's store,
> And gammons of the tuskey boar,
> And savoury haunch of deer . . .
>
> (Sir W. Scott, *Marmion*)

and how more appropriately could one begin than with Sir William Brereton's[12] entertaining account of the etiquette: 'So extreme fat are the young as that when they eat them, they are placed in the middle of the room, so all may have access about it; their arms stripped up and linen cloaths placed before their cloaths, to secure them from being defiled from the fat thereof, which both besprinkle and besmear all that come near unto it'. Harsh and socially unjust the 'good old days' certainly were, but there comes down from them a strangely evocative atmosphere, no doubt compounded of a complex and contradictory mixture, but nonetheless real. Take, again, the old bell-man of Girvan, crying his wares after three rings of his bell: 'Ailsa cocks [guillemots] cleaned and ready for the pot, tuppence each. Peaties [puffins] and strainies [razorbills] penny each, cleaned.'

Nor were sea-fowl, especially gannets, simply the seasonal luxury of the poor who could afford nothing better. The gannet used to be a delicacy at all Scottish banquets[48] – 'amongst our viands that we had I must not forget the soleand goose, a most delicate fowle which breeds in great aboundance in a little rocke called the Basse . . . It is very good flesh, but it is eaten in the forme as wee eate oysters, standing at a sideboard, a little before dinner . . . and . . . must be well liquored with two or three good rowses of sherrie or canarie sacke.' Sir Robert Sibbald, in 1648, opined that 'the art of cookery cannot form a dish of such delicate flavour, and combining the tastes of fish and flesh, as a roasted solan goose.' James V was served with them ('auce solanes') at Holyrood in 1525[48] though Charles II apparently classed them with the solemn League and Covenant, as being the two things which he disliked in Scotland. Gurney gravely puts them in their place as 'fishy dainties at best, a mixture of fish and fowl unsuited for refined palates.' In fact, to my coarse palate, they can be so delicately fishy that only the after-taste discloses it; some mute swan I ate tasted far fishier. No doubt the Irish labourers who cooked gannets by the score or hundred in brick ovens at Canty Bay, across from the Bass, found them a lot better than potatoes. Besides roasting, gannets may be pickled, dried and eaten raw, in which form I imagine they would rival cowhide, or simply boiled in water with potatoes. The annual emolument of the Vicar of the Bass (Minister of North Berwick) used to include 12 solan geese, entire.[39]

It is well known that young gannets or gugas are not only highly edible but their fat has remarkable curative properties. In *Ein Mittelenglisches Medizin Buch* of the 15th and 16th centuries, gannet's grease is recommended, along with badger and boar fat, as a cure for gout – 'Pro gutta: Item unguentum; Also an oyntement for the same. R tak cattes grece, ganates grece, banfones grece, bores grece, mery of an hors, 7 grece of a dogge, 7 alle these tempre togeder'. Again, from Canon Hector Boece, 1526, of Aberdeen, the oft-quoted passage: 'within the bowellis of thir geis, is ane fatness of singulaire medicine; for it helis mony infirmities speciallie sik as cumis be gut [gout] and cater [catarrh] disceding in the hanches or lethes [groins] of men and wemen.' Later, John Morisone, in the 18th century, wrote 'Of the grease of these fowlls (especially the solind goose) they make an excellent oyle, called the gibanistick* which is exceeding good for healing of anie sore ore wound ore cancer, either on man or beaste. ... the legg of a young gentleman which had been inflamed and cankered for the space of two years, ... yet in three weeks tyme, being my hous, was perfetlie whole be applying the foresaid oyle.' To this I add my own testimony, that it *does* relieve muscular pain. Barrels of gannet grease were so valuable that a dispute concerning some, between the Prioress of North Berwick and Robert Lauder, then owner of the Bass Rock, was arbitrated by Pope Alexander VI in 1493. As late as 1766, ten gallons of gannet grease fetched £2 13s. 5d. but by about 1860 it had been humbled from medicine to cart grease, and a little later was hardly used at all. In the Hebrides, sea-fowl fat, a mixture of several species, was used as a sheep smear.[48] As to the prices fetched by gannets, in 1643 they fetched 2s. 1d. a-piece, in 1675 about 1s. 5d.; in 1710 2s. and after that about 1s. 8d. up until the early years of the nineteenth century. By mid-century the price had dropped to 9d., or even 6d., and in another decade the trade in gannets as food had virtually ceased. Even in those days there was inflation and Pennant wrote: 'this is the only kind of provision whose price has not been advanced, for we learn from Mr.

---

* The St Kildans termed seabird fat 'giben'. The remedy for most things was 'their great and beloved giben – the fat of their fowls with which they stuff the stomach of a solen goose, in fashion of a pudding, this they put in the infusion of oatmeal [brochan].'

Ray that it was equally dear a century ago!' Gannets used to be sold in Edinburgh at the Poultry Market, every week day in August and September ('weather permitting'), and as late as 1876 some 800 gannets a year were being taken. Many of them were wrapped in rhubarb leaves, partly cooked, and sent to the markets of industrial England, to Sheffield, Birmingham, Manchester, Newcastle and London.[48]

Gannet feathers, de-odourised by baking or standing in the sun, were sold at 10s. per Scottish stone (10·9 kg or 24 lb) in 1767, and 18s. in 1874. Later, enormous quantities of feathers (not all from gannets) were exported from St Kilda at 5s. or 6s. per stone in 1877 and sold in Edinburgh or Glasgow for 7s. to 8s. The imagination boggles at the number of birds required to produce such quantities, for 90,000 small seabirds were needed for 200 stones, and trade expanded far beyond this. Gurney records that in 1900 a London merchant could still get 10s. a stone for gannets' feathers. Almost 300 gannets were needed to stuff one featherbed. Plucking, at 1s. 6d. per day in 1876, was a grim job; the old crones, smothered in feathers, worked in the dim light of the plucking room, looking like so many witches.

Amongst the more bizarre uses to which gannets have been put are shoes, lamps (the breast bone), skin bottle (stomach and gullet) principally for fulmar oil, pipe stem (ulna) and purse (web). 'The women inhabiting this Isle [St Kilda] wear no shoes nor stockings in the summer-time; their ordinary and only shoes are made of the necks of solan geese, which they cut above the eyes, the crown of the head serves for the heel, the whole skin being cut close at the breast, which end being sewed, the foot enteres into it, as into a piece of narrow stocking; this shoes does not last above five days, and if the downy side be next the ground, then not above three or four; however there are plenty of them.' The white down of Australasian gannets was used by Maoris in their hair and attached to ears, to add to their efficacy in battle. According to their fable the gannet, because of its strength, was in the van of the seabirds in their battle with the land-birds.[99]

Finally, the gannet's egg was by no means despised. Relatively unpalatable as it is judged to be by professional egg-tasters,[21] hedgehogs, and rats ranked them second most palatable of the eggs of many species, and the St Kildans must have liked them. 'The inhabitants are accustomed to drink it raw, having from experience found it very pectoral and cephalic though strangers found them "astringent and windy"'. Thus Martin Martin: 'Our men, upon their arrival eating greedily of them, became costive and feverish.' A North Berwick advertisement of 1856 offered 'one of the most rare delicacies of the season', claiming that they were highly appreciated at the Royal Table and 'admitted to be indistinguishable from plover's eggs'. The St Kildans took thousands each year (14,000 merely from Stac Lee summit, 14 May 1902), and eggs continued to be gathered on the Bass until 1885 and on Ailsa Craig, where the harvest may have been considerable, until at least 1929. It should be added that eggs taken early in the season are usually replaced within less than a fortnight.

The St Kildans preserved them for six to eight months under ashes in stone pyramids.

The Bass has perhaps a richer history than any comparable island in Britain, and most of it bound up with gannets. Although Bass Rock yields to Lundy in that the first mention of its gannets is in 1493 against Lundy's 1274, its accessibility, fortification and teeming bird life ensured that it received a flow of visitors. There is neither need nor space to retail its history[69] in full, but I must steal a page or two for a brief excursion.

The name itself may be a descriptive term of Celtic origin, meaning a conical hill, as in 'Bass' and 'Little Bass', two hillocks near Inverurie in Aberdeenshire. The hermit of Bass Rock, St Baldred, probably a simple Presbyter, died in 606 and was doubtless well acquainted with gannets. The Anglo-Saxon poem of Beowulf, around the turn of the 6th century, mentions the 'ganet-bath' (North Sea) and is probably referring to Bass gannets.

The outer wall of most of the Bass' battlements is still in good shape. It is now, and has been for long, the nesting place of the Bass' small colony of puffins and one of its first fulmar sites. The prison and barracks were situated behind them, where the lighthouse (built in 1902) and outbuildings now are. This famous fortress is thought to have been built by Malcolm II, sometime before the end of the 11th century. Malcolm III (Malcolm Canmore) presented the castle area of the rock to Lauder, who became known as the Lauder of the Bass. It was a Robert Lauder, son of Sir Robert Lauder indented in 1531, who in 1561 changed the Lauder crest: 'this junior family made several changes upon the original family arms, for whilst they preserved the Griffon in the shield instead of the white lion used by the chief, they took angels as supporters, and instead of the rest of the chief family, a tower with a man in a watching posture looking out of it, they assumed the crest of a gannet sitting upon a rock, and the motto "sub-umbra alarum tuarum", under the shadow of thy wings, which presumably originally referred to the Griffon'. Many Kings have visited the Bass, and not all under happy circumstances. The 12-year-old Prince James, son of Robert III, was sent to France via the Bass, but taken prisoner off Flamborough Head. James II and James III had little to do with Bass Rock, but James IV visited it on 23 May 1497, and paid 14 shillings to the boatman. During James' reign the Scottish admiral, Sir Andrew Wood, beat the English off the Bass.

> *The Battle it was fiercely fought,*
> *Near to the Craig of Bass*
> *When we next fight the English Loon,*
> *May nae waur come to pass.*

Bass Rock was never taken by the English though an attempt was made as early as 1548. James VI visited the Bass in 1581 and was so enamoured that he offered to buy it for any price. As a result of this visit, legislation for the protection of gannets ensued, probably the first of its kind: 'His majesty, with advice of the saidis Lordis of his secreit counseill for the stancheing of lyk enormitie in tyme cuming, has ordaint and ordainis all skeppairs and mariners of schipps or boittes and every personis of whatsumevir, usaris of sick moyen ingyne and invention, for destraoying and slaying of the said fowlis and solane geis, to be callit and convenit befoir the baillies of Dunbar, or otheris jugeis to be depute be (Mr.) George Lauder, of Bass, and his successors, lairdis of Bass.' These orders were proclaimed at the market crosses of many towns north and south of the Forth. The eventual loss of the Bass by the Lauders, after an unsuccessful attempt by Charles I to get it, was a sad one. George Lauder, in 1628, apparently bankrupt, sought refuge there but was eventually arrested and lost the rock. Before it was acquired in 1706 by the Dalrymples, the present owners, it passed through several hands (Sir John Hepburn, Sir Andrew Ramsay and Lord Lauderdale on behalf of the Government). The fortress was effectively demolished in 1701, after four Jacobite prisoners locked out their jailers and held out for almost three years, from 1691–94, eventually naming their own terms for surrender.

Among the droves of famous naturalists who have set foot on the Bass Rock may be mentioned Thomas Pennant, Ray, Willughby, Macgillivray, Audubon and, to mention a few names that will be perhaps even more famous to posterity, Roger Tory Petersen, James Fisher, Niko Tinbergen and Konrad Lorenz. I would love to steal more space to further sing the praises of this great rock, upon which we were privileged to live for three years; to describe its moods and its birds purely for their own sake; the dusk of a late July evening when the urgent, searching chirrups of excited young guillemots about to essay that compulsive and irrevocable leap down to the dark sea punctuate the rising, swelling and dying gargle of the adults; the drollery of the sinuous shag in his darting, head-throwing courtship; the immense falls of migrants on misty October days; the awakening of the gannetry in the stillness of a mid-summer dawn; seals playing lazily in the laminarian fronds at the base of the great cliffs; kittiwakes splitting the air with their frantic cries and dying moans, the very essence of a seabird rock. And the grey, wet, windy days of cold misery. Thankfully, in this year of grace 1978, the Bass is still the same, unspoilt, uncommercialised, its birds intact – nay, increasing. Long may it remain so. To quote those two great, early authors, Boece and Major, '. . . there is nothing in this rocke that is not full of admiration and woonder; therein also is great store of soland geese . . . these foules do feed their yoong with the most delicet fish that they can come by'. And John Major '. . . at the bottom of the sea with lynx-like eye he spies the fish, precipitates himself upon it, as the hauk upon the heron, and then with beak and claw drags it to the surface; and, if at some distance from the Rock he sees another fish better than the first that has caught his eye, he lets the first escape until he has made sure of the one that was last seen . . .'

Clearly, gannets have long been valuable sources of protein, fat and feathers, offering by far the largest and easiest crop of any North Atlantic seabird. One large youngster provides over 3 kg (6½ lb) of fat and protein and it is possible to gather 2,000 birds in one raid. Can it be doubted that pre-historic man would take advantage of those gannetries he could reach? His middens of 20,000 years ago, in the Channel Islands, show that he ate great auks, captured at sea, so he must have been able to make reasonable journeys. The Bass Rock would be an easy target and Ailsa Craig quite possible. Grassholm gives less to steer by but was almost certainly visited if not lived on, whilst Lundy, the Skelligs and Scar Rocks, among present day gannetries, would have been easily exploitable and others may have been accessible on occasions. But of course it is not until relatively recent times that there is any record of the nature and extent of the 'harvesting'.

Between 1511 (the earliest date for which there are figures) and 1865, the Bass yielded between 1,000–2,000 birds a year, mostly young, with the average probably around 1,500–1,600. Then demand declined and less than 1,000 a year were taken in the 1870s (800–900 in 1874) until 1876, and probably less than 500 after that, until 1885 when culling ceased.[48,38] If there were, on average, about 4,000 young produced each year, an average cull of 1,500 would mean that about 625 young would survive to breed, instead of 1,000. At this rate, the gannetry could just about hold its own, though it would be a different matter if many adults were taken.

Ailsa Craig was the other gannetry known to mediaevals: 'an incredible noumer of soland geis [on the Bass] . . . and are sene in na part of Albion, bot in this crag and Ailsay'. It has been culled since at least 1635, and probably since before 1526, though because they were less accessible fewer were taken than from Bass Rock – probably not more than 500 per year between 1853 and 1860, or possibly 1880, when exploitation ceased. Cliff-nets took over 1,500 birds a week, mainly puffins and guillemots but some gannets.

Sula Sgeir has the distinction of being the only British gannetry from which young are still taken, the practice dating from at least 1549, and possibly from the twelfth century or earlier; the only others in the world are Myggenaes (Faeroes) and the Westmann Isles. The cull, mainly of young birds but including some adults, has often been large, compared with Bass Rock. In the 1860s, 'several thousand' yearly; 1880s 2,000–3,000; 1884 2,300; 1898 2,500; 1912 2,200; 1915 1,100; 1931 2,000; 1933 2,000; 1934 1,400; 1936 2,060; 1937 2,000; 1938 2,000.

The only modern ornithologist who has stayed on Sula Sgeir with the Noss (Lewis) men during their gannet culls, is the late James McGeoch,[70] who describes the grisly operation (see plates). The men usually cross in a seine-netter and/or an open boat which can be 'beached' on the island. Two such crews total about 18 men. The average kill on 19 raids between 1919 and 1958 was 2,360 young gannets. In 1958, McGeoch remarked on the tendency to kill larger numbers but noted, also, that the market seemed easily glutted and almost half the 1958 catch was unsold on arrival at Noss. What eventually happened to the remainder is not recorded. The birds are snatched from the ledges by spring-loaded jaws attached to a bamboo pole. They are then clubbed, passed to the top of the island and plucked and singed over a peat-fire, gutted, salted and stacked for loading into the boat.

St Kilda is the name above all others in the annals of seabird exploitation. There, an entire community built their physical and cultural life around this resource, much as the Bedouins have built theirs around the camel[90] or the Eskimos the animals of the Arctic. Before I discuss the gannet culls I cannot resist a few comments on these extraordinary Scottish islanders, whose way of life was so admirably chronicled by Martin Martin. Dr Johnson may well have said 'a man could not write so ill if he should try,' but there is a lot more interest in Martin's account than in some of those of the irascible Englishman, who probably found the wildness of Scotland ill-suited to his urban temperament and responded with the caustic wit so well expressed in his famous remark, that the finest sight a Scot can see is the high road that leads to England.

To me, the most striking thing about the St Kildans as a society (which lasted, remember, at least 600 years, from the 14th century or before, to the 1930s) was not the technicalities of their dependence on and use of seabirds, but the insight they give into the biological roots of small-group structure and behaviour, and into the satisfactions which arise from living in harmony with them. 'The inhabitants of St Kilda are much happier than the generality of mankind – there is this only wanting to make them the happiest people in this habitable globe, viz, that they themselves do not know how happy they are and how much they are above the avarice and slavery of the rest of mankind.' The sources of this happiness were self-evidently not material or environmental. I suggest that it stemmed from the deep satisfaction of belonging to a strongly-bonded group which conferred status and rôle, or identity, and demanded substantial effort, skill and courage from its members. There was the physical and mental challenge of the climb as a means of expressing the aspirations common to young males the world over. As Martin said, climbing to them was as war to the soldier; they won their spurs. There was the combination of individual rights and community rights and obligations. With regard to the first, nobody could have been more proprietorial: every dried gannet had the distinguishing mark of its owner; even the boat 'sixteen subits long, which serves the whole commonwealth' was by no means free to all 'it is very curiously divided into apartments proportionable to their lands and rocks; every individual has his space distinguished to a hair's-breadth, which his neighbour cannot encroach so much as to lay an egg upon it,' which is pretty emphatic. They were 'very jealous of their wives.' Conversely, they had a great sense of unity. 'They are very charitable to their poor, of whom there are not at present above three, and these carefully provided for by this little commonwealth; each particular family contributing according to their ability for their necessities. . . .'

Grossly anti-social behaviour, such as stealing or fighting, was virtually unknown and, in this simple, illiterate community with merely oral traditions, social intercourse was conducted with a sense and dignity that is often absent from the Mother of Parliaments. 'The inhabitants are Christian . . . neither inclined to enthusiasm nor to Popery. They swear not the common oaths that prevail in the world; when they refuse or deny to give what is asked of them, they do it with a strong asseveration . . . you are no more to have it than if God had forbid it . . . and thus they express the highest degree of passion.'

It all adds up to an impressively well-integrated society which leaves many modern ones, with all their advantages, far behind. I hope it is unnecessary to add that the lesson for us is not to live on St Kilda but to take more account of these intangibles in our political, economic and social planning.

Returning, however, to St Kildan gannets, the culls ceased in 1910. In the hey-day of the islanders, with 180 souls (never less than 71) to provide for, and seabirds their staple resource, the cull was huge, but the 22,600 gannets said to be eaten in 1696 was certainly a gross exaggeration. Neil Mackenzie, minister between 1829 and 1843, and apparently a trustworthy observer, says that 2,000 gugas and the same number of adults was the highest annual kill during his period on the island, and that they probably never took more than 5,000 gugas and 2,000–3,000 adults. Even at that, incidentally, the population could not have held its own without immigration. In June 1847, 1,100 adult gannets were said to be taken in one night, which means one every three minutes for each of 10 men, throughout a six hour night, and they probably didn't have six hours to work in. The feat beggars the imagination. In April 1885, 660 adults were killed in one night. As late as 1895, 1,280 young and 1,920 adults were taken, but in 1902 only 300 young. In Spring 1910, 600 adults were caught and this appears to be the last record.

The birds were taken with nooses plaited from strips of hide and gannet quills, or clubbed directly and thrown down into the sea to be collected from a boat. Huge numbers were lost by contrary winds and currents. The same method was used on the Bass Rock, and Gurney tells how the boatmen, drifting quietly beneath the towering cliffs whilst the killing was going on above, were lost to sight and, it being thought that they were elsewhere, the dead gannets were flung over the cliff. The impact of a nine or ten-pound gannet falling 60–90 m

(200–300 ft) is not to be despised and the men had to cower beneath the seats whilst gannets thumped into the boat, flying apart and covering them with blood and feathers. Even so, the gannets came off worst.

The Westmann Islands, too, have a long history of exploitation, which seems to have been sensible in that a variable number was taken, with a view to conserving the stock, though since we do not know how much immigration occurred we cannot judge the efficacy of their methods. Here, the flat top enabled the men to herd young gannets together before clubbing them. Some 400–500 were taken annually from Súlnasker alone.[38]

The great Icelandic gannetry of Eldey, protected since 1940, was also raided by the Westmann Islanders – 4,100 gannets culled in 1908 and an average 3,257 (2,000–4,000) between 1910 and 1939, in which year the final cull was 2,000.

Icelanders sometimes managed to take good numbers of sleeping gannets from the sea, at night, after they had gorged on herrings and other fish in Hvalfjord; and also by rowing them down when they were heavy with fish and unable to rise in the calm conditions.

It was the Canadian colonies, in particular Bird Rocks, however, that suffered most catastrophically. Audubon found that 'the Labrador fishermen were in the habit of regularly visiting this great resort of gannets to procure their flesh for bait, armed with short clubs for the purpose of killing them. The frightened birds, prevented from rising into the air by their long wings, impeded each other's progress, by which numbers were overtaken and forced to the ground, the men beating and killing old and young with their clubs until too fatigued to go on any longer'. Audubon's pilot '. . . had seen six men destroy 540 gannets in about an hour.'

From 1904 onwards, the Canadian gannets were officially protected, as ours had been since the Seabird Protection Act of 1869, but prior to that it is little wonder that the world population of gannets had been savagely reduced in the 19th century; Fisher guesses by as much as two-thirds in 60 years.

In the face of all this, present-day gannets are lucky to suffer little worse than disturbance and the isolated acts of vandals, though pollution (see below) and overfishing by man may yet be hazardous.

I would not omit from this section some mention of man's treatment of the gannet (and other seabirds) when he is not concerned with practical utilisation, for it shows a heartening trend. There seems little doubt that man enjoys killing other creatures. If he can do it for practical purposes, he does so with zest. Read, for example, the joyous abandon with which the crew of Darwin's *Beagle* slaughtered the boobies of St Paul's Rocks, ostensibly for food, but killing and maiming far more than they took. If the practical returns are negligible, man does it for socially acceptable sport. And if the 'sport' is not socially acceptable, he still has a strong urge to do it anyway. Thus Gurney's records of the casual shooting of gannets as they flew back to the colony with food, the corpses often being left where they fell. Thus the workmen building the Bass Lighthouse 50 years ago, who pelted sitting gannets to death with stones, for fun.[3] Any attempt to develop this theme would lead too far afield; my main point is that, cavil as some of us may at our consumer-orientated society with its demands on the environment, there is nonetheless a vastly more civilised attitude to wildlife. Nowadays, many hundreds of visitors land on the Bass each year, and virtually everybody admires and respects the gannets. I know from the condition of my study group, that in most years not one person has ignored my little notice asking for it to remain undisturbed. There are a few exceptions, but people generally do not wander among the nesting ranks, causing havoc, as they used to do. Those many early accounts which describe the parcels of herring and mackerel by each nest tell their own tale: 'at every second gannet's nest lay a herring or two fished up from the deep' (on Sula Sgeir). The same observations were made on Bass Rock by Booth and Gurney, and on Grassholm by Lloyd.[67] Far from being placed there as food for the young, as they seemed to think, they were vomited in panic. Sad to relate, the major culprits these days are birdwatchers themselves, in their ringing activities. This damage is unintentional, caused by the chick's habit of stumbling from its nest and ending up several yards away, from which point it may not be able to return without receiving terrible punishment from the adults through which it must pass. The answer is to move exceedingly slowly whilst amongst them, crouched or sitting, and to retrieve displaced youngsters before moving on – a slow, dirty and painful business. Photographers can also behave astonishingly badly. I will not forget the sight of a black coated figure gesticulating wildly from the middle of my observation colony, whilst chicks fled in panic and eggs were kicked out by scrimmaging adults. He was a benign old vicar, who wanted only to secure a picture of an adult flying back to its nest, from which, therefore, it had first to be encouraged to flee!

Of British gannetries, two (Bempton and Grassholm) are RSPB reserves, and ringing is not allowed on the latter (the issue does not arise at Bempton!). St Kilda is a Nature Conservancy Reserve and the Bass Rock is a Nature Conservancy Site of Special Scientific Interest Grade 1. Here and on Ailsa Craig, landing is by permission, vested in the appointed boatman (Bass) and the Factor (Ailsa). Sula Sgeir is still culled, but it and Sule Stack are so remote that other disturbance is slight. It is quite certain that destruction and disturbance by man is no longer an important pressure on the gannet, which is now increasing steadily.

This introduces the nebulous concept of competition for fish between man and gannet. 'He flies above the sea. Below him he spies a herring. Swish! Down down he drops; he dives: he has it and then there's one less fish.' Gurney presented evidence to show that the effect of gannets on commercial fisheries is utterly negligible and fishery research has since confirmed this. According to a recent estimate, *all* seabirds put together take only 5% of the annual production of pelagic fish in the North Sea, which leaves the gannet with possibly a fraction of one per cent! On the other hand, bird predators, underwater predators (seals, large fish) and man, indubitably have to compete for available stocks, and it has recently been suggested[40] that seabirds could conceivably take some 35% of annual productivity, though this is far higher than the conventional estimate. The evaluation of the factors which *do* control fish stocks is highly technical, but the main point which emerges is that man is more likely to affect the gannet (and other seabirds) by over-fishing of preferred stocks, notably herring, and then turning his attention to massive exploitation of other fish (especially mackerel and sprat, but also sand-eels) than the gannet is to affect man. Whether man's effect will be to assist gannets to increase or lead to their decrease is not, either, as simple to assess as might appear. One view already supposes that the shift in human fishing pressures is responsible for the current increase in some seabirds. This, be it noted, is probably not due to the provision of offal, which, though spectacularly consumed by seabirds in superficially great numbers, is unimportant in comparison with other factors, such as the shift in the proportions of various fish species and in the proportions of the year classes (sizes) within a species. It might be added that gannets make up probably less than 1–2% of the scavengers, which are mainly various gulls.

THE GANNET IN CAPTIVITY AND OILED BIRDS

Gannets are not difficult to maintain in good health in captivity. By far the most successful keeper was E. T. Booth,[8] who took small chicks from Bass Rock, reared them to maturity and bred successfully from them. His entire account is well worth reading. Captive gannets will take a wide variety of fishes: herring, mackerel, sprats, sand-eels, flat-fish, saithe, codling, pollack, haddock, freshwater trout, whiting, mullet, smolts, minnows, slabs of conger eel and no doubt anything else, though Booth comments that they are not fond of pilchards. Fish are taken either whole or in pieces, fresh or frozen, as two years of daily feeding showed me. The amount taken fluctuates markedly according, in part, to the weather, from about 900 g (31 oz) to little or nothing. On average, a fully grown gannet requires some 300–400 g (10–13 oz) a day. Often, they will help themselves, but it is better to feed them by throwing fish; the act of catching and handling a fish predisposes them to swallow it. A juvenile can swallow up to ten herrings at a meal. Gannets can accommodate fish up to at least 30 cm (12 inches) long, though the cormorant beats this; there is an old record of one taking a grilse kelt 50 cm (20 inches) long. They should have access to water, which stimulates them to bathe and preen, and to nest material, which stimulates play and social interaction. Commonly, captive gannets suffer from swollen webs, particularly at the heel and along the toes, which are evidently painful and often intractable. Booth cured this by providing soft turf in the enclosure. In winter they should be provided with a shed, but mine seemed little incommoded by bitter cold and storms of snow and sleet. Clearly, captivity is no life at all, and my birds were in fact injured, but under ideal conditions and in large enough numbers for social interactions, they can live tolerably well. Booth's birds swam and dived from the surface like guillemots, using half-opened wings for propulsion underwater. They caught and ate sparrows and one of them bolted a fully grown guillemot, entire! Notwithstanding comments to the contrary, they do become quite tame, and I could with impunity allow one of mine to nibble and 'swallow' my finger, whilst my friend Fred Marr, the Bass Rock boatman, has had youngsters that positively solicited touching, though others were incurably fearful and aggressive.

Sarah Wanless reared several fallen chicks on Ailsa Craig. Some of them fledged successfully and one reached African waters in record time. Their peak intake of food was at age six to nine weeks. Ideally, chicks should be fed twice daily, since they are not able to take in quite as much as they need in one meal.

Weak, oiled or injured gannets are sometimes found by bird-lovers, who naturally wish to do the best they can for them. Often, it is best to kill them, distressing and difficult though this task is. It is virtually impossible to kill a gannet by twisting its neck; you might as well wring a hosepipe, and nothing is more ghastly than a slow and unsuccessful attempt. The old fowler's trick, of dislocating the neck by tipping the head sharply back, either doesn't work or needs special skill. Chloroform is usually not available and is slow. There remain only two useful methods: if the bird is lively, I slip a rubber band or some string over the beak and, holding it in both hands, belly uppermost and wings against its sides, bring the back of the head down with all force on a suitable rock. I doubt if anything could be quicker, though death does not appear to be instantaneous; the discharge of nerve impulses after the bird is unconscious causes some muscle movement. The other method, which Sarah Wanless used on hundreds of injured birds on Ailsa Craig, is to lay the bird's head on a flat rock and bring a heavy stone down with full force at the point where skull and neck meet. Both methods are messy but effective and only the desire to save the bird from prolonged suffering makes them possible.

If the bird is broken-winged, the decision to despatch it may be clearcut. If it is weak, underweight (below about 2·3 kg (5 lb)), soiled around the vent or oiled, the decision may be more difficult. An adult which is weak only through lack of food must be a great rarity; virtually always, it will be suffering from toxic chemicals, obstruction of the gut through having swallowed some metal, plastic or wood; or it may be diseased. Starving juveniles, however, may be found and could be fed for a couple of weeks and released again, as could adults entangled in cordage or artificially prevented from feeding. And gannets are unbelievably hardy birds, capable of recovering from the most fearsome wounds. Gurney mentions one that had sustained a huge head-wound, and was still active. I once rescued a youngster that had fallen from the cliff top and landed belly down on the sea, splitting itself from stem to stern so that its guts were literally hanging out. Yet, within minutes of being sewn up, it was exercising its wings vigorously, and eventually fully recovered.

Oiled birds are a difficult problem and the best methods of treatment are still evolving. In many cases it may be kinder to despatch the bird rather than attempt treatment. At least as critical as the extent of oiling is the degree of emaciation and de-hydration. In the latter condition re-hydration is essential and can be attempted by administering a solution of glucose and table salt in warm water, by tube down the bird's throat, but expert advice should be sought. The treatment has to be repeated a number of times for perhaps two or three days. There is a variety of treatments for cleaning the plumage depending on the type of oil and the degree of oiling. After cleaning, a bird should not be released until it has resumed normal preening and swimming, probably a minimum of 72 hours later. The International Bird Rescue Centre at Berkeley, California, has produced a helpful booklet, "Saving Oiled Seabirds', and copies may be obtained free from the American Petroleum Institute, 2101 L Street NW, Washington, DC 20037.

General advice may be sought from the RSPB, The Lodge, Sandy, Beds, Telephone: (0767) 80551 or, in Scotland, (031) 556 5624·9042; the RSPCA or, in Scotland, the SPCA Inspector, (telephone numbers in the local directory).

ART AND LITERATURE

I doubt if even the confirmed literature crawler could unearth many gannet riches. Pliny's 'Chenerote' was probably a goose and the gannet is unlikely to have figured in Greek and Roman literature. Icelandic Sagas might have been expected to dwell on the gannet but apparently do not. Post-mediaeval references, mainly to Bass Rock gannets, have already been quoted (see, also, the Bibliography). More modern literature with avian connections, with the notable exception of Coleridge's albatross, looks for its inspiration to nightingales and thrushes, eagles and falcons, and rarely to the raucous seabird '. . . the gagling gaunte and the churlish chouge' Skelton (1508). The excessive poetic licence taken by Browning in 'Paracelsus', where we find Festus referring to his son Aureolis' glee when some stray gannet builds amid the birch trees by the lake of Geneva, is one of the many historic allusions to the gannet documented by Cunningham in 1866.[26] Gannets figure, too, in Stevenson's tale of Tod Lapraik in 'Catriona'. I do not know of any inn signs based on the gannet, though W. B. Alexander[1] records that the pelican (which, as fossils show, used to breed in Southern England) is commonly used in Hampshire and Wiltshire as a symbolic sign of piety.

Yet the lonely rigours of the cold northern seas stir the imagination too. Who has not responded to the gannet's white form, cutting impassively into the grey wind above a hostile sea:

All day I hear the noise of waters making moan
Sad as the seabird is when going forth alone
He hears the winds cry to the waters' monotone

The grey winds, the cold winds are blowing where I go
I hear the noise of many waters far below
All day, all night, I hear them flowing to and fro

James Joyce

and:

Icicles hung round me; hailshowers flew
The only sound there, was of the sea booming –
The ice-cold wave – and at times the song of the swan
The cry of the gannet was all my gladness
The call of the curlew, not the laughter of men
The mewing gull, not the sweetness of mead
There, storms echoed all the rocky cliffs, the icy-feathered tern
Answered them . . .

'The Seafarer', Anglo-Saxon poem from *The Battle of Malden and other old English Poems* by Kevin Crossley-Holland.

Best of all, two modern poems about the gannet have come my way. The first[98] keeps mental pace with the diving gannet, the author striving and crystallising his images all the way down:

In this moment
while the fish is dying
now the gannet turns/and peels over
out of its holding pattern/flips/and capsizes, and
falls/slowly in the foreshortened distance,
as a stone dropped from some monstrous headland
seems/while one leans,
to dawdle midway in its plummet

Wings flutter at first/then cease
held back rigid-stiff in the slip –
stream punch and buffet of the kicking air.
Then/still falling/still vertical, he is struck,
like a paper dart flung at a fan/struck and
spun like a loosened weathercock/yet
vertical still/and able
to stabilise again/and then
flip and yet fasten again/and again/and still/still
still the plunge goes on now
in this moment/last second
now while the sun strikes
and the swell gathers
and the gannet is closing
and the fish is dying.

The poem that closes this book charts the immensity of the course man has traversed since those days in which he was circumscribed, credulous of barnacles turning into geese and ignorant of his destructive potential:

Gannets
before the fall, before
the sixth day, plunged
from brow to base
a hundred feet
of the Bass cliffside
with the weight and
speed of a plummet
the slant sea riving.

Gannets no doubt
when man is redeemed
or redundant will
nest on the wreckage
of the world he leaves;
spread their wings
to the measure of man
and continue in calm
their immaculate diving.

From 'God's Dominion' by Simon Baynes

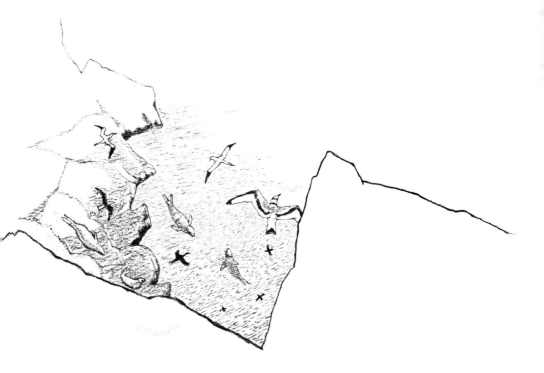

Tables

TABLE 1

Weight and measurements of the Atlantic Gannet

| | Weight (g) | | Culmen Length (mm) | | Depth (mm) | |
Area	Male	Female	Male	Female	Male	Fema
Bass Rock	2,932	3,067	100·1	99·2	35·5	34·3
	(2,470 to	(2,570 to	(93·5 to	(92·5 to	(33 to	(32 t
	3,470)	3,610)	110)	104)	40)	39)
	27 cases	27 cases	66 cases	66 cases	27 cases	36 ca
*Ailsa Craig**	3,120	2,941	98·2	97·7		
	(2,400 to	(2,300 to	(92·5 to	(92·5 to	NR	NR
	3,600)	3,600)	104·1)	100·4)		
	17 cases	18 cases	22 cases	23 cases		
Bonaventure†	3,153	3,284	101·7	101·7		
			(93·5 to		NR	NR
			107)			
	38 cases	24 cases	37 cases	24 cases		

* S. Wanless (pers. comm.)
† Poulin 1968.

Wing length (mm)		Tail (mm)		Tarsus length (mm)		Toe (mm)	
Male	Female	Male	Female	Male	Female	Male	Female
513	510·2	NR	NR	50·2	50·8	97·7	95·7
00 to	(484 to			(48·5 to	(47 to	(96·6 to	(92·8 to
635)	522·4)			51)	59)	98·8)	98·4)
cases	14 cases			3 cases	12 cases	2 cases	12 cases
				thickness			
				14 × 11·9	14 × 10·5		
				4 cases	1 case		
NR	NR	NR	NR	NR	NR	NR	NR
501	496	214·5		62·5		NR	NR
87 to	(485 to	(189·5 to		(59 to			
11·5)	503)	225·5)		65)			
10th primary							
291	300						

TABLE 2

Fluctuations in Ailsa's population, month by month, 1974–1977 (data from S. Wanless)

	F	M	A	M	J	J	A	S	O
1974					12,517	11,458	8,585	13,749	
1975	4,000		10,600 11,861	11,925 14,794	14,800	15,361	12,596	13,944	3,673 4,029 586
1976	11,529	10,353	12,309 14,215	13,387 15,035	15,814		16,222 14,359 14,759	13,310	3,500
1977			13,800						

TABLE 3
Icelandic gannetries (up to 1974)

	1939–41		1949–52		1959–62	
1. Eldey						
cliffs	628 ⎫		1,177 ⎫		2,400 ⎫	
top	8,700 ⎭	9,328	9,700 ⎭	10,877	13,900 ⎭	16,300
2. Westmann Isles						
(a) Sulnasker						
cliffs	814 ⎫		1,002 ⎫		772 ⎫	
top	786 ⎭	1,600	916 ⎭	1,918	910 ⎭	1,682
(b) Stori-Geldungur						
cliffs and top	589		652 ⎫		820 ⎫	
			150 ⎭	802	200 ⎭	1,020
Little Geldungur						
cliffs and top		4,359	111 ⎫		102 ⎫	1,122
			0 ⎭	111	0 ⎭	102
(c) Hellisey						
cliffs	1,703		2,216		1,960 ⎫	
top					115 ⎭	2075
(d) Brandur				913 / 5,534		5,315
cliffs	456 ⎫		479 ⎫		432 ⎫	
top	11 ⎭	467	8 ⎭	487	4 ⎭	436
3. Máfadrang						
cliffs (Mávadrangur)					100 ⎫	
top	0		0		0 ⎭	100
4. Skrúdur						
cliffs			134 ⎫		304 ⎫	
top	0		0 ⎭	134	10 ⎭	314
5. Stori-Karl						
cliffs (Stori-Karlinn,					0 ⎫	
Skoranhurb-Jarg)						23
top	0		0		23 ⎭	
6. Raudinupur						
(a) Sölvanöf						
cliffs			8 ⎫		33 ⎫	
top	0		0 ⎬		0 ⎭	33
Karlinn			⎬ 8			34
cliffs			0 ⎬		1 ⎫	
top	0		0 ⎭		0 ⎭	1
7. Drangey						
cliffs			1 ⎫			
top	0		0 ⎭	1	0	
8. Grimsey						
cliffs	45 ⎫		0		0	
top	0 ⎭	45				
Grand totals	13,732		16,554		22,086	

TABLE 4

Population of the Atlantic gannet, 1909–69

Region (in order of size of population) (see Table 6)	Year	No. of colonies	No. of site occupying pairs (to nearest 500)	Per cent increase 1909 to 1939	Per cent increase 1939 to 1969	Per cent per annum increase 1909 to 1939	Per cent per annum increase 1939 to 1969	Per cent (in 1969) of: East Atlantic population	Per cent (in 1969) of: World population
1. West and north Britain	1909	4	28,500						
	1939	7	34,000						
	1969	8	89,000	19	162	0·6	3·3	54	45
2. South-west Britain	1909	3	15,500						
	1939	5	16,000						
	1969	7	43,000	3	169	0·1	3·4	26	22
3. Canada (west Atlantic population)	1909	4	6,000						
	1939	6	13,000						
	1969	6	33,000	117	154	2·6	3·2	—	16
4. Faroes, Iceland, Norway	1909	4 {3I 1F}	14,000						
	1939	4 {3I 1F}	15,000						
	1969	11 {6I 1F 4N}	22,500	7	50			14	11
5. East Britain	1909	1	3,000						
	1939	2	4,500						
	1969	2	9,000	50	100	1·3	2·4	6	5
Total east Atlantic population	1909	12	61,000						
	1939	18	69,500						
	1969	28	163,000	14	134	0·4	2·9	100	84
World population	1909	16	67,000						
	1939	24	82,500						
	1969	33	196,500						
	1974	34	197,000	23	98	0·7	2·9		
	1976	34	213,000						

TABLE 5

North Atlantic gannetries

(numbers before braces refer to regions treated in Table 3)

	Colony	Founded	Year latest estimate	Approximate number (pairs)*	Comment
2	1. Grassholm	1820–60	1975	20,370	Increase at times due to immigration; considerable emigration in recent years.
	2. Little Skellig	Before 1700	1974	18,000?	Massive initial emigration after colony founded; considerable emigration most of this century.
	3. Bull Rock	1850s	1969	1,500	Initial immigration; possible emigration in recent years.
	4. Great Saltee	1929	1975	193	Increase to date due largely to immigration.
	5. Ortac	1940	1969	1,000	Initial increase due to immigration. Possibly exporting by now.
	Les Etacs	c. 1940	1969	2,000	
	6. Rouzic	1937	1965	2,600±10%	Initial increase due to immigration.
1	7. Ailsa Craig	Before 1400	1976	c. 16,000†	Curious apparent fluctuations from year to year more marked than in any other gannetry.
	8. Scar Rocks	1939	1974	482	Established and initially augmented by immigration which is now tailing off or has ceased.
	9. St. Kilda	Before 800	1973	59,000	Ancient and huge gannetry which may or may not have been receiving immigrants since 1949, depending on accuracy of estimates. Prior to that, no need to postulate immigration and probable that some emigration. Now the largest Atlantic gannetry.
	10. Fair Isle	1974	1977	c. 34	
	11. Roareim (Flannans)	1969	1975	17	
	12. Sula Sgeir	Before 1400	1972	9,000	An exploited colony which maintains its numbers by recruiting immigrants.
	13. Sule Stack	Before 1600	1969	4,000	A 'full' colony (?) which exports most of its recruits, probably many to Sula Sgeir.
	14. Noss	1914	1977	(5,498 adults)	
	15. Hermaness	1917	1976	6,012	For 20–30 years after establishment, increased rapidly by immigration. Since, Hermaness at least has had periods of substantial immigration even though the per annum increase, 1939–69, was low enough to have stemmed from the colony's own output.
5	16. Bass Rock	Before 500	1976	11,000±10%	Rate of increase at all times consistent with intrinsic production. Is exporting small numbers.
	17. Bempton	1920s	1977	c. 169	Accelerated growth in late 'sixties and during the 'seventies due largely to continuing immigration, probably all from Bass (some certainly are).

Colony	Founded	Year of latest estimate	Approximate number (pairs)*	Comment
18. *Westmanns*	Before 1600	1962	5,300	A relatively stable, exploited colony dependent for the maintenance of its numbers on immigrants.
19. *Eldey*	Before 1700	1962	16,300	A large and ancient colony which increased by some 2% per annum between 1939–62 but is probably nearly full and likely to have been exporting for several years.
20. *Skrúdur*	1940s	1962	314	New Icelandic colonies, all of which have depended on immigration and are currently increasing, except possibly Raudinupur where some cliff has collapsed.
21. *Raudinupur*	1940s	1962	34	
22. *Stori-Karl*	1950s	1962	23	
23. *Máfadrang*	1950s	1962	100	
24. *Myggenaes*	Before 1600	1966	1,801	An ancient, exploited colony which depends partly on immigration to maintain its numbers.
25. *Storebranden,* *Runde*	1946	1972	422	Recent Norwegian colonies all of which have grown by recruiting immigrants, which they are probably still doing. One breeding adult on Skarvlakken was ringed as a juvenile on Ailsa Craig.
26. *Skittenskarv-* *holmen,* *Mosken*	1960s	1972	60	
27. *Skarvlakken,* *Nordmjele*	1967	1972	103	
28. *Innerstauren,* *Syltefjord*	1961	1976	44	
29. *Bird Rocks*	Before 1500	1973	5,300	Formerly the world's largest gannetry. Increase since 1932 possibly partly dependent on immigration but could have occurred intrinsically.
30. *Bonaven-* *ture*	Before 1800	1973	17,300	The largest west Atlantic gannetry. Recently has begun to decrease (1969–1973).
31. *Anticosti* *Island*	1913–20	1972	135	A decreasing colony; somewhat unsuitable terrain. Possibly founded by birds debarred from traditional colonies by persecution.
32. *Cape St* *Mary's*	c. 1878	1972	5,300	Initially grew by massive immigration but little increase since 1934. The Bird Rock section is probably full.
33. *Baccalieu* *Island*	c. 1900–10	1973	673	A decreasing colony; also probably unsuitable terrain. Initial increase by immigration.
34. *Funk Island*	Before 1500	1972	4,100	An increasing colony, receiving immigrants.

World total 213,800 pairs

Note: Potential error in world total in my opinion could be 30,000. World total more likely to be an overestimate than an underestimate.

* This figure is *not* breeding pairs and is *not* calculable directly from photographs. For accuracy it requires several corrections to be applied.

† This is a provisional figure only: see full account of Ailsa (p. 55).

TABLE 6

The duration of incubation and guard spells, and foraging absences, of gannets from three different colonies. Figures derived from continuous (daylight hours) 48-hour checks. Age of chicks from <1–c. 8 weeks. Bempton and Ailsa Craig data from S. Wanless

		Bass Rock	Bempton	Ailsa Craig
Average length of incuba-	M	35	NR	c. 24–30
tion stints (to nearest hour)	F	30	NR	c. 24–30
Chick guard spells, chick	M	19	7	20
aged 0–45 days	F	19	7	20
Chick guard spells, chick	M	24	13	23
aged 46–91 days	F	19	8	20
Length of foraging trips	1– 4 hrs	11 ⎱ 21%	51 ⎱ 77%	11 ⎱ 36%
(no. of hours absent).	4– 7 hrs	12 ⎰	26 ⎰	25 ⎰
Percentage of total				
recorded absences fal-	7–10 hrs	31 ⎱ 65%	3 ⎱ 13%	8 ⎱ 14%
ling into each category	10–13 hrs	34 ⎰	10 ⎰	6 ⎰
	13–16 hrs	7 ⎱ 8%	5 ⎱ 10%	17 ⎱ 34%
	16–19 hrs	1 ⎰	5 ⎰	17 ⎰
	19+ hrs	6	0	16

TABLE 7

The frequency with which gannet chicks of various ages were fed by their parents, Bass Rock, 1962

Age (weeks)	Average no. of feeding bouts in 2-day watch	Average no. of entries
Singletons 0–1(5)	5·8	9·6
2–3(1)	3·0	10·0
3–4(6)	5·0	17·5
4–5(4)	5·2	19·5
5–6(6)	4·2	12·2
6–7(2)	5·0	25·0
Twins 3–4(2)	7·5	41·0
5–6(1)	8·0	25·0

Notes: 1. Figures in brackets denote size of samples. In the case of twins, it refers to the number of *pairs*.
2. Virtually all entries were successful.

TABLE 8
Fledging periods and dates of the gannet

Area	Fledging period (days)	Period in which peak fledging occurs	Comment
Bass Rock	90 (84–97) 111 cases	last week in August	possibly the earliest British gannetry
Bempton	89[1] (82–96) 44 cases	last week in August	enjoys same feeding advantages as the Bass
Ailsa Craig	91 (80–100) 230 cases	second week in Sept.	slightly later laying probably due to feeding factors
Grassholm	NR	last week in August or first week in Sept.	data not good but probably about right
Bonaventure I. (Canada)	91 (82–99)	third week in Sept.	much reduced spread of laying compared with east Atlantic colonies

[1] The shorter fledging period for Bempton, compared with the Bass, correlates with shorter foraging trips (Table 6).

TABLE 9
Differential mortality of birds fledging early and late

	Age in weeks when ringed, usually between 26 June and 7 July		
	0–2	4–6	6+
Number ringed	156	1,775	253
Number recovered (natural causes only) up to December of year of ringing	4	27	2
Percentage recovered	2·6	1·52	0·8

TABLE 10
Breeding success in the gannet

Colony	No. of years for which breeding success known	Mean percentage (and range):		
		Hatched from laid	Fledged from hatched	Fledged from laid
Bass Rock[1]	3	82 (74–87)	92·3 (89–94)	77·7 (72–87)
Bempton[2]	3	84 (80–87)	92·3 (92–93)	77·0 (73–81)
Ailsa Craig	2	81 (76–86)	92·0 (91–93)	73·7 (72–76)
Bonaventure[3]	2	38 (36–40)	78·3 (same in both years)	29·6

[1] These figures are for 1961–63, in which years data was most complete; since then, a maximum figure, for hatched-from-laid, of 96% has been recorded, but the figure for per cent fledged in this year was not obtained. Over 13 years, a figure of 73–85% breeding success (fledged from laid) was obtained and in no year was success significantly poorer.
[2] Breeding figures for 1973, 1974, 1975 only. Restricted to make comparison fairer.
[3] Low hatching success due to the effect of toxic chemicals. Fairly low fledging success due to the effects of disturbance.

TABLE 11
The difference between a cliff area ('closed' group) and a flat-ground area ('open' group) in the proportion of non-breeding birds, Bass Rock

	Average percentage[1] of *occupied sites* which:	
	contained a visible chick in July	were empty and without nest material
South-west cliff	37·2	35·3
North-west slope (colony V)	68·8	9·0

[1] These counts involved, in total, over 2,000 sites for each of the two areas over the nine years.

TABLE 12
The effect of age/experience on breeding success

Year of first breeding	No. of nests	No. of young fledged	Proportion per nest	Proportion per nest from experienced birds
1961	27	16	0·6	0·8
1962	21	13	0·6	0·9
1963	23	8	0·4	0·8

Note: The difference between experienced and inexperienced birds, in breeding success, is highly significant.

TABLE 13
Dates of return to various gannetries

Colony	Approx. dates of return[3]	Departure	Length of stay (calculated from 1 January)[1]	
			Maximum	Minimum
Bass Rock	back in force in Jan.; often many birds in late Dec.[2]	late Oct. or early-mid Nov.	$10\frac{1}{2}$ months+	$9\frac{1}{2}$ months
Bempton	back in force in late Jan.; some flying birds in late Dec. Has been returning earlier since numbers increased	late Sept. to mid Oct.	$9\frac{1}{2}$ months	8+ months
Ailsa Craig	few in Jan.; many by mid Feb.	by late Oct.	9 months	8 months
Grassholm	back in force in Jan.	Oct.–Nov.	10 months+	9 months?
Little Skellig	early to late Feb.	late Sept.– early Nov.	9 months+	$7\frac{1}{2}$ months
St Kilda	mid March	Oct.	8 months	7 months

[1] Note that, in any calendar year, about 11 months may be spent at the colony by some birds, though not necessarily by any one individual.

[2] 20 December 1974, 4–5,000 birds on Bass Rock.

[3] It must be emphasised that there is considerable variation between years; that calculations vary according to what constitutes a presence (a few, or hundreds, or thousands?) and that some colonies are more easily observed than others.

TABLE 14 – *see overleaf*

TABLE 15
The effect of the male on the laying date in the gannet

	1962		1963	
	Old male partnering new female	New male partnering new female	Old male partnering new female	New male partnering new female
Number in sample	7	23	15	25
Spread of laying dates	22 April to 16 May	27 April to 14 June	18 April to 24 May	3 May to 24 June
Mean laying date	7 May	15 May	2 May	12 May
Average number of days later than the mean for the whole group in which these pairs were situated	10	18	9	19

TABLE 14

Laying dates at various gannetries

Gannetry	Period within which:			Nature of data
	first egg laid	median egg laid	last egg laid	
Bass Rock[1]	2 March–5 April	15–20 April	up to mid July usually not beyond third week in June	systematic egg checks 1961–63; back-ageing chicks 1965–77
Bempton	25 March–early April	17–23? April	first half June	frequent observations by J. Fairhurst, enabling most nest contents to be accurately back-aged
Ailsa Craig	early to mid April	early May (possibly later some years)	early July, usually not beyond mid June	direct-ageing chicks and back-ageing (S. Wanless and pers. obs.)
Grassholm	mid March–early April	about mid April	late June	back-ageing chicks, 1975 and 1976 (pers. obs.)
St Kilda	late April	probably mid May	NR	qualitative remarks in the literature
Sule Stack	late March–early April?	early May?	June?	extremely slight. Stark (1967) records, on 15 July 1967, young all stages, some almost ready to fly. These could have been 11 weeks, but even at 9, laying must have occurred in March
Hermaness	late March–early April	late April?	June?	first egg to hatch, main cliffs, 1977, laid 2 April (from B. Sage). Remainder of my dates mere speculation
Mygennaes	late April	probably mid May	NR	qualitative remarks in the literature
Icelandic colonies	late March	second half April	NR	Gudmundsson (1953)
Westmann Isles	second week April	probably early May	NR	Gurney (1913)
Bonaventure[2]	last week April or first week May	second week May	approx. third week June	Poulin (1968)

[1] The median date was later, 1961–63, but this was due to disturbance prior to these years. Even last century, the median date was evidently around 22 April (working from data in E. T. Booth, 1879).

[2] Data for two seasons (1966: 1967).

TABLE 16
Laying dates of the same, experienced, females[1] in relation to the mean laying date of their group, in different years

Criterion	Number of cases
laying date within 3 days of the departure from the mean[2] in 3 successive years	16
laying date within 3 days of the same departure from the mean in 2 out of 3 years	45 } 66
laying date within 3 days of same departure from mean in 2 out of 2 years	5
more than 3 days' difference in departure from mean in 2 or more years out of 3	20 20

[1] In only 34 out of the 86 cases involved, were females colour ringed. However, if some unmarked females were wrongly assumed to be the same birds in successive years, this would mean that the above figures under-estimate the tendency of females to lay in the same relation to the mean in successive years. Thus, the tendency is even stronger than it appears here.
[2] e.g. If a female lays 5 days earlier than the mean in one year, and lays between 2 and 8 days earlier in other years, she lays within 3 days of the same departure.

TABLE 17
The productivity (breeding success) of 22 pairs of individually identifiable gannets that remained together over a period of several (3–11) years. The figures in the table are the number of cases in each category – e.g. – two pairs remained together for nine years and reared nine young, whilst two other pairs stayed together for nine years and reared eight young, etc.

Number of young produced	Number of years pairs remained together								
	11	10	9	8	7	6	5	4	3
11	1								
10				— no cases —					
9			2						
8			2	1					
7				1	1				
6						1			
5					1	2	4		
4						1		1	
3									3
2									1

TABLE 18
A life table for the gannet

Eggs laid per pair per year	1
Chicks fledged per pair per year	0·75
Number[1] (young) surviving to age 1 year	0·26
Number[2] surviving to age 2 years	0·23
Number[3] surviving to age 3 years	0·21
Number surviving to age 4 years	0·19
Number[4] surviving to breeding age 5 years	0·18

About 6% of adults die each year, which is 0·12 per pair (2 × 0·06) so that gannets produce in excess of their replacement needs, which is just as well since the world population is increasing!

[1] Assuming 65% mortality.
[2] Assuming 10% mortality.
[3] From now on, assuming adult mortality rate of 6%.
[4] The trouble is, of course, that these figures depend highly on accurate assessment of mortality rates and these, especially of pre-breeders, are exceedingly difficult to obtain. Very different curves for population trends can be produced by slightly varying the mortality rates upon which calculations are based.

TABLE 19
Fidelity to site and mate in the gannet

		Per cent of sample in which, in year (n + 1):						
Year (n)	No. in sample	Male and female return to same site	Male returns, female moves	Male returns, female disappears	Female returns, male moves	Female returns, male disappears	Male disappears female moves	Female disappears male moves
1961	8	87·5	—	—	—	—	12·5	—
1962	12	58	25	17	—	—	—	—
1965	14	43	7	14	22	—	7	7
1970	23	78	13	—	—	9	—	—
1971	19	74	—	10·5	—	10·5	5	—
1972	21	67	—	—	9·5	9·5	—	14
1973	17	65	6	17	—	6	6	—
1974	15	73	13	7	—	7	—	—
1975	12	42	16·5	25	—	16·5	—	—
1976	8	38	24	38	—	—	—	—
Total	149	64·4	9·4	10·7	3·4	6·7	2·6	2·6

Male returns or dies in 94% of cases and moves in 6%.
Female returns or dies in 88% of cases and moves in 12%.
The greater site-tenacity of the male is in accord with his role in establishing the site and defending it more intensively.

TABLE 20
Adult mortality rates in the gannet, Bass Rock

Year (n)	Number alive		Number alive year (n + 1)		max.% mortality	
	♂	♀	♂	♀	♂	♀
1960	27	31	27	30	0·0	3·2
1961	46	50	43	49	6·5	2·0
1962	46	47	40	43	13·1	8·5
1963	5	3	4	3	20·0	0·0
1964	4	3	4	3	0·0	0·0
1965	4	3	4	3	0·0	0·0
1966	12	13	10	12	16·7	7·7
1967	10	12	9	10	10·0	16·7
1968	9	10	8	10	11·2	0·0
1969	8	10	7	10	12·5	0·0
1970	18	22	14	18	22·3	18·2
1971	24	22	22	22	8·3	0·0
1972	26	26	24	20	7·7	23·1
1973	24	19	21	16	12·5	15·8
1974	21	15	17	11	19·1	26·7
1975	17	11	14	9	17·1	18·1

Max. mean annual mortality ♂ 11·1%
♀ 8·7%

These figures are *maxima*, due to ring-loss and bird moving undetected. 4–6% is probably nearer the true figure for mean annual adult mortality.

TABLE 21
Pollutants in gannet eggs[1]

	COLONY					
Pollutant	Nordmjele	Bass Rock	Ailsa Craig	Bonaventure	Scar Rocks	Little Skellig
PCBs (ppm fat weight)	166 ± 52·6	194 ± 29·4	412 ± 64·4	224 ± 37	NR	NR
DDE (ppm fat weight)	44·8±13·9	25·6± 3·7	54·2± 6·6	458 ± 64	NR	NR
HEOD (ppm fat weight)	2·57 ± ·55	11·4 ± 1·2	26·9± 4·1	17± 2·7	NR	NR
Mercury (ppm dry weight)	2·90 (1972) 10 eggs	2·62± 0·17 (1973–74) 18 eggs	4·54 ± 0·36 (1971–74) 29 eggs	NR	10·47 ± 0·71 (1972–73) 18 eggs	3·21 ± 0·35 (1973) 7 eggs

[1] Data from W. R. P. Bourne et al., in Nelson (1978).

TABLE 22

Organochlorines and mercury in North Atlantic gannets, 1963–1976

Origin	Sample	Liver							Other tissues				
		No.	DDE	PCBs	No.	HEOD	No.	Hg	No.	DDE	PCBs	No.	HEOD
Ailsa Craig	Juveniles	1	0·01	0·05	1	0·003	—	—	2	0·08	0·41	2	0·02
	2nd year	1	0·14	0·71	1	0·1	—	—	1	0·5	2·5	—	—
	3–4 year	5	0·72	4·62	5	0·18	—	—	5	0·96	6·15	5	0·22
	healthy adult	9	1·35	7·80	9	0·30	—	—	9	2·17	11·2	8	0·37
Ailsa and Clyde	wasted adult	4	6·15	34·8	3	1·24	—	—	5	25·3	140	3	0·45
Irish Sea	mixed	9	12·0	175	3	1·24	8	23·8	—	—	—	—	—
Bristol Channel	mixed	4	8·38	57·2	—	—	3	12·1	4	4·94	25·2	—	—
East Britain	mixed	6	3·29	12·3	2	0·08	6	11·8	4	3·14	14·7	—	—
N. Scottish Is.	mixed	6	3·21	13·0	3	0·20	2	13·1	7	2·34	9·07	2	0·24
Iceland	healthy adult?	—	—	—	—	—	—	—	1	1·5	12	1	0·34
Funk I.	healthy adult	—	—	—	—	—	—	—	10	1·14	—	—	0·06
Bonaventure I.	healthy adult	—	—	—	—	—	—	—	10	3·20	—	—	0·10
St Lawrence	dead or dying	—	—	—	—	—	1	16·0	3	11·8	24·1	3	0·69

Taken from Table 1, Parslow & Jefferies in press. Chlorinated hydrocarbons in ppm wet weight, mercury in ppm dry weight, geometric means. The other tissues were liver in the case of mercury and muscle for organochlorines except in Canada, where they were brain; five specimens of mixed origin from Britain contained geometric mean levels of 5·42 ppm DDE and 18·8 ppm PCBs in the brain. The Canadian results have been revised by J. A. Keith, who will be publishing a fuller study elsewhere. From W. R. P. Bourne *et al.* in Nelson (1978).

TABLE 23
Recoveries of gannets arranged by month and zone
(zones N. W. A. T. as on Figs 38—41)

	Zone	May	June	July	Aug.	Sept.	Oct.	Nov.	Dec.	Jan.	Feb.	Mar.	April	Totals
a														
recovered	N	—	—	8	67	143	132	36	11	6	2	2	2	409
in 1st	W	—	—	—	9	83	155	63	18	4	4	11	1	348
year of	A	—	—	—	—	—	13	25	12	9	8	1	1	69
life	T	—	—	—	—	—	1	7	13	11	7	1	1	41
	Totals	—	—	8	76	226	301	131	54	30	21	15	5	867
b														
recovered	N	1	4	25	22	15	24	16	7	4	2	1	1	122
in 2nd	W	1	8	12	11	6	9	17	15	11	5	7	2	104
year of	A	2	—	2	1	1	3	4	—	1	2	1	2	19
life	T	2	2	—	2	—	—	—	1	2	1	—	—	10
	Totals	6	14	39	36	22	36	37	23	18	10	9	5	255
c														
recovered	N	5	20	11	12	5	11	7	5	4	5	3	6	94
in 3rd	W	8	2	1	1	3	7	5	6	12	8	3	6	62
year of	A	1	—	1	—	—	—	—	2	2	—	2	—	8
life	T	—	—	—	1	—	—	—	—	—	—	—	—	1
	Totals	14	22	13	14	8	18	12	13	18	13	8	12	165
d														
recovered	N	8	10	7	12	6	12	3	2	4	3	2	8	77
in 4th	W	1	—	—	2	1	—	5	2	2	7	3	3	26
year of	A	—	—	—	—	—	—	—	—	1	1	—	—	2
life	T	—	—	—	—	—	—	—	—	—	—	—	—	—
	Totals	9	10	7	14	7	12	8	4	7	11	5	11	105
e														
recovered	N	17	20	37	18	6	11	5	3	11	10	10	24	172
in 5th	W	3	—	2	—	—	3	3	5	3	6	4	2	31
year of	A	—	—	—	—	—	1	—	—	1	—	1	—	3
life	T	—	—	—	—	—	—	—	—	1	—	—	1	2
	Totals	20	20	39	18	6	15	8	8	16	16	15	27	208
f														
ringed as	N	18	16	16	18	6	5	5	9	11	6	13	17	140
adults	W	2	1	1	—	—	2	—	3	6	2	1	1	19
	A	—	—	—	—	—	—	—	—	1	1	—	—	2
	T	—	—	—	—	—	—	—	—	—	—	—	—	—
	Totals	20	17	17	18	6	7	5	12	18	9	14	18	161

From A. L. Thomson, 1974.

TABLE 24

Age distribution of winter recoveries of gannets expressed as percentage of annual totals (from A. L. Thomson, 1974)

			Year of life			Ringed as adults
Zone	1st	2nd	3rd	4th	5th	
N	23	31	38	40	62	76
W	40	57	53	54	33	21
A	22	8	9	6	3	3
T	15	4	—	—	2	—
N + W	63	88	91	94	95	97
A + T	37	12	9	6	5	3
W + A + T	77	69	62	60	38	24

Winter is taken from November to February inclusive.

TABLE 25

Age at recovery of gannets ringed as nestlings
(after A. L. Thomson, 1974)

Ringed as nestlings		Ringed as adults	
Year of life[1] from 1 May	Number recovered	Year of life after ringing, from 1 May	Number recovered
1	867 (54·2%)	1	31 (19·3%)
2	255 (34·8%)	2	34 (26·1%)
3	165 (34·6%)	3	21 (21·9%)
4	105 (33·5%)	4	15 (20·0%)
5	69 (33·1%)	5	10 (16·6%)
6	44 etc.[2]	6	16 (32·0%)
7	42	7	12 (34·8%)
8	27	8	7 (31·8%)
9	9	9	6 (40·0%)
10	9	10	3 etc.
11	2	11	3
12	3	12	2
13	2	13	0
14	0	14	1
15	0	15	0
16	0	16	0
17	1	17	0
Total	1,600		161

[1] On average, approximately 10 years should be added to age at recovery to show actual age.

[2] Percentage figures show percentage of total remaining, not of original total (except of course in year 1). Note that in young birds, after initial high mortality, the *rate* of mortality levels out after the first year.

TABLE 26
Recoveries of Canadian gannets
(from data in Moison and Scherrer, 1973)

	Recoveries of first-year birds			Recoveries of immatures			Recoveries of adults		
	Zone 1	Zone 2	Zone 3	Zone 1	Zone 2	Zone 3	Zone 1	Zone 2	Zone 3
Mid September to December	44	22	5	15	9	6	19	4	1
January to March	1	3	37	1	4	12	0	5	6
April to June	24	8	34	24	8	7	11	2	1
July to mid September	11	4	2	9	1	1	14	0	0

Notes: 1. See Figure 43 for demarcation of Zones 1–3.
2. Note the greater tendency of adult Canadian gannets to desert home waters in winter; compared with east Atlantic gannets.

TABLE 27 – see page 314

TABLE 28
Colony-size in the Sulidae (in pairs)

Species	Maximum	Minimum	Very approx. 'typical' size at present day
Peruvian booby	360,000 (Mazorca 1960)	<400 (Coquimbo* 1972)	50,000?
Cape gannet	100,000 (Ichaboe 1956)	1 or 2 pairs (Bird Island, Lamberts Bay 1912)	20–30,000?
Atlantic gannet	55–60,000 (St Kilda 1973) 125,000 (Bird Rocks, before 1850)	2 (Bempton 1930s)	5–10,000?
Australasian gannet	6,000 (White Island 1971)	<6 (Wedge Light, early 1970s)	1–2,000
Blue-footed booby	10,000+? (Lobos de Tierra, 1930s)	2 or 3 (Tower, 1960s)	<1,000
Red-footed booby	140,000 (Tower Island 1964)	<10 (Ascension 1960s, La Plata, 1976)	2,000 or less?
White booby	5,000+ (Malpelo, 1940s)	<10 (some Line Islands)	1,000 or less?
Brown booby	8–10,000 (Desecheo 1927)	<50 (some Line Islands)	1,000 or less?
Abbott's booby	one existing 'colony' of 2–3,000 pairs, Christmas Island, Indian Ocean		

Note: The 'typical colony size' has strictly limited meaning, since (a) a 'colony' is impossible to define satisfactorily; (b) artefactual influences could be extremely important, but nevertheless it serves to illustrate certain points (see text).

* A newly discovered colony in Chile.

TABLE 29
Comparative ecology of Sulidae

Species	Habitat type	Density pairs/m²	Clutch size	Brood size	Egg wt. as % ♀	Incub. period (days)	Approx typica length o incubati stints (h
Atlantic gannet	Cliffs (preferred), slopes, flat ground	2·3	1	1	3·4	43·6	33
Cape gannet	Flat ground, preferably uncluttered	2·0–6·8 (mean 2·5?)	1	1	3·9	44·0	41
Australasian gannet	Flat ground, slopes, cliffs	2·6	1	1	3·9	43·6	27
White booby	Flat ground, slopes, rarely cliffs. Usually needs some slope, or good wind. Sometimes on or among vegetation	Highly variable 0·005–0·3	1–2 (2)	1	3·6	43·7	12–14 accordir to area
Brown booby	Cliffs and cliff-edges, slopes, flat ground. Often among or under vegetation	Highly variable 0·001–1·0	1–2 (2)	1	4·0	42·8	12–24, probabl usually <24
Blue-footed booby	Flat ground, slopes, occasionally broad ledges. Sometimes among vegetation	Highly variable 0·01 (or less)–0·5	1–3 (2)	1–3 (2)	3·6	41·0	21 Galapag
Peruvian booby	Cliffs (preferred?), slopes, flat ground	1–2·0	1–4 (3)	1–4 (3)	3·0	c.42·0	12
Red-footed booby	Trees, bushes, occasionally low herbaceous growth, very rarely, cliffs	Variable 0·003–0·6	1	1	5·0	45·0	24–60 accordir to area
Abbott's booby	Tall trees below top canopy	<·00001	1	1	7·0	57·0	52

Note: Clutch size given as 1–3 means 1–3, usually 2.
(2)

lging riod ays)	Approx. frequency with which young fed per day	Max. wt. of chick as % of adult	Length of post-fledging feeding period (weeks)	Type of post-breeding movement Adult	Young	Approx. annual adult mortality
91	2·7	137	0	Mainly dispersal	Southward migration up to 5,000 km+	6
7·2	NR but prob. c.2·0	109	0 (but see text)	Mainly dispersal	Northward migration up to 4,000 km+	5–8
02	2	138	0 (but see text)	Mainly dispersal	Westward migration up to 5,000 km	4–5
120	1·4	114	c.8	Dispersal	Wide ranging dispersal (up to 1,000s of km)	5–7
–105	Variable 1·5–2·0 ?	100–110 ?	Typically 4–8 but up to 36	Typically dispersal but may remain at breeding col.	Wide-ranging dispersal (up to 1,000s of km)	3–10 prob. c. 5
02	2·0	112	4–6	Dispersal	Less wide-ranging dispersal	?
78	3·0	120	4+?	Minor dispersal	Minor dispersal	?
–139	1·0	85–90	4–13 or more	Wide dispersal	Wide-ranging dispersal (up to 1,000s of km)	<10
68 more	1·2	<100 ?	20–40 or more	?	?	?

TABLE 27
Comparative mean measurements in the Sulidae

	Measurements (g and mm)[1]									
	Weight		Bill length		Bill depth		Wing (carpal) joint to tip		Tail	
	Male	Female	Male	Female	Male	Female	Male	Female	Male	Female
Atlantic gannet	(1) 3,100	(1) 3,100	(8) 100	(9) 99·8	(6) 35	(7) 34·3	(1) 513	(2) 510	(6) 215	(6) 215
Cape gannet	(4) 2,620	(3) 2,670	(12) 94	(14) 91	(13) 31	(10) 32	(3) 480	(4) 477	(13) 189	(12) 191
Australasian gannet	(5) 2,350	(5) 2,350	(16) 89	(16) 89	(14) 30·5	(15) 30	(5)[2] — 463 —		(6) 215	(6) 215
Masked booby	(9) 1,630	(7) 1,880	(4) 106·8	(3) 109·3	(4) 37·3	(2) 38·1	(12) 432	(9) 456	(14) 188	(11) 192
Brown booby	(17) 960	(15) 1,260	(11) 96·2	(7) 102	(10) 32	(8) 34·2	(15) 380	(13) 396	(15) 186	(16) 181
Blue-footed booby	(14) 1,280	(8) 1,800	(6) 106	(2) 114	(9) 33·5	(5) 35·3	(11) 432	(8) 457	(1) 237	(1) 237
Peruvian booby	(13) 1,300	(11) 1,520	(12) 94	(10) 99	(15) 30	(10) 32	(17) 386	(14) 429	(18) 164	(17) 171
Red-footed booby	(18) 940	(16) 1,070	(18) 86	(15) 90	(18) 27·5	(17) 28	(18) 379	(16) 385	(5) 215	(10) 205
Abbott's booby	(12) 1,500	(10) 1,600	(5) 106·1	(1) 120	(3) 37·5	(1) 39·8	(10)[3] 449	(7) 461	(3) 219	(4) 231

Note: 1. Bracketed numbers above measurements show the position of that species and sex in the 'league table' of the measurement concerned; e.g. the male red-foot is the lightest, hence number 18; the male and female Atlantic gannets are joint heaviest, hence 1. It is common for a species to hold different league positions for different characters; the species with the biggest bill may not have the longest wings etc. All combinations are interpretable in terms of adaptations for feeding and nesting.

2. Data not separated into sexes.

3. the **overall** wing length of Abbott's booby is longer than in other sulids, due to a longer humerus.

TABLE 30
Productivity in the sulids (number of young raised per pair per year)

	Produc- tion	Brood size	% breeding success	Breeding frequency (months)
Peruvian booby	1·75	2·5	70	12
Blue-footed booby	1·20	1·5	60	9 (Galapagos)
Brown booby	⌠0·45 ⌡0·65	1·0 1·0	30 65	8 (Ascension) 12 (Christmas Island, Indian Ocean)
White booby	⌠0·40 ⌡0·65	1·0 1·0	40 65	12 (Galapagos) 12 (Kure Atoll)
Red-footed booby	⌠0·24 ⌡0·70	1·0 1·0	30 70	15 (Galapagos) 12 (Caribbean)
Abbott's booby	0·35	1·0	10 or less?	24
Gannet	0·80	1·0	80	12

TABLE 31
Colonies of the African (Cape) gannet

Colony	Planar area	Population (pairs)	Density (nests) per square metre
Mercury	3	5,000 (1950)	NR. Said to be full. Some birds on cliffs.
Ichaboe	6·5	100,000+ (1956)	0·8–4·2
Possession Island	90	17,000 (1956)	3·0–4·0
Bird Island (Penguin Islet, Lamberts Bay)	Small	c.5,000 (1971)	3·76–8·6
Malagas	8·3	Conflicting reports 21,000 (1956) 35,000 (1958) 15,500 (Rand 1963)	2·5–4·0
Bird Island (Algoa Bay)	19	18,000 (1956)	1·9

Data from Rand (1963).

TABLE 32
Population of the Australasian gannet

Area and island	1946/47 census figure	1970/71 census figure	Latest figure
		Number of site-occupying pairs	
New Zealand			
Three Kings (total)		4,134	5,000
1 South West Island	824		
2 Hinemoa Rock	1,520		
3 Hole in the Wall	490		
4 Tutanekai Rock	300		
5 Arbutus Rock	1,000		
Poor Knights Islands		1,650	c.3,150
6 Gannet Stack	150		
7 Sugar Loaf	c.1,500		
Great Barrier Island			
8 Mahuki		325	1,900
Colville (Coromandel) area		1,806	3,500
9 Bush Island or Motukara-marama	1,513		3,000 (1974)
10 Double Island	5		
11 Motutakapu	288		1,000 (1964)
12 Horuhoru		1,228	1,600	1,800+(1974)
Muriwai area			
13 Oaia Islet		338	350
14 White Island		5,227	5,900
15 Kawhia (Gannet Island or Karewa)		3,715	5,800
16 Hawke's Bay complex		2,760	4,750
17 Otago (The Nuggets)		40	20
Foveaux Straits			
18 Little Solander		20	20
19 Marlborough Sounds		—	5
20 Gisborne locality		—	500
21 Mokohinhau		—	30
22 North Auckland locality		30	10
Australia and Tasmania			
Bass Straits			
1 Cat Island	c. 400	c. 12	
South of Tasmania			
2 Pedra Branca	c.1,000	c.1,000	
3 Eddystone		c. 500	
Portland, Victoria			
4 Lawrence Rocks			c.640 (1961)
5 Black Pyramid			c.450 (1961)
Port Philip Bay			
6 Wedge Light			c.6 (1972)

22,763

Total 35,843 (taking the latest counts)

References

1 Alexander, W. B. 1959. The Ornithology of Inn Signs. *Bird Notes 26*: 26–29.
2 Anderson, D. W., Hickey, J. J., Riseborough, R. W., Hughes, D. F. and Christensen, R. E. 1969. Significance of chlorinated hydrocarbon residues to breeding pelicans and cormorants. *Can. Field Nat. 83*: 91–112.
3 Anon. 1901. Letter. *Annals Scot. Nat. Hist. 10*: 181.
4 Armstrong, E. A. 1947. *Bird Display and Behaviour*. London.
5 —— 1958. *The Folklore of Birds*. London.
6 Barlee, J. 1956. Flying for business and pleasure. *Shell Aviation News*: 2–9.
7 Bewick, T. 1816. *History of British Birds*. Newcastle.
8 Booth, E. T. 1887. *Rough Notes on the Birds Observed During Twenty-five Years Shooting and Collecting in the British Isles*. London.
9 Bourne, W. R. P. *Pers. comm.*
10 ——, Bogan, J. and Wanless, S. 1978, in J. B. Nelson. *The Sulidae; Gannets and Boobies*. Aberdeen.
11 Boyd, J. M. 1961. The gannetry of St. Kilda. *J. Anim. Ecol. 30*: 117–136.
12 Brereton, Sir W. 1635. *Travels in Holland, the United Province, England, Scotland and Ireland*.
13 Broad, R. *Pers. comm.*
14 Broekhuysen, G. J., Liversidge, R. and Rand, R. W. 1961. The South African Gannet *Morus capensis*. *Ostrich 32*: 1–19.
15 Brown, R. G. B. *Pers. comm.*
16 Brun, E. 1972. Establishment and population increase of the gannet *Sula bassana* in Norway. *Ornis Scand. 3*: 27–38.
17 —— *Pers. comm.*
18 Bunce, H. O. *Pers. comm.*
19 Carrick, R. 1972. Population Ecology of the Australian Black-backed Magpie, Royal Penguin and Silver Gull. From Population Ecology of Migratory Birds: a Symposium. *U.S. Dept. Int. Wildl. Res. Rep. 2*.
20 Clyne, R. 1913. Some habits of the gannet. *The Scot. Nat.*: 164.
21 Cott, H. B. 1954. The palatability of the eggs of birds. *Proc. Zool. Soc. Lond. 124*: 335–463.
22 Coulson, J. C. 1966. The influence of the pair bond and age on the breeding biology of the kittiwake gull *Rissa tridactyla*. *J. Anim. Ecol. 35*: 269–279.
23 (Coulson and Wooler) Wooler, R. D. and Coulson, J. C. 1977. Factors affecting the age of first breeding of the kittiwake. *Ibis 119*: 339–349.
24 Coulson, J. C. and White, E. 1961. An analysis of the factors affecting the clutch size of the Kittiwake. *Proc. Zool. Soc. Lond. 136*: 207–217.
25 Cullen, M. S. and Pratt, R. 1976. A census of the gannet nests on Grassholm in 1975. *Brit. Birds 69*: 88–90.
26 Cunningham, R. O. 1866. On the Solan Goose, or Gannet (*Sula bassana*, Linn.). *Ibis (2)2*: 1–23.

27 Dixon, T. J. 1971. Estimates of the number of gannets breeding on St Kilda 1969–73. *Seabird Report* 3: 5–12.
28 Dobson, R. and Lockley, R. M. 1946. Gannets breeding in the Channel Islands; two new colonies. *Brit. Birds* 39: 309–312.
29 Dorward, D. F. 1962. Behaviour of boobies, *Sula* spp. *Ibis* 103b: 221–234.
30 Dunnet, G. M. and Ollason, J. C. 1978. Survival and longevity in the fulmar. Abstracts Aberdeen Seabird Conf. *Ibis* 120: 124–125.
31 Einarrson, Th. *Pers. comm.*
32 Elkins, N. and Williams, M. R. 1969. Seabird movements in north-east Scotland 1968 and 1969. *Seabird Report* 1: 31–39.
33 Evans, A. H. 1903. *Turner on Birds*. Cambridge.
34 Evans, P. R. *Pers. comm.*
35 Fairhurst, J. *Pers. comm.*
36 Fisher, J. 1952. *The Fulmar*. London.
37 —— and Lockley, R. M. 1954. *Sea-birds*. London.
38 —— and Vevers, H. G. 1943–44. The breeding distribution, history and population of the North Atlantic gannet *Sula bassana*. *J. Anim. Ecol.* 12: 173–213; 13: 49–62.
39 Fleming, J. 1847. Zoology of the Bass. In M'Crie: *The Bass Rock*. Edinburgh.
40 Furness, R. W. 1978. Shetland seabird communities: the possible impact of new fishing techniques. Abstracts of Aberdeen Seabird Conf. *Ibis* 120: 108–109.
41 ——. *Pers. comm.*
42 Garcia, E. F. J. 1971. Seabird activity in the Straits of Gibraltar; a progress report. *Seabird Report* 3: 30–36.
43 Gaston, A. J. 1970. Seabird migration off Cape Verde, Senegal, in April 1968. *Seabird Report* 2: 6–8.
44 Gibson, J. A. 1951. The breeding distribution, population and history of the birds of Ailsa Craig. *Scot. Nat.* 63: 73–100: 159–177.
45 ——. *Pers. comm.*
46 Gray, R. 1871. *The Birds of the West of Scotland*. Glasgow.
47 Gudmundsson, F. 1953. Icelandic birds VII. The gannet (*Sula bassana* (L.)). *Nàttùrufraedingurinn* 23: 170–177.
48 Gurney, J. H. 1913. *The Gannet, a Bird with a History*. London.
49 Harris, M. P. 1978. Variations within British puffin populations. Abstracts Aberdeen Seabird Conf. *Ibis* 120: 129.
50 —— *Pers. comm.*
51 —— and Lloyd, G. 1977. Variations in counts of seabirds from photographs. *Brit. Birds* 70: 200–205.
52 Harrison, C. J. O. 1978. In J. B. Nelson. *The Sulidae: Gannets and Boobies*. Aberdeen.
53 Harvey, W. 1651. Exercitationes de Generatione Animalium. Ref. in Gurney 1913, p. 198.
54 Henderson, A. W. 1975. B.Sc. Thesis. Aberdeen University.
55 Hopkins, J. R. 1969. Seawatching on the coast of Morocco. *Seabird Report* 1: 40–42.
56 Hopkins, P. *Pers. comm.*
57 Hounsome, M. V. 1967. The Atlantic Seawatch 1965. The Gannet. *Seabird Bull* 4: 7–20.
58 Hutchinson, G. E. 1950. The Biogeochemistry of Vertebrate Excretion. *Bull. Am. Mus. Nat. Hist.* 96: 554 pp.
59 Ingram, G. C. S. and Salmon, H. M. 1934. *Birds in Britain Today*. London.

60 Jackson, E. E. 1966. The Birds of Foula. *Scot. Birds 4 Spec. Suppl.* 60 pp.

61 Jarvis, M. J. F. 1971. Ethology and ecology of the South African gannet, *Sula capensis*. Ph.D. Thesis. Cape Town.

62 —— 1974. The ecological significance of clutch size in the South African gannet (*Sula capensis* Lichtenstein). *J. Anim. Ecol.* 43: 1–17.

63 Kay, G. T. 1948. The gannet in Shetland in winter. *Brit. Birds* 41: 268–270.

64 Keith, J. A. 1969. Some results and implications of pesticide research by the Canadian Wildlife Service. *Trans. 33rd Fed. Prov. Wildl. Conf. Can. Wildl. Service, Ottawa*: 27–30.

65 Kennedy, R. J. 1971. Preen-gland weights. *Ibis* 113: 369–372.

65aKinnear, P. *Pers. comm.*

66 Lack, D. 1954. *The Natural Regulation of Animal Numbers.* Oxford.

67 Lloyd, B. 1926. On the egg-laying of the Grassholm gannets. *Brit. Birds* 19: 309–310.

68 Lockley, R. M. in Fisher and Lockley, 1954. *Sea-birds.* London.

69 M'Crie, T. 1847. *The Bass Rock.* Edinburgh.

70 McGeoch, J. 1959. in D. A. Bannerman. *Birds of the British Isles. Vol. 8.* Edinburgh.

71 Macgillivray, W. 1852. *A History of British Birds.* London.

72 Martin, M. 1698. *A Late Voyage to St. Kilda.* London.

73 Meltofte, H. and Overlund, E. 1974. Forekomsten af Suler sula bassana ved Blåvandshuk 1963–71. *Dansk. Orn. Foren. Tidsskr.* 68: 43–48.

74 Mills, D. H. 1965. The distribution and food of the cormorant in Scottish inland waters. *Freshwat. Salm. Fish. Res.* 35: 16 pp.

75 Milon, Ph. 1966. L'évolution de l'avifaune nidificatrice de la réserve Albert-Chappelier (Les Sept Îles) de 1950 à 1965. *Terre et Vie* 20: 113–142.

76 —— *Pers. comm.*

77 Mohr, N. 1786. *Forsøg til en Islandsk Naturhistorie.*

78 Moison, G. and Scherrer, B. 1973. Déplacements saisonniers des fous de bassan de l'Île Bonaventure (Canada). *Terre et Vie* 27: 414–434.

79 Montevechi, W. A., Bursey, B., Coombes, G. and Porter, J. In press. The breeding populations of North Atlantic Gannets (*Morus bassanus*) in Newfoundland. *Canad. Field Nat.*

80 Morris, F. O. 1848. *A History of British Birds.* London.

81 Nance, 1965. Celtic Bird Names. 'Old Cornwall' 8: pp not known.

82 Nelson, J. B. 1964. Fledging in the gannet. *Scot. Nat.* 71: 47–59.

83 —— 1964. Factors influencing clutch-size and chick growth in the North Atlantic gannet *Sula bassana*. *Ibis* 106: 63–77.

84 —— 1965. The behaviour of the gannet. *Brit. Birds* 58: 233–288; 313–336.

85 —— 1966. The behaviour of the young gannet. *Brit. Birds* 59: 393–419.

86 —— 1966. Population dynamics of the gannet (*Sula bassana*) on the Bass Rock, with comparative information from other Sulidae. *J. Anim. Ecol.* 35: 443–470.

87 —— 1966. The breeding biology of the gannet *Sula bassana* on the Bass Rock, Scotland. *Ibis* 108: 584–626.

88 —— 1970. The relationship between behaviour and ecology in the Sulidae with reference to other seabirds. *Oceanogr. Mar. Biol. Rev.* 8: 501–574.

89 —— 1971. The biology of Abbott's booby *Sula abbotti*. *Ibis* 113: 429–467.

90 —— 1974. *Azraq; Desert Oasis.* London.

91 —— 1976. The breeding biology of frigatebirds – a comparative review. *The Living Bird* 14.

92 —— 1977. Some relationships between food and breeding in the marine Pelecaniformes. In Ed. B. Stonehouse and C. Perrins. *Evolutionary Ecology*. London.

93 —— 1978. *The Sulidae: Gannets and Boobies*. Aberdeen.

94 Nettleship, D. N. 1975. A recent decline of gannets *Morus bassanus*, on Bonaventure Island, Quebec. *Canadian Field Nat. 89*: 125–133.

95 —— 1976. Gannets in North America: present numbers and recent population changes. *Wilson Bull. 88*: 300–313.

96 —— 1977. Seabird resources of eastern Canada: status, problems and prospects. In *Proc. Symp.* Canada's threatened species and habitats. Canadian Nature Federation, Ottawa: 96–108.

97 Nielsen, P. 1919. *Dansk Orn. For. Tidsskr. 13*: 33–79.

98 O'Connor, M. 1975. *Hemisphere 19*.

99 Oliver, W. R. B. 1955. *Birds of New Zealand*. Wellington.

100 Palmer, R. S. 1962. *Handbook of North American Birds*. New York.

101 Parslow, J. L. F. and Jeffries, D. J. 1977. Gannets and toxic chemicals. *Brit. Birds 70*: 366–371.

102 Pearce, P. A., Gruchy, I. M. and Keith, J. A. 1973. Toxic chemicals in living things in the Gulf of St. Lawrence. *Proc. Can. Soc. Fish & Wildl. Biol.* Halifax, Nova Scotia.

103 Pearson, T. H. 1968. The feeding biology of seabird species breeding on the Farne Islands, Northumberland. *J. Anim. Ecol. 37*: 521–552.

104 Perry, R. 1946. *A Naturalist on Lindisfarne*. London.

105 —— 1948. *Shetland Sanctuary*. London.

106 Pettit, R. G. 1969. Seabird movements in north-west Spain. *Seabird Bull. 7*: 10–31.

107 Phillips, G. C. 1962. Survival value of the white colouration of gulls and other seabirds. D. Phil. Thesis. Oxford.

108 Potts, G. R. 1969. The influence of eruptive movements, age, population size and other factors on the survival of the shag (*Phalacrocorax aristotelis* (L)). *J. Anim. Ecol. 38*: 53–102.

109 Poulin, J. M. 1968. Croissance du jeune fou de bassan (*Sula bassana*) pendant sa période pré-envol. *Naturaliste Can. 95*: 1131–1143.

110 —— 1968. Réproduction du Fou de Bassan (*Sula bassana*) Île Bonaventure (Quebec) (Perspective Ecologique). M.Sc. Thesis, Laval University.

111 Probine, M. C. and Wodzicki, K. A. 1955. A note on the thermal resistance of the feathered layer of gannet skins. *N.Z. J. Sc. & Tech. 37*: 158–159.

112 Reinsch, H. H. 1969. Der Bastölpel. *Die Neue Brehm-Bucherei*.

113 Robertson, C. J. R. *Pers. comm.*

114 Ruttledge, R. F. *Pers. comm.*

115 Sage, B. *Pers. comm.*

116 Salmon, H. M. and Lockley, R. M. 1933. The Grassholm gannets – a survey and a census. *Brit. Birds 27*: 142–152.

117 Schaeffer, M. B. 1970. Men, birds and anchovies in the Peru current – dynamic interactions. *Trans. Amer. Fish Soc. 99*: 461–467.

118 Schreiber, R. W. 1976. Species account: Brown Pelican. In: Florida Committee on Rare and Endangered Plants and Animals.

119 Sharrock, J. T. R. 1973. Ed. *Natural History of Cape Clear Island*. Berkhamsted.

120 Simmons, K. E. L. 1967. Ecological adaptations in the life history of the brown booby at Ascension Island. *The Living Bird 6*: 187–212.

121 —— 1967. The role of food supply in the biology of the brown booby at Ascension Island. M.Sc. Thesis. Bristol.

122 Snow, B. 1960. The breeding biology of the shag *Phalacrocorax aristotelis* on the island of Lundy, Bristol Channel. *Ibis 102*: 554–575.

123 Spencer, R. and Hudson, R. 1975. Report on bird ringing for 1973. *Bird Study 22 (Suppl.)*: 64 pp.

124 Stark, D. M. 1967. A visit to Stack Skerry and Sule Skerry. *Scot. Birds 4*: 548–553.

125 Stein, P. 1971. Horuhoru revisited. Longevity of the Australian Gannet. *Notornis 18*: 310–365.

126 Stonehouse, B. 1962. The tropic birds (genus *Phaethon*) of Ascension Island. *Ibis 103b*: 124–161.

127 Stresemann, V. and Stresemann, E. 1960. Die Hand-schwingenmauser der Tagraubvögel. *J. Orn. 101*: 373–403.

128 Thomson, A. L. 1939. The migration of the gannet: result of marking in the British Isles. *Brit. Birds 32*: 282–289.

129 —— 1964. *A New Dictionary of Birds*. London.

130 —— 1974. The migration of the gannet: a reassessment of British and Irish ringing data. *Brit. Birds 67*: 89–103.

131 —— 1975. Dispersal of first-year gannets from the Bass Rock. *Scot. Birds 8*: 295–298.

132 Tinbergen, N. 1952, 'Derived' activities; their causation, biological significance, origin, and emancipation during evolution. *Quart. Rev. Biol. 27*: 1–32.

133 Turner, W. 1544. *A Short and Succinct History of the Principal Birds Noticed by Pliny and Aristotle*. Ed. A. H. Evans, 1903. Cambridge.

134 Urban, E. K. and Brown, L. H. 1969. The breeding biology of the great white pelican *Pelecanus onocrotalus roseus* at Lake Shala, Ethiopia. *Ibis 111*: 199–237.

135 Van Tets, G. F. *Pers. comm.*

136 Vevers, H. G. and Evans, F. C. 1938. A census of breeding gannets (*Sula bassana*) on Myggenaes Holm, Faeroes. *J. Anim. Ecol. 7*: 298–302.

137 Wanless, S. *Pers. comm.*

138 Warham, J. 1958. The nesting of the Australian gannet. *Emu 58*: 339–369.

139 Waterston, G. 1968. Black-browed albatross on the Bass Rock. *Brit. Birds 61*: 22–27.

140 White, S. J. and White, R. E. C. 1970. Individual voice production in gannets. *Behav. 37*: 40–54.

141 Witherby, H. F. et al. 1940. *The Handbook of British Birds*. London.

142 Wodzicki, K. A. 1967. The gannets at Cape Kidnappers. *Trans Roy. Soc. New Zealand 8*: 149–162.

143 —— and McMeekan, C. P. 1947. The gannet on Cape Kidnappers. *Trans. Roy. Soc. New Zealand 76*: 429–452.

144 —— and Robertson, F. H. 1953. Notes on the life history and population trends of the gannet (*Sula serrator*) at the Plateau Gannetry Cape Kidnappers. *Emu 53*: 152–168.

145 Wynne-Edwards, V. C. 1935. The Newfoundland gannet colony; with recent information on the other North American gannetries. *Ibis (13) 5*: 584–594.

146 ——, Lockley, R. M. and Salmon, H. M. 1936. The distribution and numbers of breeding gannets (*Sula bassana* L.). *Brit. Birds 29*: 262–276.

147 Young, J. 1968. Birds of the Scar Rocks – the Wigtownshire gannetry. *Scot. Birds 5*: 204–208.

148 —— *Pers. comm.*

Annotated select bibliography

The following is a selected, annotated bibliography of early accounts of the gannet, derived almost entirely from Gurney's monograph. Although I have quoted from some of these early works in the course of the book, I thought it would be useful to draw this material together in chronological order, especially since Gurney's book is no longer readily available.

Beowulf. After AD 597. *The Anglo-Saxon Poems of Beowulf*, Edited by John N. Kemble, 1833, Vol. 1, p. 129, and 11, p. 76. Uses 'ganet's bath' as figurative expression for the sea. Kemble attributes the poem's events to the 5th century and the writing subsequent to Augustine's Mission of AD 597. Another Anglo-Saxon reference to the gannet is in the *Codex Exoniensis*:

> 'At times the Swan's song
> I made to me for pastime,
> the Ganet's cry,
> and the hu-ilpes note,
> for men's laughter.'

Finally, Gurney quotes a third mention, in the Anglo-Saxon Chronicle, probably written in the 12th or 13th century.

Giraldus, Sylvester. 13th century. *History of Ireland*, mentions a white goose called a 'Gante', but this probably did not refer to the gannet.

Icelandic literature. Gurney refers to an early MS; the 'Eddubrot' (a fragment of the *Snorra Edda*) of about 1400 or earlier, which mentions the svla (sula). Gurney also presents translations from Olafsen and Polsen, 1772, *Travels through Iceland, 1752–58*, and Mohr, 1786, *Forsög til en Islandsk Natur historie*. Mohr is the only author who mentions gannets being attacked by eagles (Macgillivray's instances are said to be inconclusive).

Dunbar, William, 15th century. *The Fenyet Friar of Tungland* includes the famous lines:

> The air was dirkit with the foulis,
> that cam with yawmeris and with yowlis,
> whith shrykking, screeking, skyming, scowlis,
> and miklie noyis and showtes.

Fordun, John de. *The Scotichronicon*, alludes to the Bass gannets. The passage in question (from the *Cupar Codex*) is thought to be the work of Walter Bower (about 1447), the continuator of Fordun's work. Bower was Abbott of a monastery on Inchcolm.

Major, John. 1521. *History of Great Britain* or *Historia Majoris Britanniae*, Editio Nova, Edinburgh, pp. 22–23, refers to the Bass gannets and is the first really descriptive account of them. Major was born in 1469 at Glenhornie, within a few miles of Bass Rock. Gurney's translation is taken from the *Publications of the Scottish History Society*, Vol. V, Constable's edition.

Boece (Boethius), Hector. 1527. *The Cosmographe and Description of Albion*, Bellenden's edition, XLVII. First to mention Ailsa's gannets, and gives vivid account of the Bass Rock gannets. Boece was Canon of Aberdeen. Boece has, erroneously, been credited with the first account of the Bass's gannets, but may instead have copied in part from Major's, earlier, account.

Swave, Peter. *Aars beretninger fra det Kongeliger Geheimearchiv*. III (third volume of State papers from the Archives of Copenhagen). Edited by C. F. Wegener, 1861–65. Gurney's translation taken from *Early Travellers in Scotland*, 1891, by Hume Brown. First time the Anglo-Saxon word 'gannet' applied to the Bass birds. Swave visited Bass Rock in 1535.

Turner, W. 1544. *Avium Praecipuarum* is the first serious bird book to mention the gannet. Turner gives an account of the barnacle myth (see Chapter 7 of the present work).

Monro, Donald. 1774. *Description of the Western Isles of Scotland called Hybrides*. Describes Ailsa Craig's gannets ('Elsay an iyl ... quherin is ane great high hill ...'), but probably never visited it. Travelled in 1549 but his account not published until 1774. Described Sulisgeir and mentioned that gannets occur on Eigg and Rhum (or 'in this ile' as he puts it).

Gesner, Conrad. 1555. *Historia Animalium*, Liber III; 'de avium natura'. Repeats Turner and Boece but was evidently unacquainted with Major. Includes some advanced observations; was the first to record that the gannet incubates its egg underfoot, though this account subsequently disbelieved.

Leslie, (Bishop). 1578. *De origine, morbus, et rebus gestis Scotorum*, James Dalrymple's translation (1596). A detailed account of Bass Rock and its gannets, derived at least in part from an eye-witness. Leslie, himself, never visited Bass Rock.

Hakluyt, R. 1589. *The Principal Navigations, Voyages, Traffiques and Discoveries of the English Nation*. Contains an account of the famous voyage of the Frenchman, Jacques Cartier, in Canadian waters (1534) and his description of the Funk Island gannets, the earliest record of the Canadian gannets known to naturalists. Newfoundland had been discovered a mere 37 years previously by Cabot.

Aldrovandi, U. 1603. *Ornithologie*. Devotes Chapter XX to 'The Bass or Scottish Goose' but all of it derives from Boece and Gesner.

Carolus, Clusius, 1605. *Exoticorum Libri*, gives an account of the gannet and figures it.

Blaue, J. 1622. *Geographie Blavianae Volumen Sexten*. Describes Ailsa Craig and Bass Rock. Based on information from Robert Gordon of Stralloch. To Gordon is attributed the first mention of the oft-repeated fisherman's tale of catching gannets by nailing a herring to a board, upon which the gannet dives. Gordon also noted the union of the furculum with the keel of the sternum.

Brereton, Sir William, 1634. *Travels in Holland, the United Provinces, England, Scotland, and Ireland, MDCXXXIV-V*. Printed for the Chetham Society, 1844. Republished in *Early Travellers in Scotland*, 1891, by Mr Hume Brown. Gives an account of Bass Rock.

Harvey, W. 1651. *Exercitationes de Generatione Animalium*. Gives long account of his 1641 visit to Bass Rock though he may not have landed on it (visited Scotland with Charles I). Celebrated for his discovery of the circulation of the blood.

Ray, John. 1658–1662. *The (3) Itineraries of John Ray*. Visited Bass Rock in 1661 accompanied by Francis Willughby and Sir Philip Skippon. Willughby died 11 years later aged 37. Ray completed Willughby's *Ornithology* and published it in 1676. These two were notable pioneer ornithologists.

Willughby, F. and Ray, J. 1676. *Ornithologiae*, p. 329. Describes and figures the gannet, and describes Bass Rock. In their chapter on 'Remarkable Isles where sea-fowl build' they include the Isle of Man but make no mention of gannets there.

Sibbald, Sir Robert. 1684. *Scotia Illustrata*. Gives three figures of the gannet. Later, in a *History of the Sheriffdoms of Fife and Kinross* (1710), Ch. 11, he gives a long account of the gannet but, as Gurney puts it, he seems to have helped himself freely from earlier writers, and Gurney feels it unnecessary to quote from him.

Slezer, John. 1693. *Theatrum Scotiae*. Contains an oft-reproduced picture of Bass Rock and a lengthy but wholly derivative account of its gannets.

Abercrummie, William. 1696. 'Description of Carrick [the southern district of Ayrshire] in 1696' in *Historic Ayrshire*, 1891, Edited by W. Robertson, Vol. 1, p. 86. Tells of Ailsa Craig's seabirds and their use as food.

Martin, Martin. 1698. *A Late Voyage to St. Kilda, etc. etc. MDCXCVIII*. The first (and an excellent) authority on St Kilda's seabirds. Lived in Skye. Four editions of his *Voyage* (1698, 1710, 1749 and 1753). Some of the contents of his *Voyage* appear in his *Description of the Western Islands of Scotland* (1716), and they appear in full in the *Miscellanea Scotica* (1818). An example of his sharp powers of observation is in his description of a diving gannet: 'they descend asquint'.

Pontoppidan (Bishop). 1753. *Natural History of Norway* gives the figure reproduced on p. 16 of the present book.

Pennant, Thomas. 1766 and 1768. *British Zoology*. Visited Ailsa Craig, 1772, i.e. – after writing his main work – in which there is therefore relatively little information about gannets.

Montagu, George. 1813. *Supplement to the Ornithological Dictionary*. First description of the gannet's sub-cutaneous air-sacs.

Faber, Fredrich. 1822. *Prodromus der Islandischen Ornithologie*. Gives an excellent account of the gannet in Iceland. He refers to gannets being attacked by an infectious disease 'which destroys countless numbers'.

Audubon, J. J. 1838. *Orn. Biog.* IV. Visited Bass Rock, with William Macgillivray, in 1835, on the same day (19 August) upon which Ray and Willughby had visited it in 1661.

M'Crie, Thomas. 1847. *The Bass Rock*, contains: 'Its Civil and Ecclesiastic History (M'Crie), 'Geology of the Bass' (Hugh Miller), 'The Martyrs of the Bass' (James Anderson), (the longest section in the book), 'Zoology of the Bass' (John Fleming), 'Botany of the Bass' (John H. Balfour). A gem of a book (my comment, not Gurney's).

Macgillivray, William. 1852. *A History of British Birds*. The Shetland youth who became Professor of Natural History and lecturer on Botany, in Marischal College; and University, Aberdeen – a bearer of a fine tradition maintained by, among others, J. Arthur Thomson (father of Landsborough Thomson who wrote the papers on the migration of gannets) and V. C. Wynne-Edwards, who made pioneer observations on Canadian gannets and on seabird distribution at sea. Macgillivray's account of the gannet is one of the best of the 19th century.

Cunningham, R. O. 1866. 'On the Solan Goose, or Gannet (Sula bassana, Linn.)'. *Ibis*, V, 1–23. The first detailed historical account of the gannet, names etc., freely used (and dutifully acknowledged) by Gurney.

Harvie-Brown, J. A. 1888. *A Vertebrate Fauna of the Outer Hebrides*. Describes St Kilda, Sula Sgeir, and Sule Stack or Stack Skerry. Believed that Sula

Sgeir's gannets outnumbered those of Bass Rock and Ailsa Craig in 1887. Described Sule Stack as 'certainly one of the most inaccessible of all our Scottish islets'.

Newton, Alfred. 1893–1896. *A Dictionary of Birds*. No list of Gurney's principal debts would be complete without mention of the great and learned Alfred Newton, to whose memory (along with that of Martin Martin) Gurney so aptly dedicated *The Gannet*. Newton was largely responsible for championing the gannet and other seabirds against vandalism and pressures from commercial fishery, and helped to bring about the Seabirds' Protection Act. In addition, his great knowledge of Icelandic and other literature was of the greatest assistance to Gurney.

Wiglesworth, J. 1903. *St Kilda and Its Birds*. The fullest account since Martin Martin's.

Bibliography

Works not included in List of References.

Adams, W. H. 1964. Unseasonable record of gannet in North Carolina. *Wilson Bull.* 76: 187.

Barrett, J. H. and Harris, M. P. 1965. A count of the gannets on Grassholm in 1964. *Brit. Birds* 58: 201–203.

Boddington, D. 1959. Feeding behaviour of gannets and great black-backed gull with mackerel shoals. *Brit. Birds* 52: 383–384.

Bourne, W. R. P. 1971. The threat of oil pollution to north Scottish seabird colonies. *Marine Pollut. Bull.* 2: 117–119.

Broekhuysen, G. J. and Liversidge, R. 1954. Colour variation in the tail-feathers of the South African gannet. *Ostrich* 6: 19–22.

—— and Rudebeck, G. 1951. Some notes on the Cape gannet. *Ostrich* 3: 132–138.

Brun, E. 1967. Breeding of gannet, *Sula bassana*, in north Norway. *Sterna* 7: 376–386.

—— 1970. Gannet, *Sula bassana*, established as breeding bird in Lofoten, north Norway. *Sterna* 9: 141–147.

—— 1971. Gannet, *Sula bassana*, from Bass Rock, Scotland breeding on Andøya. *Fauna*, Oslo 24: 22–24.

—— 1974. Breeding success of gannets *Sula bassana* at Nordmjele, Andøya, north Norway. *Astarte* 7: 77–82.

Calvert, M. 1960. Gannet dispersal off the Manx coast. *Peregrine* 3: 113–118.

Clyne, R. 1916. Movements of the gannet as observed at the Butt of Lewis. *Scot. Nat.*: 55–59.

Cooper, J. and Siegfried, W. R. 1976. Behavioural responses of a young Cape gannet *Sula capensis* to high ambient temperatures.

Dathe, H. 1970. Basstölpel (*Sula bassana*) bei Berlin. *Beiträge Vogelk* 15: 455–456.

Davies, O. J. H. and Keynes, R. D. 1948. The Cape St Mary gannet colony, Newfoundland. *Ibis* 90: 538–546.

Favero, L. 1967. Notizie sulla *Sula bassana*. *Revista Ital. Orn.* 37: 258–259.

Fimreite, N., Brun, E., Froslie, A., Frederichsen, P. and Gundesen, N. 1974. Mercury in eggs of Norwegian seabirds. *Astarte* 7: 71–75.

Fisher, J. and Venables, L. S. V. 1938. Gannets (*Sula bassana*) on Noss Shetland, with an analysis of the rate of increase of this species. *J. Anim. Ecol.* 7: 305–313.

Fisher, J. and Venables, L. S. V. 1938. Gannets (*Sula bassana*) on Noss, gannet (*Sula bassana*). *Proc. Int. Orn. Congr.* 10: 463–467.

Fleming, C. A. 1947. Contributions to the gannet census. *N.Z. Bird Notes* 2: 109–111; 113–114.

—— and Wodzicki, K. A. 1952. A census of the gannet (*Sula serrator*) in New Zealand. *Notornis* 5: 39–78.

Gibson-Hill, C. A. 1948. Display and posturing in the Cape gannet, *Morus capensis*. *Ibis* 90: 568–72.

Gould, M. 1974. Gannet on Kent Island, New Brunswick. *Auk* 91: 175.

Green, R. H. and MacDonald, D., 1963. The Black Pyramid gannetry. *Emu* 63: 177–184.

Hirons, M. J. D. 1968. British Seabirds, 6. the gannet. *Animals* 10: 571–573.

Huyskens, G. and Maes, P. 1971. La migracion de aves marinas en el NW de España. *Ardeola* Special Vol.: 155–180.

Jarvis, M. J. F. 1970. Interactions between man and the South African gannet *Sula capensis*. *Ostrich* Suppl. 8: 497–514.

—— 1972. The systematic position of the South African gannet. *Ostrich* 43: 211–216.

—— 1972. A comparison of methods in a behaviour study of the South African gannet. *Zoo. Africana* 7: 75–83.

—— 1974. The ecological significance of clutch size in the South African gannet (*Sula capensis* (Lichtenstein)). *J. Anim. Ecol.* 43: 1–17.

—— and Cram, D. L. 1971. Bird Island, Lamberts Bay, South Africa: an attempt at conservation. *Biol. Cons.* 3: 269–273.

Lockley, R. M. and Salmon, H. M. 1934. The gannet colonies of Iceland. *Brit. Birds* 28: 183–184.

Lockwood, W. B. 1972. Faroese bird-name origins. 3. *Fróðskaparrit* 20: 43–53.

MacDonald, J. D. 1960. Secondary external nares of the gannet. *Proc. Zool. Soc. Lond.* 135: 357–363.

MacGregor, A. A. 1969. The skerry of the gannets; Sule Sgeir. *Country Life* 145: 1101–1103.

MacInnes, J. 1970. Gannet catching in the Hebrides. *Fróðskaparrit* 18: 151–158.

MacIntyre, D. 1950. The young gannet. *Brit. Birds* 43: 232.

McKean, J. L. 1966. Population, status and migration of the gannet *Sula bassana serrator* of Lawrence Rocks, Victoria. *Emu* 65: 159–163.

Maxwell, T. C. 1972. Spring migration of the gannet in Florida waters. *Wilson Bull.* 84: 198–199.

Melde, M. 1973. Basstölpel (*Sula bassana*) im Bezirk Dresden. *Beiträge Vogelk* 19: 224.

Monnat, J.-Y. 1969. Statut actuel des oiseaux marins nicheurs en Bretagne. 6. Hauttoégor et Guelo (de Trébeurden à Paimpol). *Ar Vran* 2: 1–24.

Moore, L. B. and Wodzicki, K. A. 1950. Plant material from gannets' nests. *Notornis* 4: 12–13.

Neven, R. 1975. Jan-van-Gent – *Sula bassana*. *Wielewaal* 41: 139.

Nettleship, D. N. and Tull, C. E. 1970. Seabird transects between Valleyfield and Funk Island, Newfoundland, summer, 1969. *Can. Field Nat.* 84: 369–376.

Olsen, B. and Permin, M. 1972. The population of the gannet *Sula bassana* on Mykineshólmur, 1972. *Dansk Orn. Foren. Tidsskr.* 68: 39–42.

Orlando, C. 1967. Catture di sule in Sicilia. *Revista Ital. Orn.* 37: 72–73.

Parslow, J. L. F. 1967. Changes in status among breeding birds in Britain and Ireland. *Brit. Birds* 60: 2–47.

Perry, R. 1950. The young gannet. *Brit. Birds* 43: 343–344.

Poulin, J. M. and Moison, G. 1968. The gannets (*Sula bassana*) of Bonaventure Island, Quebec. N.E. Fish & Wildl. Conf. Manchester, New Hampshire, U.S.A.

Rand, R. W. 1959. The biology of guano-producing sea-birds. The distribution, abundance and feeding habits of the Cape gannet, *Morus capensis*, off the south-western coast of the Cape Province. *Commerce and Industry Rep.* 39: 35 pp.

—— 1959. Conservation of the Cape gannet. *Ostrich* Suppl. 3: 31–33.

—— 1963. The biology of guano-producing sea-birds. Composition of colonies on the Cape islands. *S.A. Div. Fish Invest.* 43.

—— 1963. The biology of guano-producing sea-birds. Composition of colonies on the south-west African islands. *S.A. Div. Fish Invest.* 46.

—— 1963. Seabirds in the southern Indian Ocean. *Ostrich 34*: 121–128.

Randazzo, G. R. 1965. Nuova cattura della *Sula bassana* (L.) in Sicilia. *Atti Soc. Pelorit. Sci. Fis. Mat. Nat. 10*: 471–476.

Roberts, B. 1934. The gannet colonies of Iceland. *Brit. Birds 28*: 100–105.

Robertson, C. J. R. 1964. Observations on the black-backed gull predation at the Cape Kidnappers gannetries: 1959–1963. *Notornis 10*: 393–403.

—— 1969. Community development in the gannet at Cape Kidnappers. Ecological Society Conference.

—— and Williams, G. R. 1968. A review of gannet research at Cape Kidnappers. Report to Sanctuary Board.

Robertson, F. H. and Wodzicki, K. 1948. Contributions to the gannet census. *New Zealand Bird Notes 3*: 38–40.

Sharrock, J. T. R. 1965. The status of immature gannets off Cape Clear Island. *Brit. Birds 58*: 216–217.

Snow, D. W. 1971. *The Status of Birds in Britain and Ireland.* Oxford.

Spano, S. 1965. La sula (*Sula bassana bassana* (L.)) in Italia. *Revista Ital. Orn. 35*: 1–33.

Stresemann, E. and Stresemann, V. 1966. Der Mauser der Vögel. *J. Orn. 107*, Suppl., 439 pp.

Taylor, R. H. and Wodzicki, K. 1958. Black-backed gull – a gannet predator. *Notornis 8*: 22–23.

Uys, C. J., Don, P. A., Marshall, R. A. S. and Wells, K. F. 1966. Aspergillosis in Cape gannet, *Morus capensis. Ostrich 37*: 152–154.

Waterston, G. 1959. Gannet. In D. A. Bannerman. *The Birds of the British Isles.* Vol. 8. Edinburgh.

White, S. J., White, R. E. C. and Thorpe, W. H. 1970. Acoustic basis for individual recognition by voice in the gannet. *Nature*, Lond. 225: 1156–1158.

Wilson, J. E. 1950. Newcastle disease in a gannet. *Brit. Vet. Rec. 62*: 33–34.

Wodzicki, K. 1967. The gannet at Cape Kidnappers. 1. Population changes 1945–1964. *Trans. Roy. Soc. N.Z. Zool. 8*: 149–162.

2. Dispersal and Movements. *Trans. Roy. Soc. N.Z. Zool. 9*: 17–31.

—— and McMeekan, C. P. 1947. The gannet on Cape Kidnappers. *Trans. Roy. Soc. N.Z. Zool. 76*: 429–452.

—— and Moreland, J. 1966. A note on the food of New Zealand gannets. *Notornis 13*: 98–99.

—— and Robertson, F. H. 1953. Notes on the life history and population trends of the gannet (*Sula serrator*) at the Plateau gannetry, Cape Kidnappers. *Emu 53*: 152–168.

—— —— 1955. Observations on diving of the Australasian gannet (*Sula bassana serrator* Gray). *Notornis 6*: 72–76.

Wodzicki, K. and Stein, P. 1958. Migration and dispersal of New Zealand gannets. *Emu 58*: 289–312.

Wynne-Edwards, V. C. 1935. On the habits and distribution of birds on the North Atlantic. *Proc. Boston Soc. Nat. Hist. 40*: 233–346.

Index